Ethnic Dissent and Empowerment

STUDIES OF WORLD MIGRATIONS

Marcelo J. Borges and Madeline Y. Hsu, editors

A list of books in the series appears at the end of the book.

ETHNIC DISSENT AND EMPOWERMENT

Economic Migration between Vietnam and Malaysia

ANGIE NGỌC TRẦN

© 2022 by the Board of Trustees
of the University of Illinois
All rights reserved
1 2 3 4 5 C P 5 4 3 2 1
♾ This book is printed on acid-free paper.

Library of Congress Cataloging-in-Publication Data
Names: Tran, Angie Ngoc, author.
Title: Ethnic dissent and empowerment: economic
    migration between Vietnam and Malaysia / Angie Ngoc
    Tran.
Description: Urbana, Chicago: University of Illinois Press,
    [2021] | Series: Studies of world migrations | Includes
    bibliographical references and index.
Identifiers: LCCN 2021038168 (print) | LCCN 2021038169
    (ebook) | ISBN 9780252043369 (cloth) | ISBN
    9780252085277 (paperback) | ISBN 9780252052248
    (ebook)
Subjects: LCSH: Foreign workers, Vietnamese—Malaysia.
Classification: LCC HD8700.6 .T74 2021 (print) |
    LCC HD8700.6 (ebook) | DDC 331.6/2595—dc23
LC record available at https://lccn.loc.gov/2021038168
LC ebook record available at https://lccn.loc.gov/2021038169

To my parents, Ông Trần Quang Phong and Bà Doãn Thị Quý, for their unconditional love and support of my own transnational migration in bringing this project to completion

Contents

List of Illustrations   ix

Acknowledgments   xi

Abbreviations   xvii

Introduction   1

1. Historical, Economic, Cultural, Religious Practices of the Five Ethnic Groups   25

2. The Transnational Labor Brokerage System and Its Infrastructure   55

3. The Labor Recruitment Process and Indebtedness   74

4. Precarity and Coping Mechanisms   98

5. Physical Third Space Empowerment   123

6. Metaphorical Third Space Empowerment   150

7. Aspirations after Malaysia   173

Conclusion   199

Appendix 1. Descriptions of the Samples   209

Appendix 2. Land Issues Faced by the Five Ethnic Groups in This Study   214

Appendix 3. Chronology of the Transnational Labor
Brokerage State System, 1950s–2020   216

Appendix 4. Legal Documentation of Labor
Export Policies   218

Notes   221

Bibliography   253

Index   271

Illustrations

Figure 1. Vietnam in Southeast Asia   2

Table 1. Samples for the Five Ethnic Groups   22

Figure 2. Hrê women and children peel off the bark of *keo* trees, a cash crop, in Quảng Ngãi province in 2012   35

Figure 3. Migrants from An Giang province cross the Mekong River   38

Figure 4. Khmer social life is grounded in *wats* (temples)   41

Figure 5. Tân Châu mosque   46

Figure 6. A Chăm storefront in Ho Chi Minh City   49

Table 2. Conceptual Diagram of Ethnic Hierarchies   53

Figure 7. Vietnam and Malaysia in the transnational labor brokerage system   56

Figure 8. The Social Policy Bank uses banners to announce meetings for loan information   66

Figure 9. A migrant worker in her hostel room in Batu Pahat, Malaysia   101

Figure 10. Kinh migrants in Prague sell fish noodles, coffee, and other goods   153

Figure 11. A Hrê house funded by remittances   159

Acknowledgments

This book confirms my passionate interest in labor migration studies and my transnational fieldwork, which started in 2008 and spans several countries: Vietnam, Malaysia, Cambodia, Poland, and the Czech Republic. The more fieldwork I did, the more I learned about the richness of different ethnic groups, dispelling the narrative that Vietnamese migrants are a monolithic group. The kindness of the migrant workers and their families from the five ethnic groups who shared with me their trials and tribulations, their strategies of dissent, their success stories and optimism, kept me going even during the most arduous field trips and strengthened my commitment to shedding light on their plight and to improving their condition.

I am very grateful to many individuals in Vietnam (many of whose names I cannot mention to preserve their confidentiality) who shared with me their knowledge, sources, and time (some even accompanied me on field trips spanning over ten years). Dr. Huỳnh Thị Ngọc Tuyết, historian and social work professor, has been a role model for me owing to her strong commitment to the cause of workers and her support for fellow researchers and activists for social justice. She introduced me to Mr. Trần Văn Thạnh at a state-owned recruitment company, who supplied the context and history of the labor export policy and its implementation in Vietnam and allowed me to interview my first group of migrant returnees to Vietnam. These initial interviews were crucial because they gave me a way to contact the migrant workers who were still in Malaysia so I could expand my sample further. Trần Hoài, at the time a PhD student at the Max Planck Institute for Social Anthropology, supplied me with contacts that connected me with the Hrê in Nghĩa Hành district (Quảng Ngãi) and allowed me to explore the state resettlement policy. Nguyễn Thị Mai Thủy, from the International Labour Organization, has been very helpful in updating me on labor migration rights issues and sharing her quarterly reports on the Greater Mekong Subregion TRIANGLE project.

Vietnamese store owners and families in Warsaw and Prague offered me their hospitality and insights from socialist migrant perspectives. My Vietnam-based research assistants from the Social Science Institute in the Southern Region (Vietnam) not only helped me interview dozens of people but also transcribed hundreds of hours of conversations. My dear colleague and friend Dr. Nguyễn-võ Thu-Hương, a professor at UCLA, has been a constant source of support, advice, and ideas. There were many individuals from the Hrê, Chăm, and Khmer communities who translated for me during my interviews in their villages and communes over the years. To them, I owe a great debt of gratitude.

The role of labor newspapers is very important in understanding the labor export policy and the plight of migrant workers overseas. I'm very grateful to journalists Mr. Duy Quốc of Người Lao Động (Laborer) and Mr. Nam Dương and Ms. Lê Tuyết of Lao Động (Labor), who shared knowledge, sources, and their own investigative news articles. Mr. Duy Quốc himself conducted fieldwork in Malaysia in order to write his articles.

Two fellowships enabled me to stay in situ to do my fieldwork in Malaysia and Vietnam: the 2007 Senior Visiting Fellowship at the Centre for Asia Pacific Social Transformation Studies, University of Wollongong NSW, Australia, and the 2008 Lee Kong Chian Distinguished Fellowship on Southeast Asia, a joint appointment by Stanford University and National University of Singapore. Stanford University's Shorenstein Southeast Asia Program also created a venue for me to present and publish my earlier works on labor migration. Dr. Donald Emmerson at Stanford facilitated the Singapore connection that assisted this book project. Dr. Vicki Crinis (University of Wollongong) and Dr. Adrian Vickers (University of Sydney) created a wonderful collegial environment for me before I started my fieldwork in Malaysia, on which Vicki Crinis joined me. Dr. Lian Kwen Fee and Dr. Md Mizanur Rahman invited me to present a paper for the conference The Road Less Travelled: Mobility in Southeast Asian Societies in Brunei, where I received excellent feedback on the agency and migration patterns of the Chăm Muslim who moved between Vietnam and Malaysia.

My analysis has been strengthened thanks to comments, questions, and suggestions from the global conferences, seminars, workshops, and brownbag talks at which I presented my work in progress. Wonderful global collegiality and fellowship over the years has enabled me to bring this book to

Acknowledgments   xiii

fruition, proudly from a primarily teaching public university. I have received many constructive questions, comments, and feedback from my presentations (in English and Vietnamese) at worldwide conferences and workshops organized by the Institute of Asian Studies, the Universiti Brunei Darussalam (Brunei); the Gender and Society Research Center of Hoa Sen University, Ho Chi Minh City; the sixth Engaging with Vietnam: An Interdisciplinary Dialogue conference, jointly organized by the University of Oregon and the University of Hawaii at Manoa; the Association for Asian Studies–in–Asia (AAS-in-Asia) Conference at Doshisha University in Kyoto, Japan; the Department of Politics and Economics at Chiang Mai University in Thailand; the Vietnam Update 2008 conference at the Australian National University; and the Viện khoa học xã hội vùng nam bộ (The Southern Institute of Social Sciences) in Vietnam. In particular, Dr. Benedict J. Tria Kerkvliet, emeritus professor at the Australian National University, made excellent comments as a discussant on my presentation at the Engaging with Vietnam conference. Dr. Naomi Hosoda of Kyoto University in Japan, who was a discussant for our panel at AAS-in-Asia, introduced me to Abraham and van Schendel's work on the extralegal aspect of third spaces, which led to my passion for using the third space idea as my conceptual framework.

I have also benefited tremendously from constructive feedback received through events hosted by universities in California, including the 2009 Southeast Asian Program conference at UC Berkeley; the 2018 Southeast Asian Studies conference, Migrations and New Mobilities in Southeast Asia, hosted by UC Berkeley and UCLA; and the 2018 Southeast Asian Studies colloquium series at UC Riverside.

I deeply appreciate the constant backing and encouragement at the California State University, Monterey Bay (CSUMB), from Dr. Ruben Mendoza, chair of the School of Social, Behavioral, and Global Studies and a prolific scholar in archaeology. His collegial support of my scholarly work for over two decades speaks volumes about the interconnectedness between teaching and research. I am especially grateful to Ida Mansourian, associate dean of the College of Extended Education and International Programs, who not only has supported my desire to do traditional research but has also facilitated fantastic intellectual exchanges with faculty at some universities with whom CSUMB has signed memoranda of understanding in Vietnam, Poland, and the Czech Republic. Thanks to these exchange opportunities, I met Dr. Pawel Boski, a professor at the University of Social Sciences and Humanities in Warsaw, Poland, who shared his deep knowledge about the Vietnamese socialist migrants who live in the former Soviet-controlled Eastern European countries, especially Poland and the Czech Republic. The Psychology

xiv   *Acknowledgments*

Department's brown-bag series spearheaded by Dr. Jennifer Dyer-Seymour, Dr. Mrinal Sinha, and Dr. Justin Matthews has confirmed for me the power of bottom-up, grassroots, faculty-led efforts to sustain a passion for research on our campus. I am grateful for all the constructive comments that I have received there, especially from Dr. Sinha, Dr. Kathryn Poethig, and Ms. Joy Nguyen. I also received grants from the California State University system that contributed to my many field trips to Vietnam, including the Provost Global Engagement Faculty Development Grant at CSUMB and the California State University Research, Scholarship, and Creative Activity Award. I'm very grateful to the wonderful staff at the CSUMB Library, Rebecca Bergeon, Ryne Leuzinger, and Laura Sun, who got many Inter-Library Loan books and journal articles for me. I am also grateful to Dr. Yong Lao, who created the nice map showing where I interviewed my informants. My deep appreciation goes to my artistic cousin, Mr. Doãn Quốc Vinh, who added the migration patterns to the map to denote the different routes taken by the five ethnic groups.

My deep appreciation goes to Dr. Gerald Shenk, professor emeritus from CSUMB, one of the most inspiring colleagues in my entire teaching career. Since joining the faculty at the same time as I in fall 1996, he has continued to cheer me on, faithfully encouraging my research passion and supporting my scholarly endeavors in many invaluable ways. He painstakingly read over an early draft of the whole manuscript, pointing out holes in the arguments and suggesting important scholars to include in my intersectional analysis (race/ethnicity, class, gender). His unwavering advice has touched me deeply and has sharpened my analysis throughout the book.

Some of the research for this book has been used previously in "Migrant Labor and State Power: Vietnamese Workers in Malaysia and Vietnam," published in the *Journal of Vietnamese Studies* (co-authored with Vicki Crinis), as well as in book chapters titled "Weaving Life across Borders: The Chăm Muslim Migrants Traversing Vietnam and Malaysia" in *International Migration in Southeast Asia: Continuities and Discontinuities*, edited by Lian Kwen Fee, Mizanur Rahman, and Yabit bin Alas, and "Migrant Workers in the Clothing Industry: Networking in Christian Spaces" (co-authored with Vicki Crinis), in *Labour in the Clothing Industry in the Asia Pacific*, edited by Vicki Crinis and Adrian Vickers.

I want to thank James Engelhardt, poet–cum–acquisitions editor, who has been very supportive ever since my first query to the University of Illinois Press. He thoughtfully shepherded me through the review process, always with keen eyes, a sharp mind, and a compassionate heart. I truly appreciate the two anonymous readers, who critiqued, questioned, and made

Acknowledgments xv

constructive suggestions on the book's theoretical framework and overall organization, leading to a complete reorganization of the book! The arguments relating to the five ethnic groups are now better integrated, thanks to these insightful comments. I also want to thank Jennifer Comeau for her careful and respectful copyediting which is attentive to all the details and differences among the five ethnic groups.

During the production stage of this book, my dear father, Mr. Trần Quang Phong, sadly passed away. But his faithful support throughout the process lifts my spirit to finish the final steps of this book. Forever loving to learn new things, my mother carefully asked me to explain each and every chapter of this book to her. My loving partner, Joe Lubow, reads, discusses, and challenges everything that I write. He is the toughest critic, and in responding to his comments, I've learned to explain things in better ways. My deep appreciation goes to Joe, who also helped with the time-consuming indexing task. Without him, this book could not see the light of day. The remaining inadvertent mistakes and shortcomings are mine!

Finally, I'll never forget the tears in the eyes of the many migrants who poured their hearts out to me as they told me of their experiences and the smiles on the faces of the parents or spouses when they shared their stories. They are the ones who empowered me to finish this book and to continue on this journey to the next project, which will compare these experiences with those of guest workers in other parts of the world.

Abbreviations

71/2009/QĐTT Prime Minister Decision, "Approving the Proposal to Support Poor Rural Districts, Pushing Forward Export Labor to Contribute to Sustained Poverty Reduction in the 2009–2020 Period"

72/2006/QH11 Law on Vietnamese Working Overseas Under Labor Contracts

đ Vietnamese đồng (currency)

DOLAB Department of Overseas Labor

DoLISA Department of Labor, Invalids, Social Affairs (under the MoLISA)

GMS TRIANGLE project Tripartite Action to Protect Migrant Workers within and from the Greater Mekong Subregion from Labour Exploitation

ILO International Labour Organization

IMF International Monetary Fund

LBS labor brokerage state

MoFA Ministry of Foreign Affairs

MoLISA Ministry of Labor, Invalids, and Social Affairs

MR Malaysian Ringgit (currency)

MTUC Malaysia Trade Union Congress

NGO Nongovernmental Organization

VAMAS Vietnam Association of Manpower Supply

VGCL Vietnamese General Confederation of Labor

Ethnic Dissent and Empowerment

Introduction

Throughout modern history, nation-states all over the world have sent their citizens to other countries as temporary workers, or guest workers.[1] The term *guest worker* comes from the German term *Gastarbeiter,* first used to refer to the Turks who had started migrating to Germany in the mid-1950s for work.[2] It refers to contract workers who are recruited by their home governments to work in another country for a specific length of time and who then return to their home countries at the end of the contract.

Programs for guest workers appear all over the world. The Bracero ("strong arms") Program (1942–1964) was established between the US and Mexican governments for Mexico to send workers to work in the United States. During the 1950s, the United States also unilaterally developed the H2 visa program for temporary workers.[3] South and Southeast Asian contract workers have been sent to work in the Middle East since 1975, and the Philippine government has sent millions of its citizens to work in 120 countries since 1993.

The Vietnamese government has legislated guest worker programs for over six decades under different political regimes. As early as the 1950s, the Democratic Republic of Vietnam government was sending guest workers to several Soviet Bloc countries in the spirit of international socialist efforts to fight against the colonial French and the imperialistic United States. Then, starting in 1980, the government of the Socialist Republic of Vietnam (Vietnam's official name after reunification in 1975) signed many bilateral labor agreements to send Vietnamese contract workers to Eastern European countries in the Bloc. These programs continued until the disintegration of the Soviet Bloc in 1989.[4] Sending workers to these countries addressed many war-related problems in Vietnam, such as unemployment; repaid debt

Figure 1. Vietnam in Southeast Asia: Major Migration Pathways between Vietnam and Malaysia

accumulated during the US-Vietnam war; and provided funds and products needed for postwar nation building.

With the market system firmly established in post–Cold War Vietnam, the Politburo (the highest Vietnamese political organ) approved a policy to export labor, starting in 1999. The guest workers during the socialist era became the commodified "export labor" (*lao động xuất khẩu*). Dozens of intergovernmental agreements were established, and by December 2019 Vietnam had sent over 540,000 Vietnamese migrant workers to work in over sixty countries and territories in East and Southeast Asia (with increasing popularity of Thailand), the Middle East and North Africa, and Europe (including the former Soviet Bloc countries).[5]

Introduction 3

The Vietnamese state has used labor export policy to address domestic social and economic issues. In 2006 the state passed 72/2006/QH11, "Law on Vietnamese Working Overseas Under Labor Contracts," which sets out the procedures for all stages of the labor export process and establishes the terms for contracts with private, state-owned, and quasi-state recruitment companies (see appendix 4). In April 2009, the government introduced Prime Minister Decision 71/2009/QĐTT, "Approving the Proposal to Support Poor Rural Districts, Pushing Forward Export Labor to Contribute to Sustained Poverty Reduction in the 2009–2020 Period."[6] This policy aims to contribute to job creation. In general, every year about 1.1 to 1.5 million Vietnamese enter the labor market. The government also wants to reduce poverty and to create a source of foreign exchange income from migrant workers' remittances. Indeed, these remittances are a major source of foreign exchange income and have contributed to Vietnamese economic growth. In 2019, remittances of approximately US$16.679 billion accounted for over 6 percent of Vietnam's annual GDP, second only to the share that remittances contribute to the economy of the Philippines in Southeast Asia.[7]

As a labor scholar of Kinh descent, I have been concerned about the well-being of workers, both local and migrant. My previous book analyzed the labor movements of two ethnic groups, the Kinh (the majority) and the Hoa (the ethnic Chinese, the wealthiest minority), over a period of one hundred years. In addition to these two groups, this study brings in three other ethnic groups, the Hrê, the Khmer, and the Chăm Muslims, to underline the importance of ethnic differences in terms of cultural and religious diversity (not just socioeconomic class, which is the key factor in the policy that seeks to recruit potential migrant workers from poor rural districts).[8]

In particular, this book asks the following questions of each of these five ethnic groups: To what extent are their migration patterns similar as guest workers in Malaysia? How do they cope or resist when transnational migration policies fail to protect them? How do some bypass the labor export system altogether?

Using an intersectional framework, I argue that class analysis alone cannot explain the nuanced cultural differences among the ethnic minority workers in their relations with the Kinh ethnic officials and labor recruiters in both Vietnam and Malaysia. Moreover, within each ethnicity, different gender relations underscore how the transnational labor brokerage state system affects female and male migrants differently. Thus, this book addresses these concerns by putting ethnicity, class, and gender in the center of the analysis to understand the lives of these migrants in the entire transnational migration process (predeparture, working overseas, and return), their migration patterns, and their responses to the state system. Treating return migration as a phase of the process provides valuable insights into the contradictions between the stated goals and the actual impacts and consequences of labor export policies on the migrants and their families. Overall, by connecting these categories, I contribute a more comprehensive approach to the field of migration studies.

There is a need to study South-to-South labor migration: citizens from a developing country migrating to work in *another* developing country within the Global South. While there have been studies focusing on labor migration from Vietnam to developed countries in East and Southeast Asia such as Taiwan, South Korea (Republic of Korea), and Japan, not much has been written about workers in Malaysia, an emerging economy.[9] This study fills in this gap, exploring how Malaysia has been used as a "high potential labor market" (*thị trường lao động nhiều tiềm năng*) owing to its demand for a low-skilled labor force while requiring lower fees than some preferred labor markets, such as those in Japan, Korea, and Taiwan.[10]

Both the home (Vietnam) and host (Malaysia) countries stand to benefit from Vietnamese migrants. Malaysia is an important labor market to study because it has been recruiting Vietnamese workers who are willing to do the jobs unwanted by its local citizens. The Vietnamese state uses it as a labor export destination for its poor citizens, especially ethnic minorities in Vietnam in addition to the Kinh, consistent with the policy aiming at "sustained poverty reduction." The 71/2009/QĐTT policy provides low-interest loans, language and skills training, and health checks for migrants that allow them to work abroad, primarily in Malaysia.[11] The decision first specified that residents from sixty-one poor rural districts in the north and central provinces (such as Thanh Hóa, Nghệ An, Hà Tĩnh, Quảng Ngãi) would be eligible, but to meet the quotas, in August 2012 the state added three more poor districts in the south (Trà Vinh, Bạc Liêu, Cà Mau).[12]

Most of the migrants are young men and women from rural areas who were recruited to work in low-skilled jobs in manufacturing, construction, fishing, agriculture, domestic work, and other service industries.[13] Hahamovitch notes the conditions of precarity underlying these common experiences of guest workers: they work jobs rejected by locals, are treated like indentured servants, are expelled during economic downturns, face the threat of deportation, are not protected by local unions, and do not receive any welfare benefits from host governments.[14] These experiences of guest workers of the world are also observed in the experiences of the Vietnamese guest workers who went to work in Malaysia. Chapter 4 details the precarity and coping mechanisms of each of the five ethnic groups under study.

Women guest workers face even greater challenges. Migrant policies designed to protect women workers' rights are needed because of a pronounced preference for female workers in Malaysia and the other major destination countries (Taiwan, Japan, South Korea, and Thailand). On average, female migrants account for nearly 38 percent of the total Vietnamese migrant population working in these five countries.[15] But a higher share of women workers went to work in Malaysia: 51 percent of workers sent in 2017 were women.[16] Moreover, recent bilateral agreements with other countries have resulted in an increase in the export of female workers, especially in domestic work, where abuses are rampant. Saudi Arabia stands out in this respect: overwhelmingly, migrants sent from Vietnam to perform domestic work in Saudi Arabia were female.[17]

To frame the issue of state power in managing transnational labor migration, I use Gramsci's concepts of "hegemony" and the "manufacture of consent," discussed in his *Prison Notebooks*.[18] Gramsci talks about a capitalist state that has power in two overlapping spheres: political (ruling through force) and civil (ruling through consent). In the context of state-managed global labor migration, the labor-sending state uses its institutions to manipulate the consent of people in poor rural districts to go to work overseas, and it benefits from this process. The larger implication of this study is to assess the effects of using labor export policies to address socioeconomic problems in a multiethnic country such as Vietnam.

I argue that these transnational state bureaucracies never fully control or reap benefits from the migrants of different ethnic groups. Although states and institutions of the transnational labor brokerage state (LBS) work together to manipulate the consent of the potential migrant workers, the system faces internal contradictions and is subject to external criticisms, thus opening up spaces for workers to benefit from and subvert those states and institutions when necessary. Ethnic workers who consent to participate in the LBS system develop strategies, informed and mediated by their respective economic and cultural resources, to challenge it. They have also developed spaces of dissent to help them survive, thrive, and even bypass this LBS system altogether. Those who choose to be independent of the system demonstrate a range of migration patterns and engage in a wide spectrum of creative activities.

There exists a large literature on migrant workers (who consented to work overseas) and their attempts to fight for their rights.[19] This book focuses not only on migrants from Vietnam but also on the different migration patterns of the five ethnic groups and the different spaces of dissent they occupy. I situate each of these groups in hierarchies based on their different levels of access to economic and cultural resources (see chapter 1). Social networks inform and empower each group's migration patterns.[20]

I complement the social network concept, well established in the migration studies literature, with the concept of "third space" (developed by Homi Bhabha) to explain the forms of dissent that migrants—both guest workers and undocumented migrants—contest transnational state power. The third space concept transcends the limits of dualism (such as illegal versus legal from the perspective of the law as further elaborated on by other scholars), allowing us to acknowledge diverse forms of dissent from these five ethnic groups.[21] The third space provides an alternative arena that is socially accepted even when an action is classified as illegal by the state's legal codes. The third space accommodates a spectrum of worker responses in both physical spaces (such as restaurants, fruit orchards, factory floors, restroom stalls) and verbal metaphorical spaces (including ironic and subversive utterances and ridicule) through which workers resist injustice and empower each other or develop a hybrid culture and a negotiating space.

Integrative Theoretical Framework

The Vietnamese state becomes a labor broker, recruiting its citizens to work in Malaysia through the LBS, a structured, government-controlled system of recruiters, trainers, and funders. In response to the LBS, the migrants, their parents, and indigenous/village leaders (who can act as alternatives to the state's authority) challenge the system, and even bypass it altogether. Some of this resistance is in "third space," which may be physical or metaphorical places where survival is gained through the quiet yet active support of communities standing in opposition to the established power. Legal forms of internal/individual and structural empowerment, as well as stepwise migration, add further depth to the system and help explain the kinds of lives migrant returnees choose after their Malaysia experiences.

Labor Brokerage State

I build on the LBS concept developed by Rodriguez and Guevarra. They explain how the Philippine state acts as a labor broker to create "the great Filipino worker" and send him or her abroad.[22] The LBS must invest in a migration infrastructure that becomes self-reinforcing.[23] This coherent infrastructure of state and quasi-state institutions benefits from fees, loan interest, and the economic spillover effects of remittances. State policies, regulations, and institutions (employment agencies, banks, media, and mass organizations

Introduction 7

such as women's and peasants' unions) are needed to send migrants to work overseas. In the case of Vietnam, labor export policies are used as a strategy to create employment and reduce poverty, especially in poor rural districts inhabited by ethnic minorities. The recruitment system is critical because it is the starting point for transnational migration, which intersects with local, national, and global processes.[24]

In Vietnam, recruitment is carried out by a combination of private, fully state-owned, and quasi-state companies. This system is closely connected to mass organizations and state employment agencies at all administrative levels to recruit residents at the lowest commune and hamlet levels. After the contracts have been signed by the migrant workers-to-be, the loan application process begins, in which local state bank officials figure. This elaborate and complex system reinforces itself by creating jobs for thousands of state officials and recruiters at various levels nationwide. The recruitment system is also transnational because the Malaysian outsourcing companies work directly with Vietnamese recruitment companies to fill their job orders. All the tentacles of this system function to create and manipulate the consent of impovershed citizens by appealing to their needs and aspirations.

However, there are internal contradictions in this transnational LBS bureaucracy. Although the media in Vietnam, another dimension of the migration infrastructure, is controlled by the state and the labor unions, labor media in particular has been walking a fine line in trying to represent domestic migrant workers' rights[25] and shed light on overseas migrant workers' precarity. While the state media has reinforced the LBS by promoting its labor export policies, investigative labor journalists have from the start been criticizing these policies for not responding to the concerns of or protecting the workers in Malaysia and have exposed the wrongdoings of some elements of the LBS bureaucracy.

Moreover, external criticisms from the global civil society have intervened in the LBS system by underscoring the vulnerabilities of overseas migrant workers. The International Labour Organization (ILO) and the Tripartite Action to Protect Migrant Workers within and from the Greater Mekong Subregion from Labour Exploitation (GMS TRIANGLE project)—partially funded by the Australian government—have played a role in shaping global labor migration legislation, providing technical assistance, and monitoring Vietnam's global labor migration processes, albeit with ambiguous effects. And since 2015 some international NGOs in Malaysia and elsewhere have been more proactive in bringing international focus to the exploitation of temporary transnational migrant workers, including Vietnamese workers in Malaysia. Tenaganita, a Malaysia-based human rights and non-profit

8 *Introduction*

organization, focuses on helping and protecting migrants, refugees, women, and children from exploitation, discrimination, slavery, and human trafficking.[26] The Vietnamese-American coalition Boat People SOS and the Coalition to Abolish Modern-Day Slavery in Asia (CAMSA, a part of the global anti-labor-trafficking movement) are two international NGOs that focus on migrant workers' rights.[27]

Social Networks

The social network concept is helpful when analyzing conventional migration patterns that have been adopted by people from the same community whose members share one or more affinities.[28] Social networks illuminate common phenomena such as recruitment and remittances at the beginning of and during the migration process.

Migrant networks—social or interpersonal networks—link potential migrants in sending communities to people in receiving societies, lower the costs of international migration, and help migrants secure employment. Social networks are connected to social capital: one invests in social relationships in exchange for goods and services both tangible (via economic transactions) and intangible (the granting of approval or the pledging of allegiance). With shared allegiances, migrants can benefit from the structure of their relationships without fear of nonpayment.[29] Social bonds from the same networks can assist with the decision to migrate and help with practical matters at the beginning of life working abroad.[30]

Many social network studies have established the effects of both strong ties (e.g., relatives, friends, and neighbors) and weak ties (e.g., acquaintances, strangers, and ethnic and religious networks) on economic outcomes for migrants, and whether they are documented or undocumented.[31] These ties help them find jobs, resettle, and integrate into the receiving countries. Weak ties elucidate how migrants intending to resettle in a receiving country get help from people who are not from their own communities.[32] Collyer argues that as a result of migration restrictions, undocumented migrants use social networks differently, focusing on weaker social ties rather than strong family networks.[33] His study of the Algerian community in the UK shows that many undocumented asylum seekers receive support via weak ties provided by solidarity within well-established ethnic or religious groups instead of their family ties in France.[34]

The social network approach goes beyond the binary "legal" and "illegal" categories and explores how undocumented migrants cope with restrictions to travel and settle in new countries outside of the legal system. Boyd shows

Introduction

that family networks are central features of illegal migration in industrial nations; in particular, legal migration in the United States is associated with the illegal migration of Mexicans.[35] Aguilera and Massey find that undocumented migrants rely more on social capital, receive higher returns for their social capital, and benefit from different forms of social capital than do documented migrants. These findings confirm and extend social capital theory and underscore the importance of social networks to the understanding of migrant earnings.[36]

The permanent settlement of foreign migrants in receiving countries is the subject of a number of social network studies. Hagan focuses on changes in social networks over time, paying attention to different effects of women and men on settlement outcomes, especially with respect to opportunities to become legal, in an undocumented Mayan migrant community in Houston.[37] Pfeffer and Parra study how five Latino farmworker communities in New York used both strong and weak social ties to gain access to a broader range of labor-market opportunities outside of their ethnic enclave.[38] Bloch and McKay use the concepts of social capital and social networks to explain worker recruitment practices and employment of undocumented migrants in the ethnic business enclaves of Chinese, Bangladeshi, and Turkish-speaking communities in London.[39]

The Third Space

The concept of third space can illuminate aspects of labor migration that are not dependent on strong or weak social ties and that are not strictly related to migrants' economic outcomes (job opportunities or earnings). The idea goes beyond economic factors, recognizing broader cultural and religious resources that connect sending and receiving communities. It recognizes the soft power of ethnic competing authorities who can provide a safe space (which local or state authorities may consider illegal) that enables migrants or guest workers who engage in circular migration to Malaysia and other Southeast Asian countries to survive and move on with their lives.

The third space concept provides a way to understand the experiences of guest workers who do not plan to resettle in and integrate into the receiving countries (which is a phenomenon well studied in the social network literature). Third space enables other positions and liminal negotiating spaces, or hybridity, to emerge. It offers a means to describe migrants' liminal space of *relative* freedom and actions (such as becoming undocumented, using a tourist visa to get into the country to work) that are formally illegal but informally accepted in local communities.[40] Many Vietnamese migrants became undocumented in Malaysia by leaving abusive owners who violated their agreed-upon labor contracts. These migrants contested and effectively broke the terms of contracts that restricted them to only designated employers. The third space concept explains how these migrants gained a modicum of autonomy even after they had lost all legal standing in Malaysia and no longer had the means to return to Vietnam.

In this study, I draw on the third space concept to explain the experiences of guest workers who returned home after their migration to Malaysia for work. Physical and metaphorical third spaces can account for the cultural resources, in addition to economic support, that help migrants survive and fight for their rights. In subsequent chapters, I document the support that the Kinh, Hoa, Hrê, and Chăm Muslim migrants I interviewed received from the Malay communities and the Khmer migrants I interviewed received in Cambodia and Thailand. I also show how socialist Kinh migrants created their own cultural and economic spaces in the suburbs of Warsaw and Prague.

Third space concepts also offer a way to analyze the issues of dependency in labor migration with depth and nuance. Social networks can create well-intentioned forms of dependency that often are helpful at the beginning of the migration process but that can lock workers into the types of jobs that are suboptimal relative to their education and skills.[41] When the migrants do not adjust to structural changes happening around them, they find themselves hemmed in by "path dependency."[42] The concept of third space helps explain how migrants' newfound "freedom" helps them overcome their unintended dependency on their original social networks, allowing them to act *outside* of their comfort zone. For instance, the migrants who figure in this study would seek help from local Malaysian communities, and members of these communities would assist them in various ways, such as by informing undocumented Chăm Muslims of upcoming police raids in Malaysia or by hiring undocumented workers (of different ethnic groups) in Malaysia. Additionally, they could join temporarily with other foreign workers to act collectively, thereby achieving an elevated consciousness, or "class moments," through which they united in struggle around common issues of rights and interests.[43] In general, however, these moments were short lived; after winning some small concessions from an employer, workers retreated to their ethnic-based cultural enclaves and resumed work, lest they be sent home and lose all of their investment in terms of the loans they took to go to work in Malaysia.

Also, the concept of third space helps explain the complexity of temporary migration patterns. While social network theory recognizes that there are negative consequences (such as the hollowing out of the sending areas) and appreciates the differences between cyclical and permanent out-migrations,

Introduction 11

it glosses over the complex patterns of *non*permanent out-migrations such as circular (domestic, transnational) and stepwise migration.[44] The concept of a physical third space can explain these different trajectories that are not determined by one journey and one destination. Even with cyclical flows, migrants do not always travel to and from the same destinations, a condition assumed by social networks. Moreover, a physical third space can account for complex and diverse migration patterns, which can straddle legal and illegal spaces.

How do migrants create alternatives to their plight when they have no official voice? Scott's classic book *Weapons of the Weak: Everyday Forms of Peasant Resistance* (1985) describes forms of hidden resistance such as foot dragging, dissimulation, desertion, false compliance, pilfering, feigned ignorance, slander, arson, and sabotage.[45] Many migration scholars have used Scott's everyday forms of resistance to highlight different strategies that domestic workers use to reclaim their sense of power in relations with their employers.[46] Constable explains how these covert strategies are deployed by domestic guest workers in Hong Kong.[47] Chin discusses how domestic workers in Malaysia cope with employers who spy on them by using strategies such as talking back in subtle ways, engaging in acts of self-deprecation, taking advantage of an employer's sense of gratitude, and smiling at a nagging employer. These acts of resistance also include agreeing with their employer in a face-to-face interaction but laughing and gossiping about household affairs, behind the employer's back, to other maids and outsiders.[48] To cope with dislocations, Filipina migrant domestic workers respond in their everyday practices by manipulating the attachment that develops between them and their employers.[49] Lindquist documents how over thirty thousand Indonesian female domestic workers, for example, run away from their employers in Malaysia each year to escape debt or to return home rather than remain with the recruitment agency.[50] Crinis and Ueno explain that migrants in authoritarian states such as Singapore and Malaysia make use of more covert, subtle, and inconspicuous strategies because labor resistance may lead to work contract termination and worker deportation. Ueno analyzes how Filipina and Indonesian domestic workers in Singapore have resisted exploitation by employment agencies, employers, governments, the public, and even family members.[51]

Contributing to this large body of literature, I explain how migrant guest workers (from all five ethnic groups) who were employed in factory work deployed forms of everyday resistance. Land was not a big factor in these migrant workers' protests. Most of them were not full-time peasants but instead intermittent neophyte factory workers who created spaces of resistance when the occasion arose. Foot dragging and feigning ignorance are relevant when discussing how the returnees and their families refused to pay back the loans that enabled the migrants to work in Malaysia. Examples featuring dissimulation can be seen in the practices of migrant factory workers on the assembly line in Malaysia.

But migrants and their village and religious leaders also have engaged in open rather than hidden forms of resistance to challenge their oppression, and the third space perspective offers a nuanced, rich, and sophisticated analytical framework that can better account for such forms of opposition than social networks theory and weapons of the weak arguments.

Forms of Metaphorical Third Space

The idea of a metaphorical third space counts as discourses of dissent not only behind-the-back talking against the "masters" but also face-to-face verbal utterances that are safe for the "weak" to use. Building on Lacan's discussion of how subjects can employ certain mimicking strategies in order to survive, Bhabha develops the concept of mimicry, which he defines as the adoption of the "master's tools," such as his or her culture, assumptions, institutions, ideology, and values, in order to resist.[52] Although Bhabha's context and scholarship relates to colonial literature in India, his argument about how the poor in India adopted the British worldview to fight back is applicable to how the five Vietnamese ethnic groups—including the Kinh—challenge the Kinh government's labor export policies. In the case of Vietnam, Bhabha's notion of enunciation, which relates to the mimicry concept, opens up a metaphorical third space of dissent that illuminates how migrants embrace the labor brokerage state's labor export policies and the dreams they create in order to fight back.[53]

Building on Bhabha, Fahlander argues that mimicry can be an active, intentional, safe, and subversive strategy in unequal power relations instead of a stiff expression of the pathology of the subaltern (defined as the colonized or people of lower socioeconomic status).[54] The subaltern seems to be adjusting and assimilating to a dominant discourse, giving the impression that the colonized is "pacified and harmless," when in fact a space for hidden agendas has been opened up. This is related to Scott's concept of the hidden transcript, defined as covert and discrete forms of resistance that challenge the hegemony of the state system.[55] But active mimicry can bring the hidden agenda of the oppressed to the forefront in a safe manner. Fahlander argues that certain mocking practices may be perceived as ironic or strange, but overall, they are too subtle to be suppressed or punished by those in power. Moreover, ironic mimicry can be employed as a solidarity strengthening

Introduction

strategy that authorities will find difficult to ban. I found abundant examples of these nuanced forms of mimicry used as forms of dissent or as a means of manipulation among members of all five ethnic groups. Village/commune and religious authorities of the ethnic minority groups, who are intimately familiar with LBS policies, use subversive mimicry to safely ridicule the failure of state policies when acting on behalf of their ethnic migrants. Parents of migrants and migrants themselves use ironic mimicry to mock the very labor export policies that are supposed to lift them out of poverty.

Drawing on Bhabha's work, Massey and Soja discuss the role of social practices and how the idea of a third space transcends traditional dualism with critical spatial awareness. From the perspective of a feminist critique of dualism, Massey challenges a logic of A/not-A that, she maintains, works to the advantage of dominant social groups, defining women in terms of lack, and does not allow for a possibility of alternative forms of social order.[56] From a Marxist standpoint, Massey argues that space is constituted through social relations and material social practices and is created out of intricate networks of relations, from local to global. Soja defines the third space as a "space that draws upon the material and mental spaces of the traditional dualism (real and imagined) but extends well beyond them in scope, substance and meaning." In other words, Soja's concept of the third space allows for journeys that encompass both "real and imagined" places.[57]

The metaphorical third space can be a liminal hybrid space that calls for negotiations between two cultures or systems. It can be a space of contradiction and ambiguity that challenges essentialist oppositional polarities, such as first-world/third-world or colonizer/colonized.[58] As such, one can construct one's identities in relation to contradictory systems of meaning. Frenkel uses mimicry and hybridity to explain the discourse on multinational corporations' knowledge transfer from developed to developing countries, an example of the abstract metaphor of the third space of in-between.[59] Lee applies the third space concept to migrant domestic workers whose labor in an underground economy is not protected by explicit labor laws and regulations.[60] I draw on this liminal third space to describe the cultural hybridity and negotiations of the socialist Kinh migrants and their children who created their own identities in the commercial and cultural centers in Warsaw and Prague.

Forms of Physical Third Space

Third space enables other positions to emerge, connecting metaphorical with physical spaces. The third space can be a space of resistance, a space of

14   *Introduction*

radical openness, or a liminal, hybrid space that emerges at the margins of a new cultural politics.[61] From the legal governance perspective, Bhabha argues that the space constituted around the encounters between the colonizers and colonized is not entirely governed by laws of either ruler or ruled. Applying this extralegal aspect of third space to transnational labor migration, Abraham and van Schendel introduce the pair "licit" (socially accepted) and "illicit" (socially banned) to refer to social perceptions of activities defined by authorities as criminal/illegal. They define third space as "licit and illegal spaces," places with competing authorities that may be legally banned but socially sanctioned.[62] It is in this illegal yet licit third space that I found all five ethnic groups to have employed *metaphorical* third-space responses that are more prominent among the three ethnic minorities (the Hrê, the Khmer, and the Chăm Muslims), not the majority Kinh, in navigating, challenging, and even bypassing the LBS system.

Third space can be social and cultural spaces that offer strategies for survival. Gutierrez uses the concept in his examination of the ethnic Mexicans (not the indigenous groups living in modern-day Mexico) who lived in "Greater Mexico" in the nineteenth century.[63] This area is referred to as the US-Mexico "borderlands," roughly demarcated now by the northern states in Mexico and the southwestern states of the United States (Texas, New Mexico, Arizona, and southern California).[64] Gutierrez argues that those ethnic Mexicans were forced to devise defensive strategies of adaptation and survival in this third space, which was carved out of segregated run-down urban barrios and isolated rural colonias (unregulated settlements) that served as safe havens and as sites for the transmission of different variants of Mexican culture. Gutierrez argues that in these vibrant barrios and rural colonias, the ethnic Mexicans communicated in Spanish, practiced family customs and religious rituals, enjoyed their cuisine and music, and formed a solidarity. I draw on the idea of a physical social third space, used as a means for survival, to explain the responses of the five ethnic groups from Vietnam who operated inside the LBS system but found gaps within it to subvert, as well as those who operated outside of it (many Khmer and Chăm migrants) to survive. The concept of physical third space is also useful in explaining the development of the two major commercial and cultural centers of the Kinh socialist migrants in Europe: Marywilska in Warsaw and Sapa in Prague.

Marginalized ethnic minorities can create spaces of strength by drawing from their cultural resources and institutions. Concepts such as geographical agency and community cultural wealth help us understand physical third spaces.[65] Migrants who have economic, religious, and cultural resources can capitalize on them to make a living even when they are displaced locally, as

Introduction   15

happened in Vietnam when it moved to a market-based economy. I build on Taylor's concept of geographical agency to explain different forms of economic space created by the Khmer and the Chăm, who have transnational kinship and cultural networks that have enabled them to bypass the state system and cross many borders, from Vietnam to Cambodia, from Cambodia to Thailand, and from Thailand to Malaysia. I also use Yosso's concept of community cultural wealth to explain how the ethnic minorities I feature in this book draw on their social, religious, and linguistic resources to benefit from the LBS system when possible or to bypass it altogether.

In sum, both physical and metaphorical third spaces open up the possibility for forms of safe protest and explain various forms of dissent on the part of migrants, their parents, and their village and religious leaders. However, ethnic hierarchies (which I discuss in chapter 1) and gender differences determine the nature of these resistances. I use these concepts in three theme-based chapters, one focusing on precarity and coping mechanisms, another on physical third spaces, and another on metaphorical third spaces.

Empowerment and Protest

Migrant workers also engage in public spaces, demonstrating individual initiative and participating in public protests to fight for their rights and entitlements. The interests, initiative, and agency of the migrants themselves have also driven and framed transnational labor migration, especially nonstate patterns. Worker agency can take various forms of internal and structural empowerment.

Oishi focuses on how low-capital female migrant workers in all sectors of the global economy, not just domestic and service work but also manufacturing, have consciously engaged in activities that reflect two forms of empowerment.[66] The first form is *structural* empowerment, through which they collectively combat systemic exploitation on behalf of all workers in the world, and the second is *internal* empowerment, or cognitive processes through which they individually reflect on and analyze their oppression. Oishi argues that international labor migration can be a positive internal empowerment experience that allows workers to learn new skills (such as administrative, organizing, leadership) and new languages and that encourages self-development, self-fulfillment, self-confidence, and independence.

Remittances are important forms of internal empowerment with important social meanings. They can be motivated by two purposes: altruism toward family members (indicated when workers send remittances to lower-income households to alleviate poverty) and exchange (indicated when workers send

16 *Introduction*

remittances to high-income households to pay back a loan given to them).[67] Scholars also stress that remittances are not simply monetary transactions but also social transactions with motivational aspects that are codetermined by the migrant workers and their extended families.[68] Remittances can also be considered as acts of recognition that involve performing and negotiating multiple roles (wives, mothers, daughters, or sisters, for example) so as to maintain transnational (natal and marital) family ties across distances.[69] Other scholars argue that remittances can serve to reinforce status and networks in the migrant workers' original communities. Still others suggest that men and women negotiate remittances in multiple ways and discuss how in specific Asian contexts, women tend to assume the role of remittance sender.[70]

Remittances require a lot of sacrifice. The use of debt to finance transnational labor migration and the use of remittances for debt repayment are special aspects of labor migration in Southeast Asian contexts. Hoang and Yeoh focus on how debts incurred to finance transnational labor migration affect migrant workers and their families, especially their stay-at-home parents, spouses, and children, and note that many migrants use remittances earned during their first year working overseas to repay their debts.[71]

Stepwise International Migration

Stepwise international migration refers to a process by which migrant workers move "up" from one destination country to another to improve their long-term conditions such as greater salaries, benefits, and savings and investment at home.[72] Stepwise international migration is not a state-sponsored migration program but a conscious strategy of low-capital migrants who are motivated to "follow a stepwise international migration trajectory, working their way up a hierarchy of destination countries."[73] In the case of Vietnamese migrants, after Malaysia, they would aspire to choose an East Asian country such as Taiwan, South Korea, or Japan, saving money along the way to cover the higher fees and other costs of each step upward.

Migrants taking a stepwise approach move up from unskilled jobs in lower-level workplaces in developing countries to increasingly better jobs requiring more skills in higher-tier countries after accumulating sufficient capital to do so. Other factors that underwrite stepwise migration are the restrictive immigration requirements and policies of countries at the top of the migrants' hierarchies (such as Japan), which force migrants to consider alternative destinations as stepping stones toward their preferred destination. Most migrants cannot afford to go straight to South Korea or Japan because they lack the money and language skills, so starting with Malaysia enables

Introduction 17

them to learn and save money for the next step. Middle-class and educated women have more opportunities when it comes to stepwise mobility. Parrenas provides an example of a Filipina migrant worker with good English skills who was a schoolteacher and travel agent in the Philippines. She migrated to Taiwan in the late 1980s to work as a housekeeper, factory worker, and janitor. Then she returned to the Philippines due to restrictive migrant policies introduced in Taiwan in the early 1990s. But after only three months back in the Philippines, she decided to leave directly for the United States, her real target, because "America is the land of the promises and the land of opportunities."[74] She then paid US$8000 for the use of another woman's passport in order to go to the United States. This Filipina's middle-class status and education enabled her to work in a developed country such as Taiwan and then use that work experience as a stepping stone to migrate to the United States, where she worked and sent some of her earnings home to sustain a middle-class lifestyle for her family in the Philippines.[75]

Moreover, the presence of a global diaspora (or migrant social networks) of successful stepwise migrants from the home country can serve to inspire others to follow in their footsteps. I observed this at work in the case of Kinh socialist migrants, Chăm Muslim migrants, and, to a lesser extent, Khmer migrants.

Stepwise international migration also helps account for aspiration and forms of internal empowerment that I discuss in chapter 7. I found evidence of aspiration among the many Kinh and Hoa migrants I interviewed. Many migrants had plans to work their way up "stepwise" through a hierarchy of destination countries from Malaysia to Taiwan, South Korea, or Japan. They expected to improve their condition incrementally and to save and invest along the way.

Ethnic Hierarchies

Ethnicity is important for understanding transnational migration, even when the ethnic groups come from the same labor-sending country. But ethnicity does not act in isolation. Scholars have conceptualized ethnic hierarchies as a way to embed ethnicity in a framework of other factors. Holmes develops the concept of a labor hierarchy in terms of citizenship and language in the context of undocumented farm laborers in Skagit County in Washington State.[76] This hierarchy privileges those who have US citizenship and those who can speak English: white and Asian American US citizens rank at the top, followed in descending order by Latino US citizens or residents, undocumented mestizo Mexicans (those with mixed European and indigenous ancestries),

18 *Introduction*

and undocumented Indigenous Mexicans (including the Mixtec and Triqui people from the Mexican state of Oaxaca). While mestizo Mexicans speak Spanish, the Triqui and Mixtec speak their own non-European languages indigenous to Mexico. These groups have different privileges in relation to health, financial security, respect, and control over time and labor based on their position in the hierarchy. Quesada, Hart, and Bourgois discuss ethnic hierarchies in terms of nationality and indigeneity in the context of the vulnerability of Latino migrants as economically disenfranchised laborers in US society, which regards them as criminals and devalues their individual and cultural worth.[77]

My ethnic hierarchies are based on two dimensions: economic factors (landownership and access to finances, education, and health care) and cultural factors (transnational networks, language capabilities, and religious affinity). These economic and cultural factors inform how migrants empower themselves and engage in different spaces of dissent. I have found that cultural factors are very important, helping some ethnic minorities overcome lower rankings in terms of economic factors. For instance, religious affinity explains the Chăm Muslim case nicely. Overall, these contexts inform how the five groups coexist and resist the LBS system and highlight their cross-ethnic differences.

In chapter 1, I elaborate on where the five ethnic groups are situated in these multidimensional hierarchies constructed on different levels of privilege or uneven power relations with the Kinh, the major ethnic group. The economic and cultural contexts signal the readers on what to look for in subsequent chapters on how migrants of these five ethnic groups respond to the risks, precarity, and opportunities associated with their overseas work in Malaysia and their return—a full circle in the LBS system. Then, in subsequent theme-based chapters, I show how these ethnic hierarchies affect each ethnic group's forms of empowerment and third spaces differently.

Gender Differences

Analysis of the impacts of ethnicity in response to the LBS system must also take gender differences into account. I use Patricia Hill Collins's broad definition of intersectionality as an analytical strategy to understand the different types of gender relations in each of the ethnic groups with respect to their migration patterns, their experiences in Malaysia, and their reactions to transnational migration throughout the process. Intersectionality references the critical insight that race, class, gender, ethnicity, sexuality, age, ability, nation, and other analytical categories are best understood in relation to

Introduction 19

rather than in isolation from one another. This analytical strategy is attentive to power relations and social inequalities.[78] I focus on the interconnections among ethnicity, gender, and class, remaining conscious that women's lives are different from men's lives and that women's lives are not the same across race/ethnicity and class.

For instance, one cannot assume that Chăm men will have the same experiences as Chăm women, even when they come from the same cultural backgrounds, share the same religion, and travel together to work in Malaysia, or that the experiences of a Kinh female worker will be very different from that of a Chăm Muslim female worker just because they come from very different backgrounds. So, in each of the theme-based chapters (chapters 5, 6, and 7), I point out how gender relations are different within and across ethnic groups but can also be similar when they develop various forms of third spaces to improve their conditions.

Methodological Considerations

My findings are based on eight years of research and fieldwork interviews in both Vietnam and Malaysia (2008–15), a significant period of change in labor export policies. My data collection is based on purposive method and convenience sampling. Using a "snowballing" sampling technique, I relied on the networking of migrants and labor media as two dimensions of the migration infrastructure to procure interviewees. I interviewed over 130 individuals (migrants, their family members, and religious and village leaders) of these five ethnic groups, 30 other key stakeholders (including Vietnamese state officials and local ethnic authorities who work alongside the Kinh officials), and representatives of recruitment companies, media, mass organizations, and international NGOs. All interviewees' names are pseudonyms in their respective ethnic naming conventions. I used the real names of government workers, public officials, and directors or presidents of companies unless they advised otherwise.

The fieldwork in Malaysia was conducted with Dr. Vicki Crinis (University of Wollongong, Australian postdoctoral research fellow) in 2008. We conducted both unobtrusive observations and in-depth interviews with migrant workers in Malaysian hostels, shopping malls, bus stops, restaurants, and coffee shops in Johor Bahru. We did the same in Batu Pahat, a district about 120 kilometers from Johor Bahru, where we interviewed individuals from two migrant networks that happened to be grouped by gender and hometowns. One group included all male migrants that had come from the north and north-central provinces (Hà Tĩnh, Sơn Tây) while the other consisted of all female migrants that had come from the Mekong Delta's southern provinces (Tiền Giang, An Giang, Mỹ Tho). While these were convenience samples, they confirm that migrants from the same hometowns stayed together, and that gender affinity is an important factor that binds people together.

During the week, these migrants went to work and returned to their respective rental units in the evenings; on the weekend, they socialized with each other. We visited them over one such weekend in August 2008. We followed the leads of our two female informants, Ms. Hà and Ms. Lê, who escorted us to the workers' neighborhood to visit their fellow migrant workers from the northern and north-central provinces. We walked through a neighborhood in Batu Pahat, passing shops, restaurants, and rows of worker hostels owned by Chinese Malaysians. We were early (around nine o'clock in the morning) and the men had just awakened, but they greeted us graciously and invited us to sit on the sofa on the veranda, where we conducted our focus group interviews. Many of the fifteen men worked in plastic and paper factories. While we talked, they smoked cigarettes, drank coffee, and talked to their families in Vietnam on their mobile phones, which rang constantly.

These transnational fieldwork visits examined the full cycle of labor migration: individuals being recruited in Vietnam, working in Malaysia, and returning to their hometowns or villages in Vietnam. I treat return migration as a part of my methodology (as a way to get leads, which facilitates snowball sampling) and a conceptual element of analysis, because the objective was to understand the whole migration process (before, during, and after) and forms of protest after the migrants returned to Vietnam. Moreover, treating return migration as a phase of temporary transnational labor migration can provide insights into the contradictions of LBS policies and shed light on how migrants move on with their lives.

Convenience sampling may result in built-in biases. During my fieldwork interviews, I was escorted by local officials from labor departments, employment offices, and mass organizations at all levels (province, district, village/commune/hamlet/ward).[79] Officials often took me to specific households whose members had benefited from labor export policies, and the parents had no problem sharing stories of their children's successes with me. Therefore I cannot make generalizations. I am conscious of the potential biases reflected in the answers of the interviewees when responding to my questions in front of the state officials. But even under such close state control, the honest narratives of their own personal and family experiences reveal much about their cultural identity and their migration patterns and strategies (via state and nonstate channels). During the long interviews, when the state officials became bored and stepped out for a cigarette or coffee, I did create a third

Introduction 21

space of my own to ask some quick follow-up questions with the parents and the local leaders, hoping in this way to glean their true and nuanced feelings about the LBS system, debts, and remittances before the officials returned.

Moreover, I did manage to wander around, unescorted, and talk to other households in these ethnic neighborhoods (and one time I even ventured into a forbidden Hrê district). These invaluable moments helped me see the bigger picture and gain an uncensored understanding of their situations. On returning to their houses in the mountainous Quảng Ngãi province and in An Giang province, the returnees often began working elsewhere (in the fields or on the factory floor in other areas of Vietnam). So I interviewed their families (spouses, parents, and siblings) who stayed behind but remained in close contact with their loved ones. I also interviewed neighbors I met on the way who were curious about what I was doing in their villages. Most were very honest with me about what had happened to their children, spouses, or neighbors and about how they were doing in Malaysia at the time of our conversations.

I am also fully aware that the power relations between me and my ethnic interviewees were unequal, since I am Kinh, a member of the officials' ethnicity with privileges, and I was conscious that my questions could place ethnic members at risk, because the Kinh officials would pay attention to how they answered my questions. But here is a twist to this uneven power relationship between me (the interviewer) and the interviewees. When their indigenous leaders expressed their sentiments and directed their complaints to me, they were in fact expressing them to the Kinh officials who accompanied me and were listening to every word they uttered. Thus, in these moments, competing local authorities saw me as a mediator, a way to convey their discontent to and even at times ridicule the Kinh officials who escorted me, and so the roles of the interviewer and the interviewee were flipped. In addition, while a native speaker of Vietnamese, I do not speak the languages of the other ethnic groups, and thus I was dependent on translation, which was often provided by the ethnic members who worked as translators in local state offices or by independent guides such as local journalists.

I also interviewed other stakeholders in the LBS system. They include officials from Department of Overseas Labor (DOLAB), under the Ministry of Labor, Invalids, and Social Affairs (MoLISA), who understood the legislation and implementation of labor export policies; officials in key state banks and state-owned labor export companies; the Vietnam Association of Manpower Supply (VAMAS, a quasi-state agency that represents recruitment companies); officials from the Vietnam General Confederation of Labor (VGCL); and women's union members, labor union representatives, and ILO

22 Introduction

representatives.[80] I also interviewed owners of private recruitment companies (in person and through email correspondence) and key labor journalists who had written many articles on the effects of the labor export policies on migrant workers. These investigative journalists not only gave me helpful insights into labor migration but also supplied me with leads to follow concerning recruitment companies and employment services agencies, which then led to further interviews.

Moreover, I used mixed methods by triangulating many sources of information. I integrated primary sources (in-depth interviews) with secondary sources, including official reports from local people's committees, MoLISA, the VGCL, and the ILO; hundreds of news articles from Vietnamese media coverage; and valuable anthropological and historical information gleaned from the work of Vietnamese scholars and experts who have done extensive fieldwork research on the Hrê, the Khmer, and the Chăm in Vietnam over time.

Table 1 summarizes the number of people that I interviewed: migrants and their family members and other stakeholders in the LBS system for each ethnic group. I supply detailed explanations of my data collection methodology for each ethnic sample in appendix 1.

Book Organization

The book begins with the rationale for this study, the integrative theoretical framework and methodology that explains the transnational migration process and migrant responses. I then describe the historical contexts the reader needs to be familiar with in order to understand the cultural and economic resources that sustain different Vietnamese migrant ethnic groups. I move on to explain the intricacies and power of the transnational LBS system and how it secures the consent of the migrants to work in Malaysia. From

Table 1. Samples for the Five Ethnic Groups

	Kinh & Hoa	Hrê	Khmer	Chăm	Row total
Number of migrants and family members	32	35	20	33	120
Number of other stakeholders in the LBS system (state officials, mass organizations, recruiters, local indigenous leaders)	9	17	5	7	38
Column total	41	52	25	40	158

Introduction 23

there, the book explores the lives of the migrants, their differing patterns of migration including stepwise, circular, and domestic migration, and how they used third space. I conclude with findings on cross-group differences that highlight the third space dissent, the aspirations of migrants, and the intersectionality of ethnicity, gender, and class; these insights into ethnic hierarchies are important contributions to migration studies. Finally, I issue a call for action that is informed by the findings and analyses to improve the conditions of migrants from different ethnic groups in Vietnam.

1 Historical, Economic, Cultural, Religious Practices of the Five Ethnic Groups

A socialist cosmopolitan from Nam Định in Vietnam who migrated to the Czech Republic stays there with her extended family after the fall of the Soviet Bloc in 1989 to supply simple women's clothes, assembled in Vietnam, to working-class customers in these formerly communist markets. A young Chăm Muslim seamstress in An Giang designs and employs her siblings to assemble traditional Muslim garments to be sold in modern-day Malaysia with the help of her aunt who lives there. Born far apart (Nam Định is in the north of Vietnam and An Giang is in the south), these two entrepreneurs' paths demonstrate the effect of history and different migration patterns on their lives, yet they share a spirit of dynamism and creativity and a reliance on family networks that transcend national borders. A Khmer hamlet deputy chief in An Giang provides insights on the significant role of the *wats* (Khmer Buddhist temples) in preserving their language and culture and criticizes the indebtedness and landlessness problems related to the labor export policy affecting his villagers. A Hrê village leader in a mountainous district in Quảng Ngãi province (central of Vietnam) reminds Kinh officials of the traditional spirit of mutual aid among the Hrê migrants who left their villages to work in another country for the first time, hoping to fulfill the dreams promised by the labor export policy. Both indigenous leaders in provinces a thousand kilometers apart advocate for their respective villagers who participated in the labor export program in Malaysia and returned to Vietnam with debts they acquired in the process.

This chapter explains the historical and cultural contexts of and differences between the ethnic groups under consideration. I examine how different levels of access to economic resources—land, finance, and education—have placed each of the five ethnic groups on different levels of the ethnic hierarchies (table 2). At the same time, I examine some century-old cultural practices—national and transnational networks, language, and religion—that nearly reverse the rankings, empowering the Chăm and the Khmer. In the conclusion, drawing from the ethnic hierarchies, I signal factors that ground their strategies for survival and that even allow them to thrive in the labor brokerage state (LBS) system. These insights enable cross-group comparisons in subsequent chapters.

Kinh and Hoa Migrants in the Socialist and Market Eras

The history of mobility of socialist Kinh migrants parallels that of the non-Kinh migrants in Malaysia who received support not only from their extended family networks but also from the transnational communities in which they lived and worked. During the Cold War in the 1950s, the newly established Democratic Republic of Vietnam, north of the seventeenth parallel, had already become an LBS.[1] The first waves of Vietnamese migration in the 1950s and 1960s were based on the spirit of international socialist brotherhood to support Vietnam's anti-colonial French (in the 1950s) and anti-US imperialism (1960–75) wars.[2] The governments of the Soviet Union, East Germany, and other Eastern European countries invited Vietnamese students, workers, and cadres to their countries for further academic and vocational training as well as party training at Communist Party schools and through apprenticeships. To pay debts to these socialist allies and to alleviate problems of unemployment and poverty in Vietnam, the Vietnamese government exported labor to Eastern Europe.[3]

After winning the US-Vietnam war in 1975, Vietnam was reunified into one country, the Socialist Republic of Vietnam, but it faced almost twenty years of a US trade embargo (1975–94). External pressures such as the crisis with China and the Chinese attack on Vietnam in 1979 also pushed Vietnam closer to the Soviet Bloc, culminating in Vietnam becoming a full member of the Council for Mutual Economic Assistance in 1978.[4] Internally, Vietnam faced budget difficulties, reduced aid, and increased pressure to pay wartime and nation-building debts to the Soviet Bloc. So, between the 1980s and the end of the Cold War in 1989, the Vietnamese socialist state became a socialist labor broker, signing and implementing many bilateral labor agreements with the USSR, East Germany, Czechoslovakia, Poland, Bulgaria, and other countries to send them a combined total of about three hundred thousand low-skilled Kinh guest workers. As Vietnam opened its economy to the market system and eased price controls, Vietnamese seized the opportunity to

Practices of the Five Ethnic Groups   27

mobilize capital (money) and goods to sell abroad and to bring back foreign goods to consume in Vietnam. Under this socialist labor export policy, these early socialist guest workers established a global diaspora to welcome and support subsequent waves of migrants, mostly from north of the seventeenth parallel.

After the fall of the Berlin Wall in 1989 and the disintegration of the Eastern Bloc in 1991, all the bilateral agreements became void. Many socialist migrants, who were still working under these contracts, had to make difficult decisions: either to return to Vietnam as required by the host countries or to stay and establish underground markets to sell Vietnamese products, forms of third spaces discussed in chapters 5 and 6.

The policies of the Cold War *socialist* LBS foreshadowed twenty-first century *capitalist* LBS practices in Vietnam and Malaysia embedded in the global system, when the Vietnamese state began sending migrants of different ethnic groups to work in Malaysia (chapter 2). The main difference, however, is that the contemporary guest workers include Kinh migrants from throughout Vietnam and a small number of the ethnic Hoa (the ethnic Chinese in Vietnam) and other ethnic minorities.[5]

Cultural Resources

In most studies about Vietnam, the Kinh are usually grouped together with the Hoa, who are highly assimilated with the majority Kinh. Over one thousand years of Chinese imperial and colonial rule left indelible economic, social, cultural, and religious influences in Vietnam that have persisted into the modern day. Mahayana Buddhism entered Vietnam by Silk Road traders and missionaries through southern China and the coast, and Chinese administrators and settlers brought Confucian philosophy, ideas, technologies, and words to Vietnam. Three basic Confucian ideas that spread to Vietnam and that continue to influence modern-day Vietnam are subjects' loyalty to the king, sons' piety toward their fathers, and wives' submission and fidelity to their husbands and sons.[6]

The Vietnamese resisted sporadically during this thousand-year rule, beginning with the short-lived but famous Trưng Sisters uprising for independence between 39 and 43 CE. Within the context of Chinese colonial rule, the Vietnamese sense of national cultural identity is manifested in veneration of national mothers and fathers. Scholars have studied the pairing of mythic mothers with mythic fathers. Their specific interest is the development of Mother Goddess Liễu Hạnh's cult (revered by spirit mediums) and the association it has come to have with the cult of Trần Hưng Đạo, the hero who

28   CHAPTER 1

defeated the invading Mongol and Chinese armies in the thirteenth century and who is revered as a Father of the Nation.

The Kinh-Hoa majority also have advantages over the ethnic minorities because of their access to social capital such as family networks and their use of Vietnamese, the official language of Vietnam, which enables them to acquire the skills and knowledge needed to make a living.[7] A nationwide quantitative study on sources of inequality between the majority and the ethnic minorities shows the powerful role of language (Vietnamese) in privileging the Kinh majority and indicates that the removal of this language barrier could substantially reduce inequality between the Kinh majority and the other ethnic groups, especially in terms of access to education.[8] Many Hoa also benefit from being able to speak the language of most employers in Malaysia: Chinese. A qualitative study undertaken by Thulstrup shows stark differences between the Kinh majority and the Co ethnic minority in terms of language, culture, and family relations. Thulstrup shows that the Kinh, through their social networks, have greater mobility and more connections in lowland areas where larger markets and wood-processing industries are located. The strength of Kinh social networks explains how they were able to invest early on in acacia (keo tree) plantations, which gave them access to the best land for establishing cash-crop production and inadvertently forced the Co ethnic minority in that area to clear areas further away from the commune, including in areas of protected forest.[9]

Economic Resources

The Hoa and the Kinh have greater access to key economic-based factors (such as land, finance, education, and health care) compared to the other three ethnic groups studied in this book. While the Hoa account for less than 1 percent of the population (over nine hundred thousand people), they command financial power and are the wealthiest minority.[10] Chinese companies invest in what is known as the "greater China zone," which includes Hong Kong, Taiwan, mainland China, and Southeast Asian countries, and to protect these investments, they rely on their ethnic connections—via social, cultural, language, and personal ties—and networks that they have established through globalization.[11] Overall, the Hoa have better access to financing, surpassing the four other ethnic groups, including the majority Kinh.

The Kinh and the Hoa have a higher standard of living than the other ethnic groups in Vietnam. This standard is also reflected in higher school enrollment rates and greater access to health services.[12] Major factors that account for the divergence include greater landownership, better access to credit, control of the means of production (such as farm tools or machinery), know-how, and education (which is mostly conducted in Vietnamese). Even when access to credit is assumed to be the same among poor Kinh and the Hrê, the Khmer, and the Chăm Muslims, the outcomes still benefit the majority Kinh more than the others. An empirical study on the socio-economic impact of rural credit in northern Vietnam shows that while Hoa and poor Kinh use credit to increase their income, members of the other three ethnic groups use it to create jobs, enhance nutrition, and secure access to medical services. This differential impact requires an understanding of preexisting unequal socioeconomic conditions beyond access to financial credit. The Kinh-Hoa are substantially richer than the other three ethnic groups in terms of monthly income per household, so they can afford to invest in making more money, whereas the other groups need to spend on survival essentials, such as jobs, food, and medical services.[13]

The issues of land distribution and acquisition are complicated, and landlessness is a problem that affects not only the poor ethnic minorities but also the poor Kinh majority. Nguyễn, McGrath, and White found that inequality in land distribution tends to be higher in delta regions such as the Red River Delta and the Mekong Delta (an area of abundant land). For instance, landlessness in the Mekong Delta is the result of a cycle of chronic poverty: peasants mortgage their land in response to ill health, business failure, an increase in the cost of agricultural inputs, or a decrease in output prices for cash crops.[14] All of these factors, along with participation in the labor export program, can give rise to indebtedness, which compels poor peasants to sell their land. However, indebtedness affects poor ethnic minorities more than the Kinh majority. The majority of poor people in the Mekong Delta are landless; most are Khmer. Around 4 million people (out of the delta's population of 18 million) are classified as poor. Out of these poor peasants, 2 million are landless and around 1 million are Khmer (which is half of the total Khmer population).

Kerkvliet's study shows that since the early 1970s, the large influx of mostly Kinh migrants from the lowlands to the central highlands, often with state encouragement and assistance, has negatively affected communal land use of many ethnic minority highlanders. The increasing densities of the Kinh's population in the area resulted in the decline of shifting cultivation, a practice integral to the minorities' way of life (see appendix 2).[15]

With respect to education, a UNICEF report on enrollment and attainment in public schools shows how education corresponds to each group's economic resources.[16] The Hoa had the lowest dropout rate, followed by the Kinh, the Khmer, and the Chăm.[17] Most Hoa households, as part of the wealthiest ethnic minority, can afford to send their children to public schools, which require tuition at the preschool and lower secondary levels. They also have the means to ensure that their children stay in school until graduation. Moreover, the Hoa also have private schools to teach their children the Chinese language and other subjects to complement the curriculum at the Kinh public schools.[18]

In sum, the Hoa and the Kinh rank the highest in economic categories compared to the other three groups. The Kinh and the Hoa benefit from speaking Vietnamese (the language of the majority in Vietnam), and the Hoa from speaking both Vietnamese and Chinese (the language of many employers in Malaysia). However, they do not have the transnational social and religious connections in Malaysia, a predominantly Islamic host country. Thus, they have to rely on their own resources (mostly from their families) to go to work in Malaysia and to make a living upon returning to Vietnam.

The next ethnic group, the Hrê, is on almost the opposite end of the spectrum from the Kinh and the Hoa, having the least access to both economic and cultural resources that would allow them to fare well in Malaysia.

The Hrê

Village Governance, Gender, and Cultural Practices

The Hrê minority is one of the key target groups for Prime Minister Decision 71/2009/QĐTT the labor export policy. It is the smallest and poorest ethnic minority group in this study and is also academically the most understudied group; there are very few English-language studies (although there are more in Vietnamese). Studies tend to focus on historical and anthropological aspects.[19] As of 2015, the total Hrê population in Quảng Ngãi province, where they are concentrated, was 132,745.[20] Most of the Hrê live in the mountainous districts of Quảng Ngãi province where I did my fieldwork.

Traditionally, the Hrê relied on farming, hunting, gathering, and fishing to make a living in the mountains of central Vietnam. They resided in a cluster of villages, each consisting of several hundred households, located far away from major thoroughfares. Their main livelihood was derived from planting wet rice or rice terraces in addition to swiddening, the practice of planting food crops on a rotational basis in the mountains. Lưu Hùng, a well-known Vietnamese anthropologist, argues that the Kinh had influenced the Hrê on wet rice cultivation when the two groups came into contact in the sixteenth and seventeenth centuries (by way of the Vietnamese feudal court and the

Practices of the Five Ethnic Groups

upland migration of Kinh soldiers and Kinh migrants). By the nineteenth century, the practice of wet rice cultivation had become the Hrê's main activity, surpassing swiddening.[21]

The Hrê also had a great tradition of weaving fabrics with raised designs or brocade (*dệt thổ cẩm*) for their own use and for external sale. Unfortunately, their centuries-old livelihoods have been eroded, and they have replaced rice and other food crops with cash crops, such as the acacia mangium trees (keo), which are processed into pulp chips and sold at low prices to the Kinh (and the Japanese) to make paper.

Village governance plays a significant role in their lives.[22] The Hrê live in villages (*pplay*), often named after a nearby river, mountain, hill, field, or other physical landmark.[23] The highest authority is the village elder (*già làng*), who is revered by all villagers due to his (not her) seniority and knowledge of the land on which they settled. The second-highest authority is the medicine man (*thày cúng* or *bgau*), who leads the rituals and ceremonies and can become the village elder if he gains sufficient respect from the villagers.[24] The third-highest authority is the village chief (*trưởng thôn*) or administrative leader, who is voted into his position by the Hrê villagers. The village chief liaises with Kinh officials and decides which of his villagers will be interviewed by researchers. In chapters 5 and 6, I demonstrate how these indigenous leaders interact with various levels of Vietnamese administrative system, including province, rural district, commune, and hamlet.

In 2015, I met a knowledgeable and influential Hrê, Mr. Lê, in Hành Dũng commune, Nghĩa Hành district, a government-created area to which dozens of Hrê households had been relocated (see chapter 7 for a discussion of this relocation policy and commune). Mr. Lê, who comfortably switches between Hrê and Vietnamese languages, worked as a contractor, receiving job orders from local Kinh employers in other provinces and then recruiting workers from his commune to fulfill these orders. He explained to me the critical role that the two highest leaders in the village play: "The village elder only has power over the villagers mainly due to his seniority. The village chief, on the other hand, communicates, establishes, and mediates relations with the Vietnamese society at large. He brings back information and knowledge to disseminate among the villagers." I was informed later that Mr. Lê was aiming to become the village chief of his village.[25]

Spiritual rituals are important in village life, so much so that migrants go back to practicing them upon returning to the villages, and even the young Hrê, who have integrated into the Kinh system and who work alongside the Kinh at commune and district levels, still practice them. Rituals are especially important for coping with the extreme annual weather patterns of the area:

32 CHAPTER 1

rain and floods for three months and sun and drought for nine. The Hrê's main religion is animism, which instills in them respect for and a desire to worship all living things, including plants, trees, and especially the spirit of the rice paddies.[26] Since water is the quintessential element of their wet rice cultivation, the Hrê incorporate it into their animistic rituals that worship the god (*thần*) of rain, wind, lightning, mountains, and trees. In these rituals, the village elders select a medicine man (*pdâu* or *padau*) to prepare all offerings for the rituals.

The Hrê also perform rituals when their people are ill, as a village elder in Sơn Hà district points out: "The Hrê worship whenever they are sick" (*Người Hrê hễ đau là cúng*).[27] For instance, when one feels fatigue, one's family interprets that one's soul has gotten lost somewhere and so asks the medicine man or the village elder to perform a ritual to "summon the soul" back. This spiritual system is intended to offer them a peace of mind so they can return to work. Another common ritual is a blessing ceremony in which a group of people sit around the altar and the medicine man puts cotton strings on it and prays and blesses the strings. Afterward, the medicine man ties a string to each participant to preserve their health and their soul.[28]

Some anthropological studies suggest that compared to the Kinh and the Hoa, gender relations in traditional Hrê households are relatively equitable and that men and women are afforded the same level of respect. Lưu Hùng states in his 1983 study that "one cannot assert that the Hrê are either patriarchal or matriarchal, and it is inaccurate to conclude that the Hrê women's position is subsumed under the men's."[29] Instead, the Hrê practice double filiation (*song hệ*), which means that each offspring can choose to practice either matrilineality or patrilineality, which is shown in their names. The Hrê treat these two lines equitably, and they distribute their property equally among both daughters and sons, not privileging sons.[30] Inheritances serve as seed money for purchasing items that are important to their livelihoods (land, buffaloes, seedlings) and rituals (gongs, jars).[31]

However, the patriarchal nature of Kinh society has begun to make an imprint on the Hrê's tradition of greater gender equity as the two groups have come into greater contact. The Hrê have started to give men more power to make major household decisions and a more prominent role in representing their families in external social relations. Hrê women, on the other hand, have been shouldering more responsibilities than men, working in the fields and doing all the household chores (processing the rice harvests, raising pigs, cooking, managing household money, tending to seedlings), along with childbearing and rearing.[32] This pattern explains why Hrê men are more likely to go to work in Malaysia while the women stay home to continue making a living in the fields (relying on both wet rice and swiddening cultivations) and to take care of their families.

Unhealthy habits have set in with the advent of the market system. Traditionally, the Hrê drink wine as a community celebration when there are rituals or when they have guests. When visiting their households during my 2011–13 fieldwork, I was offered homemade *rượu cần*, a light organic wine fermented from local herbal roots (*men rừng*). We sat around a big vat with long straws made out of bamboo and drank together in a circle of community members. Our Hrê host couple, Ms. Khanh and her husband, told me that they made the yeast from the roots she found in the mountains. But as of 2011, she said, people use industrial yeast, which is faster, stronger, and more toxic and addictive. In Malaysia, the Hrê workers drink excessively, alone or with peers, at the end of a long workday or on the weekends, to release stress and manage depression, which can lead to critical, and at times fatal, health problems.

The Hrê have limited access to education and rank very low in the ethnic hierarchies for this category. Most of the Hrê I interviewed did not finish high school, consistent with the findings of Baulch and colleagues.[33] They speak and read little Vietnamese, so most have a hard time reading and reviewing labor contracts. The public school system in Ba Tơ district is very poor. The commune offers schooling only up to sixth or seventh grade (which means most do not even secure a lower secondary education).[34] To get access to public high schools, Hrê students have to go to the district center, a long distance from their communes. It is even harder to get access to college: the Hrê have to travel at least sixty kilometers from Ba Tơ district center to the Quảng Ngãi city center. The distances are even longer for those whose houses are up in the mountains. The poor road conditions make the trip arduous, especially during the floods of the rainy season. These factors help explain their low school enrollment rates. During my fieldwork trips, I walked on these hilly and mountainous slopes in both rainy and sunny seasons, so I experienced firsthand the substandard infrastructure, wading knee-deep in the mud where the flooded roads had turned into big ponds of water. The destruction of public roads, caused by the big trucks carrying tons of paper pulp to be sold in downtown Ba Tơ district, is a testament to the costly lifestyle changes under a global market system.

Land Issues

Historically, the Hrê had large communal lands of three types: lowland wet rice fields, mountainous land for swiddening, and riverine land. Villagers were permitted to build their houses on land that was not yet occupied by other families, and they respected the rights of fellow villagers who first claimed previously unoccupied land to plant, harvest, and exploit water conduits. Before the fall of Saigon in 1975, the Hrê used their land to plant rice paddies and other food crops (cassava and sugarcane). Back then, most of the Hrê in Ba Tơ district owned private land and used buffaloes to till the rice terraces.[35]

After the onset of the market system in the early 1980s, the Hrê accumulated private land as communal lands were commercialized.[36] Mountainous lands had been owned by just a few Hrê, who created massive plantations of industrial crops such as the acacia and manioc for food (and/or animal feed). The richer Hrê and the Kinh who resettled in these mountainous districts annexed the land of poorer Hrê households, leading to more land conflicts and greater inequality.[37] Land has been commodified with values based on yield, location, and access to water.[38] The closer it is to residential areas, the higher the value. As seen throughout the history of the development of capitalism, poor people's loss of their land and livelihoods impels them to switch from planting food crops to cash crops (such as the acacia).[39]

Moreover, as the market system developed, environmental problems arose. Growing acacia, which is a seven-year-cycle cash crop, on a continuing basis on the former swiddening land (which they used to rotate crops on) means that more nutrients are being extracted from the soil without giving it enough time to replenish before new trees are planted and can lead to a deterioration of land quality and an increase in the use of pesticides and fertilizer, a vicious cycle of environmental degradation.[40] Throughout the five years of my fieldwork (2011–15) crisscrossing this province, I witnessed the replacement of beautiful rice terraces by massive forests of acacia trees, while the Hrê's poverty lingered on. This bleak situation is consistent with a metaphor aptly expressed by Larry Lohman: "The market economy is a corrosive acid bath which dissolves most of the diversity-protecting practices it comes into contact with."[41]

The local Hrê semi-process this cash crop for a very low price. During my fieldwork, I witnessed how Hrê women and children worked under the hot sun peeling the bark off the long trunks of chopped-down acacia trees and then loading them onto big trucks to be transported to facilities (mostly owned by the Kinh and the Hoa) in the district center for further processing into paper chips for export to Japan. Not only do the Hrê earn meager incomes from these activities, but planting these trees contributes to a cycle of debt because this cash crop needs land, pesticides, fertilizer, and water, the last being an element that is in short supply due to extreme weather

Figure 2. Hrê women and children peel off the bark of the *keo* trees, a cash crop, in Quảng Ngãi province in 2012. Credit: Author

patterns.[42] Now, scarce resources such as land and water are being devoted to cash crops whose prices have fluctuated in the marketplace.

In 2011, Ms. Giáo, a pale, twenty-two-year-old Hrê woman in Ba Xa commune, explained to me the precarity of this cash crop and how land is allocated in her family:

> Here we work on the land of my parents-in-law; our income depends totally on planting and harvesting and selling the acacia trees; still our income is unstable. We also plant rice to eat, but not enough to sell. Both families rely on farming on the small plots of land we own. My parents don't give land to daughters but to my brother who stays with them to grow rice and fruits. No one in our two families works overseas.

Her story shows that land is being used more for cash crops, leaving them only small plots on which to grow an amount of food that is barely enough for their own consumption. This process of land commodification does not result in a stable livelihood, given the price fluctuation of commodities such as acacia. Moreover, it reflects the patriarchal influence (from the Kinh) in which the sons in both families inherit the family land and take care of their parents in their old age. Ms. Giáo's parents relied on their own son to till the land and take care of them. Their daughter, Ms. Giáo, while living within walking distance in a nearby commune, would come by for visits only.

36   CHAPTER 1

However, Hrê commune practices, in the form of mutual aid, remain strong even as they are being put to the test in the market system.[43] Brotherhood and friendship among those from the same village but not necessarily from the same families still compel those owning land to negotiate with poor villagers to share mountainous swiddening lands for temporary planting and harvesting.[44]

The Significance of Buffaloes

The Hrê attach high value to buffaloes not only as draft animals but also as important symbols in religious rituals in which they are sacrificed.[45] The buffaloes are indispensable and are the preferred means of tilling rice terraces on the slopes of Quảng Ngãi mountains. Mr. Đoàn Lân, a Hrê elder in Ba Tơ district and father of a migrant, said that his son's remittances helped him buy one buffalo (which was roaming around and feeding on the mountain during our interview) that he used to till the rice terraces on which the tractors cannot operate. Mr. Bao, the father of another migrant worker who was still working in Malaysia at the time of the interview, told me that they owned two buffaloes that they used to cultivate the rice fields, their main source of income. Pointing to a plot of land surrounding their house, without any farm animals roaming around (a common sight in rural villages and farms), he explained: "We used to raise pigs, chicken and ducks, but an epidemic wiped them all out, so now we only rely on planting the rice and doing odd jobs in the village." Thus, the two buffaloes are essential to this family's survival.

Understanding the animal's importance to the Hrê, the LBS system has used the buffalo as a symbol to promote its labor export policy, as aptly captured by a newspaper article titled "Working Overseas to Buy Buffaloes and Build Houses."[46] These state narratives also dangle motorbikes, a necessary item in the daily lives of the Hrê, as another reward designed to induce them to participate in the labor export program. I witnessed firsthand the great utility of owning a motorbike to maneuver the treacherous and muddy roads during the rainy season, which became flooded and impassable even for all-terrain vehicles.

In their animistic belief system, the Hrê also value buffaloes for rituals. Buffaloes, being closest to their everyday activities and contributing the largest part to their very existence, are the most valuable commodity they can offer to their god.[47] The rituals are meant to ward off the negative elements of the past year and to bring in the best elements of the new year for the local villagers. Mr. Đoàn Lân told me about the traditional rituals: "The Hrê do these rituals, stabbing the buffaloes [đâm trâu], to pray for strong and healthy buffaloes and for the fertility of female buffaloes so they can bear many calves in the future." When asked who selects which buffalo (could be young or old, male or female) to sacrifice, he first responded "the family" but then followed up by adding that "it could also be the village elder [già làng] and the rest of the village."[48] This shows the staying power of customs and the role of village elders in maintaining this Hrê spiritual practice.

Next comes a sizable minority group in Vietnam who live in a region that, centuries ago, was part of their homeland, Cambodia.

The Khmer

Land, Cultural Resources, and Governance Structure

The Khmer is one of the target groups of the Prime Minister Decision 71/2009/QĐTT. The Khmer migrants I interviewed used both the official state and unofficial nonstate pathways to work transnationally. I focus on the resources that enable the Khmer to bypass state channels by crisscrossing the Cambodian border and others to make a living.

The Khmer population in Vietnam is estimated to be over 1.4 million people (or 1.5 percent of the total population).[49] Many of them reside in An Giang, a Mekong Delta province, which shares a hundred-kilometer border with Cambodia, separated both by land and by the Mekong River. An Giang is therefore a convenient launching pad for the Khmer (as well as the Chăm) to enter Cambodia.[50] According to the official An Giang province statistics, there were 90,271 Khmer in the province, accounting for over 4 percent of its population.[51]

This proximity is not by coincidence: historically, An Giang was Khmer land. Centuries of conflict set the stage for present-day tensions between the Vietnamese and the Khmer.[52] Angkor was the site of the capital city of the Khmer empire (802–1431). Angkor Wat was built in the twelfth century.

In the eleventh century the Khmer king periodically sent tribute to the Vietnamese monarchs to encourage diplomatic relations and peaceful trading.[53] But in the twelfth century, the new leader of Angkor Wat turned the tables and demanded that Vietnam send tribute instead.[54] When Vietnam rejected that request, the Khmer initiated campaigns to attack Vietnam by way of sea and land and sent thousands of troops to plunder Nghệ An province in north-central Vietnam.[55] The warfare escalated when both the Khmer and the Champa invaded Vietnam, briefly seizing Nghệ An, which was retaken by the Vietnamese several years later. The Khmer empire ended with the fall of Angkor in the fifteenth century.

Figure 3. Migrants from An Giang province cross the Mekong River in 2014, a porous border that facilitates entry into Cambodia and other countries. Credit: Author

After the decline of Angkor, Burmese, Thai, and Việt state builders moved southward into the fertile alluvial basins of the Mekong River and rolled back the Khmer empire. Now severed from the Khmer empire, the indigenous Khmer people had begun calling themselves Khmer Krom (krom means "below"), indicating that they lived in the lower Mekong River valley, or the southeastern-most territory of their ancient empire (modern-day Saigon and the Mekong Delta).[56] Vietnamese scholars call this region Lower Cambodia or Kampuchea Krom.[57]

In the 1630s, the marriage between a Cambodian king and a Vietnamese princess led to the Vietnamese court setting up customs posts in the Mekong Delta, still at that time inhabited largely by the Khmer. Then this area was incorporated into Vietnam by the Nguyễn lords' "push to the south" (nam tiến) in the early eighteenth century.[58] By the late eighteenth and early nineteenth centuries, the Kampuchea Krom region (Mekong Delta) was completely under the control of the Nguyễn empire, and Vietnamese immigrants were moving into the area. In the nineteenth century, Emperor Minh Mạng

Practices of the Five Ethnic Groups 39

ordered the Khmer Krom in the Mekong Delta to assimilate by learning the Chinese and Vietnamese languages and made it clear that there would be consequences for noncompliance and rewards for compliance: "Forbid them from going to their own monks to learn. Whoever learns Chinese (*hán chữ*) will be appointed head of the village, so let them know what is demanded. Afterwards, let them also learn the Vietnamese language (*hán nhân ngôn ngữ*), clothes, and food."[59] This expansion in the south resulted in the expulsion of tens of thousands of ethnic Khmer from this former Cambodian jurisdiction, leading to a legacy of Cambodian resentment and anti-Vietnamese feelings among the Khmer residents inside Cambodia.

As with the Hrê, historical struggles to keep their land loom large in the Khmer's consciousness. But the Khmer benefit from local Khmer authorities who use their bilingual language capabilities to advocate for their rights with Kinh officials. As a result of land conflicts and collective petitions lodged by the Khmer residents, Kinh officials came to recognize the power and usefulness of local Khmer leaders and have tried to recruit their services and draw on their loyalty to help manage their own people at the hamlet level.[60]

Historical, linguistic, and cultural ties to Cambodia facilitate the sharing of knowledge and strategies for criss-crossing the 100-kilometer border between An Giang and Cambodia among the Khmer.[61] Those in the delta maintain strong ties with their relatives in Cambodia, crossing the An Giang–Cambodia border for family visits, life-cycle rites, and seasonal festivals.[62] They maintain Khmer customs, culture, and language and teach Khmer history, legends, and myths while adapting to changes in the places they live.[63] The Khmer I interviewed from Tri Tôn district, one of the two districts with a concentration of Khmer, have established cross-border networks with Chinese traders to whom they trade rice harvests and forest products in exchange for consumer goods.[64] During my 2012 and 2014 fieldwork, I myself crossed this porous border in An Giang province by taking a short boat ride to enter Cambodia for a few hours' visit. I saw that many Khmer residents enter Cambodia to do business and then return to Vietnam on the same day.

Each hamlet's governance reflects the power of local authorities and dictates the ensuing negotiations between Khmer leaders and the Kinh officials.[65] During my fieldwork, I witnessed a division of authority at the hamlet level. The Khmer local leaders know exactly how indebted each household is, but the chief and deputy chief appear to have different priorities. The Khmer hamlet chief (*ấp trưởng*) is a political figure who liaises between his people and the Kinh officials. He tends to interact positively with his Kinh

40   CHAPTER 1

counterparts. On the other hand, the hamlet deputy chief (*ấp phó*) is more connected to the needs of his fellow Khmer villagers and thus represents their interests better.

Religious and Linguistic Resources

Between 1965 and 1968, over seventeen thousand Khmer, including twenty-three hundred Theravadist Buddhist monks, fled from the then Republic of Vietnam (south of the seventeenth parallel) to Cambodia to escape the escalation of the US–Vietnam war.[66] These Buddhist monks established communities of support in Cambodia, facilitated border exchange visits, and joined forces at ceremonies.

Understanding Khmer household and religious activities at the most basic level, hamlets (*phum*), is key to comprehending the Khmer's forms of third space, discussed in chapters 5 and 6. Their phum is very important to them because it is also a religious center where they practice Theravada Buddhism.[67] According to the 2018 Unrepresented Nations and People report on the Khmer-Krom, there are more than 450 temples and over 10,000 Theravadist Buddhist monks in the Mekong Delta region.[68]

The Khmer ignored the nineteenth-century emperor Minh Mạng's order to learn Chinese and Vietnamese. Instead, they have relied on their monks to teach them the Khmer language. These monks are not only spiritual leaders but also educational leaders who try to preserve their language and cultural practices. *Achars*—the lay Buddhists, usually over fifty years of age—assist the monks in leading traditional Theravadist Buddhist rituals intended to enrich the lives of the Khmer migrants and their communities. In particular, the monks preserve and spread the rich Khmer legends, myths, epic poems, proverbs, fables, commandments, humorous stories, folk songs, and improvised dramas for educational purposes.[69] Senior Khmer Krom monks often obtained an education in local Khmer temples and then studied further in Cambodia.[70]

Most Khmer live close by to a temple, or *wat*, as it is called in the Khmer language. These temples are a central hub for all Buddhist activities and also for educational, cultural, and social aspects of Khmer life.[71] They are spaces in which Khmer traditions and the language are preserved. The wat contains classrooms where local novices take elementary level courses in the Buddhist curriculum and village children learn Khmer taught by monks and achars. Some wats serve over two thousand households and have over one hundred monks in residence.[72]

Figure 4. Khmer social life is grounded in *wats* (temples) like this one photographed in An Giang province in 2014, where ritual ceremonies and teaching are integral activities. Credit: Author

The Khmer have poor educational attainment with respect to public education.[73] The Khmer's low school enrollment is due to a lack of income, distance from schools, and difficulty with the Vietnamese language.[74] Unlike the Hoa, they cannot afford to send their children to private schools. Instead, they rely on their religious resources in the wats, where Buddhist leaders continue to command respect from the Khmer villagers living in traditional hamlets.

In the two districts in An Giang province in which the Khmer are concentrated (Tri Tôn and Tịnh Biên) where I did my fieldwork, the parents send their children to the Buddhist temple to take classes in the evening or during the summer. The acquisition of the Khmer language helps the children retain their sense of cultural identity. Many retain a basic form of the language and use it at home but switch to Vietnamese when interacting with the Kinh. As one of the people I interviewed, Neng Angkeara, who took some Khmer lessons when she was a little girl, explained, "I can speak and read Khmer, but I write it very little because there are many diacritical marks. . . . I forget

42   CHAPTER 1

a lot [of it] because I have not used it often. Still, at home, we speak Khmer only. Only when we go to the market do we speak Vietnamese."[75]

In an in-depth interview, Châu Anurak, a knowledgeable Khmer, conveyed his passion about the importance of preserving the Buddhist rituals at the Khmer temples to enrich the lives of Khmer residents. He showcased the range of the functions of the wats:

> We have lively religious activities here. Thanks to our head monk who raised money for us, we now have electricity. All thirty-six bulbs light up twenty-four hours per day for the whole village. Now we have a budget of đ53 million. The head monk raised money when people came to the temple to worship on the fifteenth day of the month. Moreover, on that day, people also had opportunities to learn Buddhist teaching/philosophy, the Khmer and Vietnamese languages, as well as internet skills. There are twelve computers in the temple for people to use. Every night during the two-month summer, the head monk taught Khmer at no charge to the children. In the summer, they [the children] do not learn the Kinh language. When the regular fall semester comes, the Khmer class stopped.[76]

The Khmer Buddhist temple is not only a site in which religion is practiced but also a place where the Khmer language, religion, and culture are taught and preserved.[77] Further, by providing electricity, a vital element of the public infrastructure, for the whole hamlet, the hamlet Khmer leaders have strengthened their authority in relations with Kinh officials.

Gender

Men and women are not treated the same in Khmer culture. The distinction starts with the naming convention: the men's names start with *châu*, while the women's names begin with *neng*. Then, as they grow up, young women do not have the opportunities afforded men to obtain a higher education in the temples. Many young men from Khmer villages spend several years living in the temple as novices, learning from the local monks and becoming ordained monks, garnering prestige in the local Khmer community. By contrast, many young Khmer women, upon reaching adulthood, are permitted to go to the temples only for meditation retreats, not for language lessons.[78] Neng Angkeara explained to me why older female teenagers are not allowed to take the Khmer language classes in the temple:

> When I was a child, I hung out with a lot of Kinh friends and spoke Vietnamese because I used to live near downtown. Also, I was discouraged from learning Khmer because it is difficult. So, when I was in my teens, other

Practices of the Five Ethnic Groups   43

[Khmer] friends asked me to study Khmer with them. I liked that idea very much because by then I had become conscious of and embarrassed [by the fact that] I'm Khmer but did not know how to read Khmer! I was able to study in the temple for only one day: my family did not allow me to return because they feared rumors from the village that I might "seduce" the monk who was teaching Khmer there.[79]

The thought that the young monk and the female novice would have a liaison, according to Neng Angkeara, was based on the fact that the young monk "teacher" was only two or three years older than her.

In sum, the Khmer's historical land tensions with the Kinh simmer to the present day. But they benefit from deep-rooted historical, cultural, language, and religious ties with Cambodia, which they maintain to travel to Cambodia and beyond to make a living.

The Chăm Bani and the Chăm Sunni Muslims

Of the five ethnic groups analyzed in this study, the Chăm are the most mobile, traveling both within Vietnam and to neighboring countries such as Cambodia. At first, the Chăm were not included in the original sixty-one poor rural districts in the north and central provinces that were targeted by the Prime Minister Decision 71/2009/QĐTT. But three years later, the state added poor districts in the Mekong Delta area, such as An Giang, and then recruited migrants, including the Chăm, to go to work in Malaysia.

Over 162,000 Chăm people live in Vietnam today. About 10 percent of the Chăm population in Vietnam practice Sunni Islam, and they construct their ethnicity (and the basis for community membership) around a version of Islam that has connections with the Malay world and the global Islamic community. The remaining 90 percent, the Chăm Bani, construct their ethnicity genealogically, based on their ties to the Champa kingdom.[80] The Chăm Bani (or Chăm Awal) reside in the south-central coast region (Bình Thuận and Ninh Thuận provinces), where they practice unique forms of Islam and Hinduism. In their "indigenized" (bản địa hóa) version of Islam, they worship many spirits (in plants and animals), heroes/heroines, and ancestors in addition to Allah.[81] Complex historical forces led the Chăm Sunni population to migrate to Cambodia and the Mekong Delta.[82]

I focus on the Chăm Sunni Muslims, who live in three major Mekong Delta provinces (An Giang, Tây Ninh, and Đồng Nai) and Ho Chi Minh and its environs.[83] Those in the Mekong Delta region are largely concentrated in An Giang, where over 12,500 Chăm practice the Sunni Islamic faith.[84] Within An Giang province, I focused on the five communes in An Phú

44 CHAPTER 1

district, a Chăm-concentrated area, where about 5,900 Chăm live. Their devout religious practices set them apart from the other ethnic groups, and their migration stories both within Vietnam and to Malaysia are powerful. Historically, the original Chăm came from Malaysia, Cambodia, Indonesia, Thailand, and the Middle East, as well as from the kingdom of Champa in Panduranga, formerly located in present-day Vietnam.[85] It is important to note that throughout the period of Champa's prominence (roughly AD 300 to 1500), maritime trade and tribute relations with China were crucial. The Champa sent periodic tribute faithfully to China to obtain Chinese assistance against local rivals, including the Khmer and the Vietnamese.[86]

It is important to understand the Champa kingdom in the larger context of the maritime networks that evolved in Southeast Asia. Its merchants frequented the ports of Southeast Asia before the seventeenth century.[87] In the thirteenth century, Arab traders spread Islam to the Chăm on the south-central coast.[88] In the fourteenth century, diplomatic missions between Champa and Java (Indonesia) also brought Islam to the Champa kingdom, before the Champa began using the Malayo-Muslim port states in the fifteenth century, when Java fragmented.[89]

History of the Chăm in Vietnam and Cambodia

The Chăm's complex history in Vietnam and Cambodia unfolded simultaneously. Scholars agree that the Chăm and the Malays came into contact in the sixteenth century, leading to the spread of Islam to Champa.[90] Also in the sixteenth century, the Malays sent tribute to the Champa coast for religious and cultural ceremonies. At the end of the sixteenth century, the Chăm king was still strong enough to send help to the sultan of Johor, the ruler of the Malays, in the Malays' fight against the Portuguese.[91] The spread of Islamic faith was thus strengthened as a consequence of the close connection between the Malays and the Chăm, a relationship forged by the Champa's alliance with the Malays against the Vietnamese, Khmer, and Portuguese.[92]

By the seventeenth century, most of the Chăm in Champa had become Sunni Muslims and followed the Shafi'i school, but they retained their traditional beliefs and practices.[93] Both the Malaysians and the Chăm use an adapted Arabic alphabet in their writings, and they pronounce some words similarly, enabling them to understand each other in their interactions in modern-day Malaysia.[94] Ms. Chamkili, a Chăm salesperson from An Giang province who worked in a retail shop in Ho Chi Minh City selling dresses for the Malaysian Muslim women who visited Vietnam, told me that she had crossed the border to Malaysia by bus several times. She indicated that when

Practices of the Five Ethnic Groups 45

she spoke Chăm (her mother tongue) in Malaysia, the Malays could understand her because of their shared alphabet and some similar pronunciations. In the seventeenth century, the Nguyễn dynasty in Vietnam completely annexed the Champa kingdom, leading to the exodus of the last king of Champa. Many Chăm, mostly Muslims from the present-day Phan Rang (central Vietnam), fled to Cambodia for refuge.[95] The Chăm who remained in Bình Thuận and Ninh Thuận followed two religious traditions embedded in Chăm culture: Hinduism (the majority religion in these two provinces) and Islam.[96]

The Chăm who fled to Cambodia ended up largely under the protection of the Khmer king.[97] The exodus lasted from the end of the seventeenth century to the beginning of the eighteenth. They were settled in two areas of Cambodia: Udong (the former Khmer capital and residence of members of the old royal Champa family, who had special status as exiles in Cambodia,) and Kampong Chăm (a Chăm colony established in Cambodia in the fifteenth century northeast of Phnom Penh, near the Tonlé Sap, Mekong, and Bassac Rivers, where the Chăm commoners reside).[98]

From the end of the eighteenth century to the middle of the nineteenth, Vietnamese authorities brought many of the Chăm from Cambodia to Tây Ninh and Châu Đốc (Mekong Delta provinces) to populate the military colonies. Essentially, the Vietnamese turned the Chăm into border soldiers (*lính biên phòng*) who built military posts and guarded the newly established villages from attacks from Cambodia and protected the Vietnamese who were exploring and developing these frontier areas.[99]

Then, between the 1860s and the beginning of the twentieth century, the Chăm who had migrated to Tây Ninh and Châu Đốc and the Malays (the Chăm and the Malays in Cambodia) became commercial agents of the French protectorate in Cambodia and the middlemen in the cattle trade to the Philippines and Cochinchina (the south of Vietnam, whose principal city was Saigon, now Ho Chi Minh City).[100] In 2008, the Kampong Chăm's population was 1,680,694 (or 12.6 percent of the total Cambodian population), reflecting a 0.44 percent growth from 2007.[101] As of October 2017, the estimated population of Cambodia is 16,074,658, and the estimated Chăm population is 1,748,433.[102]

It is important to emphasize the long-standing presence of Chăm Sunni Muslims in Cambodia, Vietnam, and Thailand who were influenced by the Malay form of Islam. By the fifteenth century, the Chăm Sunni Muslims had already established a colony in Cambodia and allied with the Malays living there.[103] Fieldwork studies by Vietnamese anthropologists, citing the French colonial government's census statistics in 1911, reveal that in that year the Chăm and the Malay populations in Châu Đốc province combined

Figure 5. Sunni Muslims pray and socialize at Tân Châu mosque in 2013, An Giang Province. Credit: Author

were over six thousand people.[104] This historical transnational coexistence (in Cambodia and Mekong Delta provinces) of the Chăm community and the Malays helps to explain the impact of the Malay way of practicing Islam on the Chăm Muslims.[105]

On the other hand, the Chăm migrant population in Ho Chi Minh City is made up of Chăm from all over Vietnam and includes even the Chăm Bani from the south-central coast with their "indigenized" form of Islam. In a broader development of the Islamic circuit of the Malay world, the Chăm have participated in the religious networks linking various learning centers in Patani (southern Thailand) and Kelantan (Malaysia).[106]

Geographical Agency

Only a small number of Chăm migrants participated in the labor export program in Malaysia. For centuries, the Chăm have maintained their mobile and peripatetic lifestyle by drawing on their cultural competencies. These itinerant and independent retailers travel throughout Vietnam from the Mekong Delta provinces (such as An Giang, Tiền Giang, Long An) to Ho Chi Minh City,

Practices of the Five Ethnic Groups 47

the south-central coast, and Hanoi to sell their wares.[107] But they also travel transnationally, crossing the Vietnam-Cambodia, Cambodia-Thailand, and Thailand-Malaysia borders.

Relying on their own cultural and economic networks, not the state system, they sell all types of sundries that they can invest in short term, from fabrics, blankets, and used and new clothes to gas stoves. This retail trade competency is handed down from one generation to another. Mr. Vijaya, a thirty-four-year-old man with three children, confirmed this: "My parents did retail sales, selling old clothes and fabrics throughout Vietnam. Wherever they went, I followed their footsteps." So he learned the retail way of life from his parents and then taught the trade to his own children.

The Chăm cross over the Cambodian border on a daily basis by taking a short boat ride to the western bank of the Mekong River, which is where the border between Vietnam and Cambodia is in this area. There they make their living by fishing and selling sundries. The riverine border is porous: I crossed it myself in 2014 in a small boat and was not asked for any identification. Ms. Alvi, whom I interviewed three times starting in 2012, had worked in Malaysia in 2008 and then returned home to the Chăm's peripatetic way of life. When she first returned to Vietnam, she worked for a factory in the south but quickly quit due to low salary. Then she returned to what she could do efficiently: buying from local sources to sell sundries such as thread, blankets, and clothing items: "I drive around with my motorbike to sell stuff and return home, all in a day. I sell in local areas, and also in Cambodia, and return home in the evening. But sometimes when the rain is hard, I have to stay overnight in my relatives' houses."[108] Again, this shows the significance of religious and kinship ties with the Chăm Muslim communities in Vietnam and Cambodia that continue to provide support for them.

In 2012, I interviewed a poor fisherman, Mr. Davi, at the doorstep of his simple house, donated and built by the local government, which provided homes for the poorest households in his hamlet. His family owned no land, so this house gave them shelter, and their boat was their means of making a living. All members of the family had to contribute to the task of bringing food to the table. Mr. Davi worked with his wife and the three children who still lived at home; three older children had already married and lived on their own with their children.

> My wife and I fished (*mần cá*). I dove 30–40 meters deep and stayed in the water for several hours to unhook the fishing net that got stuck in the tree roots deep down there. Water got into my lungs, and I got sick with asthma. So much money had to be spent at the doctor's office. Our children helped us by going around town to sell clothes, mosquito nets, and blankets.

The children engaged in selling sundries in nearby areas, whereas their father made daily trips to Cambodia to sell fish and other items: "I bring the freshly caught fish to sell in Cambodia within the same day. I sell everything: mosquito nets, hammocks, pillows, clothes."

In 2015, I followed Chăm migrants to Ho Chi Minh City, which has a large community of Chăm Muslims. As devout Muslims, the Chăm maintain their religious way of life by living near a mosque so that they can come and pray five times every day. I visited the Ho Chi Minh City Muslim Representative Committee in Phú Nhuận district (about seven kilometers from the downtown) so that I could see how a Chăm community functions in the city.[109] But the office was closed for Ramadan, so I went to Jamiul Muslimin Mosque next door, a nice, small mosque facing a big boulevard. In the prayer room on the second floor, there was a posting of the hours for praying as well as seven clocks prominently mounted on the wall to guide the Chăm prayers. When prayer time approached, the Chăm men arrived in their Muslim attire from nearby neighborhoods, either by walking or driving their motorbikes. I had a chance to talk to Mr. Shimani, a friendly Chăm, while he was getting ready for prayers in the main hall upstairs:

> Most of the Chăms here are from An Giang. They came here mainly to make a living. But most have returned to their villages for Ramadan and the new-year celebration right after that. Here, most of them engage in retail sales, the most convenient way to make a living. No one wants to work for the government. The reason is because we do not want to be restrained; we prefer the freedom to make a living by ourselves. That is the Chăm's way of life.

Even with their peripatetic lifestyle, most Chăm return to their communes (*xã*) during the holiest season: Ramadan. Mr. Shimani maintained this religious connection with his hometown in An Giang province. When we talked inside the mosque, he had just returned to Ho Chi Minh City after a four-day trip to donate money to the poor in the Chăm communes in his village:

> During Ramadan, if we made money [profit], then according to our Muslim faith, we set aside some money to give to the poor. I just went back to my commune to give them money for food after fasting. This year, my son and I donated đ100,000 [about US$5][110] each to four hundred households in several Chăm communes in An Phú district. To us, this is only a small amount, but it means a lot to these poor people.

For the poor Chăm, having food after the fasting period of the Ramadan is a big treat. Mr. Shimani and his son visited not just their home commune but also other Chăm communes. Their donations to these poor families during the holiest season show their respect for century-old practices in these communities. This annual one-time financial support can be considered a form of remittance that shows a commitment to the social network of Chăm Muslims.[111]

After visiting the mosque, I walked around the nearby Chăm Muslim neighborhood to see what their social networks looked like. Small sewing shops (selling Muslim-style dresses and scarves) and restaurants with halal foods lined the narrow alleyways. Then, following Mr. Shimani's directions, I made my way to a popular Chăm retail shop that he owns on the "Chăm street," a small street right across from the well-known hustling and bustling Bến Thành market. This area is vibrant with hotels, clothing and tailoring shops, and restaurants catering to throngs of Muslim tourists walking up and down the street. Most came from Malaysia and other Muslim countries to shop.

The Chăm's mobility is a unique factor that sets them apart from the other ethnic groups in ways that Philip Taylor's notion of geographical agency does

Figure 6. A storefront in Ho Chi Minh City in 2015, where the Chăm's entrepreneurship in making and selling garments to global Muslim customers is on display. Credit: Author

50   CHAPTER 1

not adequately account for, as they reproduce their economic space and draw on their religious and cultural networks even beyond the Vietnam-Cambodia border. Their historical connections with the Muslim Malays explain the better treatment that the Chăm working in Malaysia receive.

However, migratory lifestyles adversely affect their children's education. The UNICEF report finds that for all school-age enrollment categories, the Chăm children in An Giang have the highest out-of-school rate. The report points out that the lifestyle of the Chăm—living temporarily on boats in the river, helping their parents in fishing businesses or at junk shops—is the likely cause. These activities not only make children tired but also interrupt their schooling, resulting in poor class performance, so they skip classes, which in turn leads to dropping out.[112] Thus, while the Chăm's mobile lifestyle sustains their livelihoods, it has an unintended negative consequence on their children's education, which my interviews also documented.

The Hierarchy of the Five Ethnic Groups

To understand how these five ethnic groups relate to each other, I use a conceptual framework of ethnic hierarchies (see Table 2). The hierarchy positions each of these five ethnic groups in terms of their respective access to key economic factors (land, finance, and education) and their cultural resources (networks, language, and religion), offering a way to understand their strategies for surviving in the LBS system or for bypassing it altogether.

The Hoa and the Kinh rank the highest in economic categories—access to land, finance, and education. The Hrê rank the lowest in many economic categories, except for access to land, since they do own some land (around their houses on the hillsides and mountain ridges) and engage in wet rice, cash-crop, and swiddening cultivation for survival. The Chăm rank the lowest on landownership, since historically they have had a peripatetic lifestyle, selling sundries across Vietnam and in neighboring countries.

The costs of preschool and lower secondary public education make it difficult for the poorer ethnic minorities, including the Kinh poor, to get access to education.[113] Primary schools have lower dropout rates because primary education is free.[114] Migratory lifestyles also have adverse effects on students. More migrant than nonmigrant children drop out of school.[115] These migrant students are from districts with high concentrations of ethnic minorities, such as the Khmer and the Chăm, who account for the majority of the dropouts.[116]

Overall, the poor access to education is an important reason why many Khmer and Hrê (less so Chăm) interviewees mentioned that they wanted

Practices of the Five Ethnic Groups   51

more education for themselves and their siblings to help their respective communities. I found a strong passion for additional education among several Khmer women as well as Hrê women and men who desire to teach in their own communes and hamlets. But to teach, they have to graduate from high school, which is difficult for ethnic minorities given the low official enrollment status for the Khmer and the Chăm in An Giang and the lack of access to high schools for the Hrê who live in remote mountainous areas. Among the Chăm, a desire for religious studies was expressed prominently by the men but not the women whom I interviewed. However, my sample was small, so this issue requires more research. I found one case that shows women's religiosity and empowerment. Following up on a lead given to me by a local women's union leader in a Chăm district in An Giang, I visited a women's mosque created by the Chăm women themselves and separate from the main mosque. There, I found short ritual messages written in Arabic, which may mean that they read Arabic.

The language barrier in the state schools using Vietnamese only is cited as one of the key issues for Khmer and Chăm students: many do not understand class lessons taught in Vietnamese and receive no help from their parents, who are not equipped to help them with their homework. Consequently, they get discouraged and then drop out.[117] This is consistent with what I found in my interviews: the religious Khmer and the Chăm learned to speak their own languages in wats and mosques respectively but had difficulty with Vietnamese. However, young Khmer women do not have access to the wats and young Chăm Muslim women generally do not have access to mosques, so they are at even more of a disadvantage.

Taylor correctly rejects oft-cited reasons for these poor school-based educational attainments, such as the claim that parents maintain a low-skill traditional agricultural lifestyle and fail to appreciate how education could help them escape poverty. He recognizes the informal, community-based pathways through which knowledge is reproduced and communication networks are preserved, and he points out that nonstate schools maintained and attended by the Hoa, Chăm, and Khmer ethnic groups offer diverse vocational paths for their respective communities.[118] This explanation is consistent with Yosso's concept of community cultural wealth: in this context, these alternative pathways of knowledge and skill sets constitute a form of cultural capital that is nurtured through these ethnic groups' aspirations and their social and linguistic resources.[119]

Interestingly, the ethnic hierarchies' rankings are reversed for three cultural categories: language capabilities, national/transnational networks, and religious affinity. While the ethnic minorities face language barriers in Vietnamese state schools using Vietnamese only, they thrive, relatively speaking, when migrating to neighboring Southeast Asian countries.

Knowing the language of one's employer can help one's bargaining skills and improve labor-management relations. In the context of Malaysia, migrants who can speak directly with Malaysian employers in their languages (such as Chinese, Malay, and English) can become independent agents, negotiate for better terms for contract renewals (especially for jobs calling for technical skills), or bypass the LBS system altogether. In these cases, both sides benefit: well-trained workers can renew contracts after they fulfill the original three-year contract, and management can save money because they do not need to train their existing employees.[120]

The Hoa rank the highest in terms of language since they benefit from speaking Chinese, the language of most employers in Malaysia. A few Kinh interviewees who speak some Chinese also benefit from this language skill. Also, the Chăm can communicate very well with Malay employers and local residents, in both speaking and writing, since both peoples use Arabic-based written languages with slightly different yet recognizable pronunciations. The Khmer speak their mother tongue, the Khmer language, so they have an edge when crossing the border to Cambodia.

Surprisingly, the Kinh's language capability is the most limited; they are able to speak only Vietnamese and are not as facile in the other three languages as the other ethnic groups. My interview notes with the journalists who worked closely with the Hrê indicated that the Hrê speak English better than the Kinh.[121] Perhaps this is due to the fact that the Mon/Bahnaric-Khmer (the Hrê language), a member of the Austroasiatic family, is entirely atonal, whereas Vietnamese is tonal; it may be easier for the Hrê to pronounce the atonal English language.[122]

National/transnational networks are very much connected with religious networks. On these factors, the Chăm and the Khmer rank the highest, even when they lose out on landownership. Ancient histories of the Khmer and the Chăm inform their connection to Cambodia and Malaysia and to an extent Thailand (by way of towns bordering Malaysia, such as Pattani). Ancient histories also explain deep religious affinity: the Khmer's Buddhist connections to Cambodia and the Chăm's Islamic connections to Malaysia as well as Cambodia.

Comparative Remarks

The five ethnic groups have different experiences and histories, and I have elaborated on these unique circumstances so that we can understand what

Table 2. Conceptual Diagram of Ethnic Hierarchies

Hierarchy Privilege	Landownership	Financial Access	Education Access	Networks*	Language Capability	Religious Affinity
Most/highest	Kinh/Hoa (wet rice cultivation)	Hoa/Kinh (from kinships, banks, social networks)	Hoa (in public and private schools)	Chăm	Hoa Chăm	Chăm
	Khmer (wet rice cultivation)		Kinh (in public and private schools)	Khmer	Khmer	Khmer
	Hrê (wet rice cultivation, swiddening)	Khmer, Chăm, Hrê (from kinships & social networks)	Khmer (in *wats*) Khmer women studying to be teachers Chăm men's religious studies in mosques (local and global)	Kinh/Hoa	Kinh/Hrê	Kinh/Hoa Hrê
Least/lowest	Chăm (peripatetic lifestyle, retail)		Hrê individuals studying to be teachers Other Hrê individuals (in remote areas with very few schools)	Hrê		

* National and global

Source: Angie Ngọc Trần, 2019 (based on Holmes 2007)

grounds their strategies for survival in the LBS system. The cultural resources of each ethnic group inform how the migrants—on their own or in solidarity with others—cope with precarity while in Malaysia, create physical and metaphorical third spaces in Malaysia and Vietnam, and sustain their aspirations after their Malaysia experiences.

The Chăm's and the Khmer's lack of access to financial capital is compensated for by community capital. Both groups have limited access to economic resources, and their income is low and unstable due to seasonal work. Many migrate with their siblings to work for low wages in export processing and industrial zones in cities and provinces in the south. However, their community wealth—cultural and religious networks and language—helps them in crossing the border to Cambodia, Thailand, and Malaysia to make a living. Both groups find strength in their cultural resources and use them as strategies to safeguard themselves. Deep-rooted historical, cultural, linguistic, and religious ties with Cambodia help the Buddhist Khmer and the Chăm Muslims travel to and beyond Cambodia.

Language capability is a factor in metaphorical third spaces of dissent. The yardstick of educational standards from the Kinh public schools does not recognize the value of the language and skill sets the Khmer and the Chăm children learn in the wats and the mosques, respectively. These skill sets are vital for their survival and even for capital accumulation.

2 The Transnational Labor Brokerage System and Its Infrastructure

The transnational labor brokerage system (LBS) benefits all levels of the governments of Vietnam (labor-sending country) and Malaysia (labor-receiving country), which has the effect of reinforcing the system. Vietnam has a large number of people who need work, while Malaysia needs workers to do the jobs unwanted by most Malaysians, the so-called three-D (dirty, dangerous, and demeaning) jobs. The two countries agreed to allow Malaysian employers and their outsourcing companies to work directly with Vietnamese recruitment companies to fill their job orders. Vietnam's LBS bureaucracy creates jobs for thousands of state officials, recruiters, and mass organization members at various levels nationwide. Overall, this state-managed global labor migration system manipulates the consent of poor citizens by appealing to their needs, dreams, and aspirations. Figure 7 depicts the key stakeholders and how they connect.

The transnational LBS is challenged by its own internal contradictions (the state media, for example, walks a fine line in order to shed light on migrant workers' rights while meeting its responsibility to encourage participation) and external criticisms from global civil society organizations and union entities in Malaysia, as well as from organizations that set global labor standards.

I first outline the regional context and then describe the transnational LBS infrastructure, its key players, and the contradictory relationships they create as they manage and benefit from this system.

Labor Markets in East and Southeast Asia

Most studies of contemporary Vietnamese migrant workers have focused on workers' experiences in developed Asian countries. Wang and Bélanger find

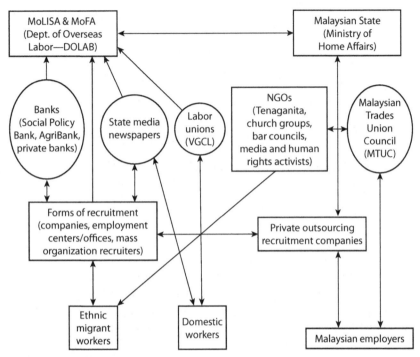

Figure 7. Vietnam and Malaysia in the Transnational Labor Brokerage System. Source: Author

that transnational recruitment intermediaries and Vietnam's and Taiwan's migration and work policies dictate the migration process and lead to a vicious cycle of debt bondage for Vietnamese migrant workers.[1] In another study, Bélanger and colleagues find that labor migrants prefer host countries such as Japan, Korea, and Taiwan because they offer higher pay, but most poor workers do not meet the educational and skills requirements and cannot afford the costs of predeparture training (language and legal instruction).[2] Hoàng and Yeoh explored interesting contradictions between stereotypes of Vietnamese women's sexuality and the fluidity of actual sexual practices in real-life contexts in their study of Vietnamese female migrant workers in Taiwan.[3]

Fewer studies focus on Vietnamese labor migration to Southeast Asia, especially to Malaysia, which is the de facto main labor-receiving market affected by Prime Minister Decision 71/2009/QĐTT, aimed at creating jobs for local residents from sixty-four targeted poor rural districts.

The Malaysian Labor Brokerage State

In the neoliberal era, Malaysia, dubbed the "market for the poor," became the first labor-receiving market established when Vietnam and Malaysia signed a bilateral agreement in 2002. Out of all labor-receiving countries (including South Korea, Taiwan, Japan, and Gulf states such as the United Arab Emirates and Qatar), Malaysia's jobs require the lowest fees and skill levels.

While being the easiest to qualify for, this labor market causes anxiety for many low-skilled Vietnamese migrant workers because of the vulnerabilities, dislocation, and alienation they experience.[4] Migrant workers in Malaysia are powerless and immobilized because their passports are taken and kept by their Malaysian employers upon their arrival.[5] Female migrant workers not only experience alienation and the pain of family separation—as do male workers—but also are subject to inhumane gender-specific migration policies, such as pregnancy tests, from both sending and receiving countries.[6] Chin focuses on domestic service workers and analyzes how they use everyday acts of resistance to reclaim power in their relations with their employers.[7] Some studies of Vietnamese workers in Malaysia examine how social relations of production have been transformed through neoliberal trade policies and transnational labor migration.[8] Lê has researched the impacts of the Malaysian recruitment process on Kinh migrant workers from the north of Vietnam. She finds that over 50 percent of total migration expenses come from migrants having to pay Vietnamese recruitment companies and Malaysian outsourcing (or recruitment) companies to find them jobs.[9] In subsequent chapters, I show that all five ethnic migrant workers had to pay both sides even higher fees: up to 75 percent of the total loan amounts.

Malaysian employers pressured the Malaysian government to allow migrant workers from poorer countries into the region to fill the low-skilled manufacturing jobs not wanted by the locals, and since these manufacturing jobs were mostly in the export industry, manufacturers wanted the government to keep the wages low to entice foreign investors.[10] Workers were required to have a passport and work permit, to sign a contract for one to three years, to pay levies and fees (until a 2019 change in the law), and to return home at the end of the contract.[11]

Since July 2005, the Malaysian government has allowed two recruitment systems to manage foreign workers, the government's one-stop recruitment center and private outsourcing companies that recruit for employers who require fewer than fifty workers. The outsourcing companies work directly with Vietnamese recruiters to fill job orders. In both systems, a migrant worker must work for the employer listed on the employment contract, so that workers have someone to name if they are underpaid or if their contract is violated in other ways. The government system is better and more reliable than the private one because when a worker is employed via the government's recruitment center, the factory employer's name is listed on the contract.[12] The factory employer is thus made legally responsible for the worker. In principle, as of the start of 2019, migrant workers in Malaysia are entitled to the same work-related injury benefits as national workers.[13]

If a worker is employed by a private outsourcing company, the outsourcing company's name is listed on the contract. However, many private outsourcing companies lack accountability in fulfilling contracts and have been reported to engage in corrupt practices. The factory owner has no responsibility to the worker if the worker's employer of record is a private outsourcing company.[14] This outsourcing recruitment system exposes the workers to greater exploitation and complicates the complaint mechanisms when they want to report excessive overtime, production speedups, poor housing, and denial of basic benefits and rights (such as health care, sick time, and on-time payment).

In August 2015, the Malaysian government, in a modest effort to address complaints by Vietnamese migrant workers, signed a memorandum of understanding (MOU) with the Vietnamese government to attempt to close loopholes that had enabled recruitment and labor exploitation. As a result of this agreement, foreign workers now have the right to retain their passports and personal documents. Workers are required to carry their passport at all times, and employers (not labor recruiters) must pick up migrant workers from the airport within six hours of their landing in the country.[15] This new version of the labor contract holds Malaysian employers, labor recruiters, Vietnamese workers, and recruitment enterprises responsible and sets regulations on wages and working hours. While this agreement is a good first step, without binding provisions and transparent enforcement mechanisms, it does not help the migrant workers who are stuck with abusive employers, the ones who were listed on contracts but failed to comply with them. Migrant workers have no power to change employers even if their current employers do not comply with the labor contracts. Their only recourse is to go to a trade union office, Tenaganita (a Malaysian-based NGO), or the Vietnamese Embassy to file a complaint. In principle, their complaints will be looked into, but there is a time limit after which the workers must return to Vietnam.[16] In practice, as shown in subsequent chapters, many move into licit third spaces and work for other Malaysian employers (not stated on their original contracts) who took a chance and hired them.

The Malaysian Minimum Wage and Levy System

Malaysia has received two side benefits from foreign workers: levies paid to the government and fees paid to the outsourcing companies. The Malaysian government originally established a levy system that Malaysian employers, not the workers, were supposed to pay. However, the government has gone back and forth on this policy, sometimes allowing the employers to deduct the costs from wages.[17] This changing policy reflects opposing interests within Malaysia, including management, proworker Malaysian unions, and local and international NGOs.

In 1993, the government began charging Malaysian employers a levy of RM1,200 per year for each foreign worker they hired as a way to protect jobs for native Malaysian workers, who were exempt from this tax. Malaysian employers would pay this annual levy to the government before foreign workers entered the country. But as reimbursement, the employers shifted the responsibility of paying the levy onto the foreign workers by deducting RM100–130 per month from their monthly paychecks. This practice ended in 2008 thanks to the Textile, Clothing, and Footwear Workers Union of Australia and the Committee to Protect Vietnamese Workers, who exposed the Malaysian employers (e.g., Nike suppliers) for deducting the levy from workers' wages.[18]

Then, in 2012, the minimum wage was equalized for Malaysian and foreign workers. The intention behind making the minimum wage the same for both Malaysians and migrant workers was to create an incentive for Malaysian employers to hire Malaysian workers over migrant workers. The government was also keen on increasing the skills and education of Malaysians so that they could apply for the higher-skilled and higher-paying jobs.[19] Once the minimum wage policy took effect in 2013, the Malaysian government again allowed employers to deduct the levy from the monthly paychecks of foreign workers (mostly working in the manufacturing, construction, and service sectors) to recoup some of the extra wages migrant workers were now receiving under the new legislation.[20] The government justified its actions by claiming that the move to impose a levy on foreign workers would not be a burden on them, as the levy required was less than the mandated salary increases.[21] But the Malaysian government has been benefiting from the levies, collecting revenues of about RM2.5 billion in 2016 (or about US$598 million).[22] In 2016, the monthly levy was also raised to between RM1,500 and RM2,500 due to the minimum wage increase in July of that year.[23]

The question of who, employers or foreign workers, ought to have to pay the levy has been the subject of an ongoing struggle that shows the power of solidarity among foreign workers, Malaysian unions, and local

NGOs. Pressure from the labor unions and NGOs such as Tenaganita led the Malaysian government to announce that as of January 1, 2017, employers (not migrant workers) would assume responsibility for levy payments, but it then postponed enacting this decree due to pressure from Malaysian employers.[24] In September 2018, the Malaysian government ruled that employers, instead of foreign workers, must bear the full cost of the original levy payment structure.[25] Employers were not happy because they had proposed that they pay only 20 percent of the annual RM10,000 levy for each foreign worker while the foreign workers would pay 80 percent. The foreign workers and the unions won the day, however, by arguing that the workers could not afford to pay their portion, amounting to RM8,000. In another twist, in May 2019, responding to pressure from Malaysian employers, the Malaysian government allowed employers in the construction, manufacturing, and service sectors (where most Vietnamese guest workers have been hired) to pay a reduced levy of RM6,000 annually for each foreign worker. The government allowed employers to extend the employment of foreigners with a decade of experience for another three years, but the reduced levy would be valid for only the first additional year; thus, for the twelfth and thirteenth years of the migrant worker's extended contract, the employer would be responsible for paying RM10,000 annually.[26]

The media in Malaysia report on labor injustice, but overall there is little criticism directed at employers or the Malaysian government due to the Printing Presses and Publications Act of 1984. Under this legislation, the minister of home affairs is given "absolute discretion" in the granting and revocation of licenses and can also restrict or ban outright publications that are likely to endanger national security interests or create social unrest. There is a heavy penalty of RM30,000 and jail time for those considered offenders by the Ministry of Home Affairs. The risks have discouraged the reporting of migrant worker exploitation in mainstream newspapers. Labor newspapers in Vietnam are more proactive and even run a hotline for reporting labor violations,[27] so Vietnamese workers find it hard to adjust to the silent media in Malaysia. It is a frustrating loss of a potential ally.

The Vietnamese Socialist Labor Brokerage State

From the labor-sending perspective, Vietnam has already been a labor brokerage state in the socialist system that predated labor export to Malaysia. In the early years after the establishment of the Democratic Republic of Vietnam in 1945, Vietnam agreed to send a number of guest workers to USSR and the Soviet Bloc countries to repay them for their support of the new socialist state. The government distributed these quotas among the ministries, which in turn spread them among the provinces and lower levels. Tens of thousands of people were sent to work in various Council for Mutual Economic Assistance countries.[28] In one estimate, the number of people sent abroad to work was ten times that of cadres, students, and scholars.[29] At the height of this program, over seventy thousand contract workers were sent to work in East Germany and eighty thousand guest workers were sent to the USSR.[30] Smaller numbers went to Bulgaria, Poland, Hungary, and Romania. About forty thousand students and young workers were sent to Czechoslovakia.[31]

While Beresford and Đặng did not indicate where the quotas were distributed, they appear to have assumed that most socialist migrant workers came from the north, given the historical commercial links between the Democratic Republic of Vietnam and the Soviet Union and the Eastern European markets (*chợ Đông Âu*). Potential guest workers had to be connected to families of cadres and government officers and have social networks that would allow them to mobilize capital and borrow money from relatives, friends, and neighbors in a shareholding system.[32] These social networks were formed by (1) the enterprising Kinh university students attending advanced programs, (2) the teachers translating for delegations sent for diplomatic and trade missions (as in the story of the Cosmopolitan Socialist Entrepreneur), (3) the cadres attending special training, and (4) the workers studying vocational courses. However, while these social networks helped the socialist migrants financially, they also locked them into certain career pathways (creating a path dependency) that may have prevented them from realizing their full potential and make it difficult to adjust to political economic structural changes happening around them.[33]

Key Players of the Capitalist Labor Brokerage System

After the fall of the Eastern Bloc in 1989 and the ensuing loss of an important source of income, the Vietnamese government made a concerted effort to address poverty and unemployment by sending workers to other countries. Since 1989, labor export quotas have extended beyond the former communist bloc. By the end of 2019, Vietnam had sent workers to over sixty countries and territories all over the global market system. Starting with the Politburo's approval of labor export in 1998, the government created a set of labor export policies whereby the poor could be recruited to work in Malaysia, where there was a need for low-skilled labor and where there were low fee requirements to work.[34] In 2002, the Vietnamese government signed a bilateral agreement with Malaysia to establish a legal framework for contract terms, including

62   CHAPTER 2

wages, taxes/levies, and working conditions, for a Vietnamese migrant who would be sent to work in this labor market and then return to Vietnam at the end of a three-year contract (see appendix 3).

The Vietnamese state has developed an intricate bureaucracy to control the three key stages of export labor: the predeparture period in Vietnam, the work period in Malaysia, and the return period after the worker has moved back to Vietnam. In 2006 the state passed Law 72/2006/QH11, Law on Vietnamese Working Overseas Under Labor Contracts, which set out the procedures for all stages of the labor export process and established the terms for contracts with private, state-owned, and quasi-state recruitment companies (see appendix 3). The period between 2002 and 2006 was the peak, when up to thirty thousand workers were sent to Malaysia, the largest labor market of that time. Vũ Minh Xuyên, a retired high-ranking official in Department of Overseas Labor who was later appointed to be the director of a major state-owned recruitment company, explained that there was a macroeconomic logic to the labor export policy: "During the 2004–6 period, the Malaysian wage was three times higher than the Vietnamese minimum wage. That's why many Vietnamese were enthusiastic to borrow money to go work in Malaysia. But an increase in the minimum wage in Vietnam starting in 2006 led to a decrease in the number of migrants nationwide going to work in Malaysia."[35]

It was not the goodwill of the Vietnamese state that instigated the annual increase in the minimum wage starting in 2006 but rather the collective actions of thousands of workers.[36] The corresponding decrease in the number of migrants who went to work in Malaysia may have contributed to the labor export policy that targets rural and mountainous areas in the name of "sustained reduction in poverty" in Vietnam. Prime Minister Decision 71/2009/QĐTT set quota goals for three periods using rigorous outreach strategies to send migrants, 80 to 95 percent of whom came from poor Kinh and ethnic minority households.[37]

The transnational LBS system stayed on course and was able to navigate global fluctuations, allowing Vietnam to benefit from sending its citizens to work in Malaysia. Between 2005 and 2015, Vietnam sent 220,000 Vietnamese workers to Malaysia, 104,948 in 2007 alone.[38] Although the 2008 global financial crisis tanked the Malaysian economy, leading to thousands of Vietnamese migrants losing their jobs and reducing the number of migrants going abroad to 68,433 by 2010, in mid-2009, only a year after the onset of the crisis, many Malaysian outsourcing companies reemerged seeking to satisfy an increased demand for low-skilled (*lao động phổ thông*) workers in electronics, mechanics, sewing, jewelry, and latex glove production, construction, restaurants, and seafood farming.[39] They had a clear preference for female workers. Mr. Paul Wong, the president of a Malaysian outsourcing company, said: "We want to recruit female workers because they are hardworking, smart, and disciplined."[40] In 2015 about eighty thousand Vietnamese migrants were working primarily in manufacturing, garment sewing, and construction in Malaysia.[41]

The Ministry of Labor, Invalids, and Social Affairs (MoLISA) is the key ministry that oversees all stages of the labor export policy. MoLISA has issued a series of legal documents on sending migrant workers abroad to strengthen the labor export legal framework (see appendix 4). To implement Prime Minister Decision 71/2009/QĐTT, the state distributes labor export quotas to all administrative levels of the sixty-four rural districts, whose job it is to recruit migrants from the poor households there. All members of the LBS system work to meet those quotas, including recruitment companies, local employment agencies and centers, and local mass organizations (such as the women's unions and the peasants' unions) who are tasked with visiting potential migrants and their parents at their homes to recruit them.

Moreover, the state has established a presence where migrants work and search out labor markets worldwide. In 2013 MoLISA created the Department of Overseas Labor (DOLAB), setting up branch offices throughout the sixty receiving countries to manage Vietnamese migrant workers on short-term labor contracts.[42] In collaboration with the consular departments of the Ministry of Foreign Affairs (MoFA), DOLAB explores foreign labor markets, monitors the trends in labor demand around the world, and publishes country-specific requirements for temporary workers on the DOLAB website.[43] DOLAB is also charged with resolving grievances and complaints lodged by the Vietnamese migrants. In Malaysia, however, their office is located in the Vietnamese Embassy in Kuala Lumpur, far away from provinces and cities where many Vietnamese migrants are sent to work.[44] During my fieldwork, many workers complained that the embassy failed to respond to their repeated complaints.

However, DOLAB activities pale in comparison with those of the more established Philippine labor brokerage state.[45] The Philippine government has several agencies that manage overseas Filipino workers all over the world, including the Philippine Overseas Labor Office and the Philippine Overseas Employment Administration, both of which have offices in every Philippine embassy and consulate around the world.

The LBS system is not monolithic: state institutions have been competing to gain control over and benefit from labor export policies. Overall, MoLISA and MoFA have benefited the most from the whole process. They have implicitly competed for positions in the Vietnamese embassies that offer the financial advantages of working overseas. In particular, MoFA controls the number of officials stationed in all Vietnamese embassies, including the one in Malaysia, and reserves those positions for its staff. Therefore, the state-sanctioned Vietnamese General Confederation of Labor has not been able to station personnel there on a consistent basis to assist Vietnamese overseas workers.[46]

How the LBS Benefits from the System

The Vietnamese LBS system benefits from migrant workers' remittances, just as socialist migrants' contributions helped pay wartime debts to the Eastern Bloc. The state receives recruitment fees (deducted directly from the loans) and benefits from the cash generated by the remittances sent from Malaysia. The remittances have increased over time, from US$10.6 billion in 2013, to $12 billion in 2015, to $13.2 billion in 2016.[47] These high remittance figures, estimated using data from IMF and World Bank World Development Indicators, seem to account for both official and unofficial channels. The official Vietnamese remittance figures are much lower: remittances of migrant workers going through the official channels added up to only about US$3 billion in 2014.[48] This means that around 75 percent of total remittances (from all countries) were sent to Vietnam through unofficial channels.

Vietnamese researchers highlight the macroeconomic benefits of remittances at national and provincial levels.[49] In terms of financial and socioeconomic impacts on Vietnam, remittances have surpassed the Official Development Assistance (ODA) and foreign direct investment (FDI) sources. Dinh Van Hai has argued that remittances provide stable inflows of foreign currencies for economic development that can avoid negative results often associated with FDI (such as environmental pollution) or ODA (debts and interest payments). Moreover, remittances can help eliminate hunger and reduce poverty while contributing to national savings. Vu also found that remittances have positive effects on economic growth at provincial and national levels.

On the required health checkups as part of the predeparture procedure, the benefit to the companies is clear, but the benefit to workers is ambiguous. At this final stage of the process, the recruitment company has already received money for contracting the worker and the worker has already incurred debts to get set up for working overseas. The recruitment companies benefit from being efficient, saving time by arranging the health checkups at the state-certified hospitals near international airports for workers' flights to Malaysia. For instance, if the health checkups are in Ho Chi Minh City hospitals, the workers can fly out from Tân Sơn Nhất airport, and if checkups are in Quảng Ngãi hospitals, they can fly out from the nearby Đà Nẵng airport.[50] However, if a checkup finds a health issue, the contracted worker would not be able to work in Malaysia to repay the debts already incurred. During some interviews, I was told that sometimes workers hid existing illnesses so that they could go to work in Malaysia.[51] Workers have an incentive to hide their illnesses so that they can repay their debts and fulfill their expectations and aspirations. In short, getting so close to departure is akin to the point of no return.

Costs to Work in Malaysia and Loan Policies

It is costly to go to work in Malaysia. Migrant workers and their families have to pay fees to the Vietnamese recruitment companies, state agencies, and the Malaysian outsourcing company as well as fees to secure a work permit and travel documents (passports, visas) and the costs of cultural orientation classes, health checks (including, for female workers, an initial pregnancy check and mandatory periodic pregnancy tests while they are working in Malaysia), and airfare.[52] Moreover, migrants from far-flung provinces have to pay room and board in cities such as Hanoi and Ho Chi Minh City while attending the orientation classes, which cover cultural topics and provide basic English language lessons, both required to qualify for a visa to work in Malaysia.

Most of the costs come from paying the recruitment and outsourcing companies in home and host countries respectively. When the Prime Minister Decision 71/2009/QĐTT Program got under way in 2008 and 2009, the loan principal of US$900–$1,000 covered these fees and some other costs. In the 2009–14 period, each migrant had to take out a larger loan, between US$1,300 and US$1,500, but ended up with less to cover other costs upon arrival in Malaysia. Over 80 percent of the loan amount was used to pay recruitment costs (US$650 to the Vietnamese recruitment companies, US$350 for Malaysian outsourcing fees), the one-way airfare (US$200 for a flight on Malaysian airlines), and processing fees (visa, passport, and health checkup). After all these deductions, not much was left for the workers' personal needs once in-country.[53]

Evidence from my fieldwork shows that the LBS state has been doing all it can to recruit migrants. To entice them, it offers them different kinds of low-interest loans (0.325% per month) to finance their work in Malaysia. Prospective workers who own land can use it as collateral, and their parents can cosign the loan application.[54] The state allows landless migrants to borrow on a trust basis (*tín chấp*), which does not require collateral. Over 91 percent of migrant workers had to borrow money to work overseas, and two-thirds had to borrow the full amount. The main sources are their family networks and state and private banks. Those unable to tap personal or state sources for loans may turn to loan sharks.[55] In this way, the state has facilitated indebtedness, which triggers third space dissent.

The two main state banks, the Social Policy Bank (the bank for the poor) and the Agriculture and Rural Development Bank, are tasked with lending potential workers up to 80 percent of the initial costs to get set up to work overseas. Starting in 2009, MoLISA recommended that the Social Policy Bank lend 100 percent of the total labor export costs to very poor households, but the amount was not to exceed đ30 million (less than US$1,500). Private banks likewise lend money to potential migrant workers, but they charge higher commercial interest rates.[56] The local mass organizations have to vouch for the character of migrants from very poor families so that the state will lend them money.

Figure 8. The Ba Tơ district branch of the Social Policy Bank uses banners to announce monthly meetings in local communes for loan information and signups in 2012. Credit: Author

Risk Management and Debt Collection Policies

The LBS creates an elaborate financial infrastructure to reduce the costs and risks of the program so that it can benefit from sending workers overseas. It has detailed policies on setting up money transfers to repay loans and guidelines whereby banks pay recruitment companies directly.[57] Transnational banking technology between Vietnam and Malaysia enables the Social Policy Bank to deduct money directly from migrant's monthly wages to ensure loan payment, and this money is deducted before the workers have any chance to withdraw money themselves.[58] This practice mimics that of the historical Vietnamese socialist state, which deducted money directly from the socialist guest workers' salaries to pay the Eastern Bloc countries in the 1980s.

If for various reasons the state cannot recoup the loan via money transfers while the migrants are still working in Malaysia, it has devised a system to collect the debt after the migrants return to Vietnam, using a local debt collection team (*ban chỉ đạo thu hồi nợ*) that includes local government officials (down to the ward/commune level) and mass organizations (such as the women's unions) who visit the returnees and their families at home every month to try to collect payments.[59] Moreover local state officials can threaten to sue returnees who default on their loans. However, Mr. Nguyễn Anh Tuấn, the vice president of Social Policy Bank in An Giang, told me that this strategy is not often used.[60]

Another way to entice a steady stream of export labor is to adjust the loan policies, even to the point of giving a "second loan." My fieldwork interviews in 2015 suggest that the government seemed to capitulate to the debtors by providing them with three repayment options. The first is to spread out the loan repayment over an extra three-year period (*dãn nợ*). The second is to postpone payment of the loan with no interest charged for a set term (*khoanh nợ*) while the debtor goes to work in a higher-paying country such as Korea or Japan. The third option is complete loan forgiveness (*xoá nợ*), which supposedly can be used only when the parents are deceased and the children can no longer work. However, as we will see in subsequent chapters, there are many exceptions to the conditions set for all three options. With the postponement option, the state allows debtors to obtain a *second* loan to cover the costs of going to work in a higher-paying country. Local bank officials in the hamlet (*xã*), the rural district (*huyện*), and the province Employment Service Center must verify that the migrants did apply to go to work overseas. While more evidence is needed to examine the real effects, the repayment options seem to entice the returnees, now with experience, to move on to better labor markets.

68 CHAPTER 2

Complaint Mechanisms

The LBS has been eager to send migrants abroad, but it has inadequate mechanisms for responding to the countless worker grievances that are lodged by migrants while they are in Malaysia and upon their return. Wanting to sustain the LBS system, the Vietnamese LBS introduced several laws to deal with workers' complaints: Law 021/2011/QH13, which outlines the processes and procedures for making complaints and the time frame for doing so; Decree No. 95/2013/ND-CP, which describes the penalties for violations against labor, social insurance, and overseas manpower supply regulations; and Decree No. 119/2014/ND-CP, detailing the handling of complaints on a range of issues, such as the dispatch of Vietnamese workers for overseas employment by recruitment companies. But the implementation of these laws is weak because of conflicts of interest: MoLISA and MoFA, the very state bureaucracies that are the subjects of migrant complaints, are charged with enforcing the laws.

Indeed, most of my interviewees received inadequate responses (or none at all) from the recruitment companies and state officials regarding their concerns over contract violations. Many felt that their voices fell on the deaf ears of state bureaucracies. An International Labour Organization (ILO)–funded study found that the mechanisms in place for addressing migrants' problems such as contract violations and other emergencies were ineffective and inadequate. This study interviewed returnees from Malaysia and Libya who had been identified as having had problems during the migration process, but out of the forty-four workers interviewed, nearly 30 percent did not even lodge a complaint because they did not know where, or how, to lodge it or believed they would not be supported.[61] Only a third received responses to their formal complaints, but everyone in this subgroup stated that their complaints were not settled satisfactorily. Overall, 85 percent were still in debt upon their return to Vietnam.[62]

The Vietnamese General Confederation of Labor

There is only one general labor union in Vietnam, the state-sanctioned Vietnamese General Confederation of Labor (VGCL), which is organized by administrative area (city, district, workplace) and by industry (textile/garment/footwear, commerce, railroads). But in reality, as part of the LBS infrastructure, the labor unions have limited ability to help the Vietnamese migrant workers overseas. The VGCL was not given a role in Law 72/2006/QH11, designed to defend migrant workers' rights while working overseas, and, as already noted, it has no representation in the Vietnamese embassies and consulates.

The VGCL has been limited to strategizing and assisting with lawmaking because without a physical presence in countries where the Vietnamese migrants are sent to work, it is unable to respond to workers' complaints there.[63] Recently, it has been advocating for a more equal footing with the recruitment companies and MoLISA, requesting that it be able to participate in the labor legislation process. Additionally, the VGCL has requested that it have a role in the grievance/complaints process (as specified in Decree No. 119/2014/ND-CP and Law 021/2011/QH13), be able to participate in legislative processes related to the labor export policy (as specified in Decrees No. 95/2013/ND-CP and 119/2014/ND-CP), and offer input into predeparture policies.[64]

However, global factors such as international labor standards and legislation in labor-receiving (host) countries have facilitated more active participation from the VGCL to advocate for migrant workers' rights overseas. Seizing on a regional initiative, Tripartite Action to Protect Migrant Workers within and from the Greater Mekong Subregion (GMS) from Labor Exploitation, the ILO funded and provided technical support to the Labor Migration GMS TRIANGLE Project office in Hanoi. In turn, this office has been working closely with MoLISA and the VGCL to help them represent and protect migrant workers' rights overseas in line with international labor standards. In 2011, the VGCL participated in the project and developed a four-point action plan: to enhance the rights of migrant workers who work overseas; to increase networks among the Vietnamese government, employers, recruitment companies, and foreign counterparts; to ensure representation of labor organizations; and to improve the VGCL's capacity in organization, mobilization, and policy making.[65]

All these efforts have had some effects, and the VGCL has started to reach out to the Malaysian trade unions. On March 16, 2015, the VGCL signed a memorandum of understanding (MOU) with the Malaysian Trades Union Congress (MTUC) for the protection of the rights of Vietnamese migrant workers in Malaysia.[66] Although this is a good first step, the VGCL has no power to enforce the protections outlined in the MOU. The ten-point "Joint Action and Cooperation Between the Parties" outlined in the MOU includes the ratification of some ILO conventions as well as some safety and health protections, particularly in hazardous industrial sectors.[67] It promotes "respect for workers' rights and interests" based on international labor standards and legislation in both countries. But it does not provide for cost sharing, and no resources are earmarked for implementation of those standards. In addition,

70   CHAPTER 2

the MOU does not clarify which "focal units" will provide implementation, though when asked about this, Mr. Trần Văn Lý, the vice president of the VGCL at the time, mentioned two VGCL departments: Social Economic Policy (Ban Chính Sách, Kinh Tế, Xã Hội) and International Relations (Ban Đối Ngoại).[68]

Almost three years later, in February 2018, steps were finally taken to implement the MOU. With Mr. Trần Văn Lý at the helm, the VGCL delegation developed a joint plan with the MTUC to beef up the protection of Vietnamese migrant workers' rights in Malaysia. The plan outlines the steps that these two parties have to commit to taking to achieve this goal, including using Vietnamese recruitment agencies, migrant workers resource centers, mass media, and other stakeholders to disseminate "targeted information" to Vietnamese migrant workers both before they depart Vietnam and during their employment in Malaysia. The MTUC also committed to providing "targeted support services," including access to legal support, to Vietnamese migrant workers through its three migrant resource centers. However, it remains to be seen how these information and support services will address the very different needs of these five ethnic groups.[69]

Internal Contradictions within the LBS System

The VGCL-controlled media has to walk a fine line between promoting labor export policies and criticizing them. The two VGCL-controlled newspapers, *Người Lao Động* (Laborer) and *Lao Động* (Labor), broadcast information about labor export policies and state loans that migrants can apply for to cover fees to work in places such as Japan, Korea, Taiwan, Malaysia, Brunei, Libya. and Algeria.[70] For the Malaysia market, they publicize low-interest state loans and other special programs intended to entice the migrants to work there. Other state-owned news outlets, such as *Tuổi trẻ* (The Young), *Tuổi Trẻ Online*, *Thanh Niên* (Youth), and *VietNam Net*, also cover labor migration issues. Being censored by the state, however, these state-run newspapers steer clear of exposing human rights violations inside and outside of Vietnam.

But whenever possible, the two labor newspapers perform a similar role to the MTUC's online *Labor Bulletin* by reporting abuses of migrant workers and calling on the government to protect them. Pro-migrant investigative journalists have had to strike a difficult balance between serving the LBS's interests (promoting labor export policies) and advocating for migrant-worker rights (exposing abuses of the state brokerage system) and reporting on the precarity that migrants face while working abroad.

Transnational Labor Brokerage System   71

After Vietnam signed the bilateral agreement with Malaysia in 2002, the media promptly reported violations in both Vietnam and Malaysia and used creative, metaphorical titles for their articles to criticize the LBS system for abandoning the very migrants they were claiming to help. They exposed state and quasi-state recruitment companies in Vietnam who worked with unauthorized individual recruiters to find potential migrant workers in rural areas and charged them up to US$2,000 per person.[71] These timely reports led to state sanctions of these practices. Other news articles provided an early wake-up call by exposing violations in Malaysia. A critical article aptly titled "Another Case of Leaving a Baby Stranded in a Marketplace" exposed the irresponsibility of a Vietnamese quasi state-owned recruitment company and its Malaysian outsourcing company counterpart in great detail, providing the names of these companies and laying out their failure to fulfill contract terms and their abandonment of the workers after they arrived in Malaysia (workers had to wait ten months for full-time employment) and also when they returned to Vietnam (it took two months for their employment files to be closed, a step that allowed them to get their deposits back).[72]

When the Prime Minister Decision 71/2009/QĐTT labor export program was introduced in 2009, investigative journalists sharply criticized its flaws, pointing out weak state investigators who turned a blind eye to known corruption and irresponsibility on the part of recruitment companies.[73] These journalists noted that only about 30 percent of these companies operated effectively.[74] They also criticized the state for failing to discipline unscrupulous recruiters for blatant violations and decried the lack of communication between recruitment companies and the embassies and consulates (under the management of the Ministry of Foreign Affairs) in labor-receiving countries—communication that would have helped give migrants some protection.[75] Moreover, they exposed violations by quasi-state recruitment companies formed by local people's committees and the VGCL (discussed in later chapters).

Thanks to these investigative journalists, there has been more of an effort on the DOLAB and Vietnam Association of Manpower Supply websites to expose bad labor export companies. In particular, the DOLAB website has improved its transparency, making it possible for migrants to check whether a given company legitimately sends workers overseas. It posts not only comprehensive information about countries that are looking for specific lines of work (including job descriptions and requirements) but also lists the Vietnamese recruitment companies that have accepted Vietnamese workers (and the corresponding host countries' companies). They also list recruitment companies whose licenses were withdrawn.[76]

Some investigative labor journalists even traveled to Malaysia to investigate these problems in situ. Duy Quốc, a seasoned investigative journalist specializing in Vietnamese labor migration all over the world, went to Malaysia on short-term visits to interview the workers there. In 2007, he interviewed workers in their dormitories and reported on their complaints of and protests in response to serious labor violations and disputes. After returning to Vietnam, he maintained contact with the migrant returnees and even gave them his mobile phone number so they could call him for legal advice to help them get back their security deposits or demand other rights.[77] In the 2014 summary article directly titled "Failure of Project Worth Thousands of Billions of Vietnamese Đồng," Nguyễn Duy sharply criticized the Prime Minister Decision 71/2009/QĐTT policy for failing to help the targeted migrants in poor districts. He pointed out that six years into the labor export policy with a US$250,000 budget, the state had been able to send only 9,000 migrants from the sixty-four targeted poor districts nationwide to work overseas, mostly in Malaysia.[78] This modest achievement does not come close to meeting the policy's quota of 50,000 such workers for the 2011–15 period.[79] This dismal record was corroborated by the LBS system itself: the Ministry of Labor reported that more migrant workers broke their contracts in 2015 compared to 2013–14 and that it had proved difficult to protect the rights of recruitment agencies and migrant workers who complied with the laws.[80]

Conclusion

Structurally, while this transnational state-managed labor migration system is self-reinforcing, balancing demand and supply of low-skilled labor, its hegemony is not complete. Paradoxically, each country is challenged by its own elements. The Malaysian government is challenged by MTUC (Malaysian unions) and Tenaganita (an NGO) to release foreign workers from having to pay levies (which have been the employers' responsibility) and to allow workers to move freely among employers. The Vietnamese LBS system is pressured by global labor standards and global civil society organizations (such as the GMS TRIANGLE Project) to look after the welfare of their migrant workers. Under global pressure and critical media coverage about the shortcomings of the labor export policies, the VGCL has been more actively responding to migrant workers' plight.

Moreover, many migrant workers have been actively reaching out to the LBS system to ask for help. They have also reached out to the media to report problems, both while they were still in Malaysia and after they returned to

Vietnam. Some returnees called and sent letters to labor newspapers and other news outlets to complain about the irresponsibility of the recruitment companies and the DOLAB office in the Vietnamese Embassy in Kuala Lumpur. Other returnees directly contacted specific journalists who had written articles in support of their plight, letting them know about contract violations perpetrated by Vietnamese recruiters and Malaysian companies.[81]

To manage labor export policies, the state has developed an elaborate recruitment system to reinforce state regulation in order to achieve stability, or infrastructural involution, of sending workers to jobs overseas.[82] Chapter 3 explains how the recruitment system works.

3 The Labor Recruitment Process and Indebtedness

Once labor migration policies are in place, the recruitment system implements those policies and, intersecting with local, national, and global processes, reinforces a robust network of states and institutions. The recruitment system in Vietnam is complex and features not only state and private companies but also quasi-state companies and mass organizations that are charged with recruiting residents from province and city down to the commune, hamlet, and household levels.

To gain the consent of ethnic minority groups, the state appeals to the real desperation of under- or unemployment in poor districts and works hard to convince these groups to overcome their fears of the unknown so they will go. For many Kinh, who are not part of the sixty-four poor districts, going to work in Malaysia has been a voluntary decision in the hope of improving their circumstances.

Understanding how these recruiters gain the local residents' consent, especially convincing them to take on loans, is crucial to understanding migrants' indebtedness and precarity in Malaysia, which leads to their forming spaces of dissent.

Recruitment Process and the Key Players

The Ministry of Labor, Invalids, and Social Affairs (MoLISA) oversees the entire labor recruitment process (recruiting, training, documentation). In 2015, it granted licenses to 247 labor export/recruitment companies: 193 of these companies, mostly connected to the state ministries and former state-owned corporations, are in the north, 6 are in the central part of the country,

Labor Recruitment Process and Indebtedness   75

and 48, which are connected to local state agencies, are in the south.[1] The geographical distribution of these recruitment companies shows their intimate connection to the power structure of LBS institutions: they are heavily concentrated in the north, where the headquarters of all the ministries are, and have a large presence in the south, near the Ho Chi Minh City's Tân Sơn Nhất International Airport, out of which migrants fly to Malaysia. The recruitment companies have also created their own association, the Vietnamese Association of Manpower Supply (VAMAS, a quasi-state entity with retired state officials at the top), to represent their interests.

The labor export market in Vietnam is not completely deregulated because a large number of state or quasi-state recruitment companies (under the control of ministries such as MoLISA) and mass organizations (such as women's unions) coexist with private companies, which have grown since 2003. These "tentacles" spread out and reach down to the lowest administrative units, such as wards or hamlets, to recruit migrant workers, but the companies do not have permanent offices in Malaysia to provide timely responses to workers' complaints. They send representatives to Malaysia only when there are crises needing urgent intervention. The lack of offices in Malaysia means that many worker grievances fall on deaf ears.

The Vietnamese recruitment companies search for job orders from Malaysia and then connect with the local state agencies to recruit workers. The Malaysian companies provide specific information about recruitment terms and conditions.[2] Then a contract is signed between the Vietnamese recruitment companies and the Malaysian manufacturing companies whereby the recruitment companies are tasked with recruiting Vietnamese workers for the manufacturers.

In the next step, the Vietnamese companies work with local LBS agencies such as local branches of state employment agencies and mass organizations. Through these elaborate recruitment networks they are able to reach potential migrants in remote areas. Employment centers (*trung tâm giới thiệu việc làm*) managed by the city and district departments of MoLISA are recruitment hotspots. At the lowest commune or hamlet level, most employment offices (*phòng giới thiệu việc làm*) are managed by the local people's committees, whose recruiters visit households to convince parents to allow their adult children to work in Malaysia and to convince the children that it is a good idea.

The local employment centers are also involved with the loan process, first signing a contract with the recruitment companies. The employment centers then work directly with prospective migrants to help them with labor contracts and loan papers. Once the contracts are signed, then the state banks

76 CHAPTER 3

lend money to the potential migrant workers. Let us start with an example of Sovilaco, a recruitment company operated by MoLISA. Mr. Vũ Minh Xuyên, Sovilaco's director, explained the process of obtaining loans to me: "We visited the An Giang province employment agency, which recruited migrants for us; then we signed an agreement with the agency [who would oversee the signing of the contract with the migrants]. The language of the agreement allows the recruits [Hrê migrants] to go to the state banks to borrow money."

Recruiters sometimes enlisted migrants and obtained loans even before a contract with a Malaysian company was finalized or before there were job orders that needed to be filled. Mr. Cung, a Hrê man, was waiting to go to work in Malaysia when I interviewed him in 2011:

> I have been waiting for three months now. I hope to be able to leave in about ten days. While waiting, I'm helping my parents working in the field. I already got a đ24 million loan to go to work in Malaysia. I've called the employment center many times to check on this situation. Here I learned to work on electronics, but when I go to Malaysia, the company there will train me and find me work.

I did not have a chance to do a follow-up interview with him to find out what ultimately happened to him, but the fact that he got the loan even *before* knowing who his Malaysian employer would be shows how desperate the local government was to meet the state-mandated quotas for their districts.

In the early 2000s, the situation became even worse, when Malaysian human resource companies started to source labor for Malaysian factories directly. Some Malaysian human resource companies opened branch offices in Vietnam to directly monitor all recruitment procedures; then they received the workers in Malaysia, providing introductory training before "hand[ing] them over to the employers."[3]

Because there are so many intermediary recruiters in both countries and there is no clear *transnational* oversight, it is difficult to hold them accountable when it comes to the terms and conditions promised to the workers. This system often results in contract violations, including employer failure to meet contract terms that relate to type of job, salary level, raises, and availability of overtime work. These common violations have caused angry and disillusioned workers to take matters into their own hands by becoming undocumented and finding or creating third spaces.

Contract and Loan Papers: Signing a Carte Blanche

Recruiters at various levels work closely together to pressure prospective migrants to sign contracts and loan papers to secure the low-interest state

Labor Recruitment Process and Indebtedness   77

loans that will finance their overseas trips. This contract and loan process is similar for all ethnic groups in Vietnam and is also observed in China and Indonesia. In the case of Vietnam, the migrants in my sample had incomplete information about the Malaysian companies that hired them. In principle, the district labor department office is supposed to provide support and guidance on all paperwork. But in reality, many migrants were asked to sign a "carte blanche" document that could be used to match them with *any* jobs that the Malaysian outsourcing/human resource companies needed to fill.[4]

At the time of departure, the migrants often do not know the specific Malaysian company they will work for, the actual terms of employment, or the benefits they are supposed to receive. Most of my informants only knew of a general job announcement to recruit workers without any particular company's name mentioned. The general job announcement may include the key job requirements and the benefits that migrants should receive. In one such announcement from 2007, one significant line jumps out of the page: it states, "The employer pays the tax/levy for workers," but as we have seen, that wasn't true before September 2018 (see chapter 2).[5] The listed benefits, which workers are supposed to receive during the entire three years working in Malaysia, often include no additional fees, exempted passport fees, free health exam, food, pocket money, dormitory housing, transportation, and cooking utensils. But there is no verifiable connection between the generic application form (without a Malaysian company's name) that the workers signed and the job requirements stated on the general announcement.

My informants gave me sample loan application forms from recruitment companies, Suleco and Sovilaco, from 2013 and 2015, showing the Vietnamese recruitment company's name but not naming a particular Malaysian factory that will hire the worker. These sample applications contain a blanket paragraph stating that the applicant has read all the information related to Malaysian cultural practices and working and living conditions; promises to comply with all the regulations of Vietnam, Malaysia, and the recruitment company; and agrees with the terms of the contract, which are not elaborated on the sheet of paper they are being asked to sign. At the end, it asks for the worker's personal information, including passport number, and it provides a place to sign and date. Nowhere does the form state the responsibilities of the LBS system (in either country) or the recruitment company.

While the carte blanche contract does not indicate management's responsibility to workers, the loan application (offered by the Social Policy Bank in the local district) is very detailed as to how migrant workers will be held accountable for their loans. It indicates the loan amount, the state-subsidized monthly interest rate of 0.325 percent per month, the due date (by which the

78   CHAPTER 3

loan must be repaid), and predeparture fees to be paid using money from the loan.

Moreover, many ethnic migrants in this study have trouble understanding the Vietnamese language used in the documentation, in addition to the content, and most are unprepared or unable to read the contracts carefully before they sign. Since the paperwork is written in Vietnamese, it privileges the Kinh who can read it at the expense of the other ethnic groups. Worse yet, in many cases, the recruits are rushed into signing it. Additionally, the content may be different between the Vietnamese version (presented by the recruitment company) and the English version (presented by the Malaysian company), although it is very challenging to assess this particular claim, because most migrants do not keep the hard copies of their contracts as evidence in case of conflict. But some parents did preserve their children's contract documentation.

In 2011, I was fortunate to meet one such cautious parent, Ms. Oanh (a Hrê mother), at her home in Sơn Hà District (Quảng Ngãi). Her son (Mr. Khôi, a twenty-year-old man) was still working in Malaysia at the time, and she shared with me all of the labor contract forms he had signed before leaving for Malaysia.

Before 2011, some Christian (Kinh) groups had attempted to recruit the local Hrê in Sơn Hà District to their faith. This had led to extreme government paranoia about these religious groups; the government feared that the groups had antigovernment and prodemocracy motives behind their religious façade. Neverthless, I managed to visit this politically sensitive Hrê district unaccompanied by any state officials.

My uncensored, in-depth interview with Ms. Oanh revealed many valuable insights that would not have been available to me had I been escorted by state officials. Unlike most Hrê families, Ms. Oanh's preservation of her son's paperwork was very rare. Mr. Khôi had only finished grade 11. He left for Malaysia only five months before this interview, on a three-year contract, with a group of sixteen other Hrê men. With strong ethnic-group bonding, they stayed together, pooling their money so each member of the group would have an opportunity to send a lump-sum amount home.

In sum, all of these loopholes and lack of accountability from the companies (in both Vietnam and Malaysia) explain the root cause of workers' complaints and their precarity in Malaysia, especially problematic when there has been no oversight to ensure proper implementation of contract terms.

Orientation Classes

There is one positive intention of the LBS system: the orientation classes that recruitment companies, funded by MoLISA, offer to the workers to prepare

Labor Recruitment Process and Indebtedness 79

them before they leave for Malaysia, for which the fees are waived.[6] The LBS system has the infrastructure and personnel to bring large groups of workers from various districts to a regionally based setting for these classes, which often last about one month. The intention of orientation classes is good, aiming to prepare migrants to work in a predominantly Muslim country. However, in reality, they fall far short of their original intention. Most migrant workers are ill prepared to go to Malaysia and are especially challenged when it comes to respecting Muslim customs and Malaysian traditions.

Most of these classes cover Malaysian cultural practices (such as dietary restrictions in this Muslim country) so that migrants will not violate them. As Mr. Nguyễn Văn Lâm, director of the employment center of the Department of Labor in An Giang, explained to me, migrants

> need to know Malaysian cultural and religious practices and know what to do and what to avoid. They need to know how to relate to their bosses, how to ask for what they need, how to enquire about wages, daily work hours, rest hours, overtime work, and compensation. Moreover, these classes introduce a list of manufacturing jobs, such as assembling electronics, for them to choose from to match their abilities and health conditions. Then after three months, these students can decide which jobs would be appropriate for them, given their level of preparedness. At the end of this class, they will register for the appropriate jobs and the recruitment office will assign a job that matches the qualifications of each person.[7]

However, the reality shows that these orientation classes are ineffective and not really benefiting the migrants. First, organizing such large classes in the center of a city or province (such as Hanoi, Ho Chi Minh City, or Quảng Ngãi) places an additional cost burden on migrants from far-flung provinces who have to pay not only transportation costs but also living expenses. Second, while some local provinces did subsidize these expenses for the poorest migrants, the migrants were still ill prepared after the class, which covers many cultural topics and basic English language skills. Mostly they learned basic vocabulary related to what was expected of them—their job responsibilities, not their rights. Mr. Sadat, a Chăm worker, said, "In the two months of basic English class, we learned the names of the machines and equipment, and phrases of work orders." Mr. Ngãi, a Kinh worker, complained that two months was too short a time to learn English so as to be able to speak it effectively. Many other Kinh workers I interviewed said that they did not speak enough Malay, English, or Chinese to interact effectively with other foreign migrant workers, and many were not familiar with Muslim religious practices. Ms. Hạnh, a Kinh worker, said that she learned English in her orientation class, but when she tried it with her Malay bosses, they did not

80 CHAPTER 3

understand her at all. At wit's end, she found a basic Malay language lesson book and studied it during break time, and eventually she understood her Malay bosses' orders and ended up speaking half English and half Malay.

State-Owned Recruitment Companies and Employment Agencies

The LBS relies on many state-owned and quasi-state recruitment companies that benefit from exporting labor. Historically, many recruitment companies were large state-owned corporations (originating and based in the north), the general corporations formed in 1991 (*tổng công ty 91*). As the state sought to enter the neoliberal market system in the twenty-first century, it was pressured by neoliberal institutions such as IMF and World Bank to undergo a privatization process (*cổ phần hóa*). During this period, the state transformed state-owned corporations into various kinds of private companies, such as joint-stock companies (in which over half of the shares were owned by the state), joint ventures, and one-member companies (in which the state was the limited-liability owner).[8] Exporting labor has become one of the many functions of these formerly state-owned companies. For instance, Việt Hà Company (located in Hà Tĩnh province in north-central Vietnam) was originally a state-owned corporation that exported wood products. It became a joint-stock company that focused on the exportation of labor to Taiwan, Malaysia, and the Middle East in 2004 by a decision of the People's Committee of Hà Tĩnh Province.[9] Some of my interviewees were recruited by the labor export and recruitment department of the Vietnamese Steel Company, which also controlled the production and export of other products, such as coal, oil, and natural gas. In this way, the state has commodified labor just as it has natural resources. Another example is Vinatex, a state-owned corporation that nevertheless in 2011 oversaw sixty privatized textile and garment factories and training and service centers; one of the latter functions as a recruitment center for export labor.[10]

Many state-owned recruitment companies originated from MoLISA and are managed by former state officials. MoLISA's Sovilaco, for example, is now managed by Mr. Vũ Minh Xuyên, who used to grant labor export licenses to recruitment companies at MoLISA. After retirement, he moved to the quasi-state side, being appointed by MoLISA to run Sovilaco owing to his insider's knowledge of labor export policy and his wealth of connections from his decades of working as a state official.

A number of migrant returnees that I interviewed in 2008 had been recruited by Suleco, which at that time was still a state-owned overseas manpower service company under the management of MoLISA in Ho Chi Minh City.[11] By 2015, it had become a private joint-stock company that offered training services to workers and professionals planning to work in Japan.[12] Others were recruited by Lasec Human Power Company, which had been part of the Ministry of Construction.[13] Still others were recruited by Traconsin (Hanoi), which became a joint-stock company in 2004 but was still connected to the Ministry of Transport.[14] And others were recruited by Vilimex Joint Stock Company (Nghệ An province in north-central Vietnam), which specializes in agricultural produce and products and may be under the control of the Ministry of Agriculture and Rural Development.

Quasi-State Organizations

Mass organizations are political and social institutions that are supposed to be independent from the government. However, in Vietnam they are under state control and help recruit migrants for the state labor export policy. In return, mass organizations also benefit from labor export policies. They have established their own recruitment companies at both central and local levels. At the central level, the Vietnamese General Confederation of Labor (VGCL) formed Latuco International Labor Supply Company to recruit migrants. In 2010 it unceremoniously ceased to exist because of many complaints from migrant workers. The laments of Ms. Thu, a Kinh worker from a northern province who decided to work underground, resonated the most with me. She complained bitterly about how Latuco failed to respond to her grievances: "I called them [the two Latuco officials], one in Vietnam and the other in Malaysia, many times but only got their excuses that they will have to investigate this problem. Thus far, they have not gotten back to me."

Labor federations at the local levels also have their own employment offices. For instance, the Employment Center of the Ho Chi Minh City Labor Federation (Trung Tâm Việc Làm của Liên Đoàn Lao Động) serves as a liaison to connect recruitment companies to potential migrant workers.

Parliamentary committees (parallel to government ministries) also formed recruitment companies. For instance, the Ethnic Committee formed Milaco Joint-Stock Company, which recruited some of this study's interviewees.[15] It became a joint-stock company in 2007, and since 2008 it has been sending thousands of migrants to work in Japan, Taiwan, Korea, Brunei, Malaysia, and the Middle East.

In rural areas, local mass organizations, such as the women's unions and peasants' unions, work closely with these employment centers to recruit local residents. These grassroots recruiters know the local conditions best. Many come from mass organizations that have their own employment centers, such as peasant employment centers (*trung tâm giới thiệu việc làm nông dân*).[16] They visit the households in their communes and villages periodically to meet with the parents and prospective migrant workers in order to fulfill the labor export quotas imposed by the state, especially in the sixty-four targeted poor districts.

In January 2013, I followed Ms. Bạch, one such recruiter, a local Kinh women's union leader who led me up the mountains in Sơn Hà district to reach the poor Hrê households in remote locations at the foot of the Quảng Ngãi mountains. While this was the most rigorous field trip I made to conduct research for this book, to her it was just another day at work. For several hours we waded barefoot on mud roads, which had been destroyed by the huge trucks transporting acacia trees, and climbed up the mountain slopes to where the Hrê households were located. As I looked at the steep slopes ahead with some trepidation, this courageous woman cheered me on by telling me her life story and by describing the livelihoods of the Hrê households she worked with. She was well acquainted with the population in her commune, which consisted of over four thousand people (about thirteen hundred households), of which almost all were ethnic minorities with a heavy concentration of Hrê. She said that the Hrê sustain their cultural traditions and continue to make a living from agricultural work such as planting rice, cassava, and acacia trees and raising pigs. But she kept repeating that their lives were "difficult" and that the government did make an effort to improve their lives by implementing infrastructure projects to build houses, roads, schools, and health clinics and to connect electricity to each commune. Given her deep knowledge regarding the condition of these thirteen hundred households and her access to this Hrê community, it was not difficult for her to spread the word about the labor export policy to Malaysia and to recruit the Hrê young adults there.

The Case of Châu Hưng Recruitment Company

Aside from mass organizations, companies that have close connections to government agencies can also be thought of as quasi-state entities. Châu Hưng Recruitment Company is an example of such an organization; it has very close connections to the LBS system. It is one of the ten companies selected by MoLISA to focus on recruiting the Hrê (from the sixty-four poor districts) to work in Malaysia. It not only uses the state media to secure contracts with prospective Hrê migrants but also manipulates the Hrê, encouraging them to dream of a better future by appealing to their cultural practices and survival needs. In 2011, with an introduction from journalist Duy Quốc,

Labor Recruitment Process and Indebtedness 83

I had an interview with Mr. Tống Thanh Tùng, the director of Châu Hưng, and learned how closely a local labor newspaper, *Người Lao Động* (Laborer), worked with a recruitment company to promote the idea of sending the Hrê to Malaysia and other countries for work.[17]

Two months before Law No. 72/2006/QH11, the "Law on Vietnamese Workers Working Abroad Under Contract," went into effect in July 2007, *Người Lao Động* organized a "direct dialogue" meeting (*chương trình giao lưu trực tuyến*) in Hanoi to promote the labor export policy and then published the proceedings verbatim in print. This newspaper brought together the key LBS representatives from MoLISA, the Department of Overseas Labor (DoLAB), and seven key recruitment companies, with Tống Thanh Tùng from Châu Hưng playing a key role.[18] During this meeting, they responded to over three hundred questions from potential migrant workers from all over Vietnam about the costs, wages, requirements, benefits, and risks in many international labor destinations, including Malaysia.[19]

Châu Hưng's recruitment strategy shows a clear preference for female workers, specifically in assembly work in Malaysia. In the town hall meeting, Tống Thanh Tùng recruited female workers for jobs in garment and electronics factories in Malaysia. In 2010, he continued to advertise assembly jobs for such factories, specifically for female workers for Panasonic and Sanyo factories. This practice recalls a similar pattern from over three decades ago explained by Aihwa Ong in her classic 1987 study on young neophyte Malaysian Muslim female factory workers and their resistance against both the state and capitalist discipline in Japanese factories in Malaysia.[20]

Châu Hưng's strategy is very clear: to dispel the Hrê's worries about going to work in Malaysia. Châu Hưng revealed how savvy it was to appeal to cultural and spiritual resources that were significant to prospective Hrê migrants and their families. A 2009 *Người Lao Động* newspaper article Tống Thanh Tùng wrote, titled "Working Overseas to Buy Buffaloes and Build Houses," documents how recruiters appeal to the Hrê's aspirations.[21]

Everyone was of one mind: export labor is the only way to reduce poverty in a swift and sustainable way as stipulated by the state. . . . Overcoming the language barrier [with the Hrê], we gave them a simple explanation about the benefits of export labor: "After three years of working overseas, *upon returning home, you will buy buffaloes and motorbikes and build and enlarge your house.*" Most Hrê participants [in these house visits] were able to understand and imagine these concrete goals. Listening to our talk, they smiled happily and said, "Those [items] have been our dream for generations." Then, we came up with some simple ways to advise them about the basic work hours, overtime hours, and types of allowances.[22]

84   CHAPTER 3

Tống Thanh Tùng dangled not only objects significant to the Hrê—buffaloes and houses—but also motorbikes, which are needed to drive on roads that have been badly damaged by big trucks transporting cash crops. Clearly the "simple ways to advise them" about pay and working conditions was very manipulative, glossing over the difficulties of working in Malaysia and not preparing the migrants well.

After the 2008 global financial crisis, governments and recruitment companies tried to rebuild guest worker confidence. In 2010, Châu Hưng stepped up efforts to entice potential guest workers—both those who had come home during the crisis and new recruits—to return to Malaysia.[23] The company established a program to attract prospective migrants (*chương trình tạo nguồn*), which was advertised in *Người Lao Động*. Incentives included waiving the đ1 million fee, which covered the visa, health examination, and other fees for the first group of migrants.[24] Several recruitment companies, including Châu Hưng, extended migrants' loan repayment schedules. For instance, a worker recruited through Châu Hưng for garment stitching, with an average loan of US$1,000, would be allowed nine months of the first year's work to repay the loan, and an electronic worker, with an average loan of US$1,200, would be allowed eleven months.

Private Recruitment Companies

Vietnamese private recruitment companies play an important role in sustaining the transnational LBS system because they serve as a crucial link between Malaysian employers and outsourcing companies.[25] They are proactive in searching for contracts with labor-receiving countries to feed to the elaborate state employment agencies. Many are not responsive to the complaints of the workers they send to Malaysia. I interviewed two unambiguously private companies: Trường Giang Company in Ho Chi Minh City and Hanic Company in Hanoi.

The case of Trường Giang Company shows that belonging to a tight-knit ethnic Hoa transnational network and speaking the language of the Chinese Malaysian employers give management an advantage if they want to maintain a permanent presence in Malaysia. Since 2010, Trường Giang has been sending workers, mostly from the Mekong Delta provinces such as Đồng Tháp and Sóc Trăng, to Malaysia. Through an introduction arranged by journalist Duy Quốc, I was able to interview the company's general president, Mã Bạch Phụng, a Hoa woman who speaks three languages (Chinese, Vietnamese, and French), and executive president Hồ Trường Sơn, a Kinh man. Mã Bạch Phụng has tight-knit connections with the Hoa communities in Malaysia:

"It is easy to deal with Chinese Malaysians because we understand each other well. I only dealt with ethnic Chinese (Malaysian) recruiters." With her established ethnic network, Mã Bạch Phụng has been able to secure a lot of job orders but not enough migrants to fill them: "The Hoa migrants often work in restaurants [where Chinese is spoken] whereas the Kinh workers often work in factories [owned by the Chinese Malaysians]." She also noted that her company provided free oral language classes for those who needed to learn to speak Chinese. She then took me to a room where a group of young students, migrant workers in training, were studying; they stood up and greeted me in Mandarin. They have a permanent representative, who is also a Hoa, in Malaysia, whose job is to respond promptly to migrants' needs. Mã Bạch Phụng herself often goes to Malaysia for several days to set things up and then returns to Vietnam.

The Trường Giang case also shows the advantage of having connections to the LBS system, in particular to MoLISA. Hồ Trường Sơn (the executive president) had worked for DOLAB as a labor export consultant: "I am trusted by and receive support from DOLAB, having worked there for fourteen years." He did not specify the form of state support he was receiving, but no doubt he had cultivated relationships that helped him secure access to low-interest loans for the migrants they recruited and get job postings listed in the state-owned newspapers such as *Người Lao Động*. Indeed, while we were talking in his office, he picked up the phone and called Duy Quốc to ask him to post a call for jobs available in Malaysia.

The second case, Hanic Company in the north, also shows the importance of having a connection to the LBS system. It received a corporate social responsibility prize from VAMAS, a quasi-state association for recruitment companies (see appendix 3). They are able to use their award for "voluntary social compliance" to global labor standards as a public relations strategy to procure more contracts with labor-receiving countries. Dr. Nguyễn Lương Trào, VAMAS president, introduced me to the leaders of this company, Ms. Nguyễn Thị Tuyết Mai, the president, and Mr. Lê Quốc Hùng, the vice president, for an interview. Both are Kinh. Hanic has less of a physical presence on site in Malaysia than Trường Giang Company. There is no permanent Hanic representative office in Malaysia. Lê Quốc Hùng has only a one-month tourist visa, so he would stay two to three weeks in Malaysia each month, fly back to Vietnam to renew his visa, and then return to Malaysia.

The Hanic case also shows the effects of a social network path dependency that can lock migrants into a trajectory that may or may not help them. Nguyễn Thị Tuyết Mai relies on the veteran migrant workers, that is, returnees, to convince potential migrants to follow in their footsteps.

86 CHAPTER 3

This support network could be helpful if the new migrant workers are able to use the lessons learned by returning migrants to avoid the precarity the returnees likely experienced in Malaysia. Unfortunately, I did not have an opportunity to interview their recruits to see if this was the case. What I was told is that since 2008, Hanic Company has been recruiting workers for Malaysian factories, their traditional labor market. They have been able to recruit directly rather than through intermediaries, and 85 percent of their recruits were Kinh workers from poor provinces in the north.

Hanic's recruitment strategy demonstrates a clear management preference for a gender division of labor, similar to Châu Hưng company, especially with respect to electronics assembly work in Malaysia. These Malaysian employers prefer female workers, and they try to entice them with lower recruitment fees (about US$800–900) compared to that for male workers (US$1200). Most women were recruited to work in electronics factories in Penang. According to Nguyễn Thị Tuyết Mai, "Managers prefer young women with good eyesight for scope work and nimble fingers. . . . Some contracts specifically ask for 100 percent women in electronics because they don't drink, don't brawl, and love to work overtime. Those [women] working in electronics were younger than those in sewing." At the time of the interview, her company had sent thirty-five hundred migrants to Malaysia, of which 15 percent were from ethnic minority groups including some Khmer from An Giang who were trained by Hanic staff in Hanoi for one to two weeks before they headed off to Malaysia.

Indebtedness

Migrants and their families incur debts through this elaborate recruitment system. Indebtedness starts when the workers sign the loan documents.[26] The workers subsequently try to save up and use their remittances to repay multiple layers of debts. But when they run into problems with their contracts while in Malaysia, their debts (both principal and interest) continue to mount.

There are mechanisms at work that can keep migrants in a vicious cycle of debt. According to Oishi, migrant workers extend their contracts because they get trapped by debt and have to continue working. Migrants are trapped by the recruitment process (which can be aggressive), the outsourcing system in Malaysia (which is opaque to migrant workers, resulting in many not even knowing the name of their Malaysian employer at the point of departure), and their ability to manage money.[27]

Most migrants need to borrow money to pay recruitment fees and other expenses, and many migrants' families are already in debt before the migrant

Labor Recruitment Process and Indebtedness 87

signs up to work in Malaysia. A nationwide study (2010–11) in eight provinces with high concentration of overseas labor returnees (from Japan, Taiwan, Korea, and Malaysia) showed that over 91 percent of migrant workers surveyed had to borrow money to work overseas.[28] Of these, two-thirds had to borrow enough to cover all fees and expenses. The main sources of money are family networks and banks (state banks, such as the Social Policy Bank, and private banks). About 10 percent borrowed from loan sharks who charged exorbitant interest rates above the official limits. For those households that owned land, the land was used as collateral.

Debts and Remittances among the Kinh and the Hoa

I asked all the migrants I interviewed about whether they had taken out loans and whether they still had debt owed from those loans. Among my thirty-six Kinh and Hoa migrant interviewees, only twelve (33 percent) had received loans from the state banks. The other twenty-four (67 percent) did not mention any debt, so I assume that they either borrowed from family members and friends or private banks, and had paid their debts.

After part of the money borrowed from a branch of the Social Policy bank was used to pay recruitment fees and expenses, these Kinh and Hoa migrants received the remainder, which was less than 25 percent of the total loan amount. The 33 percent who had obtained state loans all still had outstanding debts, ranging from đ4 million to đ20 million. In cases where the parents were poor, without any land to use as collateral, the prospective migrant was able to secure a loan based on trust (*tín chấp*). In five of the twelve debt cases, parents dragged their feet and did not pay off the outstanding amounts.

Mr. Việt is a mature thirty-seven-year-old veteran who did two-year mandatory service in the military (1994–96). The recruitment process he went through was efficient, conducted jointly by the employment office of the An Giang Labor Federation and the Sao Thái Dương Recruitment Company in Ho Chi Minh City. He completed his three-year contract (2005–8) in Malaysia and returned home, still đ20 million in debt:

> I was studying in the employment office of the An Giang Labor Federation. Still without a labor contract. When I went to the Sao Thái Dương Company in Ho Chi Minh City [for a two-day visit], on the first day they gave me a fifteen-page labor contract on A4 size paper with a lot of conditions and constraints. They told me that once I had paid the fee, it was not refundable. So, this means that when I came to this recruitment company office, the deal was already sealed. Several days later, when I finished the orientation course at the An Giang Labor Federation office, I left my phone number there. Then a day later, I received a

88 CHAPTER 3

phone call informing me that the Malaysian company had accepted workers, so I signed the loan paper to borrow đ19 million with a 0.5 percent monthly interest rate from the Social Policy Bank, transmitted my application, and said good-bye to my family the day after to fly to Malaysia. The departure was so abrupt. . . . I missed my children very much during the three-year separation.

Mr. Việt was pressured into signing the contract, even before he had a chance to read and review the lengthy document. He was also misinformed about the interest rate, which turned out to be 0.65 percent per month, not 0.5 percent. The Sao Thái Dương Recruitment Company deducted đ18 million to pay itself all the fees, including the đ5 million deposit that the company did not refund to him after he finished the three-year contract, which they were legally required to do, as stipulated in Circular 21/2013. Mr. Việt got to keep only đ1million to buy items necessary for his first overseas trip. He was very bitter about this recruitment company, which was quick to take money from his loan but did not respond to him when he faced problems in Malaysia. Many other migrants I interviewed likewise were rushed into making a decision without an opportunity to review the terms of the contract and were then ignored by the recruitment companies once they were working in Malaysia.

Ms. Kim-Ly, an ethnic Hoa who lived with her mother in their family home in downtown An Giang province (Long Xuyên City), received a đ15 million low-interest loan. She was able to obtain a second loan of đ2 million with a 0.1 percent monthly interest rate with certification from the ward-level state office to cover her expenses in Malaysia. It is possible that she received support for two loans in what was a swift recruitment process because the local government needed to meet its labor export quota. This recruitment was conducted by the now defunct Latuco Recruitment Company, owned by the VGCL, and the employment office of the An Giang Labor Federation. They sent her to work in a factory, owned by a Malaysian of Chinese descent, that made electronic products. She returned home after completing her contract in Malaysia still owing đ7 million(about US$350) with interest accruing monthly.

Most of the Kinh and Hoa migrant workers I interviewed, both men and women, aspired to send remittances home to their parents and families, as other studies have also indicated.[29] A nationwide study (mostly about the Kinh) conducted by the Institute of Social and Labor Science likewise shows that over 90 percent of migrant guest workers sent money home every two to three months to help with their families' most pressing needs. This same study shows that families used about 34 percent of total remittances to repay previous debts and debts that were accumulated to fund the migration, about

Labor Recruitment Process and Indebtedness 89

28 percent to build or repair houses, and the rest to buy household appliances or to save and invest.[30] The migrants that had to take out new loans in hopes of paying off old debts found themselves in a vicious cycle of debt that made it impossible to escape poverty.

According to Hoàng and Yeoh, it is particularly burdensome for guest workers to use remittances to pay debt during the first year abroad because their debts eat up most of their income.[31] My interviewees likewise expressed how difficult this was. This one-year average for guest workers to repay the debts incurred for their global migration is within the range estimated by other scholars.[32]

Many of those who do manage to pay off their debts in the first year do not save and invest their earnings over the remaining two years (if they complete their contracts) but use the money to take care of their families, demonstrating what Lã and Leung call "altruism towards family members."[33] However, migrants who come from families that own property or land were able to remit money (after paying off the debt in the first year), which the family then saved for them to use upon their return.

In September 2008, I visited Ms. Hà and Ms. Lê, Kinh migrants at their hostel in Batu Pahat province in Malaysia. Both are from Hải Dương (a northern province) and are married with children. They were close friends and roommates, and they pooled their money to send home. Ms. Hà described the grueling work she undertook in order to be able to send money home to her family:

> I worked continuously from 6 a.m. to 3:30 p.m. without break or food. I came in early to check the machine and worked continuously. That is the only way to catch up with the speed of the machine and to make more money, because the base pay here is very low. Very hard work, but I don't stop. With savings, I can send money home: every month I remit đ2 million. I have an eleven-year-old son [she proudly showed us a photo] who is being cared for by my parents.

Ms. Lê added that "our main goal in coming here is to make money and send it home for our parents to take care of our children and send them to school. Then later on we use our savings to build a house for our children." Neither mentioned saving any money for themselves. Ms. Liên, from Cần Thơ (a southern province), was recruited by Suleco to work in a cookie factory. She did not mention any bank debt, and she managed to remit RM14,000 over three years for the care of her parents: "My family is poor, with seven children. My mother is sick all the time. So, I only studied up to grade nine and went to work in Malaysia to send money home to take care of my parents. I did a lot of overtime work in order to have money to send home."

90   CHAPTER 3

Debts and Remittances among the Hrê

During fieldwork, I often heard about the cycles of debt related to their own or family members' health issues. Among the Hrê, it is common for migrants to use remittances to pay off previous debts instead of the loan that allowed them to go to work in Malaysia. Đinh Thị Phương Lan, a half-Hrê and half-Kinh woman, benefits from her mixed ethnicities in performing her job. She uses her linguistic skills (fluent in both Hrê and Vietnamese languages) in her job as the vice chair of the DoLISA office in Ba Tơ district to understand and shed light on the Hrê migrants' conditions. She attributes preexisting debts to medical bills migrants accrued due to poor public health services. Many Hrê interviewees likewise attributed preexisting debts to the poor health of the workers' parents. Laments over the poor public health system was a refrain in many of my interviews with the Hrê women in Quảng Ngãi. Most had an illness of one sort or another and did not look well.

In January 2011, I interviewed Ms. Khanh, a forty-four-year-old half-Tày and half-Hrê woman. She and her forty-eight-year-old husband had a nineteen-year-old son (Mr. Phúc) working in Malaysia. I visited their home in Ba Tơ district accompanied by four official escorts who monitored my interviews. Clearly, this was a "model" household: their son had already paid back 60 percent of the loan after only six months of working overseas (a pace that would allow the family to pay off the loan in less than the one-year time frame advertised by the LBS).[34] From the remittances they received, Ms. Khanh and her husband used only a small amount, đ1.4 million (about US$60), to cover family necessities and her health expenses. She recounted a near-death episode when she had an appendicitis attack and had to be rushed to a hospital for emergency surgery. The medical expenses put her in debt, which she used part of their son's remittances to repay.

When I asked what they would do after they paid off the loan, Ms. Khanh referred to health status several times:

> If we, the parents, face difficulties, then we have to spend on medicines and hospital stay. . . . After we pay off the debt to the bank, and if we have no illness, then we will put the money he sent home into the savings account for him. . . . He works very hard so when he comes home, he'd be encouraged to see that there is some savings put aside for him as seed money to invest in a small business.

The Hrê may also cede land to pay debts incurred by illnesses or by important life events such as funerals, weddings, and religious rituals.

Labor Recruitment Process and Indebtedness 91

Khmer Debts and Land Ceding

In the case of the Khmer, the recruitment companies—not the local employment centers—receive the loans and disburse them to different constituencies. Mr. Nguyễn Văn Lâm, the An Giang Employment Service Agency director, said:

> Concerned that the migrants might use the loans for "non-labor-export" purposes, right after the migrants sign the loan papers with the bank, the bank wires money to the recruitment companies to pay all expenses such as the airfare, travel documents, and fees. Then they give the remainder to the migrants to buy some necessary items for their trip overseas.

Like the Kinh and the Hoa interviewees, the Khmer interviewees complained about receiving only a tiny fraction of the loans they took out: a few million đong to buy personal items for Malaysia. The average loan amount was about đ18–19 million (about US$900-$1,100), but many Khmer interviewees complained that they received only 15–20 percent of the total. All fifteen of my Khmer interviewees used loans from the Social Policy Bank to finance their transnational labor migration. Seven of them obtained collateral-free loans on a trust basis (*tín chấp*) because they had no land to serve as collateral. Of these seven loans, four were signed for by the workers' parents and three by the migrants themselves. In the other eight cases, their families used land as collateral. Of the fifteen cases, only two migrants had paid off their debts by the time of the interview.

The state recruitment system made sure that potential migrants were able to borrow money. The recruiters from the lowest administrative levels come from three units: (*ấp*) hamlet officials, representatives of women's unions, and representatives of peasants' unions. They encouraged the parents to sign the loan documents. For example, Neng Suvanna, a thirty-eight-year-old Khmer returnee, told me that her mother borrowed đ19 million on a "trust" basis. The family had no land to use as collateral.

Khmer migrants' families may also cede land to cover debts incurred by their participation in the LBS system. Land ceding exacerbates the Khmer's historical problem of landlessness, the result of long-standing tensions between Vietnam and Cambodia and subsequent political events. One Khmer father I interviewed, Châu Sethsak, took out a loan of đ18 million for his son, Châu Tiro, so he could go to work in Malaysia.[35] The son worked there only eight months because the company went bankrupt during the global economic crisis, and by that point the father had repaid only đ4 million of

92   CHAPTER 3

the debt. The son was not able to save anything to send home. Consequently, the father had to sell part of his land—at the time he owned seven to eight công, more land than most of other Khmer interviewees—to fly his son home and to pay the debt and related expenses.[36] The father explained, "Trúng đất trả được một mớ"; this means that they owed a lot of money. Fortunately, the state gave them money for their land (although probably not much since the land was designated for agricultural rather than industrial use), enabling them to pay back some of their debts. In the rural areas where I did my fieldwork, land that the government plans to use for roads is assessed at significantly lower value than that in industrial zones in downtown An Giang. Agricultural lands (*đất nông nghiệp*) in the far-flung districts I visited are also compensated at very low rates. These poor Khmer landowners therefore get little money for their land. In Tri Tôn district, most lands are zoned for low-valued agricultural use.

Most Khmer households do still own some lands, usually several hectares for homestead (*thổ cư*) and cultivation (*canh tác*) only. They maintain the cooperative tradition of rotating the land-use rights (but not ownership) to each child in the family to provide for everyone equitably. Priority of land use tends to be given to the siblings with families who have more mouths to feed. It remains to be seen how families who own only a smaller portion of land will preserve this equitable distribution of land-use rights among their children.

Historical tensions between the Khmer and the Kinh over land have contributed to the Khmer's precarity and exacerbated indebtedness and landlessness for many Khmer households. The twentieth-century Cambodian border wars displaced both the Kinh and the Khmer, but the Khmer Krom community was permanently affected. Khmer survivors of the 1970s Khmer Rouge atrocities and mass abductions were unable to reclaim their land when they returned to Vietnam from Cambodia. Their land had been appropriated by Vietnamese (Kinh) who migrated from urban centers in An Giang. Phan Văn Dốp, a Vietnamese anthropologist, explains the complex nature of the tensions between these two groups over land:

> The Khmer in Tri Tôn and Tịnh Biên districts were relocated to Sóc Trăng and Trà Vinh provinces in order to be kept safe during the 1979 border war with Cambodia. While the Kinh who returned to Tri Tôn and Tịnh Biên [after 1979] were able to reclaim their land, the Khmer were not. . . . The government divided the land among the Kinh in An Giang, which increased the tension between the Khmer and the Kinh there. There were many rounds of state efforts to address this tension: the government gave the Khmer public land or money to buy land.

Phan Văn Dốp also points out that the government's relocation program was well intentioned; it was an effort to protect the Khmer from abduction by the Khmer Rouge. Indeed, the Kinh villagers, who had stayed behind in An Giang, suffered horrific atrocities at the hands of the Khmer Rouge in 1979–80, including the Núi Tượng massacre. Local Kinh villagers had assumed that they would be safe in their own homes because the Khmer Rouge were also Buddhists. Sadly, hundreds perished gruesomely.[37]

The Khmer Krom lost their land for other reasons as well: indebtedness, the high input cost but low sales price of rice, and mounting health and educational expenses.[38] Since the implementation of Decision 71/2009/QDTT, the Khmer have lost even more land. When workers are recruited to go to Malaysia, they and their families are encouraged to borrow money, backed up by land collateral or by trust. When jobs do not work out in Malaysia, many migrants return home with debts.[39] Many, like Châu Sethsak, are forced to sell farmland to repay the debts. Once they are landless, they have to switch from farming to retailing and laboring for wages.

During the global economic crisis of 2008–9, many Malaysian companies lost orders (some even went bankrupt) and laid off migrant workers as a result. Many workers were left stranded, and their parents in Vietnam had to come to their rescue, often having to cede their land to bring their children home and to pay off the LBS debts.

Châu Anurak explained:

I know of three cases where the parents had to buy the tickets home for their children. So they had to use their land as collateral to get the money to buy the plane tickets. . . . They had to put it under "fiducia" [cầm cố]. For some really poor families who ceded the little land they had, only several công, the parents became landless and had to resort to petty trade, such as selling fruits and banana leaves in the local market to make a living. They make as little as đ20,000–30,000 per day [about US$1.50].

Land ceding can lead to landlessness. Fiducia is a practice whereby a signee temporarily surrenders control over and use of her or his land for the duration of indebtedness. This practice predates labor export policy, but the labor export policy led to increased use among the Khmer. Parents ended up ceding segments of the same piece of land in several rounds until they completely lost the use of their land. For instance, in the first round, they might only cede one hectare; when they pay the money, they can get back their land. But if they need more money before they are able to regain control of the ceded land, then in the next round, they cede an additional hectare, and in this way gradually lose their land. In this part of the vicious cycle of indebtedness,

94   CHAPTER 3

after many rounds of ceding, the parents will have lost their land and their livelihood.

Debts and Remittances among the Chăm

Of the small number of Chăm interviewees, seven people participated in the official labor export program to Malaysia. Those who did participate followed the same recruitment process and incurred the same debts as other ethnic groups. The local brokers from An Giang Employment Services Agency helped them through all steps to secure the loans to finance their trips to Malaysia. Most Chăm are landless, so the loans disbursed to them are on a trust basis, no collateral required.

Like the other ethnic groups, Chăm returnees and their parents received only a small fraction of the loan amount while the transnational LBS system got the lion's share. The Social Policy Bank also recouped the interest by deducting money directly from the workers' paychecks. Upon the migrants' return, these families also found themselves stuck in a vicious cycle of poverty with no way to repay the loans. But for all the migrants and their families, it was the stalemate via all forms of protest that brought the state to tacitly forgive the debt, as will be discussed in chapters 5 and 6.

State Management of Debts

The state has had a difficult time dealing with loan defaults. State officials have to conduct periodic face-to-face meetings with local offices to monitor loan repayment and the whereabouts of migrants. The state categorizes the migrants into four groups: still working in Malaysia, having returned after completing their contracts, having returned home before the end of the contract, and working underground in Malaysia. The state pushes migrant workers to pay interest on their loans every three months from the beginning so that the interest will not be compounded on top of the principal, resulting in a high total debt (up to đ30 million) at the end of three years. With online direct money transfer technology, the transnational financial institutions (one of the key LBS infrastructures) at least recouped interest payments from workers' paychecks while they were still working in Malaysia.

I witnessed an extreme instance of the use of a government dragnet to monitor migrant debt in August 2012 in the Hrê-concentrated Ba Tơ district in Quảng Ngãi province. Attending a series of meetings among different levels of government, I observed a village meeting. It was led by two district officials

Labor Recruitment Process and Indebtedness   95

from the DoLISA office in Ba Tơ district: Mr. Nguyễn Văn Triệu, the chair (who was Kinh), and Ms. Đinh Thị Phương Lan, the deputy chair (who was half-Kinh, half-Hrê). There were also eight Hrê local representatives from several communes in the district; three of them were village leaders, four were from mass organizations, and one was from a people's committee. Mr. Triệu opened this meeting by instructing the local Hrê representatives on how to monitor and enforce repayment from Hrê migrant workers:

> For those who have been gone for two years and have not sent home any money, we need to work with the Vietnamese recruitment company and the Malaysian company to get them to fax that migrant's pay stub so we know how much he makes monthly and why he did not send any money home and pay the interest. For instance, if the pay stub shows only đ2–3 million per month that is OK [because the wage is too low to even consider remittance], but if he makes đ5–7 million per month then we need to work with the Vietnamese recruitment company to request the pay stub for further actions.

Đinh Thị Phương Lan confirmed this high level of state monitoring by telling me that as long as she has access to monthly pay stubs, she can find out whether a worker makes enough money (or not) to repay debt and/or send money home.

The key concern of these state officials is the migrant's ability to repay the debt, not necessarily lifting them out of poverty. In meetings like this, state officials cajoled the Hrê parents by enthusiastically describing the benefits of working overseas (saving money to bring home) but also pressured them to convince their children to finish their contracts in Malaysia and to not return home before the contracts were completed. Mr. Triệu explained that "at some communes, there were migrants who returned before the end of their contracts; each owed over đ20 million and thus far have not been able to repay any money [*chưa trả được đồng nào*]. So, coming home before the end of the contract has created a burden for the parents who will have to repay the debts of their children."

State officials stepped up the pressure in cases in which migrant workers went underground, threatening them with law enforcement in Malaysia. "Except for illness," which is a legitimate reason to take off work, Mr. Triệu noted that "if they don't communicate with their families, then the real reason they have gone underground could be drinking, brawling, or altercation. These led to police arrests and imprisonment. The Malaysian police informed me often about missing workers." This shows how closely Vietnam officials work with Malaysian officials in connection with labor export. Moreover, state officials try to elicit information from parents about their children's

96   CHAPTER 3

whereabouts and whether they are sending money home and if not, why not. Mr. Triệu even raised the specter of Malaysian police punishing migrants: "When the runaway workers call home, the parents should inform them that the police are searching for them and should tell them to promptly return to the [Malaysian] company [on their contract] because otherwise they will be put in jail if they are caught."

Later that day, I had a rare opportunity to witness a candid discussion between district and commune state officials on the labor export quota. This closed meeting revealed how the LBS system pushes to export labor from poor communes in Ba Tơ district to meet the labor export quota. Mr. Triệu told Mr. Xuân (a lower-ranking state official) that "You need to push people to register to work in Malaysia; after that they need to do the health check [and] take the orientation class." Mr. Xuân replied by explaining that they "faced difficulty [in recruiting people] for three reasons: most were keen on growing and taking care of the keo trees up on the clearing in their mountains, finding garment jobs in other provinces [in Vietnam], or harvesting rice."[40]

The state rationalizes workers' indebtedness by suggesting that it is due to their own misconduct and to the effect of external global factors. According to Mr. Vũ Minh Xuyên:

> Honestly, it was not because migrants did not have the ability to repay their debts, but there are other reasons. Top of the list is the lack of savings, drinking, and gambling. Then came the global financial crisis in 2008–9 that affected Malaysia's overall economy, especially the construction industry, and sent thousands of Vietnamese workers home before the end of their contracts. This created loan defaults and bad debt problems for the state banks.

Mr. Vũ stressed some "common negative behaviors" (*tật*) of Vietnamese workers in a Muslim country: drinking, gambling, brawling, and changing their minds about working in Malaysia once there.[41] These behaviors should not be construed as everyday forms of resistance of the weak, to invoke James C. Scott's terminology, because regardless of whether these migrants are conscious or unconscious of their actions, the effects of their actions do not help improve their working conditions or weaken the LBS system. After a night of drinking and gambling, they still have to return to work the following morning. If their productivity is not up to par, they would be sent home (and have to pay their own airfares) for not fulfilling their contract. The drinking, gambling, and brawling also point to the failure of the mandatory cultural orientation classes that are supposed to prepare these migrants before they move to Malaysia and start working there.

Conclusion

In sum, the totality of the labor recruitment process (recruiting, training, and documentation) can be destabilizing to the migrants' lives in this uneven power relation. This system has benefited every stakeholder in the LBS—the recruitment companies, local mass organizations, banks, and Malaysian industries and airlines—leaving the migrants with a small remainder and a huge debt. This indebtedness can trigger migrants' engagement in physical and metaphorical third spaces of dissent. But it could also lead to some positive empowerment and independence. The next chapter analyzes these mixed effects of the LBS system, including its lack of accountability in response to workers' complaints, leading to their precarious lives and uncertainties while working in Malaysia.

4 Precarity and Coping Mechanisms

The transnational labor brokerage state (LBS) system gives rise to many forms of precarity that make guest workers vulnerable while they are working in Malaysia. However, the system never fully controls or reaps benefits from these poor ethnic groups' migrants. The workers use their cultural resources—networks, language, and religion—to push back, do the best they can, exploit the system, and seize opportunities that arise.

This chapter discusses commonalities and differences in the precarity and coping mechanisms of the five ethnic groups, paying special attention to different gender responses within each of these communities because gender, ethnicity, and class are best understood in relation rather than in isolation from one another. When applicable, I highlight forms of internal empowerment (such as those that derive from feminism or from a specific worldview) and forms of structural empowerment (such as strikes and protests).

Different forms of precarity are triggered by the LBS system's need to manage workers and to ensure economic stability and growth for both Vietnam and Malaysia. The methods they use to manage migrants include passport impoundment, one-employer contracts, police harassment, appeal to fluctuating global conditions to excuse employers' misdeeds, and using inhumane recruitment protocols that target female workers both before they leave Vietnam and while they are working in Malaysia. Other forms of precarity are even worse: unsafe working and living conditions, robberies accompanied by sexual violence, and sudden death.

The guest workers are vulnerable as soon as they arrive in Malaysia because their passports are impounded by management. Each is given a work ID card and a photocopy of his or her passport. Passport impoundment effectively

Precarity and Coping Mechanisms

ties them to a particular employer and prevents them from working for better employers. In 2015, the passport law was changed to allow foreign guest workers to keep their passports, but this law has not been implemented consistently.[1] According to SUARAM (Suara Rakyat Malaysia), an independent human rights organization in Malaysia, employers often hold on to foreign workers' passports as "insurance," to keep the workers under their control.[2]

The one-employer contract law ties workers to the transnational LBS system, one of the key stipulations that results in precarity for workers. It forbids migrant workers from changing employers, regardless of any violations on the part of the employer or a problem with the migrant's contract.[3] While there are laws from the Vietnamese side regarding the handling of complaints and fines for violations against labor and recruitment companies, there is no effective implementation. Therefore, workers have no way to address labor violations or breach of contract. For instance, after arriving in Malaysia, many migrant workers found that they were given jobs that were different from what the contract stated, that their wages were less than what the contract had promised, and that there were no overtime opportunities to earn additional income, another contractual promise. They also had no access to timely support from their recruitment companies; most of these companies did not have a permanent office nearby or anywhere in Malaysia to address worker grievances (the DOLAB office in Kuala Lumpur, for example, was not only hundreds of miles away from most work sites but also unresponsive).

Members of all five ethnic groups have been harassed by the Malaysian police and have been subject to extortion. Mr. Thức, a Kinh worker in Malaysia, described the vulnerability of migrant workers at the hands of the Malaysian police:

> Life in Malaysia is full of insecurity. While walking on the street, many times we got stopped by the Malaysian police, who searched and frisked us. If they found money in our possession, they took it. I personally got frisked by a [Malaysian] policeman, although I could not really tell whether he was a real policeman or a fake one, because he wore a police uniform and drove a police car. At that point, I was traveling on a bus with two male friends, on the way to visit other male friends working in a lumber factory in a remote palm tree area. The police asked for my papers, searched my wallet and took all of my money, then returned the empty wallet to me.[4]

While the Malaysian 2015 passport law specifies that employers cannot hold foreign workers' passports, still migrant workers face this vulnerability as of 2017.[5]

Fluctuating global conditions affect the migrants greatly because they are stuck in the LBS system. The 2008 global financial crisis disrupted migrant workers' lives in ways beyond their control. When the Malaysian economy tanked, resulting in many company bankruptcies, migrant workers were the first casualties. The ones that lingered in Malaysia did not receive help from the state bureaucracy that had sent them there. Worse yet, returning home meant adding to their existing debts.

Female migrant workers have faced inhumane gender-specific labor migration policies, including requirements to take pregnancy tests both during recruitment and periodically once they are in Malaysia. Moreover, both female migrant workers in Malaysia and wives in Vietnam whose husbands were working abroad lamented about family breakups and divorce.[6] These findings are consistent with the findings of other migration studies scholars.[7]

Another form of precarity is the pain caused by separation from home and family. Both genders in all ethnic groups referred to this; the separation takes a toll on their families and can result in family breakup, as studies have shown.[8] But the circumstances of separation, the ascription of gender roles, and the experiences of each group are different.

Most workers I interviewed faced oppressive working conditions in Malaysia. For example, to maximize machine productivity, factories often operate on a twenty-four-hour schedule, with three shifts. Management rotates workers among the three shifts on a weekly basis without regard to the consequences of frequent schedule changes. These constant rotations disrupt workers' circadian rhythms and lead to exhaustion, fatigue, and even accidents on the factory floor. Occasionally workers engaged in collective action to address problems with working conditions, pay, or employer-provided housing.

In addition to collective actions, migrant workers coped by participating in religious and cultural networks and becoming financially empowered. Remittances can be motivated by a sense of altruism, and their use is negotiated and determined collectively by the migrant workers and their families.[9] For most migrants, sending remittances home is a source of pride and a coping mechanism. They not only help pay for their families' necessities but also preserve the status of their families in their home communities.[10] Remittances can, however, have unintended consequences that add to the burden of migrant workers. The family's expectations can increase the stakes of remittances. When migrants are unable to send money home, including for reasons beyond their control, they internalize the shame associated with that inability, which can lead to a cycle of indebtedness and induce a downward spiral.

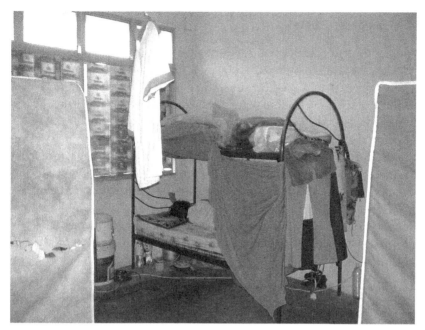

Figure 9. A migrant worker in her hostel room in Batu Pahat, Malaysia, in 2008, exhausted by weekly shift rotations. Credit: Author

Precarity of the Kinh and the Hoa

Because my interview sample reflects the majority of the migrants working in Malaysia, the Kinh (and some Hoa), in this section I discuss and give examples of their various forms of precarity. In later sections, I address similar situations for other ethnic groups, focusing on how these groups' experiences differ from the majority.

Gender Differences

As mentioned earlier, many forms of precarity affect female and male workers differently. Ms. Kim-Ly, a Hoa worker, recalled how the pregnancy policy forces women to make difficult choices: have a back-alley abortion or return home at their own expense. Ms. Hà, a Kinh worker from Hải Dương province, said that she knew of many abortion cases where poor women workers had to pay RM1000 to unscrupulous doctors. Both Ms. Hà and her friend Ms. Lê, also from Hải Dương province, told us that women tend to absorb their pain and suffering to complete their contracts and minimize their losses.

102   CHAPTER 4

The Pain of Separation

Among the Kinh, both wives and husbands went to work in Malaysia and left their children to be cared for by their grandparents or other relatives. Many migrants told me how much they missed their children. Ms. Hà proudly showed me a photo of her son, who was being looked after by her parents-in-law. She lamented how she was not at home to be part of his growing up. Mr. Vũ noted that he missed his children "very much during the three-year separation" and lamented that his abrupt departure from Vietnam did not give him time to say proper good-byes to his wife and children. Another Kinh returnee from Sơn Tây (a province in the north) mentioned a "case in which the wife was working overseas, and her husband at home dated and married another woman. The former wife was devastated upon returning home, and then decided to work overseas again as an escape!"

Working Conditions

Shift rotations are a common source of complaint. Ms. Kim-Ly lamented: "Who can withstand working during the day one week, and during the night another week?" Another worker, Ms. Nhung (a Kinh), told me that switching the body clock like that is very exhausting and can cause accidents on the factory floor because workers end up being very tired and often fall asleep easily while operating the machines.

Another common complaint is the nature of management surveillance, which takes the form of a panopticon, a concept introduced by Jeremy Bentham and subsequently used by Michel Foucault to describe a principle of social organization.[11] The panopticon model describes a prevalent form of surveillance in factories in Malaysia. One classic method of monitoring workers is by watching them from a floor high above the assembly lines. Ms. Kim-Ly recalled her own experience of being closely monitored:

> Management has an office that is above the factory with all glass windows so they can see what we are doing down on the factory floor. One time, I put an assembled dress into a bin and then pushed the bin away with my foot. Immediately, the boss's assistant came down to my station and told me to listen to him and to not push the bin like that.

To ensure productivity, management even monitored the number and duration of workers' trips to the restroom. This practice is closely connected to

Precarity and Coping Mechanisms   103

speedup, another common feature of exploitative work regimes. Ms. Nhung shared her experience with me:

> We did not dare to go to the restroom often because we were afraid that we would not meet the productivity quota and that the boss would yell at us. Every day we each had to meet the daily quota of thousands of TV cables. If we met the quota or exceeded it, the boss would smile happily. If not, the boss's wife would come down to the assembly line to yell at us and demand that we work faster. And there were cameras to monitor who went to the restroom, how often, and for how long!

Robbery

Robbery is another common threat migrant workers face. During my fieldwork in Malaysia, I was alerted to this problem by both male and female migrant workers. Robbers often attacked workers on their payday. Mr. Việt, the retired Kinh army veteran, recounted his experience as a victim:

> Every worker had a debit card, and we did not carry any cash because we were fearful of being robbed. But still we got robbed. One time [after payday], we were sitting around [at the hostel] talking in the morning, when robbers intruded and held us at knifepoint. One went around and seized all of our cards and our cash; another threatened to cut our ears if we did not tell them our correct ATM PIN numbers so that they could withdraw all of our money. We all complied to save our lives.

The fact that the robbers came directly to their hostel means that they knew when these migrant workers received their salaries. It's possible that the robbers got information about the migrants through social networking, which could be one negative effect of relying on networks to survive as a foreign worker.

Robberies terrorize female migrants even more than male migrants because sexual violence (including rape) often accompanies the taking of their money and property.[12] I witnessed the fear of a female interviewee who had just escaped a robbery attempt right before our interview in Johor in 2008. Ms. Cúc (a Kinh from Thanh Hoá) signed a three-year contract with Sing Lun Garments, a garment-making subsidiary of Singaporean Sing Lun Holdings. Sing Lun Garments, which employs around five hundred workers in the Johor Bahru factory, is a decent company that honors labor contracts, making it possible for Ms. Cúc to save money and pay off her bank loan in the first year. While taking a taxi to meet us at a shopping mall, Ms. Cúc was almost kidnapped and robbed by the taxi driver who was taking her to see us, so we changed our plan and met her at her dorm. In the interview, Ms. Cúc told us that despite the fact that Sing Lun was a good company to work for, she did not plan to extend the contract after it ended:

> Unlike other companies, this is a pretty good company. They have kept all the promises they made in the labor contract. . . . I paid my debt to a Vietnamese recruitment company in Hanoi with my first year's earnings. . . . But I will never return to work here. Good male workers from Vietnam went bad here. They did not like their jobs or their jobs did not provide enough overtime work for them to earn enough to pay back their debts and to save a little, and so those men ended their contracts early and went underground, and many joined gangs as a way to make money or got into drinking and gambling, which got them further into debt.

Her account points to various aspects of precarity and the vicious cycle of debt that migrant workers face in Malaysia. She viewed robberies perpetrated by Vietnamese men partly as a consequence of the shortcomings of the LBS system, not the men themselves.

Another sober view pointed out extenuating circumstances that could have explained these behaviors. Mr. Thức claimed that the 2008 global financial crisis was the cause of these robberies:

> Most workers were sent there as manual workers and did not receive any formal training. They had to end their work because the companies and factories they worked for no longer had work for them and did not pay them. Committing robberies was not their intention. . . . The global financial crisis in 2008 led to the bankruptcy of many companies, resulting in high unemployment, and to the unemployed getting together to go rob other poor migrants. Over there [in Malaysia] we called them mafia.

Certainly not all male workers and former workers resort to robbery, but the pressure on these men to send money home and the guilt they experience if they cannot fulfill their family obligations is intense, as expressed in the last stanza of the poem "Where is the truth?," discussed later in the chapter.

Death

A spate of newspaper articles in 2007 and 2008 reported on hundreds of sudden deaths among the first guest workers in Malaysia. Between 2002 and 2008, over three hundred such workers, mostly male, died suddenly. In 2007 alone, over one hundred deaths resulted from an unknown, unclear, or ambiguous cause. The alleged causes were toxic working conditions (owing to chemicals), long working hours, and substandard living conditions in a harsh climate. In most cases, the surviving family members in Vietnam received only minimal compensation from the Malaysian employers and the Vietnamese recruitment companies.[13] One of the friends of Mr. Việt died suddenly:

> Six of us flew to Malaysia on the same flight, but only five returned to Vietnam. My fellow friend [from Bến Tre province in the Mekong Delta] could not tolerate the harsh weather conditions: 40 [degrees] Celsius during the day and 20 at night.[14] He fell seriously ill at 1 a.m. We immediately called the vice president to report this case, but no one arrived. [At 7 a.m.], a company car arrived to take him to the hospital, but it was too late; he was already dead. Since his family was not there, the five of us had to sign his death paper at the morgue. . . . Sao Thái Dương [Recruitment] Company told us that they would only pay the airfare to transport the body home and that once it had returned to Vietnam, his family would have to take care of the rest.

The transnational LBS system failed the young man in this case: the Malaysian employer did not respond until six hours after Mr. Việt and his friends called for help. In addition, the recruitment company representatives in Kuala Lumpur did not respond to Mr. Việt's numerous calls. It is possible that this company does not have a permanent desk in Malaysia, as is the case of other Vietnamese recruitment companies. But from the information I received, a representative could have responded from their permanent office in Vietnam. It is unconscionable that the company refused to cover at least the burial expenses for the tragic ending of a migrant they sent to work in Malaysia.

Coping Mechanisms of the Kinh and the Hoa

Again, because the majority of my informants were Kinh (and some Hoa), in this section I discuss and give examples of coping mechanisms with a focus on these two ethnic groups. Later sections address similar actions of other ethnic groups.

Religious Networks

Migrant workers in Malaysia are alienated both economically and culturally. In a Marxist sense, there are various aspects to their alienation: they are made to feel estranged from the product they make, from the labor process, from their own humanity, and from society.[15] In this context, they are owned by the employers who hire them and at the same time they are obligated to the

106   CHAPTER 4

LBS system. Most interviewees could not afford to buy the very products they manufactured (most were for export). Culturally, except for the Chăm Muslims, most did not feel that they belonged in the Malaysian communities around them, whose members spoke a different language and practiced different religions (mostly Islam).

To overcome these types of alienation, especially violence in the form of robbery, many migrants turn to their respective ethnic networks. In addition, Christian groups have reached out to migrants and created safe spaces for them. In particular, the Catholic Migrant Ministry in Kuala Lumpur has established a system through which Vietnamese workers can volunteer to help each other with court appearances and phone calls to the Vietnamese Embassy in Kuala Lumpur.[16] Vietnamese clerics and volunteers from Malaysia, Canada, and the United States have organized Christian networks in Batu Pahat and Penang to provide support, faith, and friendship to migrant workers through weekend activities that they sponsor. Quite a few Kinh migrant workers have participated in these religious groups.[17]

Conversion to Christianity has been the goal of these religious groups, and in this they have had a certain amount of success. Several factors in combination have induced some migrant workers to convert to Christianity. Ms. Cúc told us how she found comfort in this religious refuge after the robbery attempts she experienced. When working in Johor, she found a supportive community and joined the Vietnamese Family in Malaysia, a Protestant group run by a Vietnamese couple who are pastors in Malaysia. Pastors from Canada and the United States came for short-term visits. Every weekend, she participated in Bible classes and in other activities with other Vietnamese migrant workers. The pastors, in collaboration with the migrant workers, published an annual booklet in Vietnamese in which they articulated their thoughts and poignantly reflected on their experience in short articles and poems. The last stanza in a poem titled "Where Is the Truth?" captures sentiments shared by many migrants in Malaysia: the trauma of the failed attempt to work in Malaysia and the hope of rebuilding one's life upon returning to Vietnam, even with debt following them:

> Returning home, I failed completely,
> Still in debt, I am full of shame . . .
> My life now, with one simple wish:
> To live modestly and peacefully in my motherland . . .[18]

Many Kinh and Hoa workers expressed appreciation for the religious support groups in which they participated, and they promised to lead healthy and religious lives. The groups made possible forms of individual empowerment via internal reflection and analysis, a type of empowerment outlined by Nana Oishi.[19] Although these religious groups provide safe spaces for alienated migrants, it is not clear that religious belief accounts for migrants' participation. They also have attended to participate in fun activities in a place where they feel safe with other workers from their social networks.[20]

Personal Empowerment

Despite the challenges and risks, migrant workers seize the opportunities offered by transnational labor migration, which, if implemented properly, has the potential to internally empower both female and male migrants. These internal forms of agency include learning new skills and new languages, as well as a sense of self-development, self-fulfillment, self-confidence, and independence.[21]

Gaining financial independence is key for many female migrants. Several female interviewees took pride in how they generated their own income and became more confident by working overseas. Ms. Hà and Ms. Lê were recruited by an employee of the Vietnamese Steel Company. They went to Malaysia even when their husbands disapproved of that choice, and they had been sending money home. Both women told us that working overseas had given them a chance to become independent wage earners and to have more voice and influence in family matters.[22] Ms. Lê said:

> We decided to go to improve our financial situation. In Vietnam, most of us were kept at home; we only walked to the market to buy ingredients to cook. But here, every month we spent thriftily to save money to send home. Of course, our husbands did not want their wives to work overseas, but we made up our minds to go make money to help our families.[23]

They showed their independence, disregarding their husbands' wishes in this case. Meanwhile, Ms. Hà made specific arrangements to ensure that the money she sent home was used for its intended purpose, thus gaining influence on family matters. She said, "I send money home to my father-in-law, who has been taking care of my son so I can work overseas. My husband works in a construction job in Quảng Ninh [a mining town] and also sells mobile phones to make ends meet." This negotiation was only possible once she was also earning money for her household. Moreover, these women had gained self-respect, which they demonstrated by the way they took care of themselves. They went shopping together on the weekends for clothes, and they dressed nicely and fashionably when they met with me. Their sense of confidence and self-respect were palpable to me during their interviews.

108   CHAPTER 4

Remittances can bring their own type of empowerment in which their use is negotiated between the migrant workers and their families. Ms. Cúc explained her hope of supporting her parents and her younger sister's education with her remittances:[24]

> I make RM18.5 per day and spend only RM1.5 for lunch. To save money, for two years now, I have been cooking rice and bringing lunch to work. It is very expensive to eat out, and plus I can't eat Malaysian foods. In two years, I have sent home a total of đ46 million [about US$2,300] to my parents. I had wanted to dedicate the first year's amount to my parents and the second year's amount to send my younger sister to college, but my mother refused to take it because it came from my hard work. I then tried to convince her by saying that we can only gain by putting all our money into my younger sister's education, because if her future is good, then our whole family's is also good. Then my mother said they can pay for my sister's education [using their income from tilling the land for rice and all types of vegetables], and they put my remittance money in the bank for me to use in the future. I think I may take it in the future, but it is not really necessary. . . . I still think it would be better for my parents to use the money for my sister's education.

Ms. Cúc used her remittance to help her family members, not herself, motivated by a sense of altruism that is described by Lã and Leung.[25] Ms. Cúc herself did not want to return to school but to play sports instead, an aspiration that indicated the sense of self-fulfillment and independence she had developed while working abroad. She negotiated her multiple roles transnationally, as a daughter who wanted her parents to have an easier time in their old age (since they had been tilling the paddy fields all their lives) and as an older sister who wanted her younger sister to succeed in her pursuit of a college degree in agricultural science; the knowledge she would gain from her degree would be very useful in helping the extended family make money on the land that they owned.[26]

Similarly, Ms. Yến, another Kinh worker, worked two jobs to send money home for her younger sister's college education:

> I worked two jobs: one in a factory making accessories for car seats from 8 a.m. to 5:30 p.m. and one washing dishes for a restaurant from 6 p.m. to 1 a.m. They gave me food, so I ate there and even brought food home. With overtime work, I made RM970 per month, spent RM270 per month, and sent home RM700 per month for my sister to go to college in accounting.

In 2011, I called Ms. Yến's sister, Ms. Giang, who was still studying accounting in a college in Ho Chi Minh City with her sister's support, and learned that Ms. Yến had gotten her contract renewed and had returned to Malaysia for two more years.

Male migrants use their remittances for altruistic purposes and thereby reinforce their status in their families, but they also invest in enterprises at home.[27] Pooling money together and taking turns sending lump sums home (*hụi*) allows them to achieve those objectives. *Hụi* is a common practice among migrant workers who come from the same native place and stay in the same hostels. The migrants prioritize who receives the pooled money first by the urgency of each migrant's need. Most rely on informal methods to save on bank fees, such as sending cash remittances with trusted friends when they return home after finishing their contracts. Otherwise, they have to resort to the global financial system, such as Western Union or another money transfer service, post offices, and banks, which charge fees to transfer money.

Mr. Thức finished paying his debts after his first year of working in Malaysia using the *hụi* system. He sent money home during the remaining two years (every three months)[28] to help his ailing eldest brother in Vietnam, demonstrating an altruism often found among migrants, while also saving money for investment:

> We took turns sending a lump sum of money home. It is important to do this with those you trust, such as your housemates, often a group of three or four people. We sent money via Western Union, but I forget how much the fee was because it was five years ago. . . . I worked hard, sending money home but also keeping some money to invest when I returned home.

Together with his wife, Ms. Thúy (whom he met while working in Malaysia), Mr. Thức opened a mobile phone repair shop upon returning home, using their combined savings:

> I learned how to fix mobile phones, and we put together our savings to come up with đ30 million [about US$1,500] to open this repair shop. Four years have passed, and we are very happy working together: my wife helps with the retail sales while I fix the mobile phones. We bought our house, and each month we make đ7 million and bring in đ2 million in monthly rental income.

Their combined remittances were put to good use: using the front of their house for the mobile shop and renting out one room for income. Mr. Thức's parents held the remittances for them while they were abroad working. The parents own their land and a house (next door to Mr. Thức's house) and have made a living by working on their land and by doing odd jobs for their neighbors.

Other male interviewees sent money home to invest in tilling the land or other enterprises. Mr. Đại (from Hà Tĩnh), who was working in a plastic factory, explained:

> I miss my family a lot, but because of our [poor] circumstances I have to go to work in Malaysia. My wife and our two children—one is in grade nine and

110 CHAPTER 4

the other grade seven—are still in Hà Tĩnh. My wife is working in the paddy field. When I return home, I'll help her till the land with a *trâu sắt* [literally "iron buffalo," the word for a tractor]. Every month, I send home RM400–500.

Similar to Mr. Thức, in addition to wanting to help his family and improve his status in it, Mr. Đại was keen on investing in a key means of production, a tractor, to increase rice productivity upon his return to Hà Tĩnh. This also indicated that his family had land to till, which is not the case for many members of the other ethnic groups.

Mr. Kiên (also from Hà Tĩnh), who worked in a paper factory, told me:

I have a wife and four-year old daughter at home. My wife and extended family work in the paddy field, growing rice and potatoes and raising chicken and pigs. My parents are still healthy; they are in their sixties. I'm sure I will find a job when I return there. I miss my family a lot. Calling them three to four times per week is very costly: at least RM100–200 per month. Still, every month I have sent them RM800. Now that the boss needs workers, I am trying to renew my contract for one more year.[29]

Clearly, Mr. Kiên was a good worker, so his boss wanted to keep him for one more year. He even paid the round-trip airfare for Mr. Kiên to visit home after three years of separation. Mr. Kiên seemed to be very confident about finding a job upon returning home, and he likely invested his saved-up remittances in a means of production or other enterprise.

Collective Actions

Collective actions are another type of coping mechanism. Most collective actions were short lived and only addressed immediate rather than systemic problems, such as the one-employer contract system and passport impoundment. After winning small concessions from the employer, it's back to business as usual for most workers because they do not want to lose their deposit (US$300). Moreover, these protests cannot last long without strategic union organizing and collective bargaining. But from the accounts of the interviewees, I found evidence of "class moments," defined as class consciousness that emerges during times of struggle when workers, bonded together by cultural factors, become aware of belonging to the working class and of their shared interests.[30] In case of export labor in Malaysia, there is also evidence of foreign workers' multinational class moments when they fought together for some common causes.

To stabilize the LBS system, the Malaysian government requires that employers provide basic accommodations for foreign workers. However,

Precarity and Coping Mechanisms   111

in reality, as the Malaysian Trade Union Congress has pointed out, many foreign workers have been forced to live in unsafe, substandard, unhygienic, and overcrowded conditions that subject them to high levels of stress.[31] Top among the stressors is the fear of being robbed, which has been exacerbated for many female workers because of the possibility of accompanying rape.[32] So when robbers invaded their safe spaces, such as the hostels, the residents went on strike, presenting an instance of *structural* empowerment, or a collective effort to combat a common problem—lack of personal safety—that threatened many migrant workers.

In Batu Pahat, we met two sisters from Cần Thơ province (in the Mekong Delta), Ms. Liên (recruited by Suleco) and Ms. Linh (recruited by Milaco Joint-Stock Company), who supported each other when Ms. Linh's dormitory was robbed. While we were talking to Ms. Liên, who was staying at one of the hostels that we visited, Ms. Linh came to say good-bye to her sister because she had completed her contract and was returning home. Her fear of robbery quashed any desire to extend her contract. Ms. Linh told us how the Vietnamese female workers led a two-day protest in the hostel of the Gimmill garment factory in Batu Pahat to demand safety measures for the almost three hundred Vietnamese migrants staying there:

> I earn piece rate, making clothes to export to Singapore. Most workers are Vietnamese women, with only six Vietnamese men, and the rest are from Malaysia, Myanmar, and Sri Lanka. It happened once before: the robbers came to the hostel on payday and demanded workers' ATM cards and the PIN numbers. This is a small hostel, and we were nervous because there is a night shift and the alley leading to the front gate is always dark. One day in April 2008 we had just gotten paid when we heard someone yelling "robbery, robbery." We then used our mobile phones to call the Malaysian police, who did come to stop this attempt. But after that, we staged a two-day protest in the hostel, demanding more guards, a more secure gate, and better lighting in the alleyway. I do not know who sparked the protest, but I know that someone called the company's office and then all of us went on strike for our safety. We elected several Vietnamese representatives who could speak Malay to talk to the foreman. Then we walked together to the factory and sent our representatives inside to talk to the management.[33]

The image of hundreds of Vietnamese migrants walking together to the factory to talk to management is powerful. Their collective action brought a temporary solution, although some workers still voted with their feet because the company failed to develop a long-term solution to security problems. Ms. Liên (Ms. Linh's sister) elaborated: "Well, it turns out that the company only provided one additional guard [so there were now two], and they added barbed wire surrounding the hostel's wall. Nothing sturdy! Nevertheless, since

112 CHAPTER 4

then, nothing has happened, and we feel pretty safe. But after this incident, some Vietnamese workers moved out to bigger hostels; some even returned to Vietnam."

In general, these migrants used technology (mobile phones) and language skills (speaking Malay, Chinese, or English) to empower themselves to fight back. While it was only a short-term fix, these Vietnamese workers successfully forced management to improve safety in and around their hostel, at least for those who stayed.

In another case in which a hostel was a site of discontent, workers fought both for changes in the work schedule and for basic necessities. Ms. Kim-Ly described the substandard living conditions at the hostel she lived in, which housed four hundred female Vietnamese workers of Kinh and Hoa descents. The hostel was overcrowded, so each room had two occupants on different work shifts. Thus, the night workers had the rooms to themselves while the day workers were at work and vice versa: "We stayed in a very small house," Ms. Kim-Ly explained, "built for seven people, but they packed in fourteen people, working two shifts (7 a.m. and 7 p.m.), so at any time there were only seven people in the house."[34] Originally, management rotated shifts every week.

It took collective action to force management to change their shift rotation from one week to two weeks. The workers complained about the one-week rotations, arguing that they could not work like that, and successfully pressured management to make this change.

Workers in both shifts subsequently also rallied around the need for water. Ms. Kim-Ly recalled how the morning and the night workers joined forces in this short protest:

> When we returned home [from work]: no water! We wanted to take a shower, but when we turned on the faucet, there were only drops of water. . . . We had to carry buckets to the gate and compete with each other for water. Then we talked to each other and agreed that no one would go to work the next day; then the night shift folks returned and found that none of the morning shift workers had gone to work. This got the president to intervene. He came to our house and asked: "Why don't you work?" and we said: "No water to take a bath and to cook, how could we work?" He said: "OK, why don't you work, then when you return, there will be water for you." We said: "No, you have to bring water here so we can take our bath properly, after that then we go to work." Only then did he order a water truck and connect the power supply to pump the water for several hours for us to use.

These migrant workers had a sense of self-respect and a good reason for why they would not work, demonstrating their internal empowerment: "No water to take a bath and to cook, how could we work?" Also, they fought

Precarity and Coping Mechanisms 113

collectively with an ultimatum: "Water or no work." This negotiation (plus the wait for the water truck to arrive) gave the morning shift workers time to rest and wash before heading to the factory. In this "class moment," or instance of structural empowerment, workers in both morning and night shifts united on the basis of class.

More class moments transpired over the expectation of overtime, as stipulated in the contracts. Workers, finding either that there was less overtime work than promised (or none at all) to make extra money to send home, or that the overtime was excessive and not properly compensated, complained to management of contract violations. Their complaints fell on deaf ears. Neither the LBS system nor its employers have policies in place that make collective bargaining between labor and management possible. So the workers went on strike. As recounted by Mr. Việt, the strike, an example of structural empowerment that was not reported in either the Malaysian or the Vietnamese media, also registers an uphill battle to organize a multinational workforce against a transnational labor export system that pitted workers against each other to weaken their collective action.

Mr. Việt complained about many contract violations that brought them together to strike: the lack of proper overtime compensation, forced and excessive overtime work, and the lack of an on-the-job health clinic:

There were about seventy to eighty Vietnamese men from all over Vietnam working there. When the boss slapped us or scolded us like slaves, we went on strike. Over there, there was no strike policy such as in [Vietnam's] labor code, so we led the strike by ourselves. The boss threatened to cut 50 percent of our salary. We made RM18 per day, working regular administrative hours. There was no overtime policy: if a work order came, then we had to work overtime until 2 a.m. or work through the night. If we did not agree to work overtime, then we were not allowed to work the next day and would not receive our regular salary plus overtime pay. So we all had to work overtime even when we were completely exhausted. We had to work standing up; one of our coworkers got badly swollen feet and needed to have a doctor's attention, but he got none and had to continue to work. There were very few local workers; most were from Bangladesh and Libya. So when we called the [one-time] strike, only the Vietnamese workers went on strike because the Bangladeshi and Libyan workers refused to join us and did not want to lodge complaints against management for fear of losing their jobs.

Unfortunately, this strike failed to force management to rectify its contract violations. Management also used a divide-and-conquer strategy to break the solidarity of this complex multinational workforce. To those who struck, management resorted to credible threats to preempt further

114 CHAPTER 4

resistance, threatening to fire them or to dock their pay for the time they were on strike. Mr. Việt informed us that those who had participated in the strike, all Vietnamese workers, ended up losing half of their monthly salary for fighting for their rights. He also complained bitterly that no help came their way from either the DOLAB office in Malaysia or from Sao Thái Dương Recruitment Company in Ho Chi Minh City, which had recruited them.

The Hrê

Most of the Hrê, the poorest group, have never or rarely set foot outside of their communes or districts before their time in Malaysia. Thus, to those who went overseas to work in Malaysia, factory work discipline, consisting of one-employer policy, shift rotations, quotas, and overtime work, was completely foreign to them, and the effects on them were more severe.

Robbery was also a constant fear for the Hrê while working in Malaysia. But one Hrê guest worker, whose story I heard from his mother, was able to fight back and keep his property. In January 2011, I had an opportunity to listen in on a short phone call from Mr. Phúc to his parents, whom I was visiting. It was a happy moment for Mr. Phúc's parents and younger brother. The mother, Ms. Khanh, then shared her worries with me about the risk of robbery. A few months before, someone had attempted to rob Mr. Phúc:

> He was sleeping during the day because he worked the night shift. He had a habit of using his cell phone to play music while sleeping. That day, he forgot to lock the door, so a thief came to the house to steal his phone. Not hearing the music, and not really in deep sleep, my son woke up and found a thief running away with his cell phone.

His younger brother, Mr. Tú, told me the rest of the story:

> My brother slept on the second floor. The thief ran down the staircase; my brother followed right behind. He jumped down the staircase to block the thief right at the door. Well, he had watched a lot of movies so he knew how to do this. At that time, he was very nervous because the thief was much bigger than he was. He [the thief] was a "foreigner." I was scared as well, just from listening to his account. . . . My brother told me that they looked at each other for a few seconds, then he punched the thief, who reluctantly gave the cell phone back to my brother.[35]

While this incident ended well for Mr. Phúc, who had the courage and drive to fight off the thief, other Hrê workers were not so lucky and ended up losing their money and/or property.

Đinh Thị Phương Lan, a state official in Ba Tơ District, explained the combined effects of precarity and the vicious cycle of debt on the Hrê:

Recently, two workers were arrested by the local Malaysian police. These two were good workers who had already finished two and a half years of their contracts. This company required workers to work one full day and one full night and then rest the following day. Not getting enough rest and with all the intention to work more to send money home, they took a chance and went to work for another company. They had no proper ID because the original company had kept their papers. So when they got caught by the local police while going to work at the second company, they had nothing to show. So the police put them in jail, demanded payment of fines, and informed the original company that employed them. Of course, these poor workers had no money, so the original company paid the money to the police in order to bail them out. But this began a vicious cycle of debt: management deducted the "bail-out money" from the workers' salaries, so chances were slim that they would be able to save and send money home to help their families.

While the pressure to make money to send home is shared by migrant workers from all ethnic groups, the difference between those other groups and the Hrê is the abject poverty of the Hrê families back home, which puts even more pressure on the Hrê workers to find additional work. Because the LBS contract system does not allow this, moonlighters who are caught end up having to pay bail money and thus, ironically, are able to send home even less money.

The Hrê, too, have experienced a few cases of sudden death in Malaysia. But they are a closely knit group and have exceptionally strong support networks to help them cope with the risks they are exposed to in Malaysia. They use terms of endearment with each other, referring, for example, to "the brothers from Ba Tơ District," and they pool their money so that they can come to each other's rescue in times of need: to buy plane tickets for ill Hrê workers who have to go home, or even to help send home the body of a fellow Hrê who has died. Mr. Văn Đô, a Hrê representative, recounted the story of one Hrê migrant's death and how the members of the group helped one another in time of crisis:

They lend money to each other in Malaysia, and their families in their commune pay it back pretty promptly. They come to Malaysia together and always stick together. When someone is sick or has an accident [on the job], other fellow Ba Tơ migrants, even those working forty to fifty kilometers away, rush to visit them and pool money to lend to those in need. One case was the sudden death of a Ba Tơ fellow migrant worker, Mr. Thạch [from Ba Giang commune]. The cause of his death is not known, but his heart failed after excessive overtime work in a factory that used a lot of chemicals. So, upon learning this sad news,

116 CHAPTER 4

other Ba Tơ workers immediately donated several million đong to send directly to Mr. Thạch's family.

This practice of offering mutual aid, which is nurtured through the Hrê's tight-knit village life in Ba Tơ district, is an example of what Tara Yosso calls "cultural wealth."[36] They may be poor in money, but they are very generous in rescuing each other in times of crisis, especially when they are away from their communes. Another moving story shows the bond among these Hrê workers: they helped out an early returnee, Mr. Thành, who had to leave before the end of his contract due to illness. Mr. Thành, whom I met at one of the meetings with the Kinh officials on debt management, had a prolonged ear infection that had started in Vietnam but got worse in Malaysia due to a toxic work environment. He told me how his fellow Ba Tơ Hrê workers pooled their money to lend to him so he could return to Vietnam for proper treatment. Unfortunately, he ended up with partial deafness due to a lack of timely care.

Among the Hrê, mostly men went to work in Malaysia, leaving their wives at home to take care of their children and elder parents. I heard about the pain of separation only from the wives, whose husbands were still working in Malaysia at the time of my fieldwork in Quảng Ngãi. Ms. Hân was one of these wives. She had been raising their child by herself while her husband had been working in Malaysia for over three years. Ms. Hân talked about the uncertainties of her husband's job:

> In three years working overseas, he only sent money home once in the first year, but nothing in the second and third year. He said that his company went bankrupt, and he complained about a toxic working environment with a low wage and not having enough money to buy food or medicine when on occasion he got sick.
>
> I have little land to grow *keo* trees and do swiddening. I miss my husband a lot. One time, I don't know whether he was drunk or not, but he told me half-jokingly that if I couldn't wait for him, then I should marry someone else. I was very sad and confused over whether he really meant it.

Long family separation has pained these waiting wives and could lead to family breakups such as divorce or separation. Ms. Hân's sentiments and laments were similar to what I heard from other Hrê waiting wives.

The Khmer

Like the Kinh and the Hrê, the Khmer also had to deal with robberies in Malaysia. Almost half of our Khmer interviewees (seven out of fifteen migrant workers) indicated that they had been robbed while working in Malaysia.

Many complained about not getting any assistance from the DOLAB office in Kuala Lumpur or from the recruitment companies when they called for help. The Khmer's coping mechanisms are similar to those of other ethnic groups. They came together to help those in need, pooled money to send home, provided cash for workers in distress, or bought air tickets for coworkers who needed to fly home before the end of the contract.[37] But there were some standout collective actions in which they joined forces with the Kinh and the Hoa and other foreign guest workers in Malaysia to fight for their migrant worker rights. In these instances of cross-ethnic structural empowerment, or "class moments," the groups fought together to force management to meet the basic terms of their contracts and to provide safe working and living conditions. I found cases where the Kinh, the Khmer, and the Chăm also bonded together to fight for proper contract enforcement when the LBS system failed to protect their rights.

Neng Kanika, a Khmer third-grade teacher at the time of this interview, had worked in a frozen seafood processing company. She recounted the fight against contract violations:

> The contract guaranteed an eight-hour workday with the possibility of three hours' overtime per day. Not only did we have no overtime, we did not even have full-time work for the whole week. We did not have enough work: only two or three full workdays per week. How could we live? So, the cookie factory next door had just opened and needed workers. We wanted to apply to work there, but Ms. Lydia, the supervisor/manager, prevented us from doing so. That's why we went on strike for seven days. Most workers there were Kinh from the north-central part of the country—Nghệ An, Hà Tĩnh, Đắc Lắc—plus a couple of dozens of Khmer. I told Lydia that we had no money to send home because we were stuck in her company. She said that if I wanted to leave, I had to pay for my own plane ticket. So, the sisters in the same work unit gave me some money so I could buy a ticket home.[38]

The Malaysian law that prohibits foreign workers from changing employers hamstrung even the Malaysian employer, Ms. Lydia, who would have otherwise allowed her workers to seek other jobs. The consequences of being underemployed are unbearable to workers who have to fulfill their families' obligations while working in Malaysia, so it is no surprise that many return early.[39]

Châu Rithi explained how he fought beside the Kinh workers for higher wages to combat exploitation in the global supply chains:

> I worked in a mechanical factory and had participated in a strike with the Kinh workers. The reason is because the boss had cut our wages. We tried to call our

118   CHAPTER 4

recruitment company and the Labor Department of the Vietnamese Embassy in Kuala Lumpur, but no one came. So we ended up striking for three days and requesting that salary be paid at the rate promised in the labor contract and that we get paid for the holidays there. Other workers [from Thailand, Nepal, Sri Lanka, Bangladesh, India, and China] also joined us in this strike. The results were somewhat "divide and conquer": while the Chinese workers got high raises, the rest of us got a very tiny raise.

"No one came to help" was a common refrain that I heard during my field-work. This cross-ethnic/race fight speaks volumes about the irresponsibility of the Vietnamese state officials and recruitment companies in Malaysia. Without intervention by the recruitment companies to address contract violations, workers are forced to take matters into their own hands. Neng Arun recounted a three-day strike in a jewelry factory owned by a Chinese Malaysian. There were forty workers, ten from Vietnam and the rest from Indonesia and Bangladesh. Some experienced Vietnamese (Kinh/Khmer) workers who spoke Malay were promoted to supervisors, and Neng Arun was one of them. Her account also demonstrates the advantage of speaking another language, which gave her an edge:

> Once I was supervising over a dozen Indonesian workers, because I can speak some Malay. I participated in this strike to demand a wage increase because after the first year we did not receive a wage increase as stipulated in our con-tract. We tried to contact our recruitment company representatives, but they could not do anything to help us. So ten of us went on strike for three days to demand a wage increase. After that [when their demand was not met], we all returned to Vietnam. The [Chinese Malaysian] boss tried to convince me to stay because he liked my [supervisory] work, but still no wage increase. So, finally, he bought a plane ticket for me to go home.

Neng Arun was fortunate because, by law, her employer was not respon-sible for her return flight, since she did not complete her three-year contract (she had worked only one year at the time of the strike). But her boss still purchased a one-way plane ticket for her, even when she struck with the others. Upon returning home, Neng Arun worked on her family's rice pad-dies to make a living. To supplement her income, she also went to work in Thailand seasonally.

A toxic work environment is another common complaint. Châu Bona, a thirty-six-year-old migrant, returned early due to low wages and unsafe working conditions. He still had đ20 million in debt but did not pay it back. He has made a living by tilling the rice paddies and driving a tractor for hire.

Precarity and Coping Mechanisms 119

While employed in a woodworking factory in Malaysia, he participated in a strike:

> We stopped work for three days due to low wages and toxic materials. Over 40 percent [of the strikers] were Kinh and Khmer; the rest were from other ethnic groups. The owner subtracted these three days from our salaries. Some did not even receive any of their salary. Then, after a month, the owner posted an announcement that we had to go home.

Other workers also fought for safety and well-being. Neng Suvanna told me about a collective effort that culminated in a strike, in which they were joined by the Kinh (the majority there):

> It was a reckless drunken bus driver who almost killed us all. Fifty of us were scared to death when he was drinking and driving for the whole afternoon, almost barreling into the huge ditches on both sides of the street. How could we survive if he were to do that? After that terrible experience, most workers decided to stay home for three days to demand another bus driver. I did not want to take off work, but I followed the other workers' decision. After three days, the boss hired another bus driver to pick us up, so that's why we went back to work.

However, there are limits to these strikes: most workers do not have enough savings to hold out for a long time—the classic power imbalance between management and workers. Thus, in the long run, most workers had to comply with management to make ends meet. When I asked Neng Suvanna whether she got paid during those three days, she said: "I don't know. I accepted what they paid me. I did not know how to calculate it to petition that they should pay me for those three days." Upon further inquiry, she told me that this company was managed by an Indian Malaysian and that the workers came from Vietnam, Bangladesh, Nepal, Myanmar, Indonesia, China, and even Malaysia. The spontaneous strike was triggered by fear for their lives.

The Chăm

Even though only a small number of the Chăm joined the LBS system, they faced many of the same forms of precarity as the other ethnic groups, including contract violations and vulnerabilities, and engaged in some of the same coping mechanisms. They include supporting each other, pooling their money to send lump sums home for their families, and joining other groups in collective actions. One important difference, however, was their faithful practice of Islam, the one factor that did not lead to the religious alienation other ethnic groups experienced in Malaysia. During Ramadan in 2012, the holy month of fasting, introspection, prayer, and celebration,[40] I had a chance to do fieldwork in An Giang. My research assistants and I interviewed many workers who had returned home for a short visit, similar to the home visits of Buddhist migrant workers at Tet. I witnessed firsthand how the Chăm Muslims do not eat or drink from sunrise to sunset each day during Ramadan, while still working during the day.

Some Chăm who had been casualties of the 2008 global financial crisis also returned home for Ramadan in 2012. Visiting one such family reunion confirmed for me many aspects of precarity facing the Chăm. I saw Mr. Chamali, a village leader and mosque keeper,[41] cleaning and attending to the Quốc Thái mosque. Mr. Chamali took us to interview former migrant Mr. Sadat, a soft-spoken, twenty-five-year-old Chăm man, and his extended family (four siblings and their spouses) at his mother's home in a ward in Quốc Thái commune, An Phú District. We talked again in 2014 in An Phú District office.[42]

Mr. Sadat had been encouraged by another Chăm, a local medical doctor from his village, to go to work in Malaysia. The An Giang Employment Services Agency recruited Mr. Sadat and twenty other Chăm migrants (including the doctor's niece) for the Latuco Company, which sent them to work in Malaysia in 2006. Mr. Sadat's mother, Ms. Baqri, took out a loan under her name on his behalf so he could go abroad to work. Her only valuable property, which she prized, was a small house without any land.[43]

After arriving in Malaysia, Mr. Sadat received no help from either the An Giang Employment Service Agency or the Latuco Company that sent him there, and his situation got worse during the financial crisis. When the Malaysian company that had hired him to solder iron bed frames went bankrupt, that company instructed Mr. Sadat to pack up and move to another factory for the remaining six months of his contract. But Mr. Sadat decided to return home six months early in order to look for a job back in Vietnam immediately instead of wasting his time in Malaysia without any guarantee of a full-time job.[44] (Many Kinh and Hoa workers likewise returned home early due to the global financial crisis.) No one in the transnational LBS bureaucracy came to their rescue. This was another case of the state, as a journalist who covers labor issues aptly described it, "Leaving a baby stranded in a marketplace."[45] Most stranded migrants ended up receiving money from their parents to buy their plane tickets home.

The few Chăm who went abroad to work experienced robbery and suffered from the pain of separation from their families, like other groups. Ms. Alvi, who went to work in Malaysia in 2005, finished her three-year contract, and returned home, lamented: "Getting there [Malaysia] is a done deal. I had to close my eyes and just work for three years. I have no money to return home early. Life there was very difficult, lots of robberies. We were very afraid. I cried day and night, missing my family."

Being the fewest in this study's sample of those who joined the LBS system, the Chăm Muslims fought alongside the other ethnic groups when the opportunity arose on the factory floor in Malaysia. Ms. Alvi recounted a strike that successfully pressured the Malaysian company to comply with the terms of the contract they signed with Latuco—a short-term victory in the ongoing battle over contract violations:

> The contract we signed stated RM18 per day [assembling electronic parts in a Chinese Malaysian factory], but when we got there, we received only RM15. Then we women workers got together to discuss how to deal with this. We decided that if it's only RM15 per day, then we would stop work. We sent a representative to talk to the boss and said that if it is RM18 per day then we will work, but if only RM15, then we won't. After that he raised our daily wage to RM18.

The fact that they sent a worker representative to talk to the Chinese Malaysian employer means that one of the workers must have been able to speak Chinese to negotiate. Again, this small victory points to the power of speaking the language of the employer.

Ms. Alvi returned home to the Chăm's peripatetic way of life, but it has been difficult for her as a sole "rice winner" for her family: "I make only enough money to pay for daily needs, no extra. My family has eight siblings, but two of my brothers have mental problems and stay with my parents; the rest are married." When she first returned to Vietnam, she worked for a factory in the South but soon quit due to the low salary. Then she returned to what she could do efficiently: buying from local sources to sell sundries such as thread, blankets, and clothing items. Ms. Alvi explains this routine: "I drive around with my motorbike to sell stuff and return home, all in a day. I sell in local areas and also in Cambodia and return home in the evening. But sometimes when the rain is hard, I have to stay overnight in my relatives' houses."[46] Again, this shows the significance of supportive religious and kinship ties between the Chăm Muslim communities in Vietnam and Cambodia.

Comparative Remarks

While all five ethnic groups face the same set of precarious elements and the vicious cycle of poverty working in Malaysia, their coping mechanisms

122 CHAPTER 4

are different and informed by the cultural resources and wealth inherent in their respective cultural practices.

The transnational LBS system affected female and male migrants differently, from the dehumanizing recruitment phase to the precarity and coping mechanisms while in Malaysia. More than the men, Kinh and Hoa women faced dehumanizing recruitment protocols (pregnancy tests) and sexual violence (including rapes during robberies) while working in Malaysia. Yet one bright spot is financial independence that some female migrants (of all four groups except for the Hrê, whose women did not work overseas) gained. They seized this opportunity with determination and confidence, even when vulnerabilities and risks envelop their lives. When these women sent money home to improve their families' livelihoods, they gained a greater voice, a better status, in the decision-making process in their families. This is consistent with migration studies literature.

On using education as a way to uplift oneself, both the Hrê and the Khmer women strive to obtain more education themselves to become teachers in order to serve their respective communities, whereas the Kinh and the Hoa women were sending money home for their younger siblings so they can obtain more education. This is a form of sacrifice of an opportunity they themselves did not have. The Chăm women also do not have access to higher education, while the men have the privilege of religious studies that are not available to the Chăm women.

Overall, class moments did enable collective actions of these ethnic groups (with other foreign workers). The Khmer fought with the Kinh and the Hoa for their shared interests, even when having some deep-rooted land tensions with the Kinh. The Chăm, a small group joining the LBS program, also participated in some collective actions alongside other ethnic groups in Malaysia. But their protests did not solve long-term problems that plagued their working and living conditions there. The glaring lack of Vietnamese union representation and collective bargaining does not help the workers to negotiate for better contracts and flexibility so they could move to better jobs in Malaysia.

The next two chapters analyze other ways of empowerment, overcoming these limits, using the concept of third space of dissent, either as physical space occupied not according to the duality of legal-illegal categories (Chapter 5) or metaphorical discourse of dissent, uttered by non-state competing authorities (Chapter 6) that are practiced by all five ethnic groups.

5 Physical Third Space Empowerment

What are the forms of empowerment that are not collective actions and cannot be explained by the social network concept? This chapter focuses on migrant responses that take place in a variety of physical spaces that do not neatly follow the duality of legal-illegal categories. Physical third spaces are segregated spaces, on the fringes of and even hidden within big cities or on the factory floor, that provide labor migrants with strategies for survival and a means of resistance against exploitation by the transnational labor export system. They can also be hybrid social and cultural spaces that are fluid and cannot be identified in terms of any particular essential cultural traits.

Actions undertaken in these physical third spaces may be deemed illegal by the terms of the labor brokerage state (LBS) framework but are treated as licit by the local (host) communities where these migrant workers reside. These actions are carried out in the open and cannot be seen as covert as what James Scott calls "weapons of the weak." In these spaces they create for themselves, they respond directly to the shortcomings of the LBS system both while in Malaysia and after returning to Vietnam.

I analyze how the five ethnic groups that are the subject of my study created different physical spaces of dissent that they occupied in opposition to the rule of law. The spaces of dissent take different forms ranging from the socialist Kinh migrants' cultural spaces in Warsaw and Prague to the Kinh and the Hoa taking naps in factory restrooms, hiding products on a factory assembly line, and becoming undocumented in the corner of a restaurant in Malaysia; to the Hrê disregarding the Malaysian labor contracts that forbid migrants from working for other employers; to the Khmer returnees working on tourist visas in Thailand; to the Chăm selling ice cream and sundries on

124   CHAPTER 5

tourist visas in Malaysia. I conclude by analyzing how cross-group differences in physical third spaces of dissent are informed and mediated by the economic and cultural factors of the ethnic hierarchies.

The Cultural Third Spaces of the Socialist Kinh Migrants

The Eastern Europe countries that received Kinh migrants as guest workers in the 1980s established a range of legal statuses, from illegal to legal, for immigrants, including illegal sojourners (those without proper visas), tolerated sojourners (those in the process of legalization), permanent residents with renewable visas, and bona fide citizens.[1] "Tolerated sojourner" is a Polish concept that refers to an immigrant who has a renewable visa that permits him or her to stay for two to three years at a time.[2] It is the most intriguing category because it admits a gray area that could include formerly legal sojourners who overstayed their visas and then retreated into a physical third space. One of the business owners I spoke with, Ms. Đào, pointed out that the food and drink vendors I met and bought foods and drinks from at the Sapa Center in Prague were most likely "tolerated sojourners." Relying on these categories, former guest workers (and their family members) have created physical third spaces on the fringes of Warsaw, Prague, and other cities in former Soviet Bloc countries. The younger generations, on the other hand, have developed hybrid cultural practices within these centers to enable upward mobility.

The history of the socialist migrants sets the stage for the emergence of two vibrant Kinh commercial centers in Poland and the Czech Republic. Third space concepts shed light on how these former socialist migrants managed to overcome their dependency on old practices and social networks that could have locked them in a suboptimal pathway that could have inhibited their growth. Collectively, these migrants moved on from small-scale household retailing to creating their own vibrant community spaces, segregated at the fringes of those city centers, relying on their aspirations and linguistic skills and their community's wealth, including financial and social resources.[3]

Marywilska Shopping Center in a Warsaw Suburb

These migrants' beginnings in Eastern Europe were humble. Back in 1989, they found ways to sew jeans and T-shirts in their dormitory rooms, with Vietnamese designs and labels, that they then sold cheaply to the local markets.[4] Making garments in their dorms was illegal, yet it was accepted socially because it met the growing Eastern European demand for consumer goods. The dorms were thus physical third spaces for these entrepreneurial migrants.

Those dorms no longer exist today; they have been replaced by a thriving shopping center that serves the Vietnamese diaspora and other ethnic groups in the area. On a weekday in June 2017, I had a chance to visit Marywilska shopping center, about 12 kilometers north of downtown Warsaw. It is in a working-class area: clean but with run-down buildings that were used during Poland's socialist era.

Marywilska perpetuates the petty trade, retailing consumer products and providing simple services, such as manicures, pedicures, haircuts, and hair styling, "path-dependency" practices acccording to Baláž and Williams's theory.[5] The Vietnamese bazaar, or "Little Hanoi" as it was known, was established by the Vietnamese at an abandoned stadium (an open-air "Euro bazaar"). For over twenty years, between 1988 and 2010, the Vietnamese held spontaneous bazaars around the stadium, trading illegally with contraband products. The tacit acceptance by the local Polish communities constituted it as a type of third space. When the stadium was to be rebuilt, the Kinh migrants moved their bazaar stalls to Marywilska.[6]

The area surrounding Marywilska has the look and feel of the collapsed socialist era: there are old apartment buildings, rusty abandoned factories, and a rundown bus station. The relocated marketplace that serves as a Vietnamese hub is at the "fringes of the city," as described by Pawel Boski.[7] Stepping inside this bazaar, which had light foot traffic for a weekday, I found Kinh traders and working-class shoppers from different ethnic groups. The traders are very closely connected to two Warsaw suburbs: Janki (which features a huge shopping center) and the nearby Wólka Kosowska, the Chinese warehouse center that supplies the Vietnamese traders at Marywilska, about twenty-one kilometers southwest of Warsaw.[8]

The inside space of this bazaar is huge, and people use electric scooters to "cruise" between stalls.[9] I talked with Vietnamese traders as they were tending to their stalls. Mr. Sơn, a middle-age man from Hải Dương (a province in the north) and a former electrical technician who interned in East Germany in the 1980s, told me, "I still do not have Polish citizenship, but I am happy with my life, living in-between two countries with flexibility. I can close up my shop for weeks and return to my hometown for a visit then return here. No problem." Mr. Sơn must have had a proper visa as a "tolerated sojourner" to work there as a shop owner. When asked why he had not gone into technical work utilizing the skills he had learned as an apprentice, he said that most jobs in that field were reserved for the Poles. So this was not a case of his

126   CHAPTER 5

having gotten stuck in a "dependency," but rather a conscious decision he made because the flexibility and mobility he has from selling wares allows him to come and go as he pleases.

Sapa Center in Prague

The biggest Vietnamese commercial center in the former Eastern Europe is the Sapa commercial center in Prague, which formed in the wake of the Czechoslovak "Velvet Revolution," when the market system replaced the command economy.[10] The Kinh migrants in the Sapa commercial center engage in wholesale trading (such as textile/garment/shoes and household appliances), selling food and drinks, and providing services (money transfers, insurance, banking, shipping, educational, medical, and legal services, among others).

In 2017, after a one-hour car ride south from central Prague, I arrived at Sapa, Prague's "Little Hanoi," which is much larger and more established than the "Little Hanoi" in Marywilska. The entrance gate conjures up the ingress to an industrial zone; the signs welcoming visitors to the commercial center are in Vietnamese and Czech.[11] This is not only the largest commercial distribution center for Vietnamese items in Europe;[12] it is also the cultural center of the Vietnamese community in Europe, where these migrants have formed a cultural third space, a place to make a living and to mediate their sense of displacement in a subtly racialized Czech society.[13] Here, they construct their cultural identities, as well as their political and religious positions in intercultural encounters. These are ways to mediate "dependency."

This third space (or enclave) on the city's fringe is akin to the run-down segregated urban barrios and rural communities (as third space) in nineteenth-century "Greater Mexico" that the ethnic Mexicans who lived there relied on to deal with their status as members of a racialized and marginalized minority. In such third space enclaves, such as in today's East Los Angeles and Santa Ana, ethnic Mexicans were able to communicate in Spanish, maintain their customs, practice their religion, teach their children Spanish, and enjoy their cuisines, music, and entertainment of home.[14] Similarly, Sapa's social spaces have become the primary sites for transmitting and preserving Vietnamese culture and ethnic identity and for forging solidarity. I heard the Vietnamese language spoken everywhere in Sapa.

But the Sapa center is not a segregated urban barrio. Upon entry, I was absolutely stunned by the scope and scale of this center, which resembles a small city of warehouses, restaurants, indoor and outdoor stalls (selling clothes, toys, shoes, bags, and every sundry one may need), covered market

Physical Third Space Empowerment 127

stalls, small grocery stores, a Vietnamese martial arts school, insurance companies, shipping stores, money transfer businesses (that handle two-way transfers to and from Vietnam), travel agencies, tax service companies, dental care offices, entertainment businesses, and places to play bingo, among many other types of services. Most of the signs are in Vietnamese, except for a handful of storefronts with Chinese names. And, except for the food and drink sold in restaurants and from carts, most products there are sold wholesale.

A Socialist Cosmopolitan: Ms. Tiệp

After leaving the enclosed clothing stalls for wholesale, I was pleasantly surprised to find a retail store owned by Ms. Tiệp, an entrepreneur whom I had interviewed in Vietnam between 2002 and 2006. The shop was closed on that day so I did not get a chance to go inside. Ms. Tiệp is an example of a proactive entrepreneur whose family business had been illegal yet tacitly accepted by locals and then became part of the economic and political fabric of the Czech Republic, finding legitimacy by filling a need during a transitional period in the country. Ms. Tiệp's story shows that the bilateral agreements between Vietnam and the former Eastern Bloc countries benefited scholars, cadres, and government officials who seized opportunities to invest in their futures.

Ms. Tiệp is a Nam Định native, an expatriate from the former Soviet Bloc who was a teacher of Russian language and literature. Back in the 1980s, she was a translator for the powerful Vietnamese Economic Management Institute during the heyday of socialism in Vietnam. In my interviews with her in Vietnam, she explained how she and other migrants created physical third spaces in the 1980s when the socialist regimes in Eastern Europe transitioned to the market system, a time when consumer products were very expensive and in short supply in the region:

> Many people in Vietnam began to send garment products to those markets, starting off with several dozen jackets sent through the post office, or sending them as carry-on luggage with people flying to visit those countries; then shipping increased to large-scale export via containers transported by commercial liners. It was very profitable at the beginning; high profit margins of up to 100–200 percent were not uncommon, even with poor quality and unattractive designs!

Smuggling apparel (such as jackets, jeans, T-shirts) and watches into Czechoslovakia in carry-on luggage was illegal but accepted behavior. Smugglers even used their own bodies to transport these consumer products by wearing

128 CHAPTER 5

several pairs of jeans and T-shirts, concealing watches in jackets, trouser pockets, and luggage and even wearing watches up the whole length of their arms.[15] After successfully getting through customs, the migrants sold these items on the black market, an illegal act that was accepted in response to widespread shortages in the Soviet Bloc.

When the socialist world crumbled around Ms. Tiệp, after the former Soviet Bloc fell to the market system in 1989–90, this "socialist cosmopolitan" decided to become a business entrepreneur and formed a partnership with her extended family. Her family had established a stronghold in Czechoslovakia, founded on education and vocational training. Her husband studied and finished his master's thesis in electrical engineering there; her siblings and their spouses had trained in technical fields and accounting in the Eastern European system. They all contributed money to this family operation as shareholders, a primary form of capital mobilization, as Beresford and Đặng argue.[16]

To some extent, she created a path of dependency on family networks. After the fall of the Soviet Bloc in 1989, Ms. Tiệp and her family decided to stay in the Czech Republic to start their garment business, mainly manufacturing women's clothes. They seized an opportunity by meeting the needs of Eastern European consumers who were longing for affordable clothing products. They started out as a small and modest enterprise in 1989 by supplying simple female apparel to working-class customers in these formerly socialist markets. Ms. Tiệp, as a former teacher, is methodical in her thinking and so is conscious of the significance of long-term trust and consistent quality. She taught herself clothing design by studying fashion catalogs and attending conferences and exhibitions on design and fabrics in China, South Korea, and Eastern Europe. Over time, her family increased the scale of its production to satisfy this market niche, and she developed more styles and sizes. How she came to create her own label for her clothing lines is a heartwarming story that demonstrates the support she received from her extended family. When she asked her two brothers what label to use, her nieces and nephews, wanting to show their respect for her innovation and hard work for the welfare of their extended family, suggested a name that incorporated her name in Vietnamese.

As the former Soviet Bloc opened up to the market system with Western Europe and Chinese suppliers, Ms. Tiệp and her family bypasssed it, using transnational family networks to move up the global supply chains. They established commercial networks between the manufacturers in Vietnam and the distributors of the final products in these countries. In particular, she participated in all stages of the supply chain, from designing clothes, to

Physical Third Space Empowerment   129

selecting fabrics, to contracting workers in Vietnam to assemble the clothes. Moreover, her mobilization of capital (from relatives and friends) to complete the supply chains was strategic: she opened kiosks in the host countries to sell the Vietnamese-assembled clothes directly to her working-class clientele there. Her intellectual, cultural, and social competencies empowered her and her family, leading to the success of their transnational business venture.

Mediating Dependency of Social Networks

Major structural changes in the late 1990s, however, reveal the limitations of social familial networks.[17] Growing economic globalization gave access to a wider range of consumer goods. Starting in the late 1990s, the socialist migrants began losing out to Chinese market traders who made cheap clothing available throughout Eastern Europe. These traders had direct relationships with individual factories in China and broader business knowledge and contacts.[18] Both the traders and the factories received support—in the form of export guarantees and credit schemes—from the Chinese government.[19] Worse yet, by 1993–94, goods from Western Europe and China began to flood the Eastern European markets, replacing Vietnamese products.

Not all entrepreneurs can adjust to those structural changes happening around them as did Ms. Tiệp and her extended family. Paradoxically, the very success created by the 1980s wave of socialist migrants had locked them into market trading jobs among Vietnamese expatriates, a path of dependency, especially when this type of work was suboptimal relative to their education and skills.[20] There was no longer a balance between agency (commercial enterprises launched by entrepreneurs) and structure (rising global market system adopted by Eastern European countries after the fall of the Berlin Wall).[21] By 2007, most Kinh traders were relying on Chinese products to sell in kiosks and other retail stores in Russia because "Vietnamese light manufacturing products could not compete with Chinese products on either price or design."[22]

Nevertheless, when I visited Prague in 2017, the Sapa commercial center demonstrated the strength of the Kinh diaspora who relied on community cultural wealth to achieve some balance in agency and structure. The Kinh traders there had moved from small-scale retail sales to wholesaling (though still with Chinese products), in addition to providing all forms of auxiliary services. I passed by many shops offering two-way money transfers between Vietnam and the Czech Republic, Western Union signs prominently on display.

Marywilska and the Sapa commercial center are social and cultural third spaces that offer migrants strategies for community survival and capital

130   CHAPTER 5

accumulation, spaces that have both illicit aspects (in both centers, there were those with illegal immigrant status) and licit aspects (they worked in the stalls and stores).[23] Commerce is more vibrant in Marywilska on the weekends, when the center is frequented by tourists and migrant workers.[24] On the other hand, commerce in Sapa center is brisk every day of the week, with Vietnamese, Czech, and global tourists alike coming to taste the foods or check out all the wares and services being offered. Both centers constitute public spaces where the Vietnamese and local residents (the Poles, the Czechs) and global tourists come together, free from oppression, embodied in their particularity and complementarity. Moreover, these centers also offer spaces for intercultural hybridity, as both Bhabha and Gutierrez describe. The younger generations in both centers have integrated into their respective host countries, speaking several languages including their mother tongue. In 2016, the Czech Republic recognized Sapa to be integral to Czech society owing to its provision of both wholesale and retail services to its citizens.[25]

Third Spaces of the Kinh and the Hoa in Malaysia

Returning to the Vietnamese labor export program to Malaysia, the Kinh and the Hoa, who taken together constitute the largest of the labor migrant groups participating in the program, have relied on diverse forms of physical third space to address the hardships imposed on them by transnational LBS system. These hardships include sleep deprivation, increased production quotas (speedup), and limited employment mobility.

Taking Naps in the Restrooms

The work schedule of the assembly line is exploitative, requiring many factories to run 24/7. In manufactured goods, such as textile/garment/footwear, machines in the assembly line cannot be started and stopped within the duration of a single shift, so management often engages in rotating shifts to ensure that machines can run continuously. Moreover, in rotating shifts, management can distribute preferred shifts across different employees. Workers are forced to rotate their work schedules every one or two weeks, disrupting their circadian rhythms, leading to sleep deprivation, exhaustion, and, at times, even tragic accidents on the factory floor. Moreover, the speed of the assembly line or demands of the piece-work quotas also exhaust workers.[26] Many interviewees complained, saying, "When I returned to the hostel, I crashed on my bed to sleep" and "We are always sleep deprived,

Physical Third Space Empowerment 131

so sometimes we go to the restroom to sleep" or "Sunday is for sleeping all day."[27]

Napping in the restrooms, if only for ten to twenty minutes, is one way to push back against factory discipline and to snag a moment of rest in a hectic work day. "Good thing that there was no limit to the number of trips to the toilet," Ms. Hảo told me. "Many times when I felt tired, I hid in the toilet stall and slept for ten minutes. We took turns sleeping in the restroom. Before we went to the toilet, we did ask permission from a Malay line leader and even told her that we would be taking a short nap." Another migrant, Ms. Tiên, said: "When we wanted to go to the restroom, we needed to ask someone to work at our station. So there was a Malay line leader who walked around the factory and would stop at any station to replace a worker if that person wanted to go to the toilet. There was no time limit, so we often took up to twenty minutes to sleep in the restroom. But the female boss [not the Malay line leader] often yelled at us."

Taking turns napping in the toilet stall created a sense of solidarity among the workers. They successfully inhabited a physical third space, using the toilet stall as a way to defy ruthless factory speedup, momentarily slowing down the global supply chain in these factories in Malaysia. The cases of Ms. Hảo and Ms. Tiên both suggest that their immediate Malay supervisors—not the bosses—were sensitive to the need of these migrants, tolerating, in effect, a paid break. After all, by turning a blind eye to this napping practice, the Malay line leaders could have reduced the number of accidents on the factory floor.

But less tolerant line leaders and employers controlled restroom breaks closely, resulting in health issues for migrants. I interviewed one migrant returnee who developed a painful kidney disease upon returning to Vietnam. The timing suggested that this disease may have been caused by restrictions on restroom visits in Malaysia. In 2012, I visited Ms. Trúc at home in downtown An Giang province. She was lying in bed, suffering from painful kidney stones while talking with me:

> Management did not allow us to bring in water. So we had to drink a lot of water at lunch. When needed to go to the toilet, we had to be replaced by another person [such as a line leader] who only allowed one to two minutes. If we needed to take longer, we were yelled at by the replacement line leader. When they refused to work at our station, we had to use our limited Malay to talk back: "If you don't replace me, I may need to release it right here!" Only then did they let us go.

While this threat brought migrants temporary relief, sadly, the health damage to workers like Ms. Trúc had lasting effects.

132 CHAPTER 5

Hiding Products to Slow Down the Assembly Line

Another strategy Vietnamese migrant workers used to fight back against oppression was hiding products in their personal space in the factory to slow down the assembly line, a form of silent collective action. To earn their daily pay, foreign migrant workers for Clipsal Corporation had to assemble a predefined number of finished products, and after they reached the day's quota, they would start to hide extras. I interviewed Ms. Bình in Ho Chi Minh City in 2008, after she had completed her three-year contract and returned home to take care of her child, who was then in grade seven. At the Selangor branch of Clipsal, an Australian company that produces small electrical boards for light switches and plugs, she assembled parts, tested switches, performed quality control, and packaged products. Ms. Bình worked twelve hours per day including overtime: "Only the Vietnamese and Indonesian workers wanted to work the graveyard shift." While working at Clipsal, she sent remittances home to her mother, who took care of her child.

At the beginning, the quota was set at forty-six hundred electric boards per day. The Vietnamese workers learned the procedures quickly and increased productivity 15 percent, to fifty-three hundred electric boards per day. This gave management a reason to raise the quota—a form of speedup—which affected all workers on the assembly line, including the Indonesian workers. Doing more than had been asked (to please the boss), a sign of false consciousness, had backfired on the Vietnamese because they had inadvertently forced other foreign workers to work faster on the line.[28] To redress their error, the Vietnamese workers found a way to fight the quota system. Ms. Bình explained: "We have a tactic to slow down work speedup whereby we save some of the 'above-quota' finished products and then bring them out in the first hour of the following day so we can work slowly with other workers." They ended up receiving the same pay yet preserved their energy for the next work day without speeding up the assembly line.[29]

Becoming Undocumented: The Garlic Peeler

Yet another tactic is to become undocumented. I found evidence of undocumented workers even in official statistics. There is a discrepancy between the Vietnamese and the Malaysian estimates of the number of Vietnamese working abroad. The Vietnamese source in 2018 provides a round number of fifty thousand, while the Malaysian source provides an exact figure of 29,039, based on the record of Vietnamese workers under contracts in Malaysia and paying levies as of 2017.[30] This discrepancy suggests that the Vietnamese

Physical Third Space Empowerment   133

government does not have control over the migrants they send to work in Malaysia and that many undocumented Vietnamese live and work without a contract in Malaysia.[31]

When the laws from both sending and receiving countries fail to protect stranded migrant workers, the workers create a less exposed, relatively safe third space to minimize the costs of their labor and to protect themselves against mistreatment by becoming "undocumented workers." But becoming undocumented is against the law and can make migrants more vulnerable or result in them being further exploited due to lack of proper documentation.[32] If caught, they have to pay a fine of about US$1,700 (đ35 million). In addition, according to Nguyễn Hồng Thao, the Vietnamese ambassador to Malaysia, if they "declined the 6P Amnesty program in 2011," they could also be put in prison and denied any future chance of working in Malaysia.[33] But many fleeing migrants nevertherless chose to occupy this form of third space after leaving exploitative employers. When doing fieldwork in Batu Pahat in Malaysia in 2008, I had a chance to interview an undocumented Kinh worker, a garlic peeler, who found this exact third space for herself after leaving an exploitative employer.[34]

In 2008, after interviewing a group of men in nearby workers' rental units, we were walking with our two informants, Ms. Hà and Ms. Lê (from the north of Vietnam), who were returning to their own units. On the way, we spotted a young Kinh woman working in a corner of a neighborhood restaurant, so we approached her. Ms. Thu was from Thanh Hóa, another northern province. She had left a garment factory before the end of her contract, thus becoming an undocumented worker. Then, she found a job peeling garlic and washing dishes in a Chinese Malaysian restaurant. Essentially, Ms. Thu worked underground for this restaurant owner. She shared her indignation:

> The Vietnamese agency sold us here. We sold ourselves to work here, but to no avail. The Latuco Recruitment Company promised that we would earn enough to save around RM300 per month to pay back our debt and help out our family. But when I came here to work for that garment factory, I earned on average only RM500 per month, and after they deducted RM100 for the levy, I did not have enough money even to pay the interest on my loan to come here. Some months, I earned as low as RM300.[35]

With such a low salary, there was no "saving of RM300 per month" as advertised. She reflected critically on her condition in noting that she had, in effect, sold herself. But she took an active step to escape exploitative working conditions by becoming undocumented, which provided a way to protest

134   CHAPTER 5

contract violations and still survive. Ms. Thu explained why she left the factory:

> No promises on the labor contract were kept. There was no health coverage when I went to the doctor, no extra pay if we worked overtime during holidays, and so forth. I signed a contract to do basic work for fixed daily salary, but when I got here, I found that I got paid by percentages [piece-rates]. When I did something wrong, the line leader scolded me badly and took deductions from my salary checks as punishment. I could not stand the big difference between the contract I signed [in Vietnam] and the real treatment in the factory [in Malaysia]. So I left that factory before the end of the contract and now work for this restaurant from 3:30 p.m. to midnight. For that, I earn RM25 per day plus two meals. I live with other female workers who also ended their contracts early with that garment factory. We pool our money to send home to pay the interest on our loans.

Clearly, Ms. Thu had a sense of self-rationalization, which Oishi refers to as a form of subjective empowerment.[36] Her independent act of leaving an abusive employer led her to this third space: a corner in a restaurant where she earned money. She subsequently received help from a network of documented workers who lived in nearby hostels. In a follow-up phone conversation with Ms. Hà in 2008, I learned that these northern female migrants had been giving clothes and food to Ms. Thu and her roommates, other undocumented female workers who had also protested and left the same garment factory.

Ms. Thu's bitter complaints expose shortcomings of the LBS system. The Latuco officials failed to respond to her repeated calls. Yet the bank in Vietnam continued to demand interest payments from her family. The Malaysian employers have the upper hand because they keep the workers' passports and charge underground migrants a fee to get their passports back. Ms. Thu understood how difficult it would be for her to reunite with her child and family back in Vietnam:

> There are many workers like us who no longer have our passports [not returned by employers because workers left before finishing their contracts]. But we all know that it would cost a worker between RM1,200 and 1,400, to be paid to Vietnamese Embassy personnel who would handle all transactions, to get back our passports, pay the airfare, the levy owed to the Malaysian government, and other fees. So if I can save RM400 per month, then I can find my way home in the next several months.[37]

As is the case for many female workers, family separation—especially not being able to see her child, who was being taken care of by her parents at

Physical Third Space Empowerment 135

the time of the interview—was hard on her. Unfortunately, I have no way of knowing how she and other undocumented migrants fared in the long run, but I know that Latuco went out of business, possibly due to repeated complaints from migrants and researchers like me.

During my 2009 fieldwork trip, I told high-ranking officials at the Vietnam General Confederation of Labor (Latuco's superiors) in Hanoi about how Latuco left workers stranded in Malaysia and did not respond to their calls for help. The officials promised to investigate these violations and take appropriate action. During my 2010 trip, I learned that Latuco had been forced to close down its business. I was unable to learn what arrangements had been made for those stranded migrant workers in Malaysia. In my interview with Dr. Nguyễn Lương Trào in July 2015, he also confirmed that Latuco's license had been rescinded and that the company was no longer recruiting workers. Damage had already been done to many migrant workers they had recruited. But Ms. Thu felt that her choice to become an undocumented worker provided a way out of the "indentured servitude"[38] and a venue to make money, which she could use to get home.

The Story of the Ghostman

A Kinh man I intereviewed found his third space in a noodle shop in a suburb district on the fringe of Ho Chi Minh City. Nguyễn Minh Ngọc (his real name)[39] also had a witty double-entendre nickname, Thằng Ma Lai, a Vietnamized version of "Malaysia" and also the name of a ghost in Vietnamese mythology. "The ghostman," a term of endearment given to him by the local people in several suburban districts on the fringes of Ho Chi Minh City, is appropriate for a man who disappeared for seven years in Vietnam after finishing only one year of his contract in Malaysia.

I interviewed him twice by phone in 2013 thanks to an introduction from Nam Dương, an investigative journalist for the Laborer. When we spoke, Nguyễn Minh Ngọc was in Móng Cái province (near the Vietnamese border with China) doing manual work building a shrimp farm there. He is from Thái Bình (another northern province) and has a ninth-grade education. In 2003, he joined the LBS program and borrowed đ19 million to go to Malaysia to work for a Chinese-Malaysian company, together with twenty-nine other men from the same hometown.

Once he arrived in Malaysia, he quickly discovered that many of the terms of his contract were not going to be kept. Instead of the electrical work he had been promised, he was assigned to be a construction worker, laboring under the hot sun all day long. While the wage was the same as stated on

136   CHAPTER 5

the contract, all other benefits were short term: room and board was free only for the first month, and there was limited opportunity for overtime work. Most migrants count on overtime work opportunities as promised by the recruitment company because when their salary is low they are unable to send money home. When the promise of overtime work was not kept, the ghostman did not earn enough money to send home or to pay his debt. Consequently, he did not recoup the investment he had made.

In August 2004 he was imprisoned, and in December he was deported back to Vietnam. Evidence shows that not speaking the language of the Chinese Malaysian boss had contributed to his imprisonment and deportation.[40] In a phone interview in 2013, he described what happened:

> It was too hot, I couldn't work. I only asked for one day off, but my boss said: "What do you do in the morning? Why are you not working? Do you want to return to Vietnam?" Then I told my boss, "You pay me a salary that is even lower than what I can earn in Vietnam, given my experience. I have lost a lot of money already. Please give me one week to think and make a decision." Then my boss fooled me by responding in a language that I did not understand. I told him to speak in Malay which I could understand better. Then I took a day off as sick leave. About 5 p.m. the following day, he informed the police and told me that if I refused to work here, then I needed to move to another construction site. I told him that I needed one week rest to regain my strength. After a while, I packed all my belongings and left with him thinking that he was moving me to another work site, only to find out that he was taking me to the police station where I was put in jail.

Once he was in jail, the labor export system failed him even further. He lamented bitterly that neither the state nor the recruitment company responded to his pleas for help. When I asked him whether he contacted the Vietnamese government in Malaysia, he replied: "I did call the Vietnamese Embassy in Kuala Lumpur, but they paid no attention, recalling the Vietnamese expression of 'leaving a baby stranded in a marketplace.'[41] They only came down after I had been in jail [about three to four months] and then gave me a plane ticket to the south (to Ho Chi Minh City) instead." This meant that he would have had to buy a domestic plane ticket to the north (to Hanoi, which is much closer to his home in Thái Bình province).

The months-long imprisonment in Malaysia had left an indelible imprint on his psyche. It shattered his self-confidence: "I felt very down. . . . I wasted time. . . . I fell down, and now to stand up it will take a lot of time. . . . I feel it is so difficult to do this." He went into hiding (in plain sight) for seven years, living in several poor suburban districts at the margins of Ho Chi Minh City because he was not able to remit any money to repay the money he had borrowed to go to Malaysia. He did not go home; the shame of not sending remittances home to fulfill his obligation to his family and anxiety about the future discouraged him from buying a plane ticket to Hanoi. In the meantime, his parents in the north ended up paying off his bank debt of đ23 million.

The fringes of Ho Chi Minh City sheltered and employed him, however, thus offering him a third space. Several local noodle factory owners gave him work and places to stay. His family and the recruitment company finally got help from two investigative journalists who tracked the ghostman down after an intensive search.[42] This story has a happy ending: after a moving family reunion, the ghostman found work in a shrimp farm in Móng Cái province (in the north, near his hometown in Thái Bình province), got married, and was expecting his first child when we talked on the phone in 2013.

Nevertheless, this happy ending does not nullify all the losses that Nguyễn Minh Ngọc and his family had endured over more than seven years, not to mention that the safe third space, the noodle factories in several districts at the margins of Ho Chi Minh City, only sustained him with bare necessities; he was not able during this time to improve his education, increase his skill set, or lift himself out of poverty. Further, in those communities, he admitted to me, he got into gambling (on soccer games), which made it impossible for him to save money. So, ironically, this social third space also nurtured unhealthy behavior in him. Moreover, this case shows the significant role played by the state media, the Laborer newspaper, and their journalists in exposing the negative side of the LBS system.

The Hrê's Third Space: Working Outside of the LBS System

The Hrê responded to the failure of the LBS program by going to work for employers not named in the contract, thus breaching the contract's terms. Many Hrê migrants entered into an illegal space that was accompanied by risk, but they were accepted by those employers who hired them, albeit on a short-term basis.

The LBS program was not successful in Ba Tơ district. The number of Hrê who returned without completing the initial three-year contract provides a way to gauge how many Hrê violated their original LBS contracts and found work outside of state channels, thus shedding light on their physical third spaces. Between 2009 and 2012, 137 returned to Quảng Ngãi province early from all overseas contracts.[43] Of these 137 returnees, 93 percent had gone to

Malaysia, the top destination for the Hrê.[44] Ba Tơ district was the hardest hit in this regard: 49 out of 137, or 36 percent, returned early. Sơn Hà district was second, with 34 out of 137, or 25 percent, returning early.[45]

Since most Hrê migrants to Malaysia were male, most early returnees were male. Hrê women have less mobility compared to the men. Only five (4 percent) of the early returnees were women.[46] Of these five women, two volunteered to return home officially, one violated some factory regulations, and two became pregnant while in Malaysia. While the pregnant woman from Tây Trà district was given đ11 million (about US$500) by Châu Hưng Recruitment Company, the other woman (from Trà Bồng district) apparently received no financial support from Sovilaco Recruitment Company. I found no additional information about their whereabouts and status.

The situation got worse over time. More Hrê left their contracts, began trying to get better jobs, and then were sent home before the end of the contracts.[47] Over half of the early returnees to Ba Tơ district between 2011 and 2015 (18 out of 35) were forced to go home because they had left their original contracts. Of the remaining seventeen who volunteered to return home early via the official channel, health played an important role in their return.[48]

Few migrant workers succeeded without language and vocational skills, and none had a religious connection to the Malaysians. Of the eighteen Hrê who tried to find other jobs in Malaysia, only three were hired with better salaries. And even for these three, opportunities were short-lived: all eighteen were sent home before the end of their original contracts. In the end, they also had to pay their return airfares, and because they returned home early, they lost their deposits, which were being kept by the local state bank.

Đinh Thị Phương Lan confirmed that the Hrê searched for work outside the original contracts, essentially with the complicity of the new Malaysian employers, because they could make more money that way: "I know in three cases, the migrants worked only the first year in the contracted electronic company for đ7 million per month; when they heard that other electronic companies offer đ8 or đ9 million per month, they switched to those higher-paying companies."[49] These decisions may sound hasty, but a đ1 to đ2 million difference per month (US$50–100) was a large amount to these poor Hrê. But these moves were a violation of the contract they had signed with the Chau Hung Company, so they were deported home at their own expense. Đinh Thị Phương Lan also mentioned other reasons why some Hrê did not complete their labor contracts as "brawling" (đánh nhau) and receiving a wage that was "less than stipulated on the contract" (đ5–7 million per month instead of đ10 million).[50] She added that the migrants had no recourse for

Physical Third Space Empowerment   139

breach of contract in Malaysia because Châu Hưng, the recruitment company that sent them there, did not have an office in Malaysia. While she did not elaborate on the reason for the brawling, she was clear about the dereliction of Châu Hưng. Nevertheless, as a participant in the program, she still praised the labor export policy in front of the local state official who escorted me to these interviews.

Interestingly, these early returnees did have leverage they could use with the LBS, since they could spread the word about what life was like in Malaysia and thereby plant doubts in prospective workers' minds about the wisdom of joining the labor export program to Malaysia. Faced with this problem, the state resorted to radio, TV, and, later, the internet to respond to any real or perceived negative comments by those early returnees that could be seen as discrediting the LBS system. In 2012, the state held a direct dialogue event (đối thoại trực tuyến) with the Hrê people to preempt this potential threat, using the state radio and TV, in collaboration with local governments, employment centers, and recruitment companies.[51]

The state appealed to other state apparatuses at all levels to communicate directly to the general public for damage control.[52] They reached out to local people's committees, labor departments, and employment centers. They threatened to use brute force, if necessary, by asking the local security police (from district to commune levels) to crush any efforts that spread "fake news" or that created "confusion" among the Hrê.[53]

The Khmer's Use of Tourist Visas to Work in Thailand

The Khmer have deep historical ties to Cambodia and rely on their kinship, religious, and cultural networks there. During fieldwork interviews in 2013–14, I learned that many Khmer bypassed the state labor export system and asserted their own geographical agency by networking with other Khmer in Cambodia and friends in Thailand and crossing through Cambodia to Thailand to do seasonal work and periodic domestic service work before returning home to An Giang.

The economic space they created for themselves transcended the political borders of at least three countries: Vietnam, Cambodia, and Thailand. I interviewed a dynamic young Khmer couple who met while working in Malaysia and then got married upon their return to Vietnam. Their subsequent border crossings were aided by their Khmer contacts in Phnom Penh, who helped them renew their tourist visas so they could cross from Cambodia to Thailand to work seasonally. Châu Rithi, the husband, had worked in Malaysia for five years. Upon returning home to An Giang, he found work elsewhere between

140 CHAPTER 5

harvests in Vietnam. He created a third space for himself by working illegally under a tourist visa for Thai employers who needed pickers to harvest their crops and so turned a blind eye. This need for labor is understandable, given that the dried fruit industry is one of the key export sectors in Thailand.

This couple would get a two-month visa to travel from Vietnam to Cambodia and then a one-month visa to enter Thailand. Then, when the one-month visa for Thailand expired, they would renew it by returning to Cambodia to apply for another one-month visa. By crossing the Thai-Cambodia border at least two times to work illegally in Thailand, they constituted an economic third space. While renewing visas is legal, using them to work is not. The recent Thai policy that allows irregular Vietnamese domestic workers already in Thailand to register for one-year work permits confirms this practice of crossing the border and indicates that the Thai government is attempting to control it.[54]

Unlike the Hrê and the Kinh, most Khmer are bilingual, speaking Khmer and Vietnamese, and some can speak other Southeast Asian languages as well, which enhances their chance of getting jobs in Vietnam's neighboring countries. Learning to speak Thai made it possible for Châu Rithi to network from one Thai employer to another:

> I learned to speak Thai, and when I worked with other Thai workers in a tourist company for six months, they introduced me to work in fruit orchards to pick seasonal fruits. Every year, during the three months without work [between rice harvest seasons in Vietnam], I come to Thailand to pick fruits between June and September, making on average đ1 million per day. I get paid by the kilogram, earning đ1,500 per kilogram. Some days, if I feel strong, I can pick up to one ton of fruit. The owner paid for room and meals. The Thai boss often drives me to the Thai-Cambodia border to renew my tourist visa. I still have to pay a fee [đ200,000 per visa renewal] to the middlemen.

This narrative shows a clear connection between language and networking: Châu Rithi's ability to talk with his Thai coworkers in their language got him a job picking seasonal fruits at orchards. The work was strenuous, but he received support from the Thai employer. Here, the fruit orchard became a physical third space in which his working on a tourist visa broke the law but was aided and abetted by the Thai employer, who needed these hardworking migrants to pick crops.

A gendered division of labor is reflected in Khmer migrants' work: Khmer couples crisscrossed Cambodia to Thailand, where the men harvested crops outside in Thai orchards and the women undertook childcare or housework inside the homes of Thai families. Neng Arun, Châu Rithi's wife, did domestic

Physical Third Space Empowerment   141

work in Thailand. She had learned to speak Malay and had received a promotion to line leader of fifteen Indonesian workers while working in Malaysia. But she had returned home six months early (before the end of her three-year contract) following a failed three-day strike for a salary increase. After returning home, Neng Arun traveled with her husband to Thailand:

> I found domestic work in Thailand. I went there by foot and worked there two to three months at a time. I worked near the Cambodia-Thailand border. The salary is not great, only enough to make a living. I stayed at a hostel paid for by the boss, but I had to pay for food myself. I have done this three times since 2007, and have to renew my [tourist] visa every two months in Phnom Penh and every month in Thailand.

Similar to her husband's situation, she benefited from her ability to speak multiple languages: Khmer (her mother tongue), Vietnamese, and Malay. As a couple, they speak four languages: Khmer, Vietnamese, Thai, and Malay. These multilingual skills facilitated their cross-border working arrangements. But working in these physical third spaces is risky. The husband, Châu Rithi, explained the complex and tenuous nature of living and working in their Thai third space: "We go to Thailand to work together. But now, we only want to stay home and work in our rice fields. In the long run, it is much better to work in our village, not in Thailand. You know, working in Thailand on a tourist visa is illegal, so we are afraid of being caught by the police. Also, it is very complex in Thailand, with a lot of people from the *xã hội đen* (loosely translated, 'underground society')."[55] For this couple, working seasonally in Thailand was only a temporary arrangement through which they hoped to save enough money for their long-term goal of rice farming in Vietnam. I learned that upon returning home to Tịnh Biên district in An Giang province, they had invested their savings in land.

Traveling the Chăm Way

The Chăm also cross national borders, relying on their friends and their families' networks in Cambodia[56] to move from An Giang to Cambodia and on to Thailand and Malaysia to work in short-term migration cycles, after which they return home for Ramadan and family visits.[57] This level of mobility brings them the most wide-ranging forms of physical third space, from outside school gates where they sell ice cream, to the factory floor and the homes of the Malays where Chăm women work. That they participate at all in the LBS system seems at odds with their entrepreneurial and independent spirit, but it shows the success of the LBS recruitment process in convincing

142 CHAPTER 5

them to go. The story of Ms. Wali is a powerful one of a resilient Chăm worker who went to work in Malaysia under the labor export policy and subsequently escaped its shackles.[58] She had finished twelfth grade but did not pass the college entrance exam, so she applied and went to Malaysia as an export laborer in 2005. She took out a đ20 million loan with her mother as a cosigner. Ms. Wali received only đ4 million to bring to Malaysia for necessities.

Low wages in the Chinese Malaysian garment factory that she worked in led her to end the contract early. Ms. Wali then escaped to a small Malay Muslim garment factory, where she worked for a sympathetic Malaysian employer. Ms. Wali explained why this Malay owner hired her, aiding her in breaking the law that forbade foreign workers from changing employers midstream in their contracts:

> He asked for my papers, and I showed him my visa and a copy of my passport because the original was held by the Chinese owner. I told him about my whole situation. Then he took pity on me because of our shared Muslim faith and hired me to work there, also stitching and earning by piece rates. But I earned four times more than what I earned in that Chinese factory.

A Malay Muslim shop owner turned a blind eye to the law and hired Ms. Wali, an undocumented Chăm Muslim, thus creating a third space for her. But her time working for this Malay garment shop owner was short due to police harassment. Ms. Wali recounted a traumatic experience:

> I worked there for several months, but not having papers, I was very afraid I would be caught by policemen when I was walking from home to work, which was about one kilometer. My fear was not about having to pay the fine but about being put in jail. One time, while walking to work, two policemen stopped me and asked for papers. I gave them the papers, but they said that my papers were expired. I used the excuse that my uncle was renewing them for me, and then I dialed my friend's number to ask him to pretend to be my uncle to talk to these policemen. Still, the policemen did not believe me. Then, at wit's end, I "threatened" them by saying, "OK, you can put me in jail now, but if something happens to me, you will be responsible for my imprisonment." The two policemen then talked to each other in low voices, and then one turned around and said, "We will let you go with a fine of RM50." I paid the fine and was happy because this was better than being put in jail. Then I came home, shaken, and was sick for two days. From then on, I did not dare to go out in the street.

Police extortion of money from vulnerable undocumented workers is a refrain I heard from many interviewees of all five ethnic groups. In this case, Ms. Wali's language ability, negotiation skills, and creativity, getting her friend

Physical Third Space Empowerment

to pretend to be her uncle, successfully got her out of trouble at that moment. But this traumatic encounter with the Malay police had left her very shaken and led her to decide to return to Vietnam through Thailand and Cambodia by foot and by car.

Ms. Wali recounted her harrowing escape, relying on leads and contacts from her Chăm friends:

> We had six to seven people in the car. The road was completely empty with forests on both sides. We had heard about vicious robbers who robbed and killed people. That's why we were so worried. [From Malaysia] We traveled two days and two nights and arrived at the Cambodia-Vietnam border [passing through Thailand]. Then, I was really scared, . . . knee deep, wading in the mud, using a cane to find our way. [It was] very arduous. . . . After crossing the border [from Cambodia to Vietnam], everyone was completely exhausted. Then I called my father to come and pick me up, using the phone that my father gave me before I left for Malaysia. . . . Everyone in my village, knowing that I had escaped through the Thailand route, had prayed for me to survive the dangers on the road. When I got home, everyone was there to greet me . . . a full house!

Still she did not escape debt, which followed her home: the escape cost her RM2,000 (over US$600, for which she had to borrow RM1,000 from friends), and she still had đ20 million (about US$1,250) in labor export debt to pay off.

The Chăm's Gendered Division of Labor in Third Space

Another Chăm story exposes the gendered division of labor in third spaces. Ms. Sayad, forty years old, and her husband, Mr. Aahil, also forty years old, had been going to Malaysia by car (via Cambodia and Thailand) to make a living since 2001, at times with their four sons. Their nomadic lifestyle, a Chăm trait, differentiates them from the other four ethnic groups. In 2013, we interviewed Ms. Sayad and Mr. Aahil at their home in An Giang. Going to work in Malaysia was a last resort for them to make a living, Mr. Aahil shared: "We had no work here in Vietnam; we worked doing manual labor, making đ80–90,000 per day, not enough money to put our children in school. We have no land, no money. So that's why we have been forced to go to Malaysia."

Arriving in Malaysia for the first time in 2001, they worked "underground for three years" on tourist visas. "We bought one-way tickets from Vietnam to Malaysia with a tourist visa, not a working one," Mr. Aahil recounted. "So, when we were caught by the police, we pleaded with them about our hard lives, and many times they sympathized with us and let us go." His mentioning

144 CHAPTER 5

that he bought a one-way ticket to Malaysia implies that he would stay in Thailand (visiting Vietnamese citizens do not require a visa) for several days to renew his expired tourist visa for Malaysia, and from there he would return to Malaysia.

Once in Malaysia, this couple followed a common gendered division of labor in which men work outside and women work mostly inside the house. Ms. Sayad would sell fabrics and clothes from door to door and take care of their children at home: "In 2001, I stayed at home to take care of our sons, while my husband sold ice cream and learned to speak Malay after two to three months there. There are some similarities between the Malay and Chăm languages, so we could guess each other's meaning when we spoke." Selling ice cream is a great option for the Chăm men but not for women because women are not allowed to sell products on the streets and in the alleyways. "Ice cream was delivered directly to our rental unit, so it was very convenient," said Mr. Aahil. On the other hand, female sellers can go door-to-door selling clothes, and Malaysian women will open their doors to them, but not to men.

These commercial activities are not permitted in Malaysia with a tourist visa: "We are not afraid while staying in Malaysia, because we had tourist visas. But we are always nervous when peddling around the streets, because that is illegal," Mr. Aahil explained. The local community, however, supported his selling of ice cream: "I left the house at 7 a.m. to sell ice cream in front of some high schools. Some high schools permitted me to sell it, but some others did not, so I wandered into some alleys to sell directly to households." Thanks to their language connection and the fact that Mr. Aahil had learned to speak some Malay after the first three months in Malaysia, the police who walked the beat let him off the hook: "When I got caught by the Malaysian police, I begged and explained our difficult circumstances to them. Then they understood my situation, had compassion, and allowed me to continue selling ice cream." The similarity between the Chăm and Malay writings (both are based on Arabic) and the fact that the Chăm have been careful to preserve their language has thus proved crucial in sustaining the Chăm's third spaces, because it helps them communicate with and receive support from the local Malays when they are working in Malaysia. Moreover, having similar languages can also support their religious connection, consistent with Weber's argument.[59]

As these accounts indicate, the Chăm follow circular migration patterns, relying on whatever forms of transportation are available to take them to Malaysia. They may start by using cars and then continue on buses or even on foot. I interviewed several families engaging in this migration pattern. Ms.

Physical Third Space Empowerment   145

Kinza made a long trip to Malaysia, passing through Cambodia and Thailand, by car with her relatives. She described her first journey to Malaysia:

> I went there on surface streets, going from Cambodia to Thailand and then to Malaysia. I went with my aunt and a group of Chăm people, so I was not afraid. It took us three days and three nights by car to get to Malaysia. I had another aunt living in Malaysia. When I got there, I was sent by an employment agency to work in different companies, but I had to renew my [tourist] visa every month when it expired. At first, I worked at a phone company, then a pesticide company . . . but had never been able to save.

Once in Malaysia, she worked for six years for many companies in various third spaces using a tourist visa, similar to many other Chăm. She accumulated social capital in Malaysia such as language skills, networks, and trust with Malaysians. She got along well with the Malaysian Muslims. "The Malaysians love the Chăm," she told me.

Mr. Vijaya, a thirty-four-year-old man who has three children, followed in the footsteps of his parents, who sold used clothes and fabrics. In 1999–2000, he drove to Malaysia via Thailand alone by car. He described his journeys using the Vietnamese expression "*đi đường dưới, đi chui*," which means traveling on "surface streets and underground." Once there, he relied on his relatives to help him find a place to stay and then lend him money to buy a cart to sell ice cream on the street and in front of elementary and high schools. When we talked in 2012, Mr. Vijaya explained how he worked in Malaysia for two to seven months selling ice cream, during which time he would renew his one-month tourist visa many times by going to Thailand as a tourist and then reentering Malaysia. These transnational patterns—circular, ground, air—are beyond Taylor's "geographical agency," which includes migration patterns within Vietnam only.

Risks of Physical Third Spaces

Paradoxically, though, while physical third spaces have enabled circular migration among the Chăm and reinforced their cultural and religious ties to the Malay world, moving within these spaces is fraught with risks and incurs real costs. Mr. Vijaya told us about police raids in some areas with Chăm concentration:

> I was working underground trying to make enough money to return to Vietnam but got caught. They found that I had overstayed my visa and put me in jail for three months. In general, when caught by the police, we were told to buy plane tickets home. Some had money and were able to buy plane tickets

146 CHAPTER 5

home; some were waiting for the Vietnamese embassies to bail them out, but this took a long time. So, during that time, we were put in jail for two to three months.

In another example, Mr. Aahil explained how the police's planned raids had forced him and his family to run for their lives:

> They would come to the areas where they knew there were Malay households housing the Chăm and would search and take those without proper papers to jail. We faced many raids when we ran for our lives, hiding here and there, leaving our belongings behind and carrying only our children. . . . We only returned home when the police were gone.

As Mr. Wasti explained, not all Malay police were supportive of the Chăm Muslims: they could be unforgiving during planned raids but more tolerant on their beat. Mr. Aahil's ice cream cart was illegal without a work permit or a business license, but it was serving the local communities, a licit third space supported by local residents and the high schools. Overall, these risks have affected the Chăm men, who work outside, more than the women. Mr. Wasti elaborated: "Many Chăm men buy ice cream and push a cart around to sell ice cream. Sometimes they also sell fabrics. But at night, many men sleep in the forest [to hide]. They don't dare to sleep in the residential areas because their passports are expired. In the morning, they resume their activities: peddling around, buying and selling ice cream."

There were more opportunities for the Chăm women. According to Mr. Wasti, many Malaysian households hire the Chăm women to work as maids doing household chores, such as washing clothes and dishes, and to take care of children. Dish washing is important for the strict Muslim halal diet, as dishes must be washed by Muslims. Moreover, local Malaysian jobbers and subcontractors would also recruit Chăm women after they got to know these hard-working Muslim migrants. Mr Wasti said: "Sometimes, the Chăm women got called to work in garment factories. Through word of mouth, some people got connected with these Chăm women, and if both sides agreed, these recruiters would prepare a passport for those Chăm women." My interviewees mentioned the use of fake papers (such as passports and work permits) that had been prepared so the Chăm could be employed as factory workers. This is similar to the "real but fake" documents in the Indonesian Riau Islands, provided by local state officials who thus play a vital role facilitating temporary labor migrants across the borderlands among Indonesia, Singapore, and Malaysia.[60]

In sum, I found three main characteristics of the Chăm way, confirmed by my fieldwork interviews. First, their many migration patterns—circular,

Physical Third Space Empowerment 147

underground, rural–urban nationwide, and transnational—add complexity to what Taylor termed "geographical agency." Second, their language skills have enabled their actions in various physical third spaces, thanks to the similarity between the Chăm and Malay writing. The Chăm are keen on preserving their language, which helps with religious training and communicating with and receiving support from the local Malays when the Chăm are working there. This is consistent with Weber's argument about the strong connection between the Malay and the Chăm, not only in religion and culture but also in their respective writings, which adapted the use of the Arabic alphabet. Third, the Chăm's peripatetic lifestyle can result in low educational achievement and high dropout rates for their children. The parents' constant traveling can disrupt school attendance or prevent the parents from directly overseeing their children's education. Mr. Aahil and Ms. Sayad took their infants with them while traveling in Malaysia, where Ms. Sayad sold fabrics and clothes door-to-door and took care of the children. When the children were older, the couple asked an aunt to look after them to ensure that they could go to school. In this case, the children got an education but without parental supervision.

Interestingly, Chăm children can also be educated in Cambodia, thanks to the historical, cultural, and religious connections to the Chăm communities there (chapter 1). Mr. Wasti's story shed light on the importance of the Chăm communities in Cambodia. After his parents passed away, there was a period of seven years when he and his family resettled in the Chăm community in Cambodia. There, his children attended a Cambodian elementary school up to grade six, learning Khmer in the morning and Islamic faith in the afternoon. Mr. Wasti himself also learned to speak Khmer and practiced speaking it with the Cambodian customers who bought his wares.

Comparative Remarks

These physical third spaces of dissent, informed by each ethnic group's access to economic and cultural resources, allow for survival and success that may or may not involve the LBS system or social networks. Survival has everything to do with the workers themselves who navigate the system based on their cultural resources and creativity. Cultural resources (especially transnational networks and religious and language affinities) opened up more physical third space for the well-connected Chăm and Khmer than for the Kinh, the Hoa, or the Hrê.

The Khmer and the Chăm, with deep historical, cultural, religious, and language connections to neighboring Southeast Asian countries, have the most diverse forms of physical third spaces. These networks and spaces allow

148   CHAPTER 5

them to challenge or bypass the LBS system, to survive, and at times even
to thrive. In these physical spaces, migrants transcend the duality of legal/
illegal by receiving tacit acceptance of the community in which they live and
work.

Of the five ethnic groups, the Chăm are the most mobile people, bypassing
the LBS system and traveling the "Chăm way." This level of mobility brought
them the most wide-ranging forms of physical third spaces (the school gates,
the factory floor, and the homes of the Malays) thanks to their historical
and religious affinity with Malay employers and local communities. The
"Khmer way" also led that ethnic group to diverse forms of physical third
spaces thanks to their historical and religious connections with Cambodia.
Learning to speak Thai also expanded their pathways to work seasonally in
Thailand.

The Hrê, unlike the Chăm and the Khmer, have limited forms of physical third space, having no religious or cultural connections outside of their
mountainous communes in Vietnam. Their forays into work outside their
legal contracts, whereby they became undocumented in Malaysia, were short-
lived because they were sent back to Quảng Ngãi promptly. Clearly, a lack of
a linguistic connection to their Malaysian hosts minimized and shortened
their opportunities to create a space outside the LBS system.

The Kinh, as the largest group, have a history of labor export dating back
to the socialist era. While the socialist migrants and their children created a
space for survival, showcasing their cultural hybridity in two centers in the
former Soviet Bloc European countries, the Kinh and the Hoa migrants in
Malaysia created physical spaces of dissent right on the factory premises (the
toilet stalls, the vault to hide extra products) or by working in local Malay
businesses as undocumented migrant workers. They have to rely on the Kinh
networks because they have no language or religious connections with the
Malays.

Different gender roles are enacted by these ethnic groups while engaging
in these physical third spaces. Many of the Chăm and the Khmer, though
working illegally, were accepted and hired by the local communities in which
they stayed and worked. For both groups, the women's space tends to be
inside the house and the men's outside the house.

Of the ethnic Hrê, mostly men went to work in Malaysia while the women
stayed at home in Quảng Ngãi to take care of their children and the elderly.
The Hrê male workers' native places of origin led to support networks in
Malaysia (for example, the "brothers of Ba Tơ district"). Their strong communal social relations remain intact, especially in helping fellow Hrê who

Physical Third Space Empowerment 149

were sent home early due to sickness or working as undocumented migrants in Malaysia.

For the Kinh and the Hoa, while there is some gender equity between women and men in terms of their abilities to go to work in Malaysia, a common gendered division of labor reflects management's preferences: compliant and nimble-fingered female workers for assembly jobs and male workers for hard labor and construction jobs.

There are limits to community acceptance in these physical third spaces: at best, they are only temporary, allowing undocumented migrants to save enough money to return home. It is important not to romanticize these gray areas, or the use of "real but fake" papers to work with tourist visas, because without proper documentation the migrants risk police raids, imprisonment, money extortion, harassment in the legal "first" space, and even deportation. These forms of precarity affect all five groups. In short, the current LBS system fails to protect these migrants in Malaysia to cope with extenuating circumstances that are, at times, beyond their control.

6 Metaphorical Third Space Empowerment

While physical third space reflects the significance and manifestation of illegal and licit "gray" areas, metaphorical third spaces—real and imagined—offer nuances that explain the negotiations, utterances, encounters, and other forms of resistance of the five ethnic groups. In this chapter, I describe how former socialist migrants and their children in Warsaw and Prague have created and maintained a hybrid culture—a fusion of the Vietnamese and respective receiving country's cultures—a liminal third space that can be contradictory and ambiguous, yet offers strategies for survival.[1] Then I turn to the labor export migrants, their parents, and the ethnic village heads and religious leaders who have created metaphorical third spaces in the form of discourses of dissent that mock the labor brokerage state (LBS) for the shortcomings of the labor export policy.

The Kinh Migrants in Eastern Europe

I visited two Vietnamese enclaves in Eastern Europe to understand how the former socialist Kinh migrants (now residents or citizens of their receiving country) and their extended families negotiate a hybrid cultural third space that draws on their religious practices and imaginations to create their own identities.

In Poland, many Kinh stall owners in Marywilska embed a religious metaphor in their places of business to establish their identities in connection to their Polish customers. The huge portraits of Pope John Paul II in a half dozen nail shops in Marywilska indicate a Catholic connection between the Kinh shop owners and their Polish customers.

Metaphorical Third Space Empowerment   151

The hybrid cultural space has been created by the next generation, the children of the socialist Kinh migrants. Walking around, I met a precocious young girl who was speaking Polish and playing dolls with her two girlfriends. When I asked in Vietnamese where her parents were, she responded in fluent Vietnamese with a northern accent. She then led me to her parents' corner shoe stall. Mr. and Mrs. Giây were very friendly and spoke to me in Vietnamese while closing up their shop. Originally from Hà Bắc province, they had come to Poland twenty years earlier and had lived there since. They focused on their work to make money and to raise their family in Poland, considering it a "social space" for upward mobility. Mrs. Giây noted that "the Vietnamese community here is very good. They have a Vietnamese language school on the weekend, and the Vietnamese Embassy takes care of the Vietnamese community here."[2]

In a phở (noodle) restaurant in Prague, Ms. Liên, the ambitious daughter of the restaurant's owners (Mr. Sơn and Ms. Lành), inhabits a third space similar to the one inhabited by Mr. and Mrs. Giây's daughter: she speaks fluent Vietnamese (also with a northern accent) to her parents and other migrants but switches easily to Czech or English when local and global customers come to dine.

Whether in a stall of Marywilska bazaar, a Prague restaurant, or another location, the offspring of the Kinh socialist migrants construct hybrid cultures that do not belong to any one of these countries but instead are an in-between third space, or a hybrid cultural third space.[3] In these spaces, these young adults can use their talents to become Vietnamese professionals in Prague and Warsaw.[4] They aspire to earn postgraduate university degrees in Western European universities. Ms. Liên studies accounting in Berlin and hopes to obtain her MBA in Australia or another country in the West. She expressed her desire to return to Prague, where her parents live and where she was born and grew up, and find a job there after earning her degrees.[5]

Another manifestation of cultural hybridity in these European enclaves is through food culture. Prague's Sapa commercial center, for example, has an especially vibrant food scene. Many restaurants, food, and drink stalls are scattered throughout the food court, operated by middle-aged women and men from the north of Vietnam. Everywhere there are men on bikes delivering food, one hand holding a tray with bowls of soup or cups of coffee and the other hand holding the bike handle, as they ride skillfully through the narrow alleys of the enclosed bazaar of clothes, shoes, bags, and toys.

The restaurant, food, and coffee carts in Sapa evoke a metaphorical third space. They offer inexpensive and satisfying northern Vietnamese cuisine of a local Viet-Prague community that hails from the same hometown: Hải

Phòng, a port town in the north. This "Vietnamese essence in the heart of Prague" is wistfully appreciated by the Vietnamese visitors from all over the world who stop by these places to get a taste of home away from home. A sign that read "Bún Cá Hải Phòng" ("Hải Phòng Fish Noodles") caught my eye. When I walked inside the restaurant, I was greeted by a friendly middle-aged woman who was selling a sweet concoction (*chè*) and other specialty snacks from her hometown of Hải Phòng.[6] She said that she had come to Prague ten years before. Parked in front of this restaurant was a man with a makeshift coffee cart adorned by a beautiful handwritten sign that read "Café Gọi" (which roughly means "call for coffee") and that gave his mobile number. People would call and he would deliver coffee anywhere within the confines of Sapa center. The cart owner was also from Hải Phòng. According to Ms. Đào, the delivery men assume this job to supplement their income or because they do not have enough money to have their own stalls. People from the same hometown support each other, and the showcasing of specialty foods from Hải Phòng suggests that there is a following of fellow Hải Phòng migrants who seek out the cuisine from their hometown. The cluster of restaurants, sweet desserts, and coffee carts—a complete dining experience—represents the significance of native place bonding.

Migrants' and Families' Uses of Mimicries

Bhabha argues that third space has two interpretations: the space where the oppressed plot their liberation (the whispering corners of the tavern or the bazaar), and the space where the oppressed and the oppressor are able to come together, free (perhaps only momentarily) of oppression itself, embodied in their particularity.[7]

I found that most discourses of dissent of the five ethnic groups I studied fall into the second category, where the oppressed (especially the ethnic minorities) and the oppressor (the Malaysian employers, the Kinh officials and recruiters) come together in some particular settings that may appear momentarily as "free of oppression." But precisely in these moments, the migrant workers strike back using various form of metaphorical third space.

Migrants and their families have used different forms of mimicry as metaphorical third space of dissent, a strategy that is intentional and subversive yet safe in the context of unequal power relations with the LBS. In this context, *subversive mimicry* refers to the act of citing state policies (such as the goals of eliminating hunger and lifting citizens up from poverty) to fight back; *ironic mimicry* can be employed to strengthen solidarity (such as joining together

Figure 10. Socialist Kinh migrants in Prague in 2017 sell fish noodles, coffee, and other goods in this cultural third space. Credit: Author

to default on loans) in ways that the state has trouble banning or that are too subtle to be suppressed or punished by the LBS state; and *performance mimicry* refers to actions that reveal how hollow the state promises to the migrants in poor districts are (unattained goals of prosperity with houses, buffaloes, and motorbikes). Overall, these ironic or mocking expressions challenge the hegemony of the LBS system.[8]

The Kinh-Hoa Migrants

The Kinh comprise the largest group who went to work in Malaysia. Many Kinh-Hoa migrants create forms of third space using subversive mimicry and ironic mimicry.

154   CHAPTER 6

A nationwide study found that about 10 percent of all migrant returnees from Malaysia, mostly Kinh and Hoa, did not repay their debts.[9] My sample had a higher ratio: 33 percent (twelve migrants out of thirty-six) still had outstanding debts after they returned, and while they were working in Malaysia, many of them did not use their remittances to pay back their debts in the first year, as Hoang and Yeoh have indicated.[10] Instead, my sample shows that even in the first year, over 30 percent of Kinh and the Hoa migrants sent money home for their families to spend and to invest in a means of production (to make a living) instead of paying back their loans.

In a few cases of debtors who had property (such as houses or land being used as collateral), the local government would go to their houses to demand debt payments. Ms. Kim-Ly, an ethnic Hoa migrant returnee, completed her three-year work contract in Malaysia and returned to Vietnam on time, but she still owed đ7 million. The local debt collection team visited her and her mother at their home every month to collect her loan payment, but they always had to negotiate with her:

> Well, there was Ms. C from the bank who came to my house to collect money. On the twelfth of every month, she would come over. Today, she came early— the eighth—so I have no money to give her. Every month, I have to negotiate to pay from đ150,000 to đ200,000, depending on how much money I make each month at home by assembling ready-cut fabrics into shirts or blouses for a retail store nearby.

She appeared to have a steady and stable job, as when I visited her house, I saw piles of cut fabrics waiting to be assembled into clothing on a table next to her industrial sewing machine, a prized investment purchased using her remittances. Clearly, she had benefited from the LBS loan and had invested in a means of production before paying her debt.

Many relied on their parents, who were often signers or cosigners on their loans and at times acted as "competing authorities" in dealing with the official state authorities who came to collect debt payments. This strategy has been shown to be effective, because the parents have nothing to lose from defaulting on a trust-based loan (given under the premise that they were poor and had no land to use as collateral). Even when they used land as collateral, the parents often invoked ill health as a reason for not being able to repay the loans.

Here are some expressions of subversive mimicries. In three of the twelve cases in which migrants did not own land and so borrowed money on a trust basis, the parents took out the loans instead of the migrants themselves. Ms. Tiên still had đ4 million in outstanding debt when she returned: she had

Metaphorical Third Space Empowerment 155

managed to pay đ6 million in her first year, but she returned home early because her company went bankrupt after she completed her first year. She expected the "bank for the poor" (Social Policy Bank) to forgive her parents' loan because her household was classified as poor. Using a subversive mimicry technique that migrants often rely on to avoid repaying loans whereby they refer to local authorities' explanations of loan policies, she cited a commune official: "For migrant returnees from poor households who cannot repay the debts, the loans will not accrue interest for one year (*khoanh lại*). After that, if the households are still poor, then the families can reapply to be considered for payment postponement." Ms. Tiên strengthened her case by stressing the fact that it was the company bankruptcy that sent her home, not her own making.

The mother of Ms. Mai, a migrant returnee, signed the loan paper on a trust basis, so the responsibility to pay the loan was on her mother alone, since Ms. Mai had already left for Malaysia. By the time Ms. Mai returned, she had paid off over half of her loan; she then used subversive mimicry effectively, citing the loan repayment policies that she had gleaned from a local authority in her commune, to avoid paying the remaining portion of her debt. Ms. Mai argued with the local official that Social Policy Bank is the "bank for the poor" and that her situation fit that definition. Ms. Hạnh, another Kinh returnee, took out a loan with her father also on a trust basis. She still owed about đ9 million on a đ17 million loan but dragged her feet in paying this remaining amount. In front of a local cadre who escorted me to this interview, Ms. Hạnh showed knowledge of the loan policies and complained about still having to pay the monthly interest even when the bank had "circled" her loan (so that it would not accrue interest). At that point, the cadre (who escorted me) spoke up to explain to her:

> It is because the bank is still assessing your loan and has not yet come to a final decision. Once they arrive at a final decision, completely "circling" the debt, then interest will stop accruing and the debt repayments will be postponed for five years.

In these two cases in which parents signed the loan or were cosigners on it, the local banks seemed to have the flexibility to assess the migrant families' ability to pay, stop the interest accumulation, and postpone the loan payments from one to five years. These vague and inconsistent loan policies confused the returnees and their families but empowered the LBS system, which has the final say on these loans. However, when the returnees pointed out these aspects of the loan policy in front of me (a Vietnamese American), the local officials accompanying me were put on the spot and called on to defend

156 CHAPTER 6

their policies and respond to the returnees' inquiries. Regardless of what actually transpired after this interview, Ms. Hạnh used subversive mimicry effectively and obtained an official response about her loan. Although she did not receive a guarantee that she would not have to pay interest, much less that her debt would be forgiven, she managed to learn more about the terms of the loan, specifically that a five-year postponement in repayment was possible. This was useful knowledge that she could parlay in her next round of challenging the state bank's authority.

Even without knowledge of the law, migrant returnees used irony, lamenting their impoverished situations and their parents' poor health to justify not paying back their loan. Mr. Ngữ came home after working only one year due to a lack of full-time work in the assigned factory in Malaysia. His mother had signed the loan paper for đ19 million on a trust basis with the Social Policy Bank, as with Ms. Mai's and Ms. Hạnh's families, Mr. Ngữ's family did not have land to use as collateral. But unlike in the case of those two families, his mother still owed the whole loan amount. He did not refer to loan policies but told me that his mother did not intend to pay it back and that her line of defense was that she was in poor health. The local officials knew that he stayed at home to take care of his frail mother, helping her with her stall selling breakfast foods and earning a pittance every day (he received đ20,000 out of the đ100,000 daily profit). Thus far, they had not come to collect loan payments, because they knew it was impossible for him to repay his debt.

Other migrants used ironic mimicry against the recruitment company and refused to pay their debts. Mr. Ngãi, a Kinh worker, signed for a loan of đ30 million and received support from the local labor department because his family was classified as a poor household. He (and other men from his hometown) returned home early because it did not work out with the company that he contracted with, and although he made numerous requests to be assigned a new job with another company, he received no help from Sona, the recruitment company that had sent him there. When he returned to Vietnam in 2003, he still owed đ8 million. He then dragged his feet for ten years, during which he worked two jobs, one as a sous-chef at a restaurant and another as a garment worker on the side, making about đ6 million per month. Still he refused to pay off his remaining debt and kept calling Sona to demand that it represent and support him. But he got no response from the company. So, when the loan officials started to come to his house to collect the debt, he had a good reason to drag his feet, pointing his finger at the unaccountable recruitment company: "As a labor service company," he explained, "it should create conditions for the workers to work overseas and for the returnees to find jobs upon returning home."

Metaphorical Third Space Empowerment   157

Having the linguistic skills to be able to speak the language of the bosses—such as Malay, Chinese, or English—is another way migrants are able to create metaphorical third spaces in which to fight for their rights. In the context of domestic work, Chin discusses how female domestic workers in Malaysia use strategies such as talking back to an employer in a subtle way to take advantage of an employer's sense of gratitude for their service.[11] In the context of factory work in Malaysia, talking back to the employers requires knowledge of and an ability to speak the language that the bosses speak. Eight Kinh and Hoa interviewees mentioned the power of language in negotiating with their bosses.[12] The migrants who could speak some Mandarin clearly had an edge because they could bargain directly with their bosses, many of whom spoke Chinese.

Ms. Kim-Ly, a Hoa, reflected on the power of knowing another language in order to fight back, lamenting her limited knowledge of Mandarin: "My mother is Chinese, but I consider myself Vietnamese. I regretted that I studied English instead of Chinese before leaving for Malaysia. When I got to Malaysia, those workers who knew Chinese could communicate with the Chinese employers, and they had advantage over me. If you can't speak Chinese, you are lost to them." Ms. Kim-Ly further explained how workers used language to stop management's verbal abuse of them:

> There was a lot of work pressure. We had a very mean-spirited and aggressive female boss. When she got mad, she became agitated, yelled out loud, and threw things at us to scare us, even though she knew that the Vietnamese are very resilient and not afraid. There were times when I could no longer stand her oppression: I talked back to her in protest, because I know some Chinese.

Two other interviewees complained about the ineffective language training in their orientation classes and elaborated on the benefits of learning to properly speak the language of the country one was going to work in. Mr. Thức learned English during his two-month orientation class but had no chance to practice it at work because his employer was Chinese Malaysian. He ended up learning Malay and used broken English and broken Malay to communicate when he was working abroad in Malaysia. Still he was shortchanged: "I didn't have enough language to talk back to the boss when I worked ten hours of overtime but they counted and paid me for only eight. This also happened to guest workers from other countries." Mr. Ngãi revealed how difficult it was to learn English in such a short period of time and offered advice on learning a foreign language:

> I studied English for two months for a certificate. But in such a short time, I only learned basic things. I couldn't communicate at the company that I was

158 CHAPTER 6

assigned to work. . . . When I returned to Vietnam, my advice to those who were waiting to go to Malaysia was that learning to speak another language is the best way to spend seed money [vốn] before going. If they only learn to speak a little, then they will have a difficult time in understanding what is being said to them. One needs to prepare well in the language so as not to be shortchanged in Malaysia.

The Hrê Migrants

The Hrê demonstrated a more robust use of mimicry than did the Kinh and the Hoa. In my fieldwork in Quảng Ngãi, I mostly met and interviewed the parents of current or former migrants, since the migrants were either working in Malaysia or doing seasonal farm work or factory work in other provinces of Vietnam. Like the Kinh and Hoa examples, most Hrê families I interviewed had dragged their feet when it came to paying off the principal loan amounts, citing poverty as their reason when officials came to their houses to demand payment. Thus they effectively used ironic mimicry.

I was able to obtain valuable internally circulated information on the Hrê migrants who returned to Vietnam prematurely. Thirty-five Hrê, mostly men from Ba Tơ district, had returned, and they all had outstanding debts with the Social Policy Bank.[13] Most of the outstanding debts were principal, because the bank already had deducted the monthly interest electronically from the workers' paychecks when they were working in Malaysia. According to Đinh Thị Phương Lan, the best repayment ratio was 50 percent of the total amount of a đ29 million loan in 2015.[14] Those who found jobs upon returning to their villages still refused to repay their debts.[15]

The Hrê have used their remittances for their families' needs instead of paying off their debts. Remittances have been used to pay health care bills, to fix or build houses, to add a storage unit for warehousing acacia trees, to buy buffaloes, to buy more land and acacia tree seedlings, and to buy farm equipment that could be rented out to generate income. In 2012 I talked to Ms. Chi, whose husband, Mr. Tuấn, had been working in a sheet-glass factory in Malaysia for the third year of his contract. When Mr. Tuấn lamented that he was missing their two sons and wanted to come home early, she tried to convince him to finish the three-year contract so that he would get the free plane ticket home. Meanwhile, she had used most of his remittances, đ35 million, to buy acacia tree seedlings and to pay family expenses, saving only a small amount to pay the loan interest.[16]

Dreams of prosperity and consumerism in which houses, buffaloes, and motorbikes figure largely have been concocted for the Hrê in recruitment

Metaphorical Third Space Empowerment 159

Figure 11. This house, built in 2012, was funded by remittances. Credit: Author

materials and newspaper accounts of the labor export program. During my fieldwork in Quảng Ngãi between 2011 and 2013, I still saw many buffaloes ploughing the provinces' beautiful rice terraces, but as acacia trees invaded the fields, the rice terraces began disappearing as if they were being burned by corrosive chemicals. The recruitment materials' suggestions that these rewards can be theirs speak to Hrê dreams of owning consumer products (motorbikes), possessing the means of livelihood (buffaloes), and securing status symbols (newer and bigger houses). These dreams also triggered peer pressure, as they saw their neighborhood friends signing the loan papers to work in Malaysia for three years.

In one of my unescorted field trips, I had an in-depth interview with Ms. Oanh in Sơn Hà district and saw firsthand how these dreams affected her twenty-year-old son, Mr. Khôi. Upon entering her dirt-floor home, I saw several big photos, encased in glass and lined up on a wall, of Mr. Khôi dressed nicely and standing proudly next to his motorbike. I saw many color photos like these throughout my field trips in Quảng Ngãi province: these dreams were vividly rendered on the walls of the parents' houses in images showing off their sons standing proudly next to their prized possessions.[17] The photo of Mr. Khôi hung up on the walls of his parents' house is a kind of "performance" mimicry, an expression of the goal of the labor export policy that renders it hollow against the backdrop of a dirt-floor house whose owners are in poverty.

160 CHAPTER 6

And the Hrê do spend money on consumer items: after all, they also want comfort in life. Đinh Thị Phương Lan confirmed: "The families that received remittances bought new family appliances and lived comfortably." Throughout my fieldwork in Quảng Ngãi, I found that parents also used remittances to buy items such as motorbikes and furniture. I witnessed firsthand the usefulness of motorbikes in mountainous Quảng Ngãi. Owning a motorbike gives a Hrê household greater mobility on very badly rutted roads, destroyed by huge tree-transporting trucks, to go to markets, schools, and hospitals. And families were also feasting when they had money, consuming "beef and Heineken beer."[18]

The state tacitly accepted the refusal of the Hrê to pay back their loans, and the local government was able to cover their defaulting. At the provincial level, Mr. Võ Duy Yên told me that the overall picture of labor export was not as grave as it seemed. He said that bad debts accounted for less than 5 percent of the total state funding for labor export and that the Quảng Ngãi People's Committee had enough revenue to cover this. However, while it is unclear whether the Quảng Ngãi People's Committee (local government) reimbursed the central government for unpaid loans, the Quảng Ngãi leaders did intend to forgive the Hrê's debt.[19]

Local officials admitted that the debt of early returnees who defaulted on their loans had been forgiven. According to Võ Duy Yên,

Many Hrê felt bad and did not come to the [employment] center to close their contracts because they had initiated the [early] return. We in Quảng Ngãi province do not want to take over people's land. And so we freeze the debts and stop the accumulation of interest. Eventually we will have to forgive these debts.

Mr. Triệu, a Kinh official, also tacitly legitimized the practice of loan default: "For the ones who sent money home, if their families were facing financial difficulties, there is no need to repay the loan installment. They should prioritize paying their families' medical bills and fixing their houses before paying the bank loans." So, it seems that at least some local officials understood the situation on the ground, showed compassion, and were pragmatic in the face of rampant poverty.

The Khmer Migrants

Like the Kinh and the Hoa, many Khmer returnees transferred debt repayment responsibilities to their parents—who signed the loan papers—knowing that it would be difficult for state officials to force the parents to pay the debts. Of my Khmer interviewees, 87 percent dragged their feet on paying their

Metaphorical Third Space Empowerment   161

loans. The tactic of delaying repayment spread like a wave, as consecutive Khmer households argued that they should not have to pay if other households were not paying. This become a solidarity strategy, a form of ironic mimicry, that the state could not ban. Mr. Nguyễn Văn Lâm, director of the employment center under the labor department in An Giang, explained:

> There has been a wave, a campaign [*làn sóng phong trào*] of returnees not paying debts to the [Social Policy] bank. There are several reasons for this: first, the migrants themselves faced real adversities [in Malaysia]; second, many returnees engaged in free-riding behavior; third, the state does not have a concrete policy to collect all the debts.

I found expressions of ironic mimicry when the Khmer seemingly adopted the "master's tools" (institutions, ideology, and values) but in reality were challenging the master. They appeared, for example, to embrace the state labor export program as a way to lift themselves out of poverty, but in fact they used its own propaganda to mock and resist it.[20] During my fieldwork, I heard the words "poor," "poverty," and "hopelessness" repeatedly from both migrants and their parents. Châu Issara owed đ19 million, but because his household was poor, bank officials were no longer asking for the money. In another case, Neng Kanika still owed đ6 million to the Social Policy Bank and promised to pay on a condition: "When I have work and make money, I'll pay the debt. If not, how can I pay? My family situation is so poor." This form of ironic mimicry reminds the collectors how hollow the promise of the labor export policy is. The Khmer claimed that they were too poor to repay the loan to fight against the very labor export policy that promised to lift them out of poverty.

During my fieldwork trips, I met many parents who stayed behind when their children, who were returnees, found work by migrating to other provinces in Vietnam; these parents used their children's income to help their families instead of paying the debt. The father of Neng Angkeara, another Khmer returnee, dragged his feet on paying their debt. He had signed the loan paper to borrow đ18 million on her behalf. After two years of working in Malaysia, she sent home the whole amount for her father to pay off the debt to avoid the interest payment, but he kept đ4 million to pay his own previously incurred debt. This resulted in a đ4 million debt on the labor export loan. She said: "The Social Policy Bank sent people to demand payment, but my father said that he is old, that he has to stay at home and cannot make any money." In a follow-up interview, she told me that the bank people had given up on coming to her father's house to demand payment.

The father of another migrant worker, Châu Hùng, told me: "My son still owes đ19 million to the Social Policy Bank. He paid all the interest but has

162 CHAPTER 6

not yet paid the principal. His debt had not yet been forgiven." The interest was still accruing on the loan; the father despaired, pointing out that his son "does not work, so how can he repay the debt?"[21] But when my official escort stepped outside for a cigarette, the father told me that his son had in fact been working in a garment factory in Đồng Nai for several years and had been sending money home occasionally. So in reality, Châu Hùng did find work in another province but sent money home to help his family instead of paying off his debt. In another case, a father left behind told me that his son, Châu Tiro, and Châu Tiro's wife left home to work in a shoe factory in Ho Chi Minh City for three years. Occasionally they send some "coffee" money, about đ100,000 (about US$5), for their father.[22]

But I also had a chance to interact directly with some Hrê migrant returnees themselves, who shared with me the methods of protest they used to demand justice for the fact that the recruitment companies that sent the migrant workers abroad failed to compensate them for contract violations not of the workers' own making. Mr. Châu Rithi had worked in Malaysia for five years and had borrowed đ16 million from the Vietnamese state bank. He had repaid only đ10 million and had sent the rest of the remittances, đ22 million, to his parents. When asked why he had refused to pay the rest of his loan, Châu Rithi said: "I have no intention of paying it because when I was in Malaysia, the terms of contract that I signed were not followed. Everyone around me also refused to pay."

In another case, Mr. Châu Amnat spoke ironically about his outstanding loan and his family's worsening conditions:

> Life was not better than before my labor export experience. In fact, it got even worse because I now have to shoulder a heavy debt of đ20 million, not even a piaster paid! At the beginning, bank officials often came knocking on my door to demand payment. But no longer, since I have no money to pay. I hope that the state will postpone my debt so I can take care of my family. If it demands payment, I do not know what I will do.

The assertion that life is not better but worse is a form of powerful ironic mimicry that exposes the unfulfilled goal of the labor export policy: poverty alleviation.

One last case shows how a Khmer returnee used her knowledge of the terms of the loan policy to fight back. Ms. Neng Suvanna's loan had been signed for her by her now deceased mother: "When my mother passed away two years ago, a Social Policy Bank official told me to sign the paperwork for loan forgiveness," she explained. Because she had learned through this encounter that the death of the loan signer is one condition under which

Metaphorical Third Space Empowerment   163

debt is forgiven, when two years after her mother's passing the bank people returned to demand payment from her, she was armed with information to challenge them.

In the meantime, she had acquired skills cutting and dyeing hair from her relatives in Cambodia and aspired to open a beauty salon. Although the state bank would not lend her money for that venture, the state did tacitly accept that her loan was forgiven when it allowed her and her young daughter to visit her brother in Australia. In my follow-up interview with her in July 2014, I learned that she was able to visit her brother for three months and had subsequetly returned to An Giang.[23]

Through word of mouth, these Khmer returnees and their parents developed a sense of solidarity (when everyone was refusing to pay) and a rationale (poverty, justice) to defy debt collection, using ironic and subversive laments that had the effect of convincing the local banks to quietly write off their debts.

The Chăm Migrants and Parents' Mimicries

The Chăm returnees likewise resisted repayment of loans; in fact, of the small sample (seven cases) of Chăm families among our interviews, all had refused to repay the loans. The debtors, six parents and one worker who signed the loan documents herself, used mimicries to drag their feet. A number of the returnees, like those in other ethnic groups, feigned ignorance of their debt and unloaded all loan payment responsibilities on their parents, who often had to deal directly with the local officials.

Like other Chăm returnees, Mr. Sadat, a returnee from An Giang, placed his family's needs before debt repayment. His mother, Ms. Baqri, took out a loan for him. When I asked whether the government had come to her house to ask for debt repayment, Ms. Baqri looked sad and worried: "Not yet. . . . Most poor people do not have enough [money] to eat, never mind repaying the debt." Later I learned that Mr. Sadat had remitted đ4 million (about US$200) to his mother via Western Union, even though he did not pay a single đồng to the Social Policy Bank. Mr. Sadat then moved on with his life, scraping by to make a living. After he returned to An Giang in 2012, he remained in poverty, a day worker in construction (earning đ75,000, or about US$3, per day). In a 2014 follow-up interview with Ms. Baqri, his mother, I found out that he had been working in a wood factory in Đồng Nai province (near Ho Chi Minh City). Then, when that company faced financial difficulties, Mr. Sadat returned to the Chăm's way of life: selling shoes on the streets in Ho Chi Minh City, barely making ends meet.

164 CHAPTER 6

I found other cases of returnees who went to work in Vietnamese cities and earned income that way but refused to pay their debts. Their parents also dragged their feet. Ms. Areen finished her three-year contract in Malaysia and stayed two more years to work underground in a restaurant without a visa. Upon returning to Vietnam, she found a job in an embroidery factory in Ho Chi Minh City. Her father, a wholesaler and distributor of blankets and mosquito nets in An Giang, did earn money, but he refused to pay the loan. Her father successfully staged a stalemate on repayment; the loan existed on paper, but it was never repaid: "I still owe đ20 million, have not paid any money. Before, officials came to our house often to demand payment, but now they no longer do that."

Ms. Alvi returned to Vietnam without much savings after completing her three-year contract in an electronics factory in Johor. In 2014, she explained that she was not going to repay her loan: "I took out the loan but do not plan to repay it because I have no money."[24] Two years later, we interviewed her again and found that she still owed đ20 million.[25] But we learned further that when in Malaysia, Ms. Alvi had twice sent money home in lump sums, by pooling money with fellow Chăm migrants, instead of paying her debt.

All these cases show that migrants and their parents used ironic mimicry, citing their impoverished existence, to justify their loan defaults. As in the case of the Khmer, the Kinh authorities implicitly accepted their refusal to pay.

The Chăm migrants, who are devout Sunni Muslims, have created religious forms of metaphorical third space both as participants in the LBS system and outside of it. A number of my informants, for example, were successful in negotiating with their employers—both in Malaysia and in Vietnam—to allow them to pray at work with pay. Securing such a third space for praying was a quiet victory for them, as they tried to find a balance between work and religious practice. In short, arguing with the employers to secure the right to pray with pay, even in makeshift prayer places inside a non-Muslim factory or in a Chinese Malaysian electronic parts factory, is a form of metaphorical third space.

Daily religious practices are very significant to the Chăm Muslims. In Malaysia, gaining the right to pray at work depended on the religion of the employers. Often, the Muslim Malaysian owners would allow the Chăm Muslim migrants time to perform their shared religious duties.[26] Mr. Wasti said: "The Malay people were very gentle. They did not cause us any problems because we are also Muslim." Malay employers also made these accommodations inside their homes when the Chăm were helping with household chores, as was the case for Ms. Lodhra, who worked as a maid for a Malay family and washed dishes for them: "The boss was very kind to me. While

Metaphorical Third Space Empowerment 165

I was working, when the time came to pray, my boss prostrated to pray in his place, and I also prostrated to pray in my place. We were doing the same thing because we have the same religion: Islam."

However, the Chăm had to negotiate and at times fight with non-Muslim or Chinese management in Malaysia and Kinh employers in Vietnam for religious tolerance and prayer accommodations. They entered into a metaphorical third space when denied the ability to pray and had to find a way to create a balance among their priorities: their livelihood, religious practices, and long-term happiness. In the non-Muslim factories, they bargained for what they could get and then made up at home for prayers missed during work time, either in the morning before leaving for work or in the evening after returning home from work.

This struggle came to the fore during Ramadan, a significant month-long religious commemoration. When the non-Muslim employers did not allow them to pray at work or to take time off for Ramadan, these migrants showed flexibility and creativity with their religious practices so as to keep their jobs. Ms. Alvi was flexible when she was not allowed to pray in a Chinese Malaysian electronic parts factory: "I was the only Chăm Muslim there, so it was very difficult for me to follow our daily praying practice. So sometimes I prayed, sometimes not."

Ms. Saadi, a Chăm returnee, was creative to make up for lost praying time at work when faced with an unaccommodating Malaysian employer:

> I was not allowed to pray at work during lunch time so I made up for it by praying as soon as I got home in the late afternoon. In the evening, I prayed three times as scheduled. I accepted this way of practicing my religion because I was very happy when I could do that. I felt relaxed and didn't worry about things.

This challenge followed the migrant workers back to Vietnam. After returning to An Giang, Ms. Rihanna, nineteen years old, worked for a small Kinh shop as an inventory clerk. At first, her employer did not understand why she needed time to pray during work hours every day. But Ms. Rihanna stood up to her employer to defend her religious practices and succeeded in earning two prayer times (with pay) at work: ten minutes in the morning and ten minutes in the afternoon. Ms. Rihanna shared her feelings about being the only Chăm in this Kinh shop:

> I do feel lonely because I am the only ethnic minority [*người dân tộc*] there, but I have a place to pray. At first, they thought what I was doing was strange. I sympathize with them, because they had not seen this before and did not know about this. But now that they know, if they "forgot" about it, I will remind them about my need to have space and time to pray [with pay].

166　　　　　　　　　　　　　　CHAPTER 6

Ms. Rihanna also prayed at home to ensure that she prayed five times per day. For instance, she prayed one time early in the morning and another two times in the evening. However, while this arrangement worked out for her most of the time, Ramadan posed more difficulties, because she needed to help her mother cook for the evening meal, when the family would break their fast. During this holy season, she sought to create a balance between making a living and practicing her religion: "I only worked in the morning, because if I were to take the whole day off, I would have no money to spend. I need to make a living. I noticed that the wife and some other coworkers were not happy that I took half the day off. But after all, they only paid me for half a day's work, from 7 a.m. to 1 p.m."

Daylight fasting during Ramadan is especially challenging for migrants who do manual and physical work. Ms. Saadi (now working in Vietnam) was satisfied with her practical solution to the problem of balancing work with religious practice. She chose to work during Ramadan because her boss offered a monthly bonus for hard workers, but this meant she had to compromise on fasting: "I tried to fast during Ramadan, but there were some days when I had to eat in order to have energy to work." She was able to rest easy by taking off on other days when she could make up for lost praying time.

The Mimicries of Competing Ethnic Authorities and Religious Leaders

Village elders or religious leaders act as *competing authorities* for the Hrê, the Khmer, and the Chăm creating a third space of dissent that contravenes the law but that is nevertheless socially accepted on behalf of their peoples.[27] These "competing authorities" appeal both to the law (when needed) and to the social perceptions of activities that are considered illegal in the name of the law (such as debt defaults).

The Hrê Village Leaders

"Competing authorities" in the Hrê context include not only the village elders and the medicine men but also the village chiefs who liaise with Kinh officials. During the Vietnam-US war (1954–75), many Hrê were recruited to join the communist insurgency, and now these former Hrê cadres (and their children) hold leadership positions in their villages and communes. In this context, the Hrê commune and village leaders used their established relations with the

Metaphorical Third Space Empowerment 167

Kinh officials to engage in both ironic and subversive mimicries to protest the Kinh's LBS policies. But the Hrê compromised when they adopted the prosperity dream with promises of motorbikes and buffaloes, and imitated the consumption patterns of the Kinh, their "oppressors."

Many Hrê officials used their knowledge of the LBS system and the labor export policy to engage in ironic and subversive mimicry to defend their fellow Hrê who had worked as migrants. In 2012, Ms. Đinh Thị Phương Lan described the vicious cycle of indebtedness that many Hrê found themselves caught in after they borrowed money to go to work in Malaysia:

> If they had already incurred medical debts before borrowing to go to Malaysia, then it becomes very difficult for them to escape poverty, having to pay two debts. So, I've been working with the Social Policy Bank to forgive about 50 percent of their debts [the debt to go to Malaysia], as it is impossible for them to pay both debts.

Her ironic mimicry, which mocks the state policy line about how the labor export program is a means of escaping poverty, was powerful because she had intimate knowledge of the poverty in her district. Her stating that loans should be partially forgiven was subversive, because after establishing that the labor export policy had not helped the Hrê escape poverty, as a bureaucrat in the LBS, she came up with a feasible solution that the state could afford to compensate for the failure of its policy.

Other Hrê commune and village leaders also used subversive mimicry to protect their fellow villagers' welfare. In 2012 I attended meetings between a Kinh official (Nguyễn Văn Triệu, head of the office of the Ministry of Labor, Invalids, and Social Affairs in Ba Tơ district) and the Hrê from three communes in the district. In one of those meetings, Mr. Văn Thanh (one of the three village heads) stood up for his fellow villagers' rights:

> In my village, there were ten who went to work in Malaysia. Three have returned and seven are still there. The seven have worked in different places, not in a single place. For the three who stayed in the same place, each was able to repay all the debt (over đ23 million per person). For the others, I know that if they made money, they sent it home. If they didn't make money, they didn't send it home. For those who wanted to renew their contracts, they came home first to finish the paperwork; then they got permission to return to Malaysia.

Clearly, this village head knew the rules of the labor export policy and defended the actions of the Hrê workers in his village who followed the law and sent money home when they could. He used subversive mimicry to show that most Hrê workers complied with the rules and to imply that the state

168 CHAPTER 6

had not. He reminded the state that when it was arranged so that Hrê could work together in the same place and stay together in the same hostel, they were able to support each other, pool their money, and repay all their debts. This condition was critically important, especially to the Hrê, who had left their villages to work in another country for the first time. He implied that the migrants could not be held to blame when the state failed to fulfill its side of the deal and enforce the terms of migrants' contracts.

In response to a Kinh official who asked for recommendations to improve the labor export program, another village head, Mr. Văn Đô, pointed out how hollow the state's promises were. He delivered a passionate speech directly to the Kinh officials, asking for loan forgiveness and post-labor-export job placement to improve the lives of his fellow Hrê migrants:

> First, the state has to inspect and work closely with the companies that employ the Hrê. For example, in the case of the Hrê man who had a prolonged ear infection, the state officials needed to verify these claims, find the reasons, and demand that the company compensate the affected worker properly. Timely action would set a good precedent for attracting subsequent potential export workers. Because the state has no policy to protect overseas workers, when they faced accidents, risks, and vulnerabilities in Malaysia, they became even poorer and got stuck in a vicious cycle of debt. The state should protect them against all these risks while they are working in Malaysia. One key area is rigorous health checkups before they depart for Malaysia. The state has to make sure that existing illnesses are discovered before they leave for Malaysia to prevent workers from failing in their jobs and so that they will not be disadvantaged by participating in the labor export policy. The will of the Hrê people is that the state ensure that its policies are reasonable and beneficial to the Hrê, not hurting them.

Mr. Văn Đô was blunt in holding the state accountable for the consequences of its labor export policy. By reminding the state officials of their responsibilities to the Hrê workers, he employed ironic mimicry: the Hrê joined this program to escape poverty, yet "they became even poorer." Moreover, he also deployed subversive mimicry by pointing out that "timely action would set a good precedent for attracting subsequent potential export workers." Mr. Văn Đô knew how important the recruitment process was and knew about the need for the Ba Tơ district officials to meet state-mandated quotas in sending the Hrê to work in Malaysia. So, the subversive part of his message informed the state that if it didn't act promptly, the Hrê would not join the labor export program. This was a credible threat, especially given the dismal record of early returnees.

Metaphorical Third Space Empowerment 169

The Khmer Village Leaders

Local Khmer leaders with knowledge of how the LBS system functions also implicitly played the role of a competing authority vis-à-vis the Kinh authorities. They used their knowledge of the law and embedded legal arguments in their subversive mimicry. At the hamlet (*phum*) level, the deputy chief, not the chief, is more connected to the needs of his fellow Khmer villagers and can better represent their interests, and so the deputy chief often plays an important role in facilitating the process of debt collection. Châu Anurak, the hamlet deputy chief in Tịnh Biên, was one of two translators who took us around to interview returnees during my 2014 fieldwork. A young Kinh female was the other one. She works with Châu Anurak on a team whose job is to go to migrants' homes and demand debt payment. She speaks Khmer fluently and helped translate for us. However, it was Châu Anurak who gave me the most valuable insights into and critique of how the labor export policy has affected his people. He not only had a keen appreciation of land ceding and landlessness problems in his hamlet but also knew exactly who owed money, how much they owed, and where they lived.

Sitting under the shade of lush green fruit trees on the property of a Khmer family and surrounded by more than a dozen of the Khmer returnees and their spouses, Châu Anurak showed off his knowledge about—and cast doubts on—the labor export policy in speaking directly to me. But when I looked around, it was clear that he was indirectly addressing the two Kinh officials (besides the Kinh interpreter) who had accompanied me:

> Several years ago, we supported sending people to work overseas, and we are very happy for those who did good work. But those who were assigned work that was not the same as that stated on the contracts, who did not receive the salary that was promised on the contract, and who trained to do one job but ended up doing another job became very risk averse to going to work overseas.

This hamlet deputy chief knew very well the precarity faced by the Khmer migrants in Malaysia and the psychological difficulties they endured upon returning home. Since the LBS system relies on word of mouth and peer pressure as part of its recruitment strategies, bad-mouthing from the returnees in a very small hamlet environment, where everyone knows everyone else, would not bode well for subsequent rounds of recruiting.

Châu Anurak knew that after returning home from Malaysia, the migrants were not making much money working on the assembly lines in big cities or other provinces. He knew that the more debt that migrants accumulated, the worse indebtedness they suffered. Relying on his knowledge of their situation and on his knowledge of the importance of the law and of invoking it, he used subversive mimicry to come to the rescue of his fellow Khmer migrants by endorsing the idea of a formal state policy that would forgive migrants' debts: "If the state created a legal document that would forgive their debts, then they would be very happy, because they have no way to repay their debts."

While not speaking directly to the Kinh officials as the Hrê indigenous leaders did, Châu Anurak still made the desperation of these poor returnees and their families abundantly clear in front of the Kinh officials and asked for loan forgiveness. This subtle form of competing authority between a Khmer village authority and local Kinh officials has yielded small victories: since 2012, the state officials in An Giang have stopped visiting the homes of Khmer migrants to demand interest or principal payments. Still, without an official policy of loan forgiveness to apply nationwide, as requested by Châu Anurak, those indebted Khmer households who used their land as collateral (or ceded it for money to bring their children home) are vulnerable and could risk losing even more land to the state.

A Chăm Religious Leader

Mr. Chamali, a local mosque keeper and a Chăm religious leader, acted as a competing authority using ironic and subversive mimicry to fight for his people's rights. Like the Hrê and the Khmer who capitalized on the power of knowing more than one language, this Chăm mosque keeper was empowered by being able to speak both Chăm and Vietnamese. The case of Mr. Sadat demonstrates how Mr. Chamali spoke up for his people's rights and helped Mr. Sadat's mother, Ms. Baqri, deal with local officials. As described earlier in this chapter, Mr. Sadat borrowed đ20 million from the state but was left with only about đ3 million (or 15 percent of the debt) to buy necessities for his trip to Malaysia. My interview with Mr. Sadat and his extended family (who all sat around on the floor to talk with me) reached a critical moment when Mr. Sadat cried while recounting his "failure" in Malaysia. He didn't finish a three-year contract because the company went bankrupt, and he chose to return to Vietnam six months early. Once home, he did not receive any help from Latuco, the union-owned recruitment company that had signed him up originally.[28] Mr. Chamali interjected and defended Mr. Sadat's actions right in front of the Kinh official who escorted me, showing that he knew the situations of the debtors in his commune very well: "I went with Ms. Baqri to see the local official [at the Social Policy Bank in Quốc Thái commune] and found out that they still owed đ26 million to the Social Policy Bank." Then Mr. Chamali requested that the Kinh government forgive Mr. Sadat's debt "because this is not his fault. He had to return to Vietnam because the company in Malaysia went bankrupt."

This competing local religious authority's remarks were forms of resistance: first, there is an element of ironic mimicry because Ms. Baqri was still in abject poverty and, worse yet, owed money to the state, even with her son having participated in a program that was supposed to lift the family out of poverty. Second, there is an element of subversive mimicry because he reminded the Kinh state officials that the contracts should have stipulations to compensate workers in extenuating circumstances that go beyond their control, such as the 2008–2009 global financial crisis that closed down many businesses in Malaysia and affected the foreign guest workers (coming from Vietnam and other labor-sending countries).

Mr. Chamali used linguistic skills (similar to the Hrê and the Khmer) to speak up for his people's rights when dealing with the local officials. Effectively, this Chăm mosque keeper had negotiated the loan forgiveness for the Chăm living in his village. A quiet debt forgiveness ensued even when there was no clear policy to forgive Mr. Sadat's loan.

Comparative Remarks

How does each ethnic group use metaphorical third space differently? All five groups used ironic mimicries (lamenting poverty) and subversive mimicries (citing state policies) to challenge the LBS system, because they are safe. The state cannot contradict its policies that promised to "eradicate hunger and reduce poverty" for these migrants. Unlike the Kinh and Hoa, the ethnic minorities, while lacking economic access, are equipped with cultural resources, such as linguistic skills, to use mimicries effectively. Their religious and village leaders, acting as competing authorities to the Kinh government officials, showed how hollow the labor export policies are. The mimicries they used reflected legitimacy and solidarity that are hard for the state to suppress. The Khmer and the Hrê village leaders and the Chăm mosque keeper invoked the "master's tools" (the LBS policies) to mock it, a safe form of subversive mimicry that resulted in debt forgiveness for their peoples.

Each ethnic group's competing authority uses different forms of mimicry. The Hrê indigenous leaders turned out to be the most outspoken, using diverse forms of metaphorical mimicry directly aimed at the Kinh officials. The local Hrê leaders were effective in using both ironic and subversive mimicries. They evoked a sense of irony—"most Hrê returnees came home poorer and were still in debt"—that used the state's narrative so the authorities could not suppress their fellow Hrê returnees. This safe strategy spread like a hashtag in social media, allowing them to control the narrative and mobilize solidarity when confronting the Kinh officials. They also used subversive mimicry because they knew both the state labor export policies and how local state officials depended on the leaders to fulfill labor export quotas. They mocked the idea that adding labor export debt to existing debts would lift the Hrê out of poverty, and they demanded state accountability on behalf of their fellow Hrê people. Migrant workers and their families defaulted on their loans by using remittances to reclaim the dreams and symbols promised to them: buffaloes, houses, and motorbikes. On the other hand, the Khmer and the Chăm leaders were indirect, addressing me as if I were the "mediator." Their intention was to relay messages to the Kinh officials who escorted me to the interviews.

The parents of all five ethnic groups also played implicit roles of competing authorities, using mimicries to demand debt forgiveness for their children. They fronted for their children (most of whom were not even home) when the bank and local officials came to their houses to demand debt payment. They used various expressions of ironic mimicry to lament their poverty conditions: poor, poorer, old age, medical debts, not having enough money to eat.

Ironically, while the local government knew that some of the returnees had found jobs after returning to Vietnam, they were not insistent about collecting loan repayment because the labor export policy had not delivered its promise to lift the workers out of poverty.

The next chapter analyzes all forms of empowerment after the migrants have returned to Vietnam and how they have moved on with their lives.

7 Aspirations after Malaysia

What do the Malaysia experiences mean to the migrants from these five groups after they return to Vietnam? This chapter shows how economic constraints hinder the ethnic minorities (the Hrê, the Khmer, and the Chăm) from achieving what they desire, but their cultural and religious resources have opened up new options so they can move forward with their lives. It also explores the similarities and differences among these five groups as to their aspirations, with attention to gender differences.

Broader Worldview and New Skills

Even if nothing else is gained, working overseas exposes migrants to new knowledge and a broader worldview. In different expressions, all five groups showed evidence of growth and development in their confidence, independence, and the ability to reflect and analyze.[1] Mr. Thao, a Kinh worker in Batu Pahat, Malaysia, eloquently summarized that sentiment in a Vietnamese saying: "Traveling one day, learning tons of wisdom"; he added that traveling offers a wealth of experiential knowledge that is not matched by "seat-time" conventional learning at school. Beyond developing a broader worldview, migrants also heightened their appreciation for different cultural practices, learned languages other than their mother tongue, and acquired new skill sets.

The largest group, the Kinh and the Hoa, attributed their newfound knowledge to the opportunity to intermingle with many groups of foreign workers in Malaysia. Mr. Ngãi said:

> On paydays we bought food and invited workers from other countries such as India, China, Bangladesh, and Indonesia, young and old of both genders, to share meals with us. We learned a lot by sharing knowledge with each other.

174 CHAPTER 7

Language competency can help facilitate activities in third spaces. Mr. Ngãi stressed the importance of speaking other languages to communicate effectively and to have more options available while in Malaysia. He pointed out that English, the common language taught in the short orientation classes right before leaving for Malaysia, was a wrong choice because most employers in Malaysia speak either Malay or Chinese. Moreover, having only one or two months of language lessons in orientation classes is grossly inadequate. He reasoned: "If I could speak Mandarin [the standard form of Chinese], I could have been hired to help with a curbside shop selling sundries, because we were permitted to do this over there."

The perception of "being permitted" is reminiscent of the case of the Kinh garlic peeler, an undocumented worker who was hired by a Malaysian restaurant owner in an illegal yet licit space. But this case also points out that knowing Chinese, the language of most Malaysian employers, can open up more opportunities to earn extra income.

Some returnees showed critical thinking about the labor brokerage state (LBS) system but also appreciated the new skills they gained from working overseas, even with limited skill transferability to jobs in Vietnam. Mr. Ngọc, the Kinh "Ghostman," shared some positive aspects of his work experience and the life lessons he learned there, regardless of the trauma he endured in Malaysia:

> One should not always believe in what one was told back in the village, because things were different overseas. I also learned new construction skills, but only some of those can be used in Vietnam due to different conditions [such as extreme climates]. And I got to know migrant workers from other poor [sic] countries, such as India, Myanmar, Indonesia, Thailand, China, and Cambodia, who came to work in Malaysia. . . . They [the recruitment company] taught me very little English, so I can speak only broken English; but then I learned to speak some Malay to be able to communicate with migrant workers from other countries.

The "Ghostman" questioned the LBS recruitment system, which made use of neighbors as local recruiters. The wisdom he shared as a returnee is invaluable for potential workers so they can avoid falling for the same traps. But reflecting on the power of language to broaden his global awareness shows internal empowerment as discussed by Oishi.[2] Learning elementary Malay language connected him to other foreign workers for camaraderie. However, only limited work skills were transferable to some jobs he found in the north of Vietnam.

Returnees from other groups also reflected on how their current jobs use skills they learned while working in Malaysia. For Châu Charya, a Khmer returnee, working overseas had given him some people skills that complemented his existing technical skills. His case also provides a positive example of a free local vocational training that did a decent job. When I visited his sidewalk motorbike shop, he stopped working on two motorbikes to chat with me. Châu Charya was happy with this job, which helps pay for his family's daily needs and serves the people in his commune:

> I went through vocational training in An Giang to fix motorbikes free of charge while making some money as a trainee. Now back here, I returned to this job, learning more techniques to fix bikes while applying some customer service skills learned from working in Malaysia. I made đ6–7 million per month [gross], with very little profit and only enough for my daily pocket change. My wife sells sundries in the market and takes care of daily food and other necessities.

So Châu Charya resumed his old job but has been doing it better, using skills he learned in Malaysia.

The remaining two groups, the Hrê and the Chăm, show some diverse patterns. It is ironic that the key target group of the labor export program, the Hrê, rarely showed newfound knowledge from their Malaysia experiences. I could not get this information from interviewing their parents, since the migrants themselves were still in Malaysia or had already left for work in Quảng Ngãi or elsewhere in Vietnam. But from a few interviews I was able to conduct with some Hrê returnees, I found that they were more focused on their migration within Vietnam (discussed below). Perhaps this implies that they would prefer to stay and work in their own province or nearby towns, where they have knowledge of the systems and can travel with their fellow Hrê neighbors while still having their family support system nearby.

On the other hand, very few Chăm participated in the LBS program. Instead, most bypassed the state system, traveling "the Chăm way" and benefiting from their diverse migration patterns.

Stepwise International Migration

Most migrant workers expressed their desire to work their way up a hierarchy of desired countries (Malaysia, Taiwan, Korea, Japan), a practice Paul coined Stepwise International Migration, to improve their long-term conditions. But stepwise migration requires independent financing to go to these desired countries, since there are no state-subsidized low-interest loans like the ones offered by Prime Minister Decision 71/2009/QĐTT, which targets poor rural districts.

176 CHAPTER 7

The specific pattern of stepwise international migration mentioned above is more feasible for the Kinh and the Hoa, who generally have access to economic resources and family connections that allow them to search for better-paid jobs in higher-tier countries. By contrast, most members of the ethnic minority groups did not have enough capital to move stepwise to those higher-tier countries. The Chăm and the Khmer instead followed regional migration patterns, relying on their historical and cultural resources and bypassing the state-managed LBS system. They tapped into their community cultural wealth,[3] established by centuries of historical and, for the Chăm, religious connections.

The presence of a global diaspora of successful stepwise migrants from the home country can establish migrant social networks (strong ties and weak ties) and inspire others to follow in their footsteps.[4] The Kinh socialist migrants have demonstrated this point most clearly by inspiring their fellow Kinh families and friends to join them in the former Soviet Bloc countries. As discussed in chapter 5, Chăm communities in Cambodia and Malaysia helped smooth the journeys of Chăm Muslims from Vietnam to Malaysia and provided the means of production, such as carts for Chăm men to use to sell ice cream on the streets. The Khmer, with historical roots in Cambodia, can maneuver their way into Thailand for seasonal farm work and domestic work and then cross back into Cambodia to renew tourist visas that grant them temporary stay in Thailand (albeit technically not permission to work).

The Kinh and the Hoa

The Kinh and the Hoa migrants, with access to financing and education, had more opportunities to work in other countries. Their family connections also assisted with this stepwise process. About one-third of all Kinh and Hoa migrant returnees expressed interest in going to Korea, Japan, Hong Kong, or Macau to improve their lives. Both groups confirmed the need for language skills and post–high school education, such as skills certification or college-level classes for Japan.

Success in Malaysia, the first step in this particular hierarchy, can ease the way for the next step. Some successful migrants capitalized on their newly gained skills to prepare for the next steps. Mr. Thức stressed technical and language skills:

> After returning home from Malaysia, I learned to speak a little English and have been improving it in a language class. I really want to go to Korea to work: any job would be fine with me, as long as the wage is high and the jobs deal with fixing mobile phones.

Aspirations after Malaysia 177

Family connections to the state—relatives who work for the government or are members of the Vietnamese Communist Party—also enabled these upward mobility endeavors. These connections would pave the way for some returnees to go on to better-paid destinations. For instance, Mr. Thao's uncle worked for the government, and this family connection would enable him to "step up" to more preferable labor markets after returning from Malaysia. Mr. Thao said that his uncle had connections in Taiwan, Korea, Macau, and the Czech Republic, and his next destination could be any of those countries. Moreover, being classified as a "revolutionary" family—a family that had fought against the French and the United States—gave them some preferential treatment.

The promise of making good money in higher-tiered countries is an oft-cited motivation, and many workers were egged on by neighbors or peer pressure. Mr. Thao shared his dream and ambition: "I want to work in other countries where I can learn as well as making money. My friends from the same ward in Nghệ An told me that they can earn more money in Taiwan and South Korea." Ms. Kim-Ly confirmed this potential financial gain: "Most people here [in An Giang province] did not want to go to Malaysia because of low wages compared to what they could have made working in Korea and Japan."

But lacking money from the very beginning can preclude the enthusiastic ones from even considering these upper-tier destinations. Ms. Kim-Ly was very realistic about the constraints she faced: "When I returned here, I really wanted to go to work in Korea. Some of my friends [returnees from Malaysia] had registered to go to Korea. But they all said that going to Korea requires a lot of money [for fees] and a [Korean] language exam." Ms. Kim-Ly gave up on the idea because her family could not afford it.

Fear of indebtedness also tempers this aspiration. Mr. Việt expressed his cautious goal of working in Korea or Japan:

> I also want to go to work in Korea, hearing that salaries are high over there, but the fee is also high: đ50–60 million. If there is no work in Korea, how can I repay this huge debt? As of May 2005, I learned that it costs đ80 million to go to Japan. Well, I can't even repay đ19 million [to go to Malaysia], so I'd be doomed if there is no work in Korea while incurring such a big debt!

The Khmer, the Hrê, and the Chăm

Stepwise migration for the ethnic minority groups—the Khmer, the Hrê, and the Chăm—takes on different forms. While these ethnic minorities have the desire to go to work in higher-paying countries, most cannot afford to follow the conventional hierarchy of destinations adopted by the Kinh and the Hoa.

178 CHAPTER 7

A Khmer village leader, Châu Anurak, clearly articulated the desire for upward mobility: "If there are better paying jobs in other countries, then they would consider going again. They especially preferred going to work in Japan rather than working for Chinese companies in Malaysia."[5] Instead, these groups' de facto stepwise migration patterns, based on their respective cultural and historical connections to neighboring countries, bypassed the state system and brought them to Cambodia and then to Thailand to do seasonal farm work or housework, as discussed in chapter 5.

Many Hrê migrants also desired to move beyond Malaysia to Korea and Japan in a step-by-step manner.[6] Like the Khmer, they didn't have the financial resources and language preparation to take on these next adventures. But unlike the Khmer, they don't have transnational historical and religious connections that enable them to bypass the state system. Ms. Đinh Thị Phương Lan told me that the state gave the Hrê a token quota to go to these desirable destinations but did not prepare them properly for their labor markets:

> The ones who returned home early for various reasons did not want to work in Malaysia but would prefer to go to some industrialized country such as Japan or [South] Korea. But these countries require high technical and language skills to warrant higher wages.[7]

In an interview in 2012, Mr. Nguyễn Văn Triệu explained: "Many Hrê wanted to work in Taiwan, Korea, and Japan. So we supported and sent ten Hrê migrants to Hanoi to study Korean language and culture for four months, but at the end they did not pass the exams, so they returned home with nothing." This statement is consistent with the returnee statistics showing that the few Hrê who were trained and then sent to work in Korea ended up returning home early.[8] Given the inadequate public education they had received—as discussed in chapter 1, many did not finish high school—this outcome was hardly surprising.

The Chăm stand out with their wide-ranging migration patterns. Religious affinity with the Malaysian Muslims helps them with some upward mobility. Their geographical agency can serve religious purposes in addition to economic ones.[9] Their stepwise migration patterns bypass the LBS system, relying on centuries of historical, cultural, and religious connections that enable them to crisscross Cambodia, Thailand, and Malaysia.

Details shared in my interviews with the Chăm on their religious studies (as an upward mobility effort) are consistent with anthropological and archaeological findings about the Islamic circuit and its two nearby religious learning centers: Pattani, in southern Thailand near the border with Malaysia, and Kelantan, in northern Malaysia.[10] Pattani is one of the four provinces of Thailand where the majority of the population—about 88 percent—are Malay Muslim. The people speak the Pattani Malay language, although most also speak Thai. The Pattani Malays are similar in ethnicity and culture to the Kelantan Malays in Malaysia. The proximity of Pattani and Kelantan, both with Muslim Malay communities, suggests different forms of movement for the Chăm, such as migrating for religious studies or using tourist visas to work in Malaysia. For example, during my fieldwork, I found some Chăm men who had traveled to Kelantan to study the Quran.[11] This is consistent with Taylor's observation that many Chăm men went to Kelantan to study Islam, sometimes with the help of scholarships from the Malaysian government.[12] More recent studies show that Malaysia has been giving scholarships to both male and female students to study in universities in Malaysia so that Chăm women, too, have been going to study in Malaysia.[13]

Aspirations for Higher Education

Education is an aspiration shared by all five groups but expressed in different ways. Also, the passion to learn languages other than their mother tongues seems to have been energized after they returned from Malaysia and reflected on the usefulness of language.

The two groups that were deprived of the Kinh public education, the Khmer and the Hrê, value direct intervention by way of becoming teachers themselves to contribute to their respective communities. Some Kinh, while having relatively more economic endowment, aspired to more education not for themselves but for their siblings. For the Chăm, education is reflected prominently in religious studies, which are for men, not women.

The Kinh and the Hoa

Most of the Kinh and the Hoa interviewees did not express an interest in continuing their own education upon returning to Vietnam. Instead, they sent money for their siblings' education. The narrative from Ms. Cúc (a Kinh) exemplified that "sacrifice" sentiment. She wanted to use part of her remittances to send her younger sister to college, focusing on agricultural science, as an investment in education that could expand her family's farming business venture. She negotiated with her parents to use the money for her sister's education, not for herself. Other Kinh wistfully recalled their educational attainment but did not wish to obtain higher education themselves. But some, like Mr. Thao, did wish they could have obtained more education: "I used to be a very bright student in high school, and received awards for

180 CHAPTER 7

twelve years in high school. I wanted to go to college, but my family is poor and has no money to send me to school," he said.

The Hrê

While the Hrê had the least access to economic resources, especially education and land, the Hrê migrants and their parents aspired to use education to improve their impoverished circumstances. Some articulated clearly the desire to become teachers to help Hrê children in their communes directly. This aspiration not only addresses the lack of bilingual teachers in these ethnic areas but also aims to improve the Hrê's access to the Kinh's public education in their remote mountainous districts. After all, the Hrê children would be happy to see teachers who could speak their language (Mon/Bahnaric-Khmer).[14] Moreover, irrespective of the probability of participating in the Kinh's public education, the Hrê preserve their language by speaking it at home and in their communes. I heard the language spoken throughout my fieldwork in Quảng Ngãi.

The following three cases demonstrate the aspirations of migrants and their parents, including some Hrê who did not participate in the LBS program.

Mr. Cung was waiting to go to Malaysia when we talked in front of his house in 2011. He showed a clear passion for education:

> I could not pass the twelfth grade, so I can't get into college or vocational school. So that's why I decided to go to work in Malaysia. I do think about better markets such as Korea and Japan, but my abilities are limited. . . . My father was an elementary [school] teacher, but he retired a long time ago. Before, I dreamed about being a teacher like my father, but a dream is only a dream.

His dream for education was supplanted by the LBS dream. His regret for not passing the twelfth grade—a requirement for elementary school teachers—had left an indelible imprint on his psyche since he kept repeating "my abilities are limited." His "teacher dream" was very different from the "buffalo, house, and motorbike" dream created by the LBS state and its media to promote the labor export program. And he was also cognizant of better markets that were beyond his reach.

Ms. Oanh told me a story of her son's passion for education. Mr. Khôi, her son, was still working in Malaysia when we had this interview. Ms. Hà had instilled an understanding of the importance of education in her children for what it could enable, irrespective of their impoverished conditions. Although I did not have a chance to interview Mr. Khôi directly, I understood that he and his siblings had received support from their mother. Ms. Oanh said, "I always advise them: although we are very poor, we still try our very best to

Aspirations after Malaysia 181

raise them and give them an education." When I asked why her son did not finish high school, she explained her son's proactive decision:

> Because we are very poor, he quit school after grade eleven so that he could help his family. He wanted to go to work overseas; no one forced him to. He wanted to learn about different places [*để biết đó đây*]. After he is done with this contract, he wants to return to finish high school. He wants to study electronics.

Economic necessity had motivated Mr. Khôi to quit school before graduating from high school, similar to Ms. Giáo (discussed in chapter 1). But he knew that working in Malaysia would be a stepping stone for him to enlarge his knowledge and skill set. In particular, his job with Samsung in Malaysia would have brought him closer to his dream once he returned to Vietnam. Ms. Hà said, "He wants to bring home the electronic skills that he learned in Malaysia. This has been his dream since grade nine."

Mr. Khôi was lucky since his work was consistent with what was stated on his contract and what he had requested on his application: an electronic assembly job in Malaysia. His stepwise plan was not to work in another country but to use his newfound skills to work in Vietnam after finishing the Malaysia contract.

When Ms. Hà was asked whether she had received money from her son, she said: "Yes, he did send money home, but not for me. My sister was poor and wanted to borrow his money to send her children to school. So he lent money to his aunt so her children could go to school." In an altruistic sense, Mr. Khôi wanted more education not just for himself but also for his siblings and relatives.

Mr. Khôi used his experiential learning to prevent his younger brother from falling into a suboptimal pathway, a negative outcome of social and familial networks discussed in the introduction. Having seen the precarious working conditions in Malaysia, he did not want his eighteen-year-old brother to follow in his footsteps. When his brother expressed interest in working in Malaysia, possibly because of peer pressure, Mr. Khôi advised him not to go; he reflected that life in Malaysia was very complex and that it would be better for his brother to stay home and finish high school. He offered to send money home for him to study whatever vocational skill he wanted in order to find a good job.

The third case is a Hrê woman who did not go to work in Malaysia but stayed at home to work the family field. Ms. Giáo expressed a strong passion to become an elementary teacher in order to teach in her own commune:

> We have been married for four years now, and we have a two-year-old son. I only finished grade nine and had to stop because I needed to work on the land

182   CHAPTER 7

> to help my family. But I would love to become a teacher. . . . I want to become
> an elementary school teacher. We teach our two-year-old son to speak the Hrê
> language at home, but he learns Vietnamese in kindergarten.

She implied that the use of Vietnamese in kindergarten made it difficult for
her son to retain his mother tongue. The lack of bilingual classes in Vietnamese public schools is a common problem facing the Khmer and the Chăm as
well. But to become a teacher who could teach bilingual classes, she needed
to finish high school, a dream that did not seem feasible when she was working in the field to make a living and taking care of their son and housework.

Ms. Giáo was very concerned about the lack of education that permeated
her whole family and also affected her husband. Most did not even finish
their high school education, having to make a living.

> I have many siblings. Most of us finished only up to grade nine, except for the
> youngest one, who finished high school and worked as a local policeman [*công
> an*]. . . . My husband only got up to grade two.

Poor infrastructure had prevented them from going to school: it was difficult
to ride a motorbike, or even walk, on roads damaged by the trucks carrying
tons of the paper pulp trees or on puddled, unpaved roads during the rainy
season. Distance could also be an obstacle; as a child, her husband had lived
too far away from upper-level schools.

The Khmer

Some Khmer returnees aspire to gain higher education to improve their
lives and to help their communities address challenges in public education.
The Kinh public schools do not help minorities learn their native languages.
While the *wat* schools have provided Khmer language classes and Buddhist
philosophy to preserve their culture, they must compete with the dominant
Kinh (Vietnamese) language and the corresponding reward system. The
Vietnamese language has become the language of trade, administration,
and intercultural communication. Most Khmer youths choose to attend
Vietnamese schools, while a few attend Khmer literacy classes held in the
temples during school holidays.[15]

Young women face even more barriers created by the patriarchal Khmer
culture, which prevents them from advancing their Khmer language acquisition. The sense of self-empowerment was very clear when several Khmer
interviewees expressed a strong desire to further their own education and
to become teachers to help educate their own communities. This pattern is

Aspirations after Malaysia 183

different from that of Kinh and Hoa migrants, many of whom remit money to improve their younger siblings' education, not their own. When I interviewed Neng Kanika in 2014, she had been teaching second and third grades in Tri Tôn district since 2011. Perseverance, not the LBS system, helped lift her out of poverty and fulfill her education dream:

> When I left for Malaysia, I knew that I wanted to save money to further my education. When I returned here, seeing that my friends were going to school, I was very sad because I knew that those folks [former classmates] were not as good as me, but they had a chance to go to school and I didn't. . . . But sadly my trip to Malaysia failed [she was unable to save any money and still owed đ6 million to the state bank], so after returning here, I worked for a shoe factory in Đồng Nai for one year. Then I quit to study full time, from 2007 to 2011, and got my teaching credential and started teaching in 2011. In the first two years I taught second grade; in 2013 I became the head teacher of third grade, teaching all [general] subjects.

The failed Malaysia experience led her to factory work in Vietnam, but that did not deter her from her education dream. She was able to become a teacher to help her community. The strict gender barrier keeping older female teenagers from taking Khmer language classes in the Khmer *wats* had limited her Khmer language ability to just simple writing. Thus, she conducts her classes in Vietnamese, but her role as a teacher still benefits Khmer students who are inspired to see someone like them in the classroom.

The Chăm

Religious studies connect the Chăm men, but not the women, to the global Islamic community, allowing for peaceful mutual understanding and communications. These devout Muslims practice their Islamic faith wherever they go, a common pattern found among many Chăm migrants. Women are not allowed to enter the main hall of a mosque but have to go up to the balcony, if there is one. If there is no balcony, they pray at home or in a women's makeshift mosque. I visited one women's mosque in a Chăm district in An Giang and found instructions in Arabic on pieces of paper taped to the inside wall.

Spiritual support from Malaysia to the Chăm in Vietnam follows centuries-old Malay-Chăm connections. The Malaysian government and private donors, including corporations, have provided scholarships to some young Chăm men for Islamic education in Malaysia, reinforcing Islamic identity. Religious migration and Islamic education are thus avenues for some Chăm men to engage in upward mobility and expand their worldviews. In addition,

184 CHAPTER 7

some Chăm Muslim men cobble together money to finance their religious studies in Malaysia.

Three examples from my fieldwork interviews show the opportunities afforded three young men in their twenties. The Hồ Chí Minh City Muslim Representative Committee plays an important role in connecting prospective students to appropriate teachers in the global Islamic community, who facilitate and support their religious studies.

The case of Mr. Abdullah, whom I interviewed in 2012 when he was twenty-eight years old, shows that Islamic study can be used to provide service to the Muslim community in An Giang province. Mr. Abdullah had studied for nine years in various places: seven self-financed years in Hồ Chí Minh City and Cambodia (most likely in areas with high Chăm concentration, such as Kampong Chăm) and then two years in Malaysia with financial support from some Malaysian donors. After the two years of studying in Malaysia, he had to return home due to illness. At the time of the interview, he wanted to complete his Islamic religious studies in Malaysia then return to his district to provide religious service in his local mosque.

Mr. Chamana, whom I also interviewed in 2012, when he was twenty-four years old, was more ambitious for personal economic upward mobility. He wanted to become a hakim, someone who is knowledgeable in Islamic law, or to work in the management team of Petronas, a Malaysian oil/gas corporation with offices in Vietnam. Petronas sponsored him to engage in Islamic studies in Malaysia.

During the Ramadan season in July 2015, I had the great fortune to interview Imam Sanes,[16] a gentle twenty-seven-year-old local religious leader, right before his sermon, in a beautiful international mosque located in the middle of trendy shops and high rises in District 1 in Hồ Chí Minh City. Imam Sanes works full-time and resides at the mosque with his wife. He shared his insights with me in the hall right outside the mosque's main chamber:

> I paid my own way to Selangor [Malaysia] to study the Quran but received free room and board when I got to Malaysia. I did not intend to become an imam but wanted to deeply understand life philosophy. After five years of study, I had memorized the whole Quran in Arabic. Every Friday, I teach the Quran [to fellow Muslims]. The hakim here manages the whole mosque, but he does not teach the Quran.

So, while not originally intending to become an imam, in the course of Islamic studies, he found enlightenment and became one.

Imam Sanes has three siblings who worked in garment factories in Củ Chi district, each making about đ3 million per month. Their parents joined

Aspirations after Malaysia 185

Imam Sanes's siblings in Củ Chi, where they lived in a Chăm migrant community. The parents and siblings led efforts to form a local mosque so they could practice their religion and continued what they had done in An Giang to preserve their centuries-old practices. Imam Sanes shared:

> My father sometimes travels around to sell sundries, but he is also an imam, leading religious ceremonies in a makeshift mosque [in Củ Chi district]. . . . They rented a regular room and converted it into a mosque open twenty-four hours a day for the Chăm Muslims to come in to pray. My mother teaches the Chăm language to the children [possibly of other Chăm migrants]. I think it originates from Arabic, and the writing is somewhat similar to Malay.

Even though Chăm women don't have the same access to religious education, global Islamic presence affects the everyday life of both men and women, from mosques to apparel. Broad support from Sunni Muslim communities in the Middle East dates back to the early 1990s.[17] During my fieldwork, I saw strong signs of influence from the UAE and Saudi Arabia, who had donated money to build some relatively big mosques for the Sunni Chăm Muslims in An Giang and Hồ Chí Minh City.[18] I also saw different styles of Muslim attire worn by women and men in An Giang's Chăm districts, reflecting influences from Islamic countries in the Gulf states and Southeast Asian countries.

Domestic Migration Patterns of Ethnic Minority Returnees

For many ethnic minority returnees, their stepwise migration is to other provinces in Vietnam. The three ethnic minorities I researched, the Hrê, the Chăm, and the Khmer, have engaged in various forms of migration after their Malaysia experiences. While the Hrê responded to the state policies encouraging resettlement to lowland areas, all three ethnic groups have members who opted to work in factories in Ho Chi Minh City and nearby provinces. But they also initiated their own pathways, drawing from centuries of cultural and religious connections with some neighboring countries.

The Hrê

The Hrê returnees created their own economic spaces near where they lived, despite the remote mountainous areas with poor road conditions. Some resumed farm work or became hired hands in their villages. They migrated to nearby provinces—for instance, Dak Lak (over 400 kilometers southwest of Quảng Ngãi) or Gia Lai (less than 300 kilometers southwest of Quảng

186 CHAPTER 7

Ngãi)—to pick coffee beans, tea leaves, and other agricultural produce. Those coffee/tea plantations became economic spaces where the Hrê returnees could generate some income.

During my home visits, many migrants were away, working on plantations in nearby provinces, so I interviewed the parents in order to understand the circumstances of their children. My interviews highlighted the vulnerabilities that migrants faced when the "contract" was informal and oral, without government regulation.

In 2013 I interviewed Mr. Ngô's father, whose son was not at home. I learned that Mr. Ngô had finished his LBS contract and returned on time. He then found a job picking coffee beans, splitting his time in two places: Buôn Ma Thuột coffee town (Dak Lak province) and Gia Lai province. For two months of work, he made a lump sum of between đ7 and đ8 million, or đ3.5–4 million per month.[19] While the workers' salaries were high compared to the low minimum wage in rural areas, they were withheld by the Vietnamese coffee plantation owners until the end of the second month (right before their time to return home) to make sure they wouldn't leave work in midseason.

A common trend of the returnees to work on farms domestically became clear after I interviewed Mr. Châu, a thirty-five-year-old Hrê at the state-resettlement area discussed below. When I asked to speak with Mr. Bình, another returnee, I learned that Mr. Bình was not at home. He had been sent to work in Malaysia by the LBS system but returned to Quảng Ngãi before the end of his three-year contract. While the reasons for Mr. Bình's early return are sketchy,[20] his job upon return to Quảng Ngãi was clear: harvesting cash crops and doing farm work. Mr. Châu shared:

> Upon returning here [Nghĩa Hành district], he worked just like me. I heard that he now lives in Lâm Đồng province [almost 600 kilometers southwest of Quảng Ngãi], working for a plantation there, picking passion fruit and help-ing with animal husbandry, raising fowl, pigs, and cows for meat. I'm not sure whether he has a yearly or monthly contract. But as a single person, he is more flexible and can work on a yearly contract. He does not have to come home after a two-month seasonal contract as I do.

This seasonal farm work in nearby provinces is common among the Hrê living in a state-relocated area.

Many Hrê migrated to other parts of Vietnam in response to the state's resettlement policy, which started in earnest in 1997–98 for the purposes of nationalizing forest lands and controlling the ethnic minorities' populations.[21] This policy has very clear goals: "to reduce poverty and manage population's residence and ethnic villages" (*giảm nghèo và quản lý dân cư, thôn bản*). The

Aspirations after Malaysia   187

goal of managing population seems to be the driving reason for monitoring the activities of ethnic minorities, as is the case with the Hrê. It is not a coincidence that the state concentrated them in lowland, downtown areas near the commune/district main thoroughfare.[22] Nghĩa Hành district, designated as the "resettlement area" (Vùng Tái Định Cư), is part of this larger resettlement policy, and my fieldwork findings contribute to the scant literature on the Hrê's livelihoods. Here, the Hrê stay in fixed residences, yet they continue their traditional combination of swiddening (*làm rẫy*) and wet rice cultivation, both activities taking place in this resettlement lowland area.[23] But within this community, limited land and water have led to a competition between residents who grow food crops (rice) and those who grow cash crops (acacia trees for paper pulp); this has made their lives more vulnerable to market fluctuations, essentially making the poverty reduction goal a pipe dream.

The state has a political motive for controlling this area. Nghĩa Hành is immediately to the east of Sơn Hà district, a politically sensitive district also in Quảng Ngãi province. Some Christian church groups in Sơn Hà had inspired religious conversions among some local Hrê, to the chagrin of paranoid state officials, who feared prodemocracy people's uprisings. State paranoia may have led to a heightened desire for state control in the name of national security. In particular, the state financed housing projects for the thirty-six poor Hrê households in this resettlement area, using funding from the poverty reduction program. Each household received đ15 million (about US$750) from the state to transform a prefabricated house into a simple brick house to meet these clear objectives: "to reduce poverty and to concentrate Hrê population in the lowland."[24] In 1999 a flood washed over this lowland, interrupting this plan, so they sought refuge in their old houses up in the mountains, not too far from this new lowland site. Then, in 2000, they returned to Nghĩa Hành district and tried to maintain their traditional lifestyle to the extent possible.

The Hrê have created an economic space for themselves by engaging in seasonal migration to make a living during this area's off-season. In 2015, I went with a local researcher to visit Hành Dũng commune in Nghĩa Hành district to understand the connection between domestic migration and transnational migration via labor export. While Prime Minister Decision 71/2009/QĐTT has stipulations to help returnees find jobs, create small-scale businesses, or use the income generated from their labor export experiences, in reality, these objectives were not realized. Therefore, the returnees have sought any temporary jobs in nearby provinces.

In Nghĩa Hành district, I met Mr. Lê (a jobber we met in chapter 1), who introduced me to several Hrê men who had been doing this seasonal

188 CHAPTER 7

migration. I learned that the male members of all of the thirty-six households left home for two to three months during Quảng Ngãi's rainy season, from September to November, to pick coffee beans in Kontum province, the nearest central highland coffee bean province to Quảng Ngãi.[25]

Thus, one can argue that Kontum is a form of economic space that supplements their income during the rainy seasons in Quảng Ngãi. But this seasonal work is also precarious: instead of formal labor contracts, everything is conducted verbally. If for any reason workers have to leave (for example, because of a family emergency), they lose all of their salary, which is paid at the very end of the harvesting season. Clearly, workers are at a disadvantage in these verbal agreements.

Walking around the resettlement neighborhood, I had a chance to talk to some residents whose houses were built along the main thoroughfare. I had a long conversation with one couple, Mr. Châu (mentioned above) and his wife, Ms. Na, one of the households in the relocated area. Mr. Châu told me that farming is still his main job, but during the rainy season he would go to Kontum province, the nearest place to do seasonal work:

> I go to pick coffee beans for exactly two months. After that I have to return home to help my family plant the young seedlings for our [wet] rice paddies. No one at home can do that but me. After two months of picking coffee beans, even when the job was not done, I had to leave to tend to our rice planting at home. My boss can find other pickers, such as the Hrê who were still single and thus could extend their work period in Kontum.

The Hrê women continue to live a hard life, still engaging in swiddening and wet rice cultivation. I talked to Mr. Châu's wife, Ms. Na, in front of their prefabricated house, donated by the state and some international NGOs. Her story is similar to that of other Hrê women who stay at home while their husbands either work in Malaysia or pick coffee beans in nearby central highland provinces. Ms. Na told me, "Every morning, I walk up the mountain to pick up wood. If by luck I find a good spot with lots of wood, then I finish my task early. If not, I have to walk to different areas to pick up wood. Then, I carry the load on my back [cõng] down the mountain." I looked with admiration at several huge bundles of wood stacked in front of her house. I tried to lift up one bundle but could not even move it; carrying such heavy loads down the mountain is truly hard labor for women. Ms. Na replied matter-of-factly when I asked how heavy each bundle was and how much she received for this work:

> I don't know.... Maybe it is around 40 kilograms [about 88 pounds] per bundle. For each bundle, I receive about đ30,000 [US$1.50] from the Kinh peddlers who

Aspirations after Malaysia   189

go around to buy them for fuel. . . . On a good day, I can pick up three bundles, earning đ90,000; if not, only two bundles. Yes, my back is a little sore, but I'm used to doing this hard work since I was a child. My family was poor so they could not afford to send me to school.

Ms. Na's story reveals her initiative. She supplements such meager daily income by pulling weeds, tending to the young acacia and cassava trees, and doing any odd jobs she can find. Her modest plan to improve their lives is constrained by a lack of seed money:

> I have some aspirations and want to have some seed money to buy cows and pigs so they can produce offspring to sell in the market and for me to build up my principal. I already asked the local women's union in our commune to lend me some seed money, but they told me that I already escaped poverty, that I am no longer poor, so they did not lend me any money.

Ms. Na protested the local women's union claim that she and her husband had escaped poverty; they were still poor and living hand to mouth. She continued,

> There is no unity among us Hrê women: some want to borrow money, some don't. The reason is the high interest rate: up to 0.7 percent per month [seven-tenths of 1 percent, or 8.4 percent annually]. Some Hrê women are afraid that they cannot pay such high monthly interest rates, so they don't dare to borrow money.

She revealed an important fact: Hrê women's aversion to indebtedness, given the many debt default cases of the migrant returnees who live among them. However, environmental constraints can result in indebtedness. Water is used for both food crops (rice) and cash crops (acacia trees), and these competing purposes exacerbate the Hrê's precarity. Ms. Na informed me:

> We really need water here. We barely have enough water from the rain during the months of September, October, and November to plant just one season of rice on our plot of land. This is barely enough for us to eat. So we ended up having to borrow from a nice Kinh woman who lent us money without any interest, and repaying her when we have some money from selling *keo* trees or other produce. When we got sick, we also needed money and had to borrow from her again.

The need for water and the lack of water irrigation to till her plot of land were repeated three times during our conversation. Apparently, land is being rotated for two purposes: planting a food crop and planting a cash crop.

The resettlement policy does not help the Hrê escape the cycle of debt. They have a hard time sustaining themselves via food crops such as rice and

190 CHAPTER 7

cassava. They need money to buy inputs (such as fertilizer and pesticides) for the cash crops and to buy medicine when they are sick. Worse yet, the cash crops can damage the soil for a long time, delaying when the Hrê can once again plant food crops on their plots of land.[26]

Even in terms of housing, the Hrê continue their traditional lifestyle in this resettlement area. Many of their houses have a cement front (of the prefabricated part) but have a makeshift traditional wooden house as a separate unit behind the prefabricated house. The wooden house is cool in the summer because it has better ventilation. Many remarked wistfully to me, "There are no more woods these days to build wooden houses like these."

They also continue to engage in swidden cultivation, using back-breaking techniques, to supplement their livelihoods. Both men and women return to their plots of land up the slopes of the mountains to collect wood and to care for and harvest their paper pulp trees. Most women stay at home and walk up and down the mountains with heavy loads of wood on their backs for very small amounts of money, and the men migrate after harvests to do seasonal work on plantations in nearby provinces.

The Khmer

After toiling in Malaysian factories, the Khmer workers came home to assembly factory work in export processing zones and industrial zones in nearby cities, with mixed outcomes. My interviews with workers in the Samho sports shoe factory indicated that most factories showed a preference for female assembly workers.

The state and its local infrastructure had plans to find jobs for all local residents of all ethnic groups in An Giang. Local officials collaborated with factories in big cities to create jobs for their residents. They offered incentives for job training and job placement in factories near Ho Chi Minh City.[27] Many Khmer who could not find jobs in An Giang were willing to work in cities away from home.[28] Local employment centers actively recruited returnees to work in export processing zones and industrial zones in and around Ho Chi Minh City and the semi-rural Củ Chi district.[29] For instance, the An Giang Employment Service Center obtained job orders from factories, such as Samho in Củ Chi district, and then recruited Khmer residents in Tri Tôn and Tịnh Biên districts.

Working in a factory in Vietnam requires no loans, unlike going to work in Malaysia. Domestic assembly work is also less risky than overseas work because the local employment centers are within reach by phone and bus,

Aspirations after Malaysia 191

and migrant workers can keep their personal documents while working in the factories.

Some Khmer returnees who did not choose factory work have relied on manual jobs in An Giang, such as construction work or jobs as mechanics for the men and domestic work and child care for the women.[30]

Many migrant returnees received subsidized bus fare, or even a free ride, to go to the factories in the south. Traveling by bus or van with others from the same village or commune to work in industrial provinces, such as Đồng Nai and Bình Dương, mimics the journeys they took to work in Malaysia. Native place and familial bonding made working away from home easier; family members often joined them at the same time or subsequently. This trend is confirmed by migration studies scholars.[31] Taking advantage of the comforting native place bonds, the state promoted this form of domestic migration by paying bonuses to informal recruiters who signed up their family members and friends. The process started with those who came to work in the cities first; then they sent messages home to encourage their families and fellow villagers to join them at the factory.

Following the footsteps of over five hundred Khmer from Tri Tôn and Tịnh Biên districts to the Samho shoe factory in Củ Chi, I witnessed the good work of an enterprise-level union. This union offers three types of service that look after workers' rights and welfare: a small library, a union shop for sundries, and a union office. There, I had the opportunity to interview some workers, the human resource director, and the union leaders in the union's office.[32] (This huge compound of factory buildings is unshaded, and the weather was oppressively hot. I learned from a worker interviewee that management "cut down all the trees to build more plants because of production needs"— another sad example of the "corrosive effect" of the market system, which destroys the environment for management's profit.)

The union office is a one-stop shop. The "library," a big bookcase with many shelves holding books and magazines, is at one end; the union shop is in the middle, selling phone cards and household sundries; and the office, where workers can pay their dues, register grievances, and get updated on the union's latest activities, is at the other end. The union president invited me to have lunch with him in the cafeteria where the workers eat. I accepted the invitation with great delight: the cafeteria is well ventilated and the lunch was nice and filling. The young workers were milling around, smiling.

In 2014 I interviewed six Khmer women in this factory to understand the scope of domestic migration. Most were recruited by friends and family members and the An Giang employment center. They did not have to take

192   CHAPTER 7

out loans. At work, they had good relations with the Kinh and participated in strikes with the Kinh when the opportunity arose. But their work experiences were mixed.

The first four cases indicate experiences in gainful employment. I interviewed a Khmer female worker, Neng Leakena, who was an informal recruiter and acted as a group leader. She told me: "I followed eight of my friends to work here. I am a union member, working in the leather stockroom to disburse this accessory; I make đ4 million per month and can only send money home (about đ2 million) when I get overtime." She had to pay for rent and meals but was able to send money home regularly to assist her aging parents. Neng Leakena shared the power of language and the incentives being offered to family recruiters:

> The Kinh are nice to me; Khmer is my mother tongue but I speak good Vietnamese because I learned it when I was a child; when I had any issue, I came to talk to the [Kinh] union representative, who resolved it for me just fine. There was no break for menstruating workers, but when I felt tired, I talked to the supervisor, who let me go home. . . . My parents stay home to till the land. My family has eight children, and I am the youngest child. Once my job was stabilized here, I returned to the village and persuaded my friends (two or three people) to come here to work with me. Then I was paid "bonuses" for recruiting my fellow villagers: the first three months I received đ150,000. I continued [to recruit] over the next 3 months and got đ150,000 again. Occasionally, I got đ300,000 as bonus.

Neng Leakena's case also shows the weak enforcement of the progressive Vietnamese labor laws related to women workers' rights. The current Labor Code entitles female workers to a paid thirty-minute break daily during menstruation.[33] But the local union is ineffective in demanding that management comply with this policy, thus leaving the female workers at the mercy of their supervisors, who then "grant" this entitlement at will. In this case, Neng Leakena's ability to speak the employer's language gave her an edge and rapport with the Kinh supervisor, who allowed her to go home early during menstruation or when she was feeling sick.

Job stability is important to these migrants. Neng Tơ shared: "I was recruited by my family [siblings] and make đ4–5 million a month, which includes overtime work. My parents work on their land; I send money home only when there is overtime work. I have some job stability after three years." This family is fortunate to have some land, which must generate the parents' main source of income.

Remittance to family can be a big incentive. Neng Rinh's story is another positive case from the Samho factory. She was recruited by her brother. At the

Aspirations after Malaysia   193

time of our interview, she had been working there only six months, checking the final products. While she missed her family a lot, she was able to send money home, and she planned to return home for the Khmer Lunar New Year in April:

> I earned around đ3 million and was able to send some money home after working two months; I feel very good [about this]. I joined the union but am not active in the union. I have normal relations with the Kinh, but I miss home a lot: crying all the time and calling home as much as I can. I will go home in April [for four days] for the Khmer New Year by taking the Phương Trang bus for six hours. I bought a ticket with a bed so I can relax.

Another case shows migrants traveling together as siblings. Neng Nuôi and her younger sister worked very hard to be able to send money home because their parents did not have any work at home.[34] Still, they looked forward to going home for their New Year: "We will go home for Tết [the Khmer new year] and use the Phương Trang bus service. We bought 'bed' tickets so we can sleep on the bus." These Khmer migrants continue to be proud of their cultural identity and faithfully practice their April celebrations.[35]

However, there were some negative experiences with domestic migration. Neng Rachana worked in the quality-control station, returning products that did not meet standards. After working there for two years, she still earned just a bit more than đ3 million per month while having to spend over 20 percent of her meager salary on rent (đ700,000 per month). As a result, she did not want to continue working for Samho, complaining that its salaries were not livable.

Some workers endured toxic working conditions, dealing with chemicals and noise without proper protection. Neng Thơ had worked there for just five months at the time of the interview. She stayed in the same rental unit as her sister, who had recruited her. She noted,

> There was only four-hour notice to work overtime. I worked in the washing assembly, washing the outer sole of the shoes (to prevent slipping). The water "ate up" our hands because we were not used to wearing gloves and ended up not wearing them when handling the soles. The water on the conveyor belt reeked with the smell of bleach and bubbled up with chemicals. It's not just the smell, but also the high level of noise. A lot of water was used in the washing. When I looked at my paycheck stub, I found that they paid for "toxic allowance." [Nevertheless,] I have not sent any money home or returned home for a visit because I have not even had enough money to eat.[36] My family has very little land, only 2–3 *công*,[37] and they do not have enough to eat. I have good relation with the Kinh, no problem.

194 CHAPTER 7

This narrative indicates the need to inform workers about the benefits of wearing gloves for protection. Neng Thơ had not yet joined the union at the time of the interview. As a result, she did not receive benefits from union representation or instructions on working conditions, such as how to deal with overtime notices or the policies for exposure to toxic conditions.

Neng Thơ's case and others show that working for a foreign factory in Vietnam does not lift these domestic migrants out of poverty. As another example, some Khmer workers cannot afford adequate childcare with their low pay. Neng Thanh, thirty-one years old, had worked at Samho for almost a year with her sister. "I am doing the job of pressing [at Samho]; the machine is pretty safe, but it requires fast action to push the button for the pressing movement to happen," she told me. The working conditions were pretty safe, but without her parents living nearby to help, she had no support for her childcare needs:

> I have four children: the eldest is twelve, the second seven, the third three, and the youngest one is just seven months old. My husband is also Khmer and doing construction work. I make đ3 million, just barely enough to feed my children. So my eldest does not go to school because she stays in the room taking care of my youngest son. I have no money to send them to childcare, so none of my children go to school.[38]

Clearly, migrant children are disadvantaged by not receiving a proper education, starting at a very young age. This is an unintended consequence of their parents' mobile, unstable, and precarious lifestyle, enacted in pursuit of making a living. The Chăm's peripatetic lifestyle is similar, although their migration patterns are informed by centuries-old histories.

The Chăm: Circular Migration and Entrepreneurship

The lives of a few Chăm who participated in the LBS program were not much better after their Malaysia experiences. Some of them found work in export processing zones and industrial zones in and around Hồ Chí Minh City, beyond retailing, as Taylor has reported.[39] Mr. Sadat, his wife (Ms. Aleena), and his siblings migrated domestically and found work in Quốc Thái commune of An Phú district. They joined thousands of migrant workers to serve the global supply chains by laboring in factories in Vietnam for very low wages. I had a chance to talk to them while they were visiting home during the Ramadan season. Ms. Aleena worked in a Korean-owned garment factory in Củ Chi district; she made about đ3 million per month with overtime pay, but she had to pay rent, utilities, and food. She sent home what she could

Aspirations after Malaysia

after all those expenses. Ms. Issra, Mr. Sadat's sister, worked in a refrigerator factory in Bình Dương province (north of Ho Chi Minh City), making about đ2 million (or less than US$100) per month. She was given a free room in a worker dormitory but had to pay utilities and her own food expenses. Still, she saved and sent home about US$50 per month—half of her salary.

However, the Chăm's geographical agency and their national and transnational cultural and religious networks have given them many more options than the other four groups. Those who traversed Vietnam and Malaysia in circular migration patterns maintained and nurtured the networks established in Malaysia long after returning to their communes in Vietnam. Ms. Tiệp (portrayed in chapter 5) relied on strong ties with her family connections in Vietnam and some Eastern European countries to build a transnational "garment empire." Similarly, one young entrepreneur, Ms. Kinza, demonstrated strong ties with her aunt who lived in Malaysia.[40] But beyond these strong ties, Ms. Kinza also revived an important Chăm tradition: working with garment/apparel products.

I visited her and her extended family in their one-room house, where sewing and stitching machines lined the wall. Ms. Kinza, a twenty-five-year-old seamstress and fashion designer, demonstrates a return to the traditional Chăm way of life, filled with dynamism and creativity. The whole family continues various aspects of the traditional Chăm way of life. Her father fishes, and her mother sells the catch. Ms. Kinza designs and sews traditional Muslim garments to be sold in Vietnam and Malaysia, with the help of her siblings and other relatives.

As described in Chapter 5, Ms. Kinza has accumulated skills and built networks, while working in a "third space" using a tourist visa. Between factory jobs, she helped the aunt who lived in Malaysia sell her garment products. Her experience demonstrates the power of historical roots; and thanks to it, she developed a customer-based network in Malaysia for her own subsequent tailoring business.

Success stories like Ms. Kinza's require a combination of factors including the help of local mass organizations. Ms. Chamis is a Kinh who has happily married into a Chăm family and converted to the Islamic faith. We had a nice interview in her small "convenience shop," which sells dried foods, drinks, and sundries for the local Chăm families in her neighborhood in An Giang. Ms. Chamis worked hard to organize free sewing lessons for the Chăm women who were interested in learning.

Upon returning home from Malaysia, Ms. Kinza and other Chăm women in the same village attended this sewing class for three months: "With my passion for sewing, when I saw that the government opened a sewing class,

196 CHAPTER 7

I immediately took it and have been sewing ever since. Now, every day, I cut five or six suits [Malay female dress suits], and then I assemble them the following day." Effectively, Ms. Kinza has practiced horizontal integration, connecting several phases of production.

Her ambition does not end there. Learning these skills and benefiting from cross-border connections with her aunt in Malaysia turned out to be a good investment for Ms. Kinza. Every year, on average, Ms. Kinza sent a hundred or more dresses to Malaysia. Her aunt in Malaysia has acted as a retailer of her products. Both aunt and niece benefit from this exchange: the aunt gets a small fee for stockpiling unsold clothes, and Ms. Kinza's business gets a budding clientele:

> I sew according to standardized sizes from the clothes that my aunt sells in Malaysia. Each set of clothes [which includes a blouse and a pair of pants] would cost me about đ150,000 (about US$7), and I can sell it for đ300,000 [a 100 percent profit].

This young entrepreneur has further built her enterprise by providing tailoring for her fellow Chăm villagers. In addition, along with her siblings and other relatives, Ms. Kinza also assembles precut fabrics, subcontracting for Chăm shops in her district. "Then I save my money in the 'piggy bank' to buy [Vietnamese] fabrics to sew clothes," she said.

Thinking long-term, she also invested some of her profits into means of production, buying more sewing machines to scale up her product lines. In this case, strong ties of family networks, nurtured during her stay in Malaysia in the shadow of third space, helped her revive and extend Chăm traditions of designing, sewing, and selling across borders. She dreams of opening up her own tailoring shop in An Giang one day.

From a piggy bank to sewing machines, Ms. Kinza shows that she was able to accumulate more capital to enlarge her operation, relying on social and historical networks. Moreover, in the long run, she might even be able to move her extended family up the economic ladder in the ethnic hierarchies discussed in chapter 1.

Comparative Remarks

Some Kinh and Hoa, with better economic resources, engage in the conventional *stepwise* destinations after Malaysia, while the other three ethnic groups engage in their own regional *circular* migration, enabled by their cultural and religious, rather than economic, resources. There is gender equity among the Kinh, Hoa, Khmer, and Chăm ethnic groups: both men and women migrate to work in other Southeast Asian countries. The Khmer migrants traverse Vietnam, Cambodia, and Thailand; the Chăm crisscross Vietnam, Cambodia, and Malaysia (via Thailand).

Of the five ethnic groups discussed in this book, the Hrê have the fewest economic resources and cultural connections and thus the fewest opportunities for transnational migration. Hrê women face more constraints on working outside of their communes or villages; they mostly stay at home to engage in a combination of wet rice agriculture and swidden cultivation. Hrê men continue strong native place bonding in their domestic migration, traveling together with fellow Hrê to nearby provinces for seasonal farmwork.

The groups that are most deprived educationally, the Hrê and the Khmer, are the most proactive in obtaining additional education for themselves so they can teach in their respective communities. For the Chăm, the strong role of religion offers religious education but privileges men over women in terms of opportunities to advance their studies overseas. Some Chăm men used such opportunities to pursue upward mobility.

Conclusion

The robust network of the transnational labor brokerage state (LBS) system never fully secures the consent of the migrants from Vietnam. On the Vietnamese side, this system faces both internal contradictions and external criticisms, thus opening up spaces for dissent. Ethnic hierarchies are important for thinking about different forms of export labor dissent, even when different ethnic groups are dealing with the same labor export policy. We cannot think about the lives of migrants without considering how gender and physical and metaphorical third spaces of dissent play into their experiences while they are working abroad and upon returning home. By combining these analyses, this book contributes a comprehensive and intersectional approach to the field of labor migration studies.

Ethnic hierarchies are also useful in highlighting the power of community cultural wealth. Many of the Kinh and the Hoa are able to partake in conventional stepwise migration thanks to their access to financing and the state system. But for the ethnic minority groups with limited access to economic resources, their cultural resources have come to their rescue. Village/commune and religious leaders, for example, make use of verbal resources in the form of metaphorical mimicries to demand justice for their peoples. These cultural resources inform their fellow villagers' responses to the LBS system or enable those who bypass it altogether.

Long-standing religious resources continue to empower the Chăm and the Khmer, allowing them to challenge and bypass the LBS system. Local religious leaders prove to be efficient competing authorities. The Chăm Muslims' faith gave them an edge while they were sojourning in Malaysia, and they received more compassionate and accommodating treatment from local

200 *Conclusion*

Muslim communities than they did from other groups. This religious affiliation was sustained even after the Chăm returned to An Giang (as in the case of Ms. Kinza, the seamstress entrepreneur). For the Khmer, the local *wats* are not only the center of religious practices but also the "keepers" of their language, traditions, and cultural practices.

A semblance of justice prevails. The state has tacitly written off many migrant workers' debts since 2013. Some local state officials have largely stopped coming to their houses to collect debt payments (unless the officials know that the returnees are gainfully employed). This unofficial debt forgiveness (as of my fieldwork in 2015) expands the official scope of loan forgiveness, which dictates that loans can be forgiven only when the parents are deceased and their children can no longer work.

Next Steps for the Five Ethnic Groups

Internal empowerment takes many forms. Migrant returnees from all five groups gained something from their Malaysia experiences that helped them improve their lives, despite the precarity and risks they faced in Malaysia. Many came home with broader worldviews, having learned new languages and experienced new cultures by interacting with other foreign guest workers. Some were able to apply relevant new skills, such as customer service skills, ability to communicate with employers, and money management, to their livelihoods at home.

Many members of all five ethnic groups aspired to move up the migration ladder, but the steps in their ladders have been different, determined by their own economic and cultural wealth. Paralleling the upward mobility of the Kinh and Hoa, who have more opportunities to participate in conventional stepwise migration than other groups, many earlier Kinh migrants of the Soviet era, with their (now adult) children, have moved beyond small-scale retailing and have become professionals with their own cultural hybrid identities, contributing to thriving Vietnamese communities in Warsaw and Prague.

Different gender patterns, informed by varying cultural and religious resources and practices, are in evidence among ethnic minority groups. Both female and male Khmer migrants traverse Vietnam, Cambodia, and Thailand and return home. Many Chăm families without government assistance crisscross Vietnam, Cambodia, and Malaysia (via Thailand) and return home. Some of the Chăm and the Khmer migrate to work in factories in Vietnam's cities and suburban areas. Moreover, some Chăm open shops in Ho Chi Minh City, where they sell garments to women from Malaysia and other Muslim countries. The Hrê men, with the fewest economic and cultural connections overseas, travel with fellow Hrê brothers to nearby provinces in Vietnam for

Conclusion

seasonal farmwork. Meanwhile, their wives stay at home, doing hard labor as they work wet rice paddies, engage in swidden cultivation, and take care of their families.

A desire for higher education is prominent among the groups that are most deprived of public education. Many Hrê and Khmer are vocal about their desire for education and are proactive in obtaining it so they can contribute directly to their respective communities. Among the Chăm, on the other hand, men are privileged over women owing to the strong influence of Islam on their communities. Only men have access to religious studies (conducted in Thailand or Malaysia), which they use as a path to upward mobility or as a platform for future community service when they return to their local mosques.

LBS Dynamics and the Need for Monitoring

Players in the transnational LBS system continue to benefit from it. According to the World Bank's statistics, 6.5 percent of Vietnam's GDP (or US$17 billion) came from remittances in 2019.[1] This source projects that due to the Covid-19 pandemic, remittance flows to Low and Middle Income Countries will decline by around 20 percent in 2020.[2] Vietnam's government also wants this system to survive because it creates jobs for people who keep it running, such as administrators and office employees of banks and recruitment companies and cadres in various mass organizations. Since 2016, the Malaysian state has also been benefiting from the LBS system thanks to an increase in tax revenue, which it secured by doubling the levy paid by foreign migrants who are working jobs not wanted by local Malaysians.

This transnational system thus has checks and balances to ensure that it is self-reinforcing and coherent.[3] The Vietnamese LBS has instituted some laws to address workers' complaints about the labor export policies. They include Law 02/2011/QH13, which outlines procedures for making complaints; Decree No. 95/2013/NĐ-CP, which decribes regulations and penalties for recruitment companies and migrants; and Decree No. 119/2014/NĐ-CP, which details how to handle complaints on a number of issues related to Vietnamese workers working abroad.

The 2019 Labor Code, effective as of January 1, 2021, applies primarily to domestic workers, but some sections also apply to overseas workers. Seeking to protect migrant laborers who work overseas, the code has stipulations on compliance with the laws of both Vietnam and host countries, as well as provisions and procedures for settling labor disputes between a worker and a recruitment organization that sent the migrant worker to work overseas after having signed an employment contract. However, while the Vietnamese

202 Conclusion

overseas workers are expected to comply with these laws, there is no mention of how they shall be protected by the laws, and there is no distinction between protections for male and female overseas migrant workers.[4]

More importantly, Law 69/2020/QH14, the recently revised law on contract-based Vietnamese overseas workers—ratified on November 13, 2020, and effective starting January 1, 2022—focuses on overseas workers. It has some key features to empower migrant workers, by adopting several ILOs' key recommendations with regards to removing obligation to pay brokerage fees; enabling migrant workers to unilaterally liquidate contracts in case of threats, sexual harassment, maltreatment or forced labor; acknowledging discrimination and forced labor; and offering legal assistance in cases of abuse, violence or discrimination while working abroad and after returning home in access to social psychological consulting service. To name just a few features:

- Brokerage fees are now forbidden. This provision protects potential workers from unscrupulous brokers who are not monitored by the government. Service fees charged by recruitment companies are still allowed, but the ceiling for rates is clearly stipulated: one month's salary for every twelve months of the contract, with a maximum of three months' salary for contracts of three or more years. If a worker's contract is renewed (after completion of an initial three-year contract), then the service fee is only half a month's salary for every twelve months of the renewed contract.
- A migrant worker can end a contract with a recruitment company if it is not implemented correctly.
- State agencies are not permitted to charge migrants service fees if they work with (foreign) not-for-profit contracts.[5]

It will be important to observe how these new laws will be enforced.

The Malaysian government signed a memorandum of understanding with Vietnam in August 2015 that aims to regulate wages and working hours and responsibilities of all stakeholders (employers, recruiters, and workers), which is a good step forward. Part of the goal of this memorandum is to ensure the implementation of the 2015 Malaysian passport law under which foreign migrant workers are allowed to keep their passports and personal documents. Other parts of this agreement demand accountability from Malaysian employers (not the intermediaries, such as labor brokers and outsourcing companies), stipulating that the employer is responsible for picking up Vietnamese workers at the airport within six hours of their arrival, and for properly implementing the terms of labor contracts.

There is also a sign of progress on the union side. Building on the 2015 MOU signed between the two unions for the protection of the rights of Vietnamese

Conclusion 203

migrant workers in Malaysia, in 2018, the Malaysian Trade Union Congress (MTUC) and the Vietnam General Confederation of Labor (VGCL) jointly developed a plan of action to increase the protection of Vietnamese migrant workers' rights in Malaysia. Specifically, this plan promises to disseminate "targeted information" to prepare workers before they leave Vietnam, and to give them access to legal and migrant support services while they work in Malaysia. Under this plan, the key Vietnamese LBS players—recruitment agencies, migrant worker resource centers, and mass media—would provide the predeparture preparation. MTUC also commits to providing "targeted support services" to migrant workers, especially legal support, through its three migrant resource centers. However, it remains to be seen how these services will address the different needs of these five ethnic groups. External groups need to monitor how well these laws and plans are carried out. Future studies can examine the implementation, monitoring, and enforcement of this plan of action to ensure compliance.

Call for Action and Future Research

One should not romanticize third spaces of dissent. Community acceptance in physical third spaces is temporary and at times fraught with risks (such as the possibility of police raids) for the undocumented migrants who are trying to save enough money to return home, and possibly for those who are harboring them. Use of ironic and subversive discourses—a type of metaphorical third space—is a safe strategy but does not have long-lasting effects if the migrants do not organize and mobilize to demand their rights from the LBS system.

Concrete action is long overdue. The VGCL can learn, for example, from the Nepalese Workers' Association GEFONT, an outgrowth of the MTUC and the Nepalese trade union council that helps Nepalese and other foreign migrant workers, including Vietnamese workers, in Malaysia.[7] The leader of the Nepalese Workers' Association, who speaks Nepalese and some English, operates a twenty-four-hour SMS hotline for foreign workers who need help with any problems that they encounter while working in Malaysia.[8] The VGCL can learn from GEFONT's success by working with the MTUC to form a Vietnamese migrant workers' support group or association to protect their rights. Such a collaboration would be one way to effectively implement the memorandum signed between the VGCL and the MTUC in 2015.

The Vietnamese LBS can also learn from the experiences of the Philippine Overseas Employment Administration, which has offices in every Philippine embassy and consulate in the world and provides on-site remedies to help overseas Filipino workers file legal complaints against employers and

204   *Conclusion*

agencies at the Philippine Overseas Labor Office.[9] The LBS system, especially the Department of Overseas Labor, should learn from the best practices of these labor offices and provide legal counsel so the Vietnamese migrant workers in Malaysia can demand justice on-site and to get their grievances addressed in a timely manner.

Global civil society organizations have provided help. Among the faith-based NGO activist groups, the Catholic Migrant Ministry in Kuala Lumpur has allowed Vietnamese workers to volunteer to help other workers with court appearances and to make phone calls to the Vietnamese Embassy and elsewhere. The ministry also has hired Malaysians as legal counsel and works with NGO activists who help Vietnamese migrant workers in other ways. However, they do not operate a direct helpline like GEFONT does. The second grouping, which includes overseas Vietnamese NGOs that are critical of the Vietnamese government (such as the Committee to Protect Vietnamese Workers, Boatpeople SOS, and the Coalition to Abolish Modern-Day Slavery in Asia), carries out some functions of trade unions to support migrant workers in global fora, but they do not mobilize labor.[10] An openness to and collaboration with such groups can help implement the memorandum of understanding between the MTUC and the VGCL and protect Vietnamese migrant workers overseas.

Fundamentally, however, the real problem is political. The VGCL has been aware of GEFONT's effectiveness in assisting its migrant workers for years. Its inaction, neglecting to form a migrant workers' support group in Malaysia, has a lot to do with the suspicion that such workers' groups may be influenced by prodemocracy and antigovernment groups. Consequently, migrant workers from all ethnic groups from Vietnam are deprived of the protection and representation they sorely need, and they miss out on joining in solidarity with other foreign workers in Malaysia. The Christian groups and other church associations that some Kinh and Hoa have joined serve only as a temporary support system while they are in Malaysia. Unlike the Nepalese Workers' Association GEFONT, these associations do not have the capacity to intervene directly for migrant worker rights.

As this book goes to press, both Vietnam and Malaysia have been under strict Covid-19 lockdown with thousands of Vietnamese migrant workers stranded, jobless, or underemployed in Malaysia.[11] In Vietnam, DOLAB has instructed recruitment companies to postpone sending workers overseas due to the resurgence of the coronavirus in Malaysia and worldwide.[12] This pause on labor export activities offers an opportunity to assess this policy. A conversation with a journalist in Vietnam in July 2021 confirmed with me that Decision 71/2009/QĐTT expired unceremoniously in 2020. This silence speaks volumes about its failure. Learning from this book's insights, the state ought to assess whether implementing labor export is an effective and humane way to alleviate poverty. While the state's intentions in offering low-interest-rate loans are good, adding labor export debt on top of existing debts is not an effective way to lift poor ethnic migrants out of poverty. The government needs to break this vicious cycle of debt. Concrete loan forgiveness policies could provide proper closure for these impoverished migrants and their families. The ban on brokers' fees in the 2020 revised law on contract-based Vietnamese overseas workers is a step in the right direction, because incurring less migration debt would empower overseas migrants to leave abusive employers with less financial consequence.

The LBS needs to learn from the experiences of Nepal and the Philippines and provide proper protection for Vietnam's citizens while they are working in Malaysia (and elsewhere). Because the Department of Overseas Labor's response to workers' grievances has been dismal and the Vietnamese government refuses to allow unions other than the VGCL to organize, it behooves the VGCL to represent workers overseas. And since the VGCL cannot function directly in other countries, it must work with unions in the receiving countries (following the Nepalese GEFONT model) to protect and defend the Vietnamese guest workers.

The 2020 law on contract-based Vietnamese overseas workers, Law 69/2020/QH14, is a revision that improves protections for Vietnamese workers abroad, but it continues to miss two important considerations.

First, there is no union protection anywhere in the revised law. When a conflict arises (among all parties), this law stipulates that its resolution will be based on intergovernmental agreements between Vietnam and the host countries, as well as international conventions that Vietnam has ratified. In other words, conflicts are to be resolved by the appropriate Malaysian entities and the Vietnamese MoLISA counterparts.[13] This means that there is no role for the VGCL in conflict resolution.

Second, there are no pathways for migrants to actually take advantage of this revised law because they have no protection while overseas. While the revised law allows migrant workers to end their individual contracts with Vietnamese recruitment companies when the contract stipulations are not implemented or are violated (Article 46, p. 23), there is no comparable law in the receiving countries to protect migrant workers against financial penalty or criminal vulnerability while they are overseas.[14] Moreover, there is no way for aggrieved migrants to redress violations or harassment that have been inflicted upon their well-being. The situation is worse in some Gulf states that use the kafala (sponsorship) system, in which the sponsor is also the employer who dictates the employment conditions. Worse yet, for workers in private homes, or domestic work, the sponsor-employer is the head of

206 *Conclusion*

household whose authority often goes unquestioned and unsupervised. In this system, foreign domestic workers are legally bound to their employers and have limited rights. The employees' physical, economic, and mental health are precarious, often resulting in overwork, underpayment of wages, and other consequences that can lead to physical and sexual abuse.[15]

For now, some stipulations in the revised law are sensitive to the rights of female migrant workers. For instance, Article 7 mentions specifically that forced labor, maltreatment, human trafficking, discrimination, and sexual harassment are forbidden, as is massage in restaurants, hotels, and entertainment centers. These stipulations are timely, as increasing numbers of female migrant workers are recruited to do domestic work in the Gulf states (such as Saudi Arabia) and in other East and Southeast Asian countries (such as Taiwan, Thailand, and Korea)—all locations where sexual and physical abuses have been documented. However, there are no mechanisms to enforce these stipulations. In the era of Covid-19, overseas domestic workers whose work takes place behind closed doors are even more vulnerable.[16]

Moreover, the state needs to provide better pre-labor-export orientation and post-labor-export opportunities for the returnees so they can truly escape poverty. Knowing the power of language in working overseas, the state needs to offer proper language training; perhaps the Chinese or Malay languages would be more appropriate for working in Malaysia than half-baked English. It should also improve public education in poor districts and offer bilingual classes, including classes that teach the languages of the ethnic minority groups so as to empower the people who are the targets of the labor export policy. Moreover, the state needs to create permanent jobs for those who complete their contracts and return to Vietnam with the hope that their efforts abroad will help them succeed at home. Incentive mechanisms can include financial support for stepwise international migration and vocational training courses so the returnees can use their newly acquired skills in jobs in Vietnam and beyond.

In rural and remote highland areas, most would-be migrants rely on informal local networks that make them susceptible to high fees, deception, and even trafficking.[17] Local governments and civil society organizations need to reach out to them and provide them with reliable sources of information on overseas work opportunities so they can have realistic expectations in terms of financial gains (compared to working in Vietnam) and the potential skills they could gain that could help them change their lives for the better. Most importantly, the would-be migrants must be aware of and learn how to avoid real risks while overseas, especially in domestic work where there is no oversight and abuses can happen in the privacy of the employer's home.

Finally, as a contribution to migration studies especially in Southeast Asia, this study has shown that state policies should be sensitive to two key factors:

ethnicity and gender. First, different ethnic groups living within each country's borders have different resources and constraints that policies need to take into account in order to help migrants overcome adversities and achieve long-term successes. To truly deliver on the poverty reduction promise of the labor export policy, the state should offer preparation in the predeparture stage and an incentive system to cover the costs of going abroad for impoverished migrants. Second, in light of a drastic increase in the number of female migrants working abroad, gender sensitivity, currently sorely missing in labor export policies, will be required in order to protect the rights of female migrant workers of different ethnic groups.

The revised law (69/2020/QH14) on contract-based Vietnamese overseas workers has very powerful stipulations, specifically empowering the migrant workers aiming to level the uneven power relations between labor and management. But to have teeth, it needs to be properly implemented starting on January 1, 2022. The global Covid-19 crisis has intensified all the precarities facing overseas migrant workers, now stranded in legal and illicit third spaces. It is all the more urgent to mobilize all forces, national and transnational, to assist and empower them.

Appendix 1
Descriptions of the Samples

The Kinh and Hoa Sample

To capture the whole transnational migration experience, I interviewed 41 Kinh and Hoa migrants and their family members over an eight-year period from 2008 to 2015, which allowed me to speak with both migrants who were still working in Malaysia as well as migrants who had returned to Vietnam. In my fieldwork, I did not come across any Kinh or Hoa migrants who bypassed the state system. Thus, I cannot make generalizations based on my convenient sample. Mr. Trần Văn Thạnh (Suleco Company president[1]) assisted with developing my sample; he helped me find the original six migrant returnees in Ho Chi Minh City, whom I then interviewed several times in 2008. These interviewees gave me information about their Vietnamese friends who were still working in Malaysia. Using these leads, I built my sample by going to Malaysia with Dr. Vicki Crinis to interview these migrant workers in 2008. From 2009 to 2014, I expanded my sample further by interviewing members of households (parents, spouses, and siblings) of the migrants who were still working in Malaysia or had returned to their hometowns (Ho Chi Minh City, An Giang, and the northern city of Sơn Tây), as well as workers waiting to migrate.

Interviews with Kinh and Hoa Individuals

All names are pseudonyms.

Ho Chi Minh City, 2008: Ms. Hảo, Ms. Nữ, Ms. Lê, Ms. Yến, Ms. Thanh, Ms. Nhung, Ms. Bình, Ms. Tiên
Ho Chi Minh City, 2011: Ms. Giang
Malaysia, 2008: Mr. Đại, Mr. Danh, Mr. Kiên, Mr. Thao, Ms. Cúc, Ms. Hà, Ms. Linh, Ms. Liên, Ms. Thu, Ms. Lê
An Giang, 2012: Ms. Mai, Ms. Trúc

210 APPENDIX 1

An Giang, 2013: Mr. Thức, Ms. Thúy, Mr. Ngãi, Mr. Tài, Mr. Ngữ, Mr. Việt, Ms.
Kim-Ly, Ms. Hạnh, Mr. Lộc Quảng Ngãi, 2013: Ms. Bạch
Other (conversations in public settings): Ms. Tiệp, intermittent interviews be-
tween 2002 and 2006; Mr. Nguyễn Minh Ngọc, phone interview, 2013; Mr.
and Ms. Giây, 2017, Warsaw; Mr. Sơn (husband), Ms. Đào (wife), and Ms.
Liên (daughter), 2017, Prague

The Hrê Sample

I interviewed fifty-two people in Quảng Ngãi province, spread out over four years
(2011, 2012, 2013, and 2015). Thirty-five were Hrê migrants, their spouses, and parents.[2] The remaining seventeen were Kinh and Hrê government officials at four
levels—provincial (*tỉnh*), rural district (*huyện*), village (*thôn*), and commune (*xã*)—
whom I interviewed to gain an understanding of the LBS recruitment system and
the indebtedness it gave rise to. I started with Ba Tơ District, home to the largest
concentration of Hrê, where I visited downtown Ba Tơ District and five of the eighteen communes (Ba Tô, Ba Tiêu, Ba Xa, Ba Vì, Ba Thành), and the Sơn Hà district,
another area with many Hrê, where I visited two communes (Sơn Cao and Sơn
Hạ). I managed to visit the Sơn Hạ district by myself once, and on that occasion I
was able to get more candid interviews. I later added a third district, Nghĩa Hành,
which gave me the opportunity to learn about the local state relocation policy as
well as the enhanced economic agency the Hrê secured by migrating to the nearby
provinces. I walked around to observe and interviewed seven Hrê who had relocated
to that area. I'm conscious that interviewees might have self-censored their answers
to my questions because of the presence of local state officials who escorted me.
But I managed to balance those interviews with others that I conducted by having
independent guides (such as local journalists) accompany me to remote communes
up in the mountains of Quảng Ngãi. There, I was able to ask questions without being censored, and the respondents were able to answer me more freely. This was
the most arduous fieldwork I did, wading knee-deep in the mud (during the rainy
season) to reach those villages.

Interviews with Hrê Individuals

All names are pseudonyms.

Quảng Ngãi, 2011: Ms. Khanh, her husband, and their sons, Mr. Phúc and Mr.
Tú; Ms. Oanh; Ms. Giáo and her husband; Mr. Cung
Quảng Ngãi, 2012: Mr. Thành, Mr. Văn Thanh, Mr. Văn Đô, Ms. Chi and Mr.
Tuấn (her husband), Ms. Hân
Quảng Ngãi, 2013: Mr. Châu and Ms. Na (his wife), father of Mr. Ngô
Quảng Ngãi, 2015: Mr. Lê, Mr. Đoàn Lân, Mr. Xuân (a low-ranking Hre state
official), Mr. Bao

The Khmer Sample

My fieldwork interviews from 2014 reflect perspectives from the household, hamlet, district, and province levels. I interviewed twenty returnees as well as their parents, because the decision to migrate, whether transnationally or domestically, is mostly a household survival strategy.[3] To understand competing authorities, I interviewed Châu Anurak (the hamlet deputy chief in Tịnh Biên district) and five Kinh officials (the vice chair of the An Giang Department of Labor, the director of An Giang Employment Center, the vice president of the An Giang Social Policy Bank, the chair of Tri Tôn District Labor Department, and a vocational instructor at Tri Tôn District Employment Center). I focused on two Khmer-concentrated districts (Tri Tôn and Tịnh Biên) in An Giang province. Over thirty-five thousand Khmer reside in the province, one-third of them in Tịnh Biên district.[4]

Interviews with Khmer Individuals

All names are pseudonyms.

> An Giang, 2014: Neng Angkeara, Neng Kanika, Châu Anurak, Châu Jivin, Châu Sethsak (father of Châu Tiro), Neng Arun, Châu Amnat, Châu Issara, Châu Virak, Châu Siha, Châu Rithi, Châu Balin, father of Châu Hùng, Châu Charya, Châu Bona
> Củ Chi district, 2014: Neng Leakena, Neng Tơ, Neng Rinh, Neng Nuôi, Neng Rachana, Neng Thơ, Neng Thanh

The Chăm Sample

My interview sample focused on the Chăm-populated An Phú district. Over fifty-nine hundred Chăm Muslims live in five commune there. My sample includes forty people: thirty-three migrant workers and their families, and seven officials and religious/cultural leaders. Between 2012 and 2015, my assistants and I interviewed thirty Chăm worker returnees and relatives (parents, sisters, and spouses) in three communes (Đa Phước, Quốc Thái, Vĩnh Trường) and three Chăm who migrated to work and worship in Ho Chi Minh City (one of the Chăm's main migration destinations).[5] Two religious leaders (one mosque keeper in Quốc Thái commune and one imam in a Ho Chi Minh City mosque) and five state officials at different levels in the LBS in An Giang province comprise the group of officials and religious/cultural leaders that I interviewed. I was fortunate to witness Chăm Muslim practices twice during the Ramadan season, once in their hometown (An Giang province) in 2012 and once in Ho Chi Minh City in 2015. On these occasions, I was able to conduct interviews with religious leaders and scholars and worshippers that provided me with a greater understanding of how they support their fellow Chăm, forge connections with the global Islamic community, enhance their internal power, and deepen their reflection.

212 APPENDIX 1

Interviews with Chăm Individuals

All names are pseudonyms.

An Giang, 2012: Ms. Wali, Ms. Areen and her father, Ms. Rihanna, Mr. Ruabi
and wife, Mr. Vijaya, Ms. Sayad and Mr. Aahil (husband), Ms. Alvi, Ms.
Kinza, Ms. Chamis, Ms. Saadi, Mr. Chamana, Mr. Abdullah, Mr. Davi, Ms.
Baqri (Mr. Sadat's mother)
An Giang, 2014: Ms. Alvi (follow-up interview), Mr. Wasti, Mr. Chamali, Mr.
Sadat, Ms. Aleena (Mr. Sadat's wife), Ms. Issra (Sadat's sister), Ms. Baqri
(follow-up interview), Mr. Salim and son, Ms. Lodhra
Ho Chi Minh City, 2015: Mr. Masood, Ms. Chamkili, Imam Sanes, Mr. Babar,
Mr. Shimani

Additional Interviews

State Officials, Company Owners, and Organization Representatives

All names in this section are real. Entries are in roughly chronological order.

Mr. Tống Thanh Tùng, director of Châu Hưng Recruitment Company, 2011
Ms. Đinh Thị Phương Lan, vice chair of DoLISA in Ba Tơ district, Quảng Ngãi,
2011 and 2012
Mr. Nguyễn Văn Triệu, chair of DoLISA in Ba Tơ district, Quảng Ngãi, 2012
Mr. Phạm Văn Thích, a Hrê official in the Ba Tơ District Labor Department,
Quảng Ngãi, 2012
Mr. Xuân, a Kinh commune official in Ba Tơ, Quảng Ngãi, 2013
Mr. Vũ Minh Xuyên, director of Sovilaco Recruitment Company, 2014
Ms. Thái Thị Bạch Lan, vice chair of An Giang Labor Department, 2014
Trần Duy Hiếu, chair of Tri Tôn District Labor Department, An Giang, 2014
Mr. Nguyễn Thành Danh, vocational instructor at Tri Tôn District Employment
Center, 2014
Mr. Nguyễn Văn Lâm, director of Employment Center of the Labor Depart-
ment, An Giang, 2014
Mr. Nguyễn Anh Tuấn, vice president of An Giang Social Policy Bank, 2014
Mr. Tôn Long Quốc Vinh, director of human resources at Samho factory, Củ
Chi district, 2014
Mr. Võ Duy Yên, director of Quảng Ngãi Employment Center, 2015
Mr. Phan Văn Dốp, Institute of Social Science and Humanities, Southern re-
gion, Ho Chi Minh City, 2015
Ms. Nguyễn Thị Nhung, Institute of Social Science and Humanities, Southern
region, Ho Chi Minh City, 2015
Dr. Nguyễn Lương Trào, director of VAMAS, Hanoi, 2015
Ms. Nguyễn Thị Tuyết Mai, director of Hanic Recruitment Company, Hanoi, 2015
Mr. Lê Quốc Hùng, vice director of Hanic Recruitment Company, Hanoi, 2015

Descriptions of the Samples   213

Journalists

Pen names are used. Entries are in alphabetical order.

Mr. Nam Dương, Ho Chi Minh City, 2010–13
Mr. Duy Quốc, Ho Chi Minh City, 2011–15
Mr. Nguyễn Quyết, Ho Chi Minh City, 2016
Mr. Tử Trực, Quảng Ngãi, 2011–15
Mr. Phạm Anh, Quảng Ngãi, 2015

Appendix 2
Land Issues Faced by the Five
Ethnic Groups in This Study

My book's context is the increasingly urbanized and commercialized countryside in Vietnam where most residents can no longer rely on traditional farming to make a living, which leads workers to resist the labor export policy that tries to replace their way of life. The Hrê still have their family plots and rice terraces on the hillsides or up in the mountains where they practice wet rice cultivation alongside their traditional swidden cultivation, or shifting slash-and-burn cultivation.[1] However, these practices have been gradually replaced by the planting of acacia trees, a cash crop that requires water, fertilizer, and seven years of growing to harvest.

The state's developmental agenda in the mountainous regions is to eliminate swidden cultivation because the state believes that swiddening is a primitive form of agriculture and leads to an "uneducated, poor, and miserable life" and also to deforestation.[2] In its place, the state has introduced sedentarization, which highlights fixed settlements, wet rice cultivation, and the integration of local peoples into a national political community, with access to modern communications and schooling.

But sedentarization has had mixed results. In his study of the Kmhmu, a tiny Mon-Khmer ethnic group in the northern uplands of Vietnam, Nguyễn Văn Chính maintains that their living conditions under the sedentarization program have failed, citing low uptake of wet rice cultivation, weak participation in schooling, high levels of poverty, alarming food shortages, and excessive indebtedness.[3] The Kmhmu people have ended up having to continue to exploit the forested slopes to make a living.

Land issues seem to affect the Hrê and the Khmer more than the Kinh, Hoa, and Chăm. The sedentarization policy also applies to the Hrê, but it has not affected their livelihoods because they already practiced a combination of sedentary wet rice cultivation and cash crop planting while also exploiting the forested slopes (by gathering wood limbs) to supplement their income. However, the 1997–98 resettlement policy, focusing on both "fixed cultivation and fixed residence," has affected the migration patterns and livelihoods of the Hrê. The Hrê's forms of resistance focus on maintaining their traditional livelihoods and keeping as much income intended for remittances as they can for themselves and their families, not the state.

Khmer families often have a small amount of land, but many parents have had to cede their landholdings to pay mounting debts, including the fees to send their children to work in Malaysia and, at times, to bring them home early in cases of contract violations. Some Kinh migrants' families own small plots of land, but most of the crops are for family consumption; their children have gone to work in Malaysia in hopes of saving up money to open small retail shops upon returning home or to participate in stepwise migration to a higher-tier country. Finally, Chăm households have little to no land and rely on their geographical agency as well as national and transnational networks to make their living.

Appendix 3
Chronology of the Transnational Labor Brokerage State System, 1950s–2020

Year	State-Managed Labor Migration Policies
1950s	The state sends workers/students/cadres to the Soviet Bloc countries.
1983	Vietnam and Cambodia sign the Agreement on Border Regulations (BBC/FE 7393 A3/1) to allow border crossing of their citizens
1988	The state sends workers to the Middle East and African countries.
1989	Soviet Bloc countries (East Germany, Poland, etc.) send Vietnamese migrant workers home because of the disintegration of the Soviet Union.
1999	Decree 152/1999/ND-CP announced. Quasi-state companies are allowed to provide labor exporting services.
2002	MOU between Vietnam and Malaysia signed to allow Vietnamese workers to hold temporary jobs in Malaysia.
2003	Decision 86/2003/QĐ-BNV by the Ministry of the Interior establishes Vietnamese Association of Manpower Supply (VAMAS).
2004	Decision 41/2004/Q Đ-BNV by the Ministry of the Interior approves VAMAS bylaws. Critical newspapers issue a number of reports about corrupt recruitment companies.
2005	Beginning in July, the Malaysian government allows two recruitment systems to manage foreign workers: the government's one-stop recruitment center and private outsourcing companies that recruit for employers who require fewer than fifty workers.
2006	Vietnam joins World Trade Organization. Law 72/2006/QH11 regarding Vietnamese labor migrants working overseas under contract passes.
2007	Law 72/2006/QH11 approving the support of poor rural districts to send them to work overseas, and going into effect in July.
2008	Social Policy Bank (No. 1034/NHCS-TD) guidelines issued.
2009	Prime Minister Decision 71/2009/QĐTT introduced.
2010	The Ministry of Labor, Invalids, and Social Affairs (MoLISA) issues Decision No. 630/ QD-LĐTBXH.
2011	Law on Complaints 02/2011/QH13 passes.

Chronology of Labor Brokerage

Year	State-Managed Labor Migration Policies
2012	MoLISA issues Decree No. 1083/QLLDNN-KHTC, which expands eligibility for work overseas with state support.
	VAMAS receives support from the International Labour Organization via the GMS TRIANGLE project to develop a code of conduct for its labor export companies.
	Malaysia revises the minimum wage policy to equalize the rates for both Malaysian and foreign workers, to be enforced starting 2013.
2013	MoLISA establishes the Department of Overseas Labor (DOLAB), to assist in managing Vietnamese workers overseas.[1]
	MoLISA establishes Circular No. 21/2013/TT-BLDTBXH.
	MoLISA establishes Circular No. 22/2013/TT-BLDTBXH.
	MoLISA and the Ministry of Foreign Affairs issue Joint Circular No. 32/2013/TTLT-BLDTBXH-BNG.
	State Bank of Vietnam issues Circular 31/2013/TT-NHNN.
	Prime Minister issues Decree No. 95/2013/NĐ-CP.
2014	Prime Minister issues Decree No. 119/2014/NĐ-CP.
	Prime Minister issues Decree No. 103/2014/NĐ-CP on the 2015 regional minimum wage average of đ2.4 million per month.
2015	The Ministry of the Interior approves changes to the bylaws.
	VAMAS member companies grow to 156.
	VAMAS introduces criteria for monitoring and evaluating the implementation of the Vietnamese code of conduct for Vietnamese recruitment companies that send workers overseas.
	On March 16, the VGCL signs a memorandum of understanding with the Malaysian Trades Union Congress (MTUC) for the protection of Vietnamese migrant workers in Malaysia.
	MOU signed by the governments of Vietnam and Malaysia in August to protect the rights of Vietnamese overseas workers.
2017	Employers are still found impounding foreign guest workers' passports when they arrive in Malaysia for work.[2]
	The Malaysian government holds employers (not migrant workers) responsible for levy payments. Implementation was postponed.
2018	In September, under pressure from labor unions and NGOs, the Malaysian government decides that employers must bear the full levy cost.
	The MTUC and the VGCL develop a plan of action as a result of the memorandum signed between them in 2015.
2019	In May, the Malaysian government reduces Malaysian employers levy responsibility from RM10,000 (annual levy for each foreign worker) to RM6,000 for the construction, manufacturing, and service sectors, where most Vietnamese guest workers have been hired. This reduced rate is valid for only one year.
	In November, Law 45/2019/QH14, a revision to the Labor Code, is ratified.
2020	On November 13, Law 69/2020/QH14, the revised law on contract-based Vietnamese overseas workers (replacing the 2006 law), is ratified, slated to become effective on January 1, 2022.
	Vietnam repatriated over 75,000 Vietnamese from the world's most severe Covid-19 hotspots.[3]

Appendix 4
Legal Documentation of Labor
Export Policies

Due to the collapse of the Soviet Union in 1989, the Politburo approved the labor export policy starting with **Decree 152/1999/NĐ-CP**, which allowed quasi-state companies (belonging to political and social mass organizations, including labor unions) to provide labor exporting services, in addition to state agencies.

The **2002 memorandum of understanding** signed between Vietnam and Malaysia established a legal framework for the terms (wages, taxes/levies, and working conditions) of three-year contracts. It also established the one-employer contract law, in which foreign workers were not allowed to change employers or employment sectors, even if an employer violated the terms of an employee's contract.

Decision 86/2003/QĐ-BNV by the Ministry of the Interior established the Vietnamese Association of Manpower Supply (VAMAS) and guidelines for governing the activities of recruitment companies and Vietnamese overseas workers.

Decision 41/2004/QĐ-BNV by the Ministry of the Interior approved bylaws under which VAMAS would represent 127 recruitment companies who were granted state licenses to send workers overseas under labor contracts.

The state began earnest enforcement of its labor export policy after Vietnam joined the World Trade Organization in 2006. Vietnamese **Law 72/2006/QH11** (Law on Vietnamese Working Overseas Under Labor Contracts) was designed to defend the rights of migrants working overseas under contract. It set procedures for all stages of the labor export process and established the terms for contracts with private, state-owned, and quasi-state recruitment companies. This law was intended to "eradicate hunger and minimize poverty" by creating jobs for peasants in poor rural districts. The Vietnamese General Confederation of Labor (VGCL) was not given a role in this law to defend migrant workers' rights while they are working overseas.

The 2008 guidelines from the Social Policy Bank (**No. 1034/NHCS-TD**) set out loan amounts, interest rates, loan disbursement, and direct payments to the recruitment companies based on the labor contract. These policies required approval from the

Labor Export Policies   219

local people's committees, who determined the loan duration, collection amounts (principal and interest), and loan deferments. Subsequent policies spelled out different ways to deal with risky loans and defaults, such as loan deferment and loan forgiveness, and described the paperwork necessary for these transactions.[1]

Prime Minister Decision 71/2009/QĐTT (Approving the Proposal to Support Poor Rural Districts, Pushing Forward Export Labor to Contribute to Sustained Poverty Reduction in the 2009–2020 Period) aimed to work toward poverty alleviation through labor exportation by creating jobs for residents from sixty-one targeted poor rural districts. (Three years later, three more districts were added.) The policy provided low-interest loans to cover migrants' costs for language and skills training and health checks, and it set labor export quotas for all administrative levels of the targeted districts. It was set to expire in 2020.

In 2010, the Ministry of Labor, Invalids, and Social Affairs (MoLISA) issued **Decision No. 630/QD-LĐTBXH** to regulate costs for vocational and language training and orientation courses for workers from the sixty-one poor districts[2] to work abroad.

Law 02/2011/QH13 outlined the procedures and mechanisms for making complaints related to violations of labor contracts and the time frame for doing so.

The MoLISA **Decree 1083/QLLDNN-KHTC** in 2012 expanded the labor export policy beyond the sixty-four poorest districts (the original districts specified in Prime Minister Decision 71/2009/QĐTT and the three districts added later) in an effort to entice poor households by offering low-interest loans (0.6 percent per month) from the Social Policy Bank. This expanded policy applied to workers who were first-degree relatives of those who sacrificed for the country, workers from poor households, ethnic minorities, and local residents who were of working age and were qualified and aspiring to work abroad under contract.[3]

To strengthen the labor export legal framework, MoLISA issued a series of legal documents pertaining to sending migrant workers abroad. The key ones included **Circular No. 21/2013/TT-BLDTBXH**, regulating the maximum security deposits to be paid by workers, to be managed by MoLISA and the state bank, and **Circular No. 22/2013/TT-BLDTBXH**, regulating labor supply contract requirements. To work in Malaysia, workers had to deposit US$300; upon finishing their three-year contracts, they had to report to the recruitment company to close the file (*thanh lý*) in order to receive their deposits back. This created a deterrent for workers to overstay their visas or fail to complete their contracts.

Prime Minister Decree No. 95/2013/NĐ-CP stipulated administrative sanctions for violations of the labor law and penalties for violations when sending workers overseas under contract.

Joint Circular No. 32/2013/TTLT-BLDTBXH-BNG, adopted by MoLISA and the Ministry of Foreign Affairs, penalized those who stayed abroad illegally after the expiration of their contract, fled assigned employment, and did not show up at the workplace as agreed to in the labor contract upon arrival in the destination country. It also applied sanctions to agencies, organizations, or individuals that violated contract terms.[4]

APPENDIX 4

Circular 31/2013/TT-NHNN permitted direct deduction of money from workers' accounts to pay their debts. This circular goes into great detail about taking money from debtors' accounts, domestically and globally, in all forms (checks and electronic), and applying it to the state budget. Section 4, "Payment and Budget," requests information on the amounts and values of debt of each individual and the amounts and values of electronic deduction.[5]

Prime Minister Decree 103/2014/NĐ-CP set the 2015 regional minimum wage average of đ2.4 million per month.

Decree No. 119/2014/NĐ-CP detailed how to handle complaints on a range of issues related to Vietnamese migrants working overseas.

On March 16, 2015, the VGCL signed a **memorandum of understanding** with the Malaysian Trades Union Congress (MTUC) for the protection of Vietnamese migrant workers in Malaysia. The ten-point memorandum included the ratification of International Labour Organization conventions regarding safety and health issues, particularly in hazardous industrial sectors.

In August 2015, the Vietnamese and Malaysian governments signed a **memorandum of understanding** stipulating the right of foreign workers to retain their passports and personal documents and requiring employers (not labor recruiters) to come to the airport to pick up migrant workers within six hours of the worker's arrival there.

In 2017 the Malaysian government held employers (not migrant workers) responsible for levy payments. This was supposed to be effective starting on January 1, 2017, but implementation was postponed until 2018, so foreign workers continued to pay the levies for their employers until then.

The Labor Code Revision, **No. 45/2019/QH14**, applied primarily to domestic workers, but some sections also applied to overseas workers. The code has stipulations on compliance with the laws of both Vietnam and host countries, as well as provisions and procedures for settling labor disputes between an employee and the recruitment organization that sent the migrant to work overseas after having signed an employment contract. However, while the Vietnamese overseas workers are expected to comply with these laws, there is no mention of how they shall be protected by the laws.

On November 13, 2020, **Law 69/2020/QH14** was ratified to protect overseas contract-based workers. This revised law on contract-based Vietnamese overseas workers replaced the 2006 law and is slated to become effective on January 1, 2022. It has three key improvements: brokerage fees are now forbidden, in order to protect potential migrant workers from unscrupulous brokers who are not monitored by the government; migrant workers can end a contract with a recruitment company if the contract is not implemented as stipulated; and migrants do not have to pay social security or income taxes twice (both in Vietnam and in a receiving country).

Notes

Introduction

1. Hahamovitch, "Creating Perfect Immigrants."
2. Ibid., 70, 72–73, 81–82, 90–93.
3. In 1986, the H2 visa program was revised and divided into the H-2A agricultural program and the H-2B nonagricultural program. Although the H-2A program was originally created to allow migrants from the Caribbean islands, at present most guest workers are from Mexico and Central America. For more information, see Southern Poverty Law Center, "Close to Slavery." The H2 program was part of the Immigration Reform and Control Act that made it illegal to hire undocumented workers (Hahamovitch, "Creating Perfect Immigrants," 93).
4. See chapter 1 for a more detailed analysis of this history and for an update on the former Kinh/Vietnamese migrants who ended up staying in Poland and the Czech Republic after the Soviet Union lost control of the Eastern Bloc.
5. Hahamovitch, "Creating Perfect Immigrants," 92; GMS TRIANGLE project quarterly briefing note, Vietnam, July–December 2019.
6. "Phê duyệt đề án Hỗ trợ các huyện nghèo đẩy mạnh xuất khẩu lao động góp phần giảm nghèo bền vững giai đoạn 2009–2020."
7. GMS TRIANGLE project quarterly briefing note, Vietnam, July–December 2019. In 2015, Vietnam's remittances of US$13.2 billion ranked third as a proportion of GDP, after those of the Philippines and Nepal. See Ratha et al., "Migration and Remittances."
8. Trần, *Ties That Bind*. There are fifty-four ethnic groups in Vietnam, including the Kinh (83 million), the Hoa (over 900,000), the Hrê (132,745), the Khmer (1.4 million), and the Chăm Muslims (162,000) (Đặng Nghiêm Vạn, Chu Thái Sơn and Lưu Hùng, *Ethnic Minorities in Vietnam*; Baulch et al., "Ethnic Minority Development in Vietnam").
9. Wang and Bélanger, "Exploitative Recruitment Processes and Working and Working Conditions of Vietnamese Migrant Workers in Taiwan"; Bélanger et al.,

Notes to Introduction

"From Foreign Trainees to Unauthorized Workers"; Hoang and Yeoh, "Transnational Labour Migration, Debts, and Family Economics in Vietnam"; Bélanger et al., "International Labor Migration from Vietnam to Asian Countries"; Hong Van and Ha Nam, "Labor Export."

10. Nhân dân [The people], "Ma-lai-xi-a, thị trường lao động nhiều tiềm năng" [Malaysia, a potential labor market]. The fees guest workers have to pay cover predeparture training, such as language acquisition, cultural orientation, and legal instructions (Bélanger et al., "From Foreign Trainees to Unauthorized Workers").

11. While Malaysia was envisioned in Decision 71/2009/QĐTT as the principal country to which Vietnamese workers would be sent, over time fewer migrants have been sent there. In 2017, there were 1,330 migrants compared to 2,079 in 2016 (GMS TRIANGLE project quarterly briefing note, Vietnam, April–June 2018). Over three years, Malaysia dropped from the third (in 2015) to the fourth major destination (in 2018), below Taiwan, Japan, and the Republic of Korea (Thailand was fifth). In 2019, according to DOLAB, Japan continued to be the favorite destination for migrant workers owing to the good jobs and salaries offered there (Vietnam News Service, "Labour Export Companies Have Licences Revoked").

12. Trần Văn Thạnh, Suleco, interview, August 15, 2012.

13. GMS TRIANGLE project quarterly briefing note, Vietnam, July–September 2018): 1–2.

14. Hahamovitch, "Creating Perfect Immigrants," 73, 94.

15. Of the 118,859 workers who went to work in the top five countries through formal channels in 2017, 44,702 were women (GMS TRIANGLE project quarterly briefing note, Vietnam, April–June 2018).

16. Of the 1,330 migrants sent to Malaysia in 2017, 675 were women (GMS TRIANGLE project quarterly briefing note, Vietnam, April–June 2018).

17. Taiwan resumed hiring Vietnamese women after the 2005 suspension on Vietnamese domestic workers (35 percent of whom were women) was lifted. The Thai government permits irregular/undocumented Vietnamese domestic workers who are already in Thailand to register for one-year work permits (GMS TRIANGLE project quarterly briefing note, Vietnam, April–June 2018). Recent TRIANGLE in ASEAN quarterly reports alerted to increasing numbers of migrant workers being sent to the Middle East, especially women workers to Saudi Arabia as domestic and care workers. TRIANGLE in ASEAN Quarterly Briefing Note, Vietnam, April–June 2018; Viet Nam, January–March 2019; Viet Nam, July–December 2020. Rampant abuses to Vietnamese domestic workers are found in this article: Yen Duong, "Overworked, abused, hungry: Vietnamese domestic workers in Saudi." https://www.aljazeera.com /features/2018/9/19/overworked-abused-hungry-vietnamese-domestic-workers-in -saudi, 19 Sep 2018

18. Heywood, *Political Ideas and Concepts*, 100–101. See also Powercube, "Gramsci and Hegemony," https://www.powercube.net/other-forms-of-power/gramsci-and -hegemony. Gramsci's notebooks were smuggled out of prison in the 1930s, published in the 1950s, and translated into English in the 1970s under the title *Selections from the Prison Notebooks*.

Notes to Introduction 223

19. Parrenas, *Servants of Globalization*; Lan, "Among Women Migrant Domestic Workers and Their Taiwanese Employers Across Generations"; Oishi, *Women in Motion*; Ueno, "Strategies of Resistance among Filipina and Indonesian Domestic Workers in Singapore"; Crinis, "Vietnamese Migrant Clothing Workers in Malaysia."

20. Trần, *Ties That Bind*; Lian et al., *International Migration in Southeast Asia*.

21. Bhabha, *The Location of Culture*.

22. Rodriguez discusses this concept in the case of the Philippine government (a sending country), arguing that the Philippine state, as a labor broker, has invested in its labor export bureaucracy by establishing a global network of embassies and consular offices that shape migration patterns of Filipinos, employment agencies, and workers' movements worldwide (*Migrants for Export*, x, xxiii, 12, 14, 24). Guevarra focuses on the experience of Filipino domestic workers and nurses working in the United States and how the Philippine state uses its multilevel labor brokering process to create "the great Filipino worker." Her multisited ethnography also reveals how the Philippine state creates and manages a racialized form of productive femininity and unique Filipina workers who are "better workers than others" (*Marketing Dreams, Manufacturing Heroes*, 206, 209).

23. Xiang and Lindquist, "Migration Infrastructure," S124, S136.

24. Lindquist, "Labor Recruitment, Circuits of Capital, and Gendered Mobility"; Xiang and Lindquist, "Migration Infrastructure."

25. Trần, *Ties That Bind*, 271–75, and news articles written by two journalists: Duy Quốc and Nguyễn Duy.

26. http://www.tenaganita.net

27. Crinis and Trần, "Migrant Workers in the Clothing Industry," 88–89.

28. Massey and España, "The Social Process of International Migration"; Wilson, "Weak Ties, Strong Ties"; Davis et al., "Domestic and International Migration from Rural Mexico."

29. Portes, "Social Capital."

30. Pohjola, "Social Networks," 437.

31. Giulietti et al., "Strong Versus Weak Ties in Migration"; Collyer, "When Do Social Networks Fail to Explain Migration?," 712–13. Mark Granovetter coined the phrase "weak ties" and argued that weak ties are superior to strong ones because weak ties involve a secondary ring of acquaintances who have contacts with networks outside of the migrants' ethnic enclaves and therefore offer new sources of information about job opportunities. See Giulietti et al., "Strong Versus Weak Ties in Migration," 111–12, and Boyd, "Family and Personal Networks in International Migration," 654–55.

32. Liu, "Migrant Networks and International Migration."

33. Collyer, "When Do Social Networks Fail to Explain Migration?"

34. Ibid., 706–7, 712–13.

35. Boyd, "Family and Personal Networks in International Migration."

36. Aguilera and Massey, "Social Capital and the Wages of Mexican Migrants," 671.

37. Hagan, "Social Networks, Gender, and Immigrant Incorporation."

38. Pfeffer and Parra, "Strong Ties, Weak Ties, and Human Capital."

Notes to Introduction

39. Bloch and McKay, "Employment, Social Networks and Undocumented Migrants."

40. Bhabha, *The Location of Culture*; Frenkel, "The Multinational Corporation as a Third Space," 926–28.

41. Pohjola, "Social Networks."

42. I use this concept to explain the trajectory of the socialist migrants who went to work in Eastern Bloc countries before the fall of the Berlin Wall in 1989. See Baláž and Williams, "Path-dependency and Path-creation Perspectives on Migration Trajectories."

43. "Class moments" is a term I coined and developed in *Ties That Bind*, 12, 86, 203.

44. Portes, "Social Capital."

45. Scott, *Weapons of the Weak*, xvi. This book predates another famous book by Scott, his *Domination and the Arts of Resistance*, published in 1990. The context for *Weapons of the Weak* is the forms of peasant resistance in a rice-farming community in a Malaysian village (the paddy-growing area of Kedah) from 1978 to 1980. One feature of the "green revolution" the peasants had to cope with was the introduction of combine-harvesters in 1976, which led to the elimination of two-thirds of the wage-earning opportunities for smallholders and landless laborers. To hold on to their land, peasants used everyday forms of resistance against the landlords who sought to extract labor, food, taxes, rents, and interest from them.

46. Constable, *Maid to Order in Hong Kong*; Chin, *In Service and Servitude*; Chin, "Diversification and Privatisation"; Parrenas, *Servants of Globalization*; Ueno, "Strategies of Resistance among Filipina and Indonesian Domestic Workers in Singapore"; Crinis, "Sweat or No Sweat"; Lindquist, "Labor Recruitment, Circuits of Capital, and Gendered Mobility."

47. Constable points out the everyday acts of resistance that situate Filipina domestic workers in a broader ethnographic study of subtler forms of power, discipline, resistance, and accommodation and argues that these forms of power coexist and compete with each other (*Maid to Order in Hong Kong*).

48. See Chin, *In Service and Servitude*; Chin, "Diversification and Privatisation."

49. Parrenas argues that migrant domestic workers who are considered family members can take advantage of the attachment to induce employers to respond to their needs (*Servants of Globalization*).

50. Lindquist, "Labor Recruitment, Circuits of Capital, and Gendered Mobility."

51. These governments implement rules and regulations to guarantee a stable workforce and seek to prevent labor resistance by canceling work permits and deporting migrants to their home countries if they are perceived as "troublesome" (Crinis, "Sweat or No Sweat"; Ueno, "Strategies of Resistance among Filipina and Indonesian Domestic Workers in Singapore").

52. Lacan is cited in Bhabha, "Of Mimicry and Man," 131.

53. Bhabha, "Of Mimicry and Man."

54. Fahlander, "Third Space Encounters," 26–27.

55. Scott, *Domination and the Arts of Resistance*.

Notes to Introduction 225

56. Massey, "Politics and Space/Time," 71–73.

57. Soja argues that this mode of critical spatial awareness is significant in the rebalanced trialectics of spatiality-historicality-sociality (*Thirdspace*, 10–11).

58. Frenkel, "The Multinational Corporation as a Third Space," 926–28.

59. Ibid., 933.

60. Lee, "Bare Life, Interstices, and the Third Space of Citizenship," 71, 73.

61. Frenkel, "The Multinational Corporation as a Third Space"; Bhabha, *The Location of Culture*.

62. Abraham and van Schendel, introduction, 22–25.

63. Gutiérrez, "Migration, Emergent Ethnicity, and the 'Third Space,'" 481–517; Thelen, "Rethinking History and the Nation-State," 485–86, 488–89, 504.

64. Thelen, "Rethinking History and the Nation-State," 484n5.

65. Philip Taylor develops the geographical agency concept in a study of the Chăm Muslims in the south of Vietnam to describe how these mobile people recreate their economic livelihood through local and extralocal trading practices that draw on and sustain their cultural competencies and institutions ("Economy in Motion," 248). Tara Yosso defines the concept of community cultural wealth in terms of the array of "cultural capital that is nurtured through aspirational, navigational, social, linguistic, familial and resistant capital" ("Whose Culture Has Capital?," 69).

66. Oishi, *Women in Motion*, 188–92.

67. Lã and Leung, "Remittances from Migrants," 10, 13. By 2006 in Vietnam, 10 percent of urban households received international remittances, versus 4.6 percent of rural households, because city dwellers were more likely to have family members migrating to work overseas (12, 16). However, evidence in this book shows that rural households, too, have received remittances from the overseas workers I interviewed.

68. Rahman and Lian, "Towards a Sociology of Migrant Remittances in Asia," 693–95, 700, 702.

69. Yeoh et al., "Between Two Families," 444. Yeoh and colleagues studied thirty Vietnamese women who married Singaporean men through commercial matchmaking agencies.

70. Yeoh et al., "Between Two Families," 443; Rahman and Fee, "Towards a Sociology of Migrant Remittances in Asia," 700, 702.

71. Hoàng and Yeoh, "Transnational Labour Migration, Debts and Family Economics in Vietnam," 297–98. Hoàng and Yeoh interviewed thirty-seven migrant households in 2009, including family members who migrated to work in Taiwan, South Korea, Malaysia, and Japan and parents and spouses who stayed at home.

72. Paul, "Stepwise International Migration."

73. Ibid., 1842, 1864–65, 1874–75, 1880.

74. Parrenas, *Servants of Globalization*, 86–87.

75. Ibid., 88.

76. Holmes, "'Oaxacans Like to Work Bent Over.'"

77. Quesada et al., "Structural Vulnerability."

78. Collins, "Intersectionality's Definitional Dilemmas," 2, 14.

226   *Notes to Introduction and Chapter 1*

79. Different Vietnamese words denote the various administrative levels of local governments: *làng* ("village"), *xã* ("commune"), *ấp* ("hamlet"), and *phường* ("ward"). I use the proper terms in subsequent chapters.

80. Hiệp hội xuất khẩu lao động Việt Nam [Vietnam Association of Manpower Supply], "Giới thiệu về hiệp hội xuất khẩu lao động Việt Nam" [About the Vietnam Association of Manpower Supply].

Chapter 1. Historical, Economic, Cultural, Religious Practices of the Five Ethnic Groups

1. Berger, "Vietnamese Workers in USSR"; Beresford and Đặng, *Economic Transition in Vietnam*; Ginsburgs, "Imported Asian Labor in the USSR"; Hardy, "From a Floating World"; Hüwelmeier, "Bazaar Pagodas"; Iglicka, "Migration Movements from and into Poland in the Light of East–West European Migration"; Schwenkel, "Socialist Mobilities"; Schwenkel, "Rethinking Asian Mobilities"; Temko, "Soviets Defend 'New Form of Cooperation'"; Williams and Baláž, "Winning, Then Losing, the Battle with Globalization"; Baláž and Williams, "Path-Dependency and Path-Creation Perspectives on Migration Trajectories."

2. Beresford and Đặng. *Economic Transition in Vietnam*, 72–75. Even then, these students/workers/cadres saved money to buy a number of second-hand consumer products and brought them back to Vietnam for their own use or to sell to cover short-term living expenses. These small assets brought back from those Soviet Bloc countries were sufficient for the Vietnamese to place a high value on studying abroad.

3. Beresford and Đặng, *Economic Transition in Vietnam*, 78–79.

4. The Council for Mutual Economic Assistance was founded in 1949 by the Soviet Union and the Eastern Bloc (Bulgaria, Poland, Romania, Czechoslovakia, and Hungary) in response to the US's Marshall Plan and Western Europe's Organization for European Economic Cooperation.

5. The Kinh constitute the majority ethnic group, accounting for about 86 percent of Vietnam's population. This figure is based on estimated statistics from 2017 (https://www.indexmundi.com/vietnam/demographics_profile.html).

6. Goscha, *Vietnam*, 18–20.

7. Baulch et al., "Ethnic Minority Development in Vietnam."

8. Nguyen Thi Minh Hoa et al., "Language, Mixed Communes, and Infrastructure."

9. Thulstrup, "Livelihood Resilience and Adaptive Capacity," 360.

10. Taylor, introduction, 23. The population estimate shows an increase from eight hundred thousand based on the 2009 census statistics used in Đặng Nghiêm Vạn et al., *Ethnic Minorities in Vietnam*.

11. Yeung, "The Dynamics of the Globalization of Chinese Business Firms," 78; Coe et al., "Globalization, Transnationalism, and the Asia-Pacific," 49; Harianto, "Business Linkages and Chinese Entrepreneurs in Southeast Asia," 137.

12. Baulch et al., "Ethnic Minority Development in Vietnam," 1151, 1166–67, 1173.

13. Tran Thi Thanh Tu et al., "Socio-Economic Impact of Rural Credit in Northern Vietnam."

14. Nguyen et al., "Agricultural Land Distribution in Vietnam," 5–6, 10, 12, 20.

Notes to Chapter 1   227

15. Kerkvliet, "Agricultural Land in Vietnam," 297.

16. This study is based on data from the 2009 population and housing census and interviews conducted in April 2013 with the education managers from the Department of Education and Training of An Giang Province. It focuses on the phenomenon of out-of-school children, defined as children between five and fourteen years of age in An Giang Province who never attended school or who had attended but later dropped out (Department of Education and Training of An Giang Province, *Global Initiative on Out-of-School Children*).

17. This study does not take into acount the ethnic private and religious schools. Also, the study focuses on the main ethnic groups in An Giang and so does not include the Hrê in Quảng Ngãi. From preschool to primary school to lower secondary school, the dropout rate of Hoa children ranked the lowest (that is, they stayed in school longer than the other ethnic groups), followed by Kinh children, Khmer children, and Chăm children. The percentages of (preschool) five-year-old out-of-school children among the five ethnic groups in An Giang are as follows: Hoa, 7.46 percent; Kinh, 22.19 percent; Khmer, 33.93 percent; Chăm, 45.16 percent (Department of Education and Training of An Giang Province, *Global Initiative on Out-of-School Children*, 10). The dropout rates in primary and lower secondary schools are similar: the lowest was among the Hoa and the highest was among the Chăm, at 45.5 percent, with the Kinh and the Khmer in between (17).

18. Taylor, introduction; Department of Education and Training of An Giang Province, *Global Initiative on Out-of-School Children*.

19. Đặng Nghiêm Vạn et al., *Ethnic Minorities in Vietnam*; Baulch et al., "Ethnic Minority Development in Vietnam"; Lưu Hùng "Sự du nhập hình thái canh tác ruộng nước vào vùng dân tộc Hrê" [The introduction of Thai rice field cultivation to the Hrê people], Viện dân tộc học [Institute of Ethnology], "Lễ trâu của người" [The Hrê buffalo ceremony]; Lưu Hùng "Mấy ghi nhận qua tìm hiểu làng của dân tộc Hrê" [A tool to record the knowledge of the Hrê ethnic minority villages], 164–66; UBND tỉnh Quảng Ngãi [People's Committee of Quảng Ngãi], Ban dân tộc [Department of Ethnic Affairs], "Sự khác biệt về tên gọi của người Hrê trong những khu vực cư trú khác nhau ở miền núi phía tây tỉnh Quảng Ngãi" [Differences in the names of Hrê people in different residential areas in the western mountainous area of Quảng Ngãi province].

20. "Theo thống kê đến ngày 31/12/2015, tổng dân số dân tộc Hrê của tỉnh Quảng Ngãi là: 132.745 người, trong đó" (According to statistics, as of December 31, 2015, the total Hre ethnic population in Quảng Ngãi province is 132,745 people) (UBND tỉnh Quảng Ngãi [People's Committee of Quảng Ngãi], Ban dân tộc [Department of Ethnic Affairs], "Dân tộc Hrê" [Hrê ethnic group], http://www.quangngai.gov.vn/vi/bandantoc/Pages/qnp-intro-gioithieu-qnpstatic-18-qnpdyn-o-qnpsite-1.html). The 2015 statistics show an increase compared to the 2009 census of over 127,000 nationwide (concentrated in Quảng Ngãi); Ban chỉ đạo tổng điều tra dân số và nhà ở trung ương/Central Population and Housing Census Steering Committee, *Tổng điều tra dân số và nhà ở việt nam năm 2009/The 2009 Vietnam Population and Housing Census*, 134.

228   *Notes to Chapter 1*

21. Lưu Hùng "Sự du nhập hình thái canh tác ruộng nước vào vùng dân tộc Hrê," 34.

22. *Tin tức du lịch* [Travel news], "Văn hóa truyền thống của dân tộc H'rê (Quảng Ngãi)" [Traditional culture of the Hrê people (Quảng Ngãi)].

23. Lưu Hùng, "Mấy ghi nhận qua tìm hiểu làng của dân tộc Hrê" [A tool to record the knowledge of the Hrê ethnic minority villages], 164–65.

24. Viện dân tộc học [Institute of Ethnology], "Lễ trâu của người" [The Hrê buffalo ceremony]. Another spelling is "pdâu."

25. Trần Hoài, email correspondence.

26. *Tin tức du lịch* [Travel news], "Văn hóa truyền thống của dân tộc H'rê (Quảng Ngãi)" [Traditional culture of the Hrê people (Quảng Ngãi)]; Viện dân tộc học [Institute of Ethnology], "Lễ trâu của người" [The Hrê buffalo ceremony].

27. UBND tỉnh Quảng Ngãi [People's Committee of Quảng Ngãi], Ban dân tộc [Department of Ethnic Affairs], "Sự khác biệt về tên gọi của người Hrê trong những khu vực cư trú khác nhau ở miền núi phía tây tỉnh Quảng Ngãi." [Differences in the names of Hrê people in different residential areas in the western mountainous area of Quảng Ngãi province].

28. Trần Hoài, conversation, May 1, 2015.

29. Lưu Hùng, "Góp phần nghiên cứu tính song hệ ở dân tộc Hrê," 41–42.

30. Although on the land issue, one of my interviewees said that her Hrê parents are being realistic and giving the land to her brother so they can stay with him and be taken care of by him in their old age.

31. Phan Hữu Đạt elaborates more on double filiation (*song hệ*) and, drawing on the evidence of a number of global cases, argues that there are differences between these two separate groupings based on matrilineality or patrilineality. These two systems play different roles in the economy and society and follow different rules regarding marriages, inheritances, and the framework of their communities ("Lại bàn về chế độ song hệ ở các dân tộc nước ta" [The division in our nation]).

32. Lưu Hùng, "Góp phần nghiên cứu tính song hệ ở dân tộc Hrê," 41.

33. Baulch et al., "Ethnic Minority Development in Vietnam."

34. UBND tỉnh Quảng Ngãi [People's Committee of Quảng Ngãi], "Thành phố quảng ngãi và các huyện trong tỉnh" [Quảng Ngãi and districts in the province], http://www.quangngai.gov.vn/userfiles/file/dudiachiquangngai/PHANV/HuyenBaTo .htm; Tran Hoai, email correspondence, May 2015.

35. Lưu Hùng, "Tìm hiểu quan hệ xã hội ở dân tộc Hrê" [Research on the social relations among the Hrê ethnic people], 34.

36 Kerkvliet also notes this troubling trend in the context of the ethnic minorities in the central highland ("Agricultural Land in Vietnam," 297).

37. Lưu Hùng, "Tìm hiểu quan hệ xã hội ở dân tộc hrê" [Research on the social relations among the Hrê ethnic people], 35.

38. Ibid., 33.

39. Being forced to grow a cash crop like trees intended to be used for paper pulp is another way of how they are alienated from their land because they cannot consume the produce that they plant.

Notes to Chapter 1

40. A similar pattern is observed in the Co's clearing of areas in protected forests, as Thulstrup notes ("Livelihood Resilience and Adaptive Capacity," 360).

41. Larry Lohman, "Who Defends Biological Diversity?," 100.

42. Trần Hoài, conversation, May 1, 2015.

43. Lưu Hùng has also made this argument; see "Mấy ghi nhận qua tìm hiểu làng của dân tộc Hrê," 166.

44. Lưu Hùng, "Tìm hiểu quan hệ xã hội ở dân tộc Hrê," 34.

45. Ibid., 35.

46. Tống, Thanh Tùng, "Đi để sắm trâu, xây nhà." [Working overseas to buy buffaloes and build houses].

47. "Lễ hội lớn nhất của người Hrê là ăn tết và cúng đâm trâu" (The biggest festival of Hrê people is to celebrate Tet and worship buffalo) (UBND tỉnh Quảng Ngãi [People's Committee of Quảng Ngãi], Ban dân tộc [Department of Ethnic Affairs], "Dân tộc Hrê" [Hrê ethnic group], http://www.quangngai.gov.vn/vi/bandantoc/Pages /qnp-intro-gioithieu-qnpstatic-18-qnpdyn-0-qnpsite-1.html).

48. Đoàn Lân, interview, 2012.

49. The 2017 nationwide population estimate shows an increase over the 2014 figure of 1.3 million (Đặng Nghiêm Vạn et al., *Ethnic Minorities in Vietnam*; Baulch et al., "Ethnic Minority Development in Vietnam").

50. Taylor, *The Khmer Lands of Vietnam*, 162.

51. Dương Thị Bích Thủy et al., "Nâng cao chất lượng vận động trong đồng bào Khmer ở An Giang." [Improving the quality of mobilization among the Khmer people in An Giang]. These statistics are much lower than the 1993 estimates cited in Engelbert, "The Khmer in Southern Vietnam," 158. Dương Thị Bích Thủy states that there are sixty-four Khmer villages with over seven hundred thousand residents in An Giang.

52. Nguyễn-võ Thu-Hương, *Khmer-Viet Relations and the Third Indochina Conflict*, 2–3. The complex and interconnected history of Cambodia and its relations with the Chăm (especially in Kampong Chăm) and the Vietnamese is documented in Chandler, *A History of Cambodia*, 58, 79, 162, 177. See also Taylor, *Chăm Muslims of the Mekong Delta*, 16.

53. Kiernan, *Việt Nam*, 157, 159.

54. Ibid., 163.

55. Goscha, *Vietnam*, 417; Chandler, *History of Cambodia*, 39, 151.

56. Chandler, *History of Cambodia*, 94, 97, 112–23.

57. Phan Văn Dốp, interview, April 2015. Phan Văn Dốp is a Vietnamese anthropologist.

58. Engelbert, "The Khmer in Southern Vietnam," 166–67; Taylor, *The Khmer Lands of Vietnam*; Phan Văn Dốp, interview, April 2015.

59. Kiernan, *Việt Nam*, 279.

60. This official document mentions the need to recruit Khmer cadres, provide training, offer special treatment, and manage them (Dương Thị Bích Thủy et al., "Nâng cao chất lượng vận động trong đồng bào Khmer ở An Giang" [Improving the quality of mobilization among the Khmer people in An Giang]).

230   *Notes to Chapter 1*

61. Engelbert, "The Khmer in Southern Vietnam," 168.

62. Cambodian border provinces include Takeo and Prey Veng, located in the southwest of Cambodia (Taylor, *The Khmer Lands of Vietnam*, 182–83, 189; Đặng Nghiêm Vạn et al., *Ethnic Minorities in Vietnam*, Engelbert, 171).

63. Taylor, *The Khmer Lands of Vietnam*, 182–83; Đặng Nghiêm Vạn et al., *Ethnic Minorities in Vietnam*.

64. Taylor, *The Khmer Lands of Vietnam*, 177.

65. Historically, Khmer village chiefs (*me khum*) had the authority to raise taxes and oversaw law and order in their administrative units. Engelbert, "The Khmer in Southern Vietnam," 171.

66. Kiernan, *Việt Nam*, 438.

67. Đặng Nghiêm Vạn, et al., *Ethnic Minorities in Vietnam*, 30; United States Department of State, Bureau of Democracy, Human Rights and Labor. "Vietnam 2013 International Religious Freedom Report." Washington, DC: United States Department of State. "https://www.state.gov/documents/organization/222393.pdf" https://www.state.gov/documents/organization/222393.pdf.

68. Unrepresented Nations and People (UNPO) report "Member Profile: Khmer-Krom; Khmers-Krom Federation (KKF). Brussels, Belgium: UNPO Advocacy Office, 2018; Đặng Nghiêm Vạn, et al., *Ethnic Minorities in Vietnam*, 35. Consistent with the statistics provided by the UNPO report, a master's thesis documented 452 Khmer Theravada temples in Vietnam: Mae Chee Huỳnh Kim Lan. A Study of Theravada Buddhism in Vietnam. Master's Thesis in Buddhist Studies, International Master Degree of Arts Programme, Mahachulalongkornrajavidyalaya University, Bangkok, Thailand, 2010.

69. Đặng Nghiêm Vạn et al., *Ethnic Minorities in Vietnam*.

70. Hodges, "Reincarnating Knowledge." They also studied in a high school in Kompong Chăm, a province right on the bank of the Mekong River (Taylor, *The Khmer Lands of Vietnam*, 103, 110, 126–27).

71. Wats also serve an environmental aspect as places where fresh water is collected and distributed (Taylor, *The Khmer Lands of Vietnam*, 47–49).

72. Taylor, *The Khmer Lands of Vietnam*, 35.

73. UNICEF Report, Department of Education and Training of An Giang Province, *Global Initiative on Out-of-School Children*.

74. Taylor, *Social Inequality in Vietnam and the Challenges to Reform*, 245, 257, 259. He uses the 2001 UN Development Programme statistics.

75. Neng Angkeara, interview, June 2014.

76. Châu Anurak, interview, June 2014.

77. Vietnam News Service, "Khmer Monks Open Summer Class."

78. Taylor, *The Khmer Lands of Vietnam*, 117.

79. Neng Kanika, interview, June 2014.

80. Nakamura, "Cham in Vietnam," 162, 167, 171.

81. Nakamura, "Cham in Vietnam"; Bruckmayr, "Between Institutionalized Syncretism and Official Particularism," 16, 20, 26; Taylor, *Social Inequality in Vietnam*

Notes to Chapter 1   231

and the Challenges to Reform, 260. Đổng Thành Danh, a Chăm Bani scholar, discusess indigenzied Islam in "Bàn thêm về sự du nhập của Hồi giáo ở Champa" [The introduction of Islam to Champa].

82. Ban chỉ đạo tổng điều tra dân số và nhà ở trung ương/Central Population and Housing Census Steering Committee, *Tổng điều tra dân số và nhà ở việt nam năm 2009: Kết quả toàn bộ/The 2009 Vietnam population and Housing Census*; Nakamura, "Cham in Vietnam," 113.

83. Taylor, "Economy in Motion," 248.

84. Trúc Quỳnh, "Vài nét về dân tộc chăm ở An Giang" [Some characteristics of the Chăm minority in An Giang].

85. Taylor, *Social Inequality in Vietnam and the Challenges to Reform*, 260.

86. Reid, *Charting the Shape of Early Modern Southeast Asia*, 43–44.

87. Manguin, "The Introduction of Islam into Champa," 289.

88. Kiernan, *Việt Nam*, 411.

89. Reid, *Charting the Shape of Early Modern Southeast Asia*, 46.

90. Đổng Thành Danh, "Bàn thêm về sự du nhập của Hồi giáo ở Champa" [The introduction of Islam to Champa], 84; Goscha, *Vietnam*, 410. Manguin argues that the Chăm-Malay connections were established in Cambodia at the end of fifteenth century as the result of a close alliance formed between the Chăm colony and the Malay colony in Cambodia ("The Introduction of Islam into Champa," 305). Given this, it makes sense that there are connections between the practices of Chăm Muslims in Cambodia and the Chăm in the Mekong Delta (Bruckmayr, "Between Institutionalized Syncretism and Official Particularism," 16, 20, 26; Weber, "The Cham Diaspora in Southeast Asia," 175).

91. Manguin, "The Introduction of Islam into Champa," 306–7.

92. Reid, *Charting the Shape of Early Modern Southeast Asia*, 46–47.

93. Kiernan, *Việt Nam*, 239.

94. Weber, "The Cham Diaspora in Southeast Asia," 174–77.

95. Trankell, "Songs of Our Spirits"; Kiernan, *Việt Nam*, 239–40. Trankell and Kiernan give different figures: Kiernan states that 5,000 individual Chăm fled, while Tranknell claims that 5,000 families fled.

96. Taylor, *History of the Vietnamese*, 322; Nakamura, "Cham in Vietnam," 151; Đổng Thành Danh, "Bàn thêm về sự du nhập của Hồi giáo ở Champa" [The introduction of Islam to Champa], 81.

97. Weber, "The Cham Diaspora in Southeast Asia," 157–8, 187–8; Taylor, *History of the Vietnamese*, 323.

98. Trankell, "Songs of Our Spirits."

99. Weber, "Exploring Cam Narrative Sources for History of the Cam Diaspora," 8–9.

100. Weber, "The Cham Diaspora in Southeast Asia," 187–88.

101. National Institute of Statistics, *General Population Census of Cambodia 2008*. As of January 2020, the population of Cambodia was 16,613,515, according to UN estimates (http://www.worldometers.info/world-population/cambodia-population).

Notes to Chapter 1

102. Oguzhakan Taskun, a representative of the World Orphan Fund in Cambodia, estimates that the number of Chăm in Cambodia was about one million (email correspondence, August 2015).

103. Manguin, "The Introduction of Islam into Champa," 305.

104. Phan Văn Dốp and Nguyễn Thị Nhung, "Quan hệ đồng tộc và văn hóa" [Ethnic and cultural-religious relations], 57–58.

105. In the twentieth century, different forms of Chăm Islam spread between Battambang, Phnom Penh, and Kampong Chăm before moving across the border to Tay Ninh, An Giang, and Saigon (Noseworthy, "Articulations of Southeast Asian Religious Modernisms," 112, 121, 124).

106. Bruckmayr, "Between Institutionalized Syncretism and Official Particularism," 27.

107. Nakamura argues that Chăm sellers of cloth and textiles went to the south-central coast in the 1960s ("Cham in Vietnam," 151); see also Taylor, "Economy in Motion," 239.

108. Ms. Alvi, interview, 2014. This is consistent with Phan Văn Dốp and Nguyễn Thị Nhung's finding that many Chăm have relatives in Cambodia that facilitate these transnational commercial exchanges ("Quan hệ đồng tộc và văn hóa – tôn giáo").

109. It is unclear whether the Ho Chi Minh City Muslim Representative Committee is related to the Vietnam Association of Islamic Muslims (Hiệp hội chăm hồi giáo Việt Nam) that was located in Saigon before 1975 and that Nakamura discusses ("Cham in Vietnam," 151). Another Vietnamese source mentions the Vietnam Chăm Association that had offices in Saigon and was established in 1960. In 1966, the Council of Churches of Vietnam's Mosques was set up in Châu Đốc and has survived to this day ("Sự du nhập Hồi giáo vào Việt Nam" [The introduction of Islam into Vietnam], http://voer.edu.vn/m/hoi-giao-o-viet-nam/d25febf0).

110. University of Pennsylvania, Exchange Rate to U.S. Dollar for Vietnam [FXRATEVNA618NUPN], retrieved from FRED, Federal Reserve Bank of St. Louis; https://fred.stlouisfed.org/series/FXRATEVNA618NUPN, December 15, 2018.

111. Lian et al., *International Migration in Southeast Asia*.

112. UNICEF Report, Department of Education and Training of An Giang Province, *Global Initiative on Out-of-School Children*, 20.

113. The economic marginalization of the Khmer Krom is thought to have been caused, inter alia, by shortage of capital, poor access to markets and services, and high levels of landlessness (Taylor, "Redressing Disadvantage or Re-arranging Inequality," 236–37, 245, 261).

114. UNICEF Report, Department of Education and Training of An Giang Province, *Global Initiative on Out-of-School Children*, 20.

115. The percentage of primary-school-age migrants who were out of school (13.7 percent) was nearly double the rate of that of nonmigrants (7.45 percent) (Department of Education and Training of An Giang Province, *Global Initiative on Out-of-School Children*, 12).

116. Department of Education and Training of An Giang Province, *Global Initiative on Out-of-School Children*.

Notes to Chapters 1 and 2   233

117. Ibid., 20, 22.

118. Taylor, *Social Inequality in Vietnam*, 258–59.

119. Yosso, "Whose Culture Has Capital?"

120. Crinis, "Vietnamese Migrant Clothing Workers in Malaysia."

121. Duy Quốc and Tử Trực, conversations, 2011–15.

122. "Hrê," *Ethnologue*; Hammarström et al.,"Hrê."

Chapter 2. The Transnational Labor Brokerage System and Its Infrastructure

1. Wang and Bélanger. "Exploitative Recruitment Processes and Working Conditions of Vietnamese Migrant Workers in Taiwan," 331.

2. Bélanger et al., "From Foreign Trainees to Unauthorized Workers ," 31–53.

3. Hoàng and Yeoh's study, "Transnational Labour Migration, Debts, and Family Economics in Vietnam," makes an important contribution to the scholarship on migration and on sexuality as self-actualization, a means of exploring freedom, and a form of empowerment.

4. Lindquist, "Labor Recruitment, Circuits of Capital and Gendered Mobility."

5. Lê Thu Hương, "A New Portrait of Indentured Labor," 883, 890; Crinis, "Vietnamese Migrant Clothing Workers in Malaysia."

6. Lim and Oishi, "International Labor Migration of Asian Women"; Parrenas, *Servants of Globalization.*

7. Chin, *In Service and Servitude.*

8. Crinis, "Vietnamese Migrant Clothing Workers in Malaysia."

9. Lê Thu Hương, "A New Portrait of Indentured Labor," 883, 890.

10. Crinis, "Global Commodity Chains in Crisis."

11. Elias, "Gendered Political Economy and the Politics of Migrant Worker Rights"; Piper, "Rights of Foreign Workers and the Politics of Migration in South-East and East Asia"; Crinis, "Global Commodity Chains in Crisis."

12. The employer's name, but not that of the recruitment company, must be listed on all contracts. But the recruitment companies must be approved by the government, and they are listed on the government's website.

13. "Foreign Workers in Malaysia Are Covered and Entitled to the Same Work-Related Injury Benefits as the National Workers," International Labour Organization, November 29, 2019. https://www.ilo.org/global/topics/geip/news/WCMS_731149/lang--en/index.htm.

14. Crinis, "The Devil You Know"; Crinis, "Malaysia."

15. Malaysia Ministry of Human Resources, Sample Contract of Employment for Foreign Workers, https://www.mohr.gov.my/pdf/Contract_of_Employment_(EU).pdf; Vietnam News Agency, "Malaysia Issues New Rules for Vietnamese Workers," http://en.vietnamplus.vn/malaysia-issues-new-rules-for-vietnamese-workers/84073.vnp.

16. Crinis, correspondence, September 26, 2017.

17. Crinis, "Sweat or No Sweat."

18. Sittamparam, "Ministry to Probe Nike Claims of Worker Abuse," 17.

234   *Notes to Chapter 2*

19. Ratha et al., "Migration and Remittances," 19.

20. Hector et al., "Employers Should Pay the Levy, Not Migrant Workers." Some employers, however, do not deduct levies from migrant workers' wages because they are scared that if they do so, they will be outed by a corporate social audit (Crinis, correspondence, August 2017).

21. "Malaysian Trades Union Congress Ticks Off Employers, Saying Probation Period Would Shortchange Foreign Workers."

22. Bernama, "Higher Levy Will Deter Foreign Workers to Malaysia."

23. Hector et al., "Employers Should Pay the Levy, Not Migrant Workers." These numbers do not include the revenues of Malaysian recruiters and Malaysian Airlines.

24. Amarthalingam, "Malaysia Defers Foreign Workers' Levy Payment to 2018."

25. Bernama, "Employers to Bear Full Levy Payment for Foreign Workers," http://www.bernama.com/en/news.php?id=1646221.

26. Carvalho and Rahim, "Reduced Extension Levy Fees for Foreign Workers Finally Enforced."

27. Trần, "The Third Sleeve."

28. According to Baláž and Williams, "Path-Dependency and Path-Creation Perspectives on Migration Trajectories," 47–48, the mid-1980s waves still consisted of educated Vietnamese expatriates.

29. Beresford and Đặng, *Economic Transition in Vietnam*, 79.

30. Schwenkel, "Rethinking Asian Mobilities," 244; Ginsburgs, "Imported Asian Labor in the USSR," 16.

31. Williams and Baláž, "Winning, Then Losing, the Battle with Globalization," 536; Beresford and Đặng, *Economic Transition in Vietnam*, 72–73; Schwenkel, "Rethinking Asian Mobilities," 239.

32. Beresford and Đặng, *Economic Transition in Vietnam*, 84.

33. Baláž and Williams, "Path-Dependency and Path-Creation Perspectives on Migration Trajectories," 47–49.

34. Bélanger et al. "From Foreign Trainees to Unauthorized Workers," 42–43.

35. Vũ Minh Xuyên, interview, July 2014. This historic increase in minimum wage was the hard-won victory of the huge Vietnamese worker strike in 2005–6 which gained 40% minimum wage increase and subsequently stipulated an annual minimum wage adjustment, to be announced at the end of the previous year.

36. See Trần, "Contradictions of multi-stakeholder labor relations in Vietnam."

37. Nhân dân [The people], "Ma-lai-xi-a, thị trường lao động nhiều tiềm năng" [Malaysia, a potential labor market]; Nguyễn Duy, "Chưa đạt mục tiêu" [Goal not yet reached]; GMS TRIANGLE project, quarterly briefing note, January–March 2017. In particular, in the first two years of 71/2009/QĐTT, the state aimed to send ten thousand migrants from sixty-four rural districts and ethnic minority groups; in the second period (2011–15), the quotas were to increase to fifty thousand migrants, again from poor rural districts and ethnic minority groups; in the last period (2016–2020), the goal is to achieve a 15 percent increase from the level realized in the second period.

Notes to Chapter 2   235

38. International Labour Organisation, "Vietnam, Malaysia's Trade Unions Ink Agreement to Strengthen Protection of Migrant Workers' Rights."

39. Crinis, "Vietnamese Migrant Clothing Workers in Malaysia"; Bộ lao động ngoài nước [Department of Overseas Labor], *Thị trường Malaysia 6 tháng đầu năm 2009* [The Malaysian market in the first six months of 2009].

40. Anh Phương, "Đơn hàng tốt từ những đối tác tốt" [Good orders from good partners].

41. "Southeast Asia: ASEAN 2015."

42. Bộ lao động thương binh và xã hội [Ministry of Labor, Invalids, and Social Affairs], "Quy định chức năng, nhiệm vụ, quyền hạn và cơ cấu tổ chức của Cục quản lý lao động ngoài nước" [Defining functions, tasks, and organizational structure of the Department of Overseas Labor].

43. Trần Văn Thạnh, interview, September 2008.

44. Kuala Lumpur is 208 miles away from Johor Bahru, where we interviewed many migrant workers.

45. Rodriguez, *Migrants for Export.*

46. Trần Văn Lý, interview, 2015.

47. The 2016 figure is an estimate, since there are no breakdown numbers for remittances sent by Vietnamese migrants from Malaysia (Ratha et al. "Migration and Remittances").

48. See International Organization for Migration, *Vietnam Migration Profile*, 66.

49. Đinh, "Roles of Remittances in the Socio-economical Development"; Vũ, "Foreign Capital Inflows and Economic Growth."

50. Duy Quốc, interview, January 2013.

51. Duy Quốc concurred with this insight. Interview, January 2013.

52. As an incentive for on-time completion of the work, the migrants are required to pay only the outbound fare. If the migrants finish the work on time, the Malaysian employer pays for the return flight.

53. Duy Quốc, email and interviews, August 2016. Many migrant returnees I interviewed also mentioned the same figures. On average, the recruitment fee for the labor export companies was about one month's salary for each year of work—that is, roughly 8 percent of the annual salary (Duy Quốc, interview, August 2012).

54. Duy Quốc, interview, 2009; Prime Minister Decision 71/2009/QĐTT, "Phê duyệt đề án hỗ trợ các huyện nghèo đẩy mạnh xuất khẩu lao động góp phần giảm nghèo bền vững giai đoạn, 2009–20" (Approval of the proposal to support poor rural districts to boost labor export and contribute to sustained poverty reduction in the 2009–2020 period).

55. These are the results from a nationwide study (2010–11) conducted by Viện khoa học lao động và xã hội (Institute of Social and Labor Science). The study, which surveyed 1,450 worker returnees from Japan, Taiwan, Korea, and Malaysia from eight provinces with high concentration of overseas labor returnees, is titled "Báo cáo tóm tắt: Đánh giá thực trạng lao động đi làm việc ở nước ngoài đã trở về Việt Nam" [Summary report: Assessment of the working status of laborers in Vietnam

236   Notes to Chapter 2

who have worked abroad]. The eight provinces are Thái Bình, Phú Thọ, Vĩnh Phúc, Bắc Giang, Hải Dương, Thanh Hóa, Hà Tĩnh, and Ho Chi Minh. See Bộ lao động thương binh và xã hội, huyện Ba Tơ [Ministry of Labor, Invalids, Social Affairs, Ba Tơ District], *Báo cáo tình hình thực hiện công tác xuất khẩu lao động 3 năm* [Report on the implementation of first three years of the labor export program], 8.

56. Duy Quốc, interview, 2009.

57. See International Organization for Migration, *Vietnam Migration Profile*, 55.

58. Mr. Thức and Mr. Việt, interviews, 2013.

59. Ms. Hoa, interview, 2013.

60. Nguyễn Anh Tuấn, interview, January 2014.

61. Letts, *Complaint Mechanisms for Migrant Workers*. When I inquired about the full report that was expected to accompany this study, I was told by Ms. Nguyễn Thị Mai Thủy, a Vietnam representative for the GMS TRIANGLE project, that it was still being vetted by MoLISA and other state offices and not yet available (email, January 2016).

62. The top three means of making a complaint are by calling the recruitment companies (100 percent of all forty-four interviewees), by sending letters to those companies and to local authorities (70 percent), and by making a visit to the communal people's committee (61 percent). The key issue was a discrepancy between conditions outlined in the worker's signed contract and what happened in actuality. In particular, the top four problems were lower salaries than stated in the contract (100 percent), no insurance even though coverage was specified in the contract (100 percent), longer work hours than workers had agreed to (95 percent), and a discrepancy between food, accommodations, and utility arrangements that were promised and what was provided (90 percent). Overall, 90 percent of all interviewees were disappointed with their labor export experiences (Letts, *Complaint Mechanisms for Migrant Workers*).

63. Tổng liên đoàn lao động Việt Nam [Vietnamese General Confederation of Labor] "Báo cáo về bảo vệ di cư lao động" [Report on labor migration protection].

64. Predeparture policies are specified in Circular 21/2013-TT-BLDTBXH, on the maximum amount of deposits required in specific countries, and Circular 22/2013-TT-BLDTBXH, which contains a sample labor contract.

65. Email correspondence with the vice president of the VGCL, Mr. Trần Văn Lý, with an attachment titled "Về Bảo Vệ Lao Động Di Cư IV. Các Hoạt Động của Công Đoàn và Sự Cần Thiết Sửa Đổi Bổ Sung Chính Sách Pháp Luật Để Tăng Cường Sự Tham Gia Trực Tiếp Của Công Đoàn Trong Việc Bảo Vệ Người Lao Động Đi Làm Việc Ở Nước Ngoài Theo Hợp Đồng."

66. Trần Văn Lý, personal communication, May 2015; text of the 2015 Memorandum of Understanding Between the Vietnam General Confederation of Labour (VGCL) and the Malaysian Trades Union Congress (MTUC).

67. "Vietnam, Malaysia's Trade Unions Ink Agreement to Strengthen Protection of Migrant Workers," https://www.ilo.org/hanoi/Informationresources/Publicinfor mation/newsitems/WCMS_353252/lang--en/index.htm.

Notes to Chapters 2 and 3   237

68. Trần Văn Lý, interview, July 2015.

69. International Labour Organization, "Malaysian and Vietnamese Trade Unions to Collaborate on Protecting Migrant Workers' Rights."

70. Nguyễn Duy, "Đi Xuat Khau Lao Động được vay đến 75 triệu đồng." [Export labor can obtain up to VND 75 million loan].

71. Nguyễn Duy, "Cục Quản lý lao động ngoài nước: Yêu cầu ngừng hợp tác với 3 công ty môi giới Đài Loan" [Department of Overseas Labor: requesting to stop working with three Taiwanese companies], March 1, 2004; Duy Quốc, "Rắc rối thẩm định hợp đồng" [Trouble appraising labor contracts].

72. Duy Quốc, "Xuất khẩu lao động sang Malaysia [Export labor to Malaysia].

73. Nguyễn Duy, "Bức tranh màu xám của XKLĐ" [Mixed results for export labor].

74. Nguyễn Duy, "Xuất khẩu lao động" [Export labor].

75. Nguyễn Duy, "Xuất khẩu lao động" [Export labor].

76. Department of Overseas Labor (DOLAB) under the MoLISA (Ministry of Labor, Invalids and Social Affairs website, http://dolab.gov.vn/BU/Index.aspx?type=dgdh&LIST_ID=1144&MENU_ID=246&DOC_ID=1561.

77. Duy Quốc, personal communication, 2008–15.

78. Nguyễn Duy, "Thất bại với đề án ngàn tỉ" [Failure of project worth thousands of billions of Vietnamese đồng].

79. Prime Minister Decision 71/2009/QĐTT, "Phê duyệt đề án hỗ trợ các huyện nghèo đẩy mạnh xuất khẩu lao động góp phần giảm nghèo bền vững giai đoạn, 2009–20" (Approval of the proposal to support poor rural districts to boost labor export and contribute to sustained poverty reduction in the 2009–2020 period), 1–2.

80. See International Organization for Migration, *Viet Name Migration Profile*, 72.

81. Duy Quốc, interview, 2015.

82. Xiang and Lindquist, "Migration Infrastructure."

Chapter 3. The Labor Recruitment Process and Indebtedness

1. As of 2017, there were 290 active labor export companies throughout Vietnam (Vietnam News Service, "Labour Export Companies Have Licences Revoked." However, only 156 member companies were listed on the official VAMAS website.

2. Job orders provide detailed information about how many workers are needed, what gender and age are preferred, nature of work, amount of wages to be paid, length of the contract period, number of working days and hours, what kind of accommodations, transportation, and food are provided, the amount of the Malaysian government levy (paid by workers) and immigration charges (paid by employers), cost, if any, of the medical examination, and what insurance, medical and other leave, paid holidays, overtime, and air passage are offered.

3. Galaxy Human Resources Development business proposal, 2005, 7.

4. At the commune/hamlet levels, the invitation from the local people's committee that informs workers of the date and time to show up in order to depart for Malaysia, highlights the role of the committee.

5. Bernama, "Employers to Bear Full Levy Payment for Foreign Workers."

238   *Notes to Chapter 3*

6. A sample application form shows that a worker would ask MoLISA to waive the orientation fees to attend classes that provided basic skills, language instruction, and information to prepare migrants to work in Malaysia. This fee waiver form was printed on the recruitment company letterhead, which means that the recruitment companies would get a refund from MoLISA for these classes that they offered.

7. Mr. Lâm also showed me the website that he showed these students to search for jobs that would match their qualifications: Global Manpower Services Joint Stock Company, "Work in Malaysia," http://www.gmas.com.vn/viec-lam/viec-lam-tai -malaysia. For more on the company, see http://www.gmas.com.vn/gioi-thieu-gmas and http://www.companiess.com/gmas_hanoi_info2441665.html.

8. Trần, *Ties That Bind*, 131–34.

9. Global labor export company Toàn Cầu, "Bulletin of the joint-stock labor export company Việt Hà-Hà Tĩnh (VIHATICO)," http://congtyxklduytin.com/ cong-ty-co-phan-xuat-khau-lao-dong-viet-ha-ha-tinh-vihatico/, accessed July 10, 2020. People's committees are executive organs of local state administration. Their responsibility is to implement the Constitution and the law; see Helpline Law, Vietnam: Constitution, "The People's Councils and the People's Committees," http://www .helplinelaw.com/law/vietnam/constitution/constitution09.php.

10. In 1997, Vinatex oversaw 52 state-owned textile and 122 garment factories; by the end of 2008, most of Vinatex factory member firms had been privatized. The service centers include a training center, industrial and fashion colleges, a trade/ export promotion center, a fashion design institute, and one medical center (Trần, *Ties That Bind*, 133–34).

11. SULECO, "Corporate History," http://suleco.vn/lich-su-hinh-thanh.

12. Suleco was supposed to become a joint-stock company by mid-2008, but it did not happen then because "the MoLISA in HCMC still had to find employment for war invalids and redundant workers in Ho Chi Minh City" (Trần Văn Thạnh, Suleco, interview, September 2008). The full name of the private company is Cổ phần Dịch vụ Xuất khẩu Lao động & Chuyên Gia.

13. Lasec's full name is Công ty cổ phần cung ứng lao động dịch vụ xây dựng thủy lợi.

14. Trường Thọ, "Phương Thành." Traconsin became Tranconsin, a manpower company; its website is https://www.gmdu.net/corp-652675.html.

15. It used to belong to Ủy ban Dân tộc, a parliamentary committee (http://milaco .vn/gioi-thieu-ve-cong-ty). The full name of the company is Công ty Cổ phần xây dựng thương mại và Dịch vụ Quốc tế MILACO. It currently focuses on training and sending workers and study-abroad students to Japan, Taiwan, Korea, and several European countries.

16. Ms. Bạch, interview, January 2013.

17. According to Duy Quốc, Tống Thanh Tùng's father used to work in a MoLISA department and thus he had connections there. Tống Thanh Tùng was forthcoming only in the first interview. After that, he came up with many reasons for not answering the followup questions I posed via numerous phone calls and emails.

Notes to Chapter 3   239

18. Duy Quốc, "Chương trình Giao lưu trực tuyến" [Direct-Dialogue Program].

19. Nguyễn Duy, "Tạo mọi thuận lợi cho người lao động" [Creating favorable conditions for all employees].

20. Ong, *Spirits of Resistance and Capitalist Discipline*.

21. Tống Thanh Tùng has also published other articles in *Người Lao Động* and posts newly established labor markets on the newspaper's employment page, as well as online at websites that Vietnamese use for finding work, such as VNExpress, phunuonline, vieclamdongthap.vn, chauhung.com.vn, facebook/vietnamtaiwan, baomoi.com, and Saigon Giải Phóng.

22. Tống Thanh Tùng, "Đi để sắm trâu, xây nhà" [Working overseas to buy buffaloes and build houses], my emphasis.

23. During this crisis the Malaysian government did not accept foreign temporary workers to work in light-industry factories, especially electronics, and many guest workers were laid off and sent home.

24. Nguyễn Duy, "Tạo mọi thuận lợi cho người lao động" [Creating favorable conditions for all employees].

25. "Outsourcing companies outsource workers to certain workplaces requiring less than 50 workers and often share workers between different workplaces. This system was outlawed in 2018 because it caused too many problems. In 2018 the government cancelled the licences of outsourcing companies," (communication with Vicki Crinis, May 6, 2020).

26. Lindquist, "Labor Recruitment, Circuits of Capital, and Gendered Mobility"; Lê Thu Huong, "A New Portrait of Indentured Labour."

27. Oishi argues that workers who have grown up in a family with no money often have similarly poor money management skills as their parents (*Women in Motion*, 139). However, evidence from my interviewees did not reveal poor money management skills; instead, depression due to precarity in Malaysia led many male migrants into drinking and gambling, which would likely have increased the debts of the migrants. I want to thank Gerald Shenk for pointing out the value judgment implication of Oishi's argument.

28. The survey included 1,450 worker returnees (Viện khoa học lao động và xã hội [Institute of Social and Labor Science], "Báo cáo tóm tắt" [Summary report].

29. Mills, "Gender and Inequality in the Global Labor Force"; Portes, "Migration and Development"; Lim and Oishi, "International Labor Migration of Asian Women."

30. Viện khoa học lao động và xã hội [Institute of Social and Labor Science] "Báo cáo tóm tắt" [Summary report], 13–15.

31. Hoang and Yeoh, "Transnational Labour Migration, Debts and Family Economics in Vietnam," 297–98.

32. Lê Thu Hương estimates eleven months "A New Portrait of Indentured Labor," 880–96 and Danièle Bélanger and her coauthors eighteen months "International Labor Migration from Vietnam to Asian Countries".

33. Lã and Leung, "Remittances from Migrants," 10, 13.

240   *Notes to Chapters 3 and 4*

34. I realized the biased nature of this interview. Still, once in it, I was able to ask critical questions when the state officials stepped outside.

35. It is possible that his land was agricultural land, which has a low value and so would not have been useful as collateral.

36. A *công* is a Vietnamese metric unit of area, used in land measurement; it is the area of one thousand square meters (or one-tenth of a hectare). A hectare is ten thousand square meters (one hundred by one hundred meters) of land.

37. Phan Văn Dốp, interview, April 2015. During my fieldwork in An Giang, I visited that museum and was deeply saddened by the exhibitions.

38. Taylor, *Social Inequality in Vietnam*, 261.

39. Châu Anurak, interview, June 2014.

40. This conversation took place during the harvesting season in August 2012.

41. Mr. Vũ Minh Xuyên, interview, 2014.

Chapter 4. Precarity and Coping Mechanisms

1. Vietnam News Agency, "Malaysia Issues New Rules for Vietnamese Workers."

2. Achariam, "SUARAM."

3. Crinis, "Continuities and Discontinuities," 1–10. This law is still in effect as of 2019. There is a long list of conditions that foreign workers must agree to, and one of those is that they will not change employers or employment sectors; see https://www.imi.gov.my/index.php/en/foreign-worker.html.

4. Mr. Thức, interview, 2013. Concerns about the Malaysian police's harassment of migrant workers were also echoed by Mr. Lộc and Ms. Hạnh, the two returnees I interviewed in An Giang in 2013.

5. Achariam, "SUARAM: Bosses must stop holding foreign workers' passports."

6. Men also mentioned the pain of family separation, but none told me that they had divorced or that their family had broken up as a result.

7. Lê Thu Huong , "A New Portrait of Indentured Labour"; Oishi, *Women in Motion*; Parrenas, *Servants of Globalization*.

8. Hoang and Yeoh, "Transnational Labour Migration, Debts, and Family Economics in Vietnam"; Crinis, "Vietnamese Migrant Clothing Workers in Malaysia."

9. Lã and Leung, "Remittances from Migrants"; Rahman and Lian, "Towards a Sociology of Migrant Remittances in Asia."

10. Yeoh et al., "Between Two Families," 443; Rahman and Lian, "Towards a Sociology of Migrant Remittances in Asia."

11. Foucault, *Discipline and Punish*. Foucault draws on Jeremy Bentham's argument that the perfect prison would be structured in such a way that cells would be viewable from a central tower to argue that the panoptic model of surveillance has been used as a principle of social organization in many realms, such as university classrooms, urban planning, and hospital and factory architecture (Felluga, "Modules on Foucault").

12. "Three rape Vietnamese worker after robberies," *New Straits Times* [Kuala Lumpur], August 18, 2013, http://www.nst.com.my/nation/general/three-rape-vietnamese-worker-after-robberies-1.339624#ixzz2yLm5iYy6.

Notes to Chapter 4   241

13. Nhã Trân, "Vì sao nhiều công nhân Việt Nam ở Malaysia bị tử vong?" [Why did so many Vietnamese workers die in Malaysia?]; Theo Nguyễn Thái Sơn, "Dột tử" [Sudden death]. In 2009 and 2014, there were a couple of tragic deaths: the cause of one was unknown, and the other was due to an accident on the job (Trần Tuấn, "Vừa đi xuất khẩu lao động Malaysia 1 tháng, lao động Việt Nam đột tử" [Only working in Malaysia for one month, Vietnamese workers suddenly died]; "Hà Tĩnh" [Hà Tĩnh];"Xuất khẩu lao động ở Malaysia" [Labor export in Malaysia]).

14. Newspapers reported that a number of male workers had to sleep in containers that exacerbate the harsh weather contrasts in certain Malaysian regions.

15. Karl Marx, *Economic and Philosophic Manuscripts (1844)*, 29–33.

16. Crinis and Tran, "Migrant Workers in the Clothing Industry."

17. See Crinis and Tran, "Migrant Workers in the Clothing Industry."

18. I was given a copy of the 2008 spring issue of the *Voice of Vietnamese Workers in Malaysia*, which includes this moving poem, signed by a pseudonym "laborer." It describes a vicious cycle of debt (the word "debt" is repeated several times), shame, sadness, fear and confusion, failure, disappointment, and husband-wife separation, and it ends with the expression of a wish to live in Vietnam.

19. Oishi, *Women in Motion*.

20. Ms. Cúc, interview, 2008. Scholars have also questioned whether, in light of the goal of converting migrants, the activities of these Christian support groups are forms of disciplining the migrant workers through the Bible. See Crinis, "Continuities and Discontinuities."

21. Oishi, *Women in Motion*, 9, 188–192.

22. Bangladeshi female migrant workers in the United Arab Emirates who sent their money home for their households in Bangladesh likewise experienced a sense of empowerment as a result; see Rahman and Lian, "Towards a Sociology of Migrant Remittances in Asia."

23. Ms. Lê, interview, 2008. She specified that she sent in the range of đ1–2 million, about US$50–100, a month.

24. This story is recounted in Trần and Crinis, "Migrant Labor and State Power."

25. Lã and Leung, "Remittances from Migrants."

26. This line of argument is similar to that made by Yeoh et al., "Between Two Families."

27. Yeoh et al., "Between Two Families," 444; Rahman and Lian, "Towards a Sociology of Migrant Remittances in Asia."

28. In this informal *hụi* system, three participants pool the money they have saved, and each participant gets the collective money as a lump sum once every three months. This enables the participants to pay less overall in money transfer fees.

29. Mr. Kiên, interview, 2008. He was finishing his three-year contract at the time of our interview.

30. Trần, *Ties That Bind*.

31. "Robbery Rape Gang Busted," *New Straits Times* [Kuala Lumpur], February 8–10, 2008; "Robber Kills Guard, Sets Building on Fire," *New Straits Times*, February 4, 2008. More recent sources focus on problems with labor brokers and how

242   *Notes to Chapters 4 and 5*

big brands want to make sure that they fulfill their corporate social responsibility but do not necessarily care about the vulnerabilities of foreign workers in Malaysia. See "Migrant Workers Issue" and Yi, "World's Top Glovemaker Vows Clean-Up as Migrant Workers Toil in Malaysia Factories."

32. Tan, "Robbery, Rape Gang Busted"; "Robber Kills Guard, Sets Building on Fire."

33. For information about this strike, see Trần and Crinis, "Migrant Labor and State Power." It is unclear whether the lack of lighting concern was attended to.

34. She also said that the night workers were very afraid of being robbed when they returned to the hostel from their shifts.

35. When I asked for clarification about whether the thief was Malaysian or another foreign worker, Mr. Tú replied that he did not know, since the thief was not caught. But he was sure that the thief was not Vietnamese.

36. Yosso, "Whose Culture Has Capital?," 70, 77–78.

37. The employer would pay the return airfare only if the migrants finished the three-year contracts.

38. "Sisters" is a term of endearment since they were not related by blood. Neng Kanika had at that point just finished two years of her three-year contract.

39. Hải Anh Lã and Suiwah Leung, "Remittances from Migrants. "

40. Ramadan is celebrated during the ninth month of the Islamic lunar calendar. The month of fasting, introspection and prayer commemorates the revelation of the Quran to Muhammad and is one of the holiest events of the Islamic faith.

41. Mr. Chamali is not a hakem ("Ông Cả," or someone who is knowledgeable in Islamic law). He is not an imam (leader of congregational prayer, under the hakem) or a bilal who issues the call to prayer. Taylor, *Chăm Muslims of the Mekong Delta . . .* 87.

42. I was interviewing an official there when I ran into her. She was transferring the house deed to her son for him to get married.

43. Ms. Baqri, interview, 2012.

44. Ibid., 2014.

45. Duy Quốc, "Xuất khẩu lao động sang Malaysia" [Export labor to Malaysia].

46. This is consistent with Phan and Nguyễn's finding that many Chăm have their relatives in Cambodia which facilitate these transnational commercial exchanges. Phan Văn Dốp and Nguyễn Thị Nhung, "Quan Hệ Đồng Tộc và Văn Hóa – Tôn Giáo."

Chapter 5. Physical Third Space Empowerment

1. Boski, "A Psychology of Economic Migration," 1084.

2. Boski, conversation, 2016.

3. Yosso, "Whose Culture Has Capital?," 69–91.

4. See chapter 1 for an account of the labor system that channeled the Vietnamese migrants to these former Eastern European countries. See also Beresford and Đặng, *Economic Transition in Vietnam,* 78, 83, 84, 87, 89, 90.

5. Baláž and Williams, "Path-Dependency and Path-Creation Perspectives on Migration Trajectories."

6. Boski, conversation, 2017.

Notes to Chapter 5   243

7. Boski, "A Psychology of Economic Migration," 1083.

8. I thank Paweł Boski for this insight. See also Boski, "A Psychology of Economic Migration," 1083, and "Centrum Janki: Basic Information," http://chjanki.pl/en/about/basic-information.

9. Compared to the Sapa center, there are fewer activities: there was no gambling in sight or food and drink delivery.

10. Thu Hằng, "'Chợ' Sapa, hương Việt giữa lòng Praha, CH Séc" ["Sapa" market: The Vietnamese Essence in the Heart of Prague]. The Czechoslovak "Velvet Revolution" was a nonviolent transition of power from the communist planned economy to a parliamentary republic, lasting from November 17 to December 29, 1989.

11. At the exit gate, I came across a large board listing regulations in the Czech language.

12. Storm, "Sapa, Prague's 'Little Vietnam.'"

13. Thông Tấn Xã Việt Nam [Vietnam News Agency], "Ra mắt Ban Thường vụ lâm thời Hội Đồng hương Nghệ Tĩnh tại Séc" [The launching of the provisional standing committee of the Nghe Tinh Association of Councils in the Czech Republic].

14. Gutiérrez, "Migration, Emergent Ethnicity, and the 'Third Space,'" 488–89, 504.

15. Beresford and Đặng, *Economic Transition in Vietnam*, 85.

16. Ibid.

17. Williams and Baláž, "Winning, Then Losing, the Battle with Globalization," 545. In another study, Baláž and Williams argue that the Vietnamese migrants in Slovakia were locked into suboptimal pathways and could not respond to changing conditions over time ("Path-Dependency and Path-Creation Perspectives on Migration Trajectories," 37–67).

18. Williams and Baláž, "Winning, Then Losing, the Battle with Globalization," 542.

19. Ibid., 541–42.

20. A second wave of migrants, who came to Slovakia in the 1990s via informal networks of families and friends to help with retail sales in the open markets, were less educated (Baláž and Williams, "Path-Dependency and Path-Creation Perspectives on Migration Trajectories," 47–49).

21. Williams and Baláž, "Winning, Then Losing, the Battle with Globalization," 547.

22. Trần Quang Vinh, "Cuộc sàng lọc nghiệt ngã," Tuổi Trẻ Online, May 12, 2007, https://tuoitre.vn/cuoc-sang-loc-nghiet-nga-200712.htm

23. Ms. Đào, phone conversation, July 2017. See also Abraham and van Schendel, introduction.

24. Marzena Indra-Gozdz, conversation, June 2017.

25. This recognition could be interpreted as an artifact of politically correct behavior that masks underlying racism in the Czech Republic, but in implementing the new tax policy, which mandates electronic records of cash sales of goods and services for tax collection purposes, Czech authorities reached out to the Sapa community and were able to affirm that the Vietnamese do their business in line with local law, thereby countering the rumor that Vietnamese enterprises evade taxes and acknowledging the crucial role played by Vietnamese wholesale and retail outlets. Voice of Vietnam

244   Notes to Chapter 5

5, "Czech Republic Considers Vietnamese Integral Part in the Society"; Voice of Vietnam, "Vietnamese Firms Updated on Czech Law on Electronic Records of Sales."

26. Workers have to produce a predetermined minimum amount of the product per day or per hour to get paid.

27. Ms. Tiên, Ms. Hảo, and Mr. Hưng, interviews, 2008.

28. *False consciousness* is defined as forms of consent and capitulation among workers to the dominant ideology, hegemonic order, and/or state policies that reproduce their subordination in capitalist production relations. In this case, the Kinh-Hoa migrants consented to the quota system in this factory. See Scott, *Domination and the Arts of Resistance*.

29. This covert resistance is similar to that of Filipina domestic workers, who engaged in "hidden" organizing and communicating (Parrenas, *Servants of Globalization*; Constable, *Maid to Order in Hong Kong*, 23–24).

30. GMS TRIANGLE Project Quarterly Briefing Note, Vietnam, July–September 2018; Kaur, "Home Ministry."

31. Ms. Nguyễn Thị Tuyết Mai and Mr. Lê Quốc Hùng, interview, July 2015. As of August 2013, there were about five thousand undocumented Vietnamese workers in Malaysia. So, in 2013, the Vietnamese Ministry of Security went to Malaysia to work with Rela (Ikatan Relawan Rakyat), or the People's Volunteer Corps, which was established in 1972 by Malaysia's Home Affairs Ministry. Members of the corps have the power to carry firearms, arrest individuals, and enter premises without permits. In particular, since 2005, they have been empowered to catch undocumented migrants ("Rela Watch: What Is Rela?," https://relawatch.wordpress.com/what-is-rela).

32. Guest workers can end up becoming undocumented because they overstay their visas or because they do not have their passports in their possession. Before the change in the Malaysian passport law in 2015, the Malaysian government allowed Malaysian employers to impound foreign guest workers' passports as soon as they arrived in Malaysia for work (GMS TRIANGLE Project Quarterly Briefing Note, Vietnam, October–December 2018).

33. Duy Quốc, "Hết đường trốn ở Malaysia" [End of the road in Malaysia].

34. See Trần and Crinis, "Migrant Labor and State Power."

35. When asked for that factory's name, she said that she was so angry about it that she did not even care to remember its name. But it could be that she was being cautious and was keeping it secret for her own safety.

36. Oishi, *Women in Motion*.

37. Ms. Thu, interview, 2008. These fees may include the embassy staff's own fees for their service.

38. Lê Thu Hương, "A New Portrait of Indentured Labor."

39. His story was widely publicized in newspapers, so I have not used a pseudonym.

40. Nam Dương, who checked these facts with the Vietnamese Customs Office, relayed this information to me. There was one month that was not accounted for, July 2004, before he was imprisoned in August 2004. During that month, he might have become undocumented.

Notes to Chapter 5 245

41. The Vietnamese expression is "đem con bỏ chợ," which literally means "leaving a baby stranded in a marketplace." The sense is of doing something half-heartedly.

42. In 2010, at the request of Mr. Ngọc's family and the state-owned recruitment company (VINATEX-Labor section) that had sent him to Malaysia, journalist Mr. Nam Dương went looking for Mr. Ngọc. Another *Laborer* journalist, Mr. Nguyễn Quyết, had written a newspaper article on March 1, 2010, titled "Đi xuất khẩu lao động rồi . . . biến mất" (Joining the labor export program, then disappeared) to trigger public leads about this case. Local resident Mr. Duy Long told them that the local people had given Mr. Ngọc the nickname "Thằng Ma Lai," knowing his circumstances and accepting him. These journalists followed the locals' leads, tracing Mr. Ngọc's movement, and finally found him at the noodle factory in its new location in a rezoned area of the suburb (District 12). The two journalists reported the story in an article, "Four Days in Search of Mr. Ma Lai," describing this search and Mr. Ngọc's moving reunion with his father, who flew in from Thái Bình to meet up with his long-lost son. So in the space of one week, from the publication of the first article (March 1) to the second article (March 8), the search ended successfully.

43. Given the paucity of data, I do not know how many Hrê went during that time.

44. Bahrain, United Arab Emirates, and Korea accounted for the remaining 7 percent.

45. About sixty percent (80 out of 137) of all Hrê returnees in Quảng Ngãi had been recruited by Châu Hưng, while 24 percent had been recruited by Sovilaco. Seventy-four percent, or 26 out of 35, of the returnees from Ba Tơ district between 2011 and 2015 were recruited by Châu Hưng and 26 percent were recruited by Global Companies Manpower Services Joint Stock Company (Phòng lao động thương binh và xã hội, huyện Ba Tơ [DoLISA, Ba Tơ district], *Báo cáo tình hình thực hiện công tác xuất khẩu lao động 3 năm* [Report on the implementation of the first three years of the labor export program]).

46. List of Early Returnees to Quảng Ngãi province and Reasons, December 2012.

47. The 2012 Quảng Ngãi province report shows that over 21 percent of the Hrê reported that they "worked outside of their legal contracts and returned to Vietnam"; 36.5 percent returned legally and voluntarily; 19.7 percent returned because they had engaged in brawling or violated factory policies; 16 percent returned due to health reasons; and 1.5 percent returned because they had not met job requirements (Viện khoa học lao động và xã hội [Institute of Social and Labor Science], "Báo cáo tóm tắt" [Summary report], 3).

48. Four returned voluntarily because of health issues, and one died of a heart attack only after six months on the job. (Phòng lao động thương binh và xã hội, huyện Ba Tơ [DoLISA, Ba Tơ district], *Báo cáo tình hình thực hiện công tác xuất khẩu lao động 3 năm* [Report on the implementation of the first three years of the labor export program]).

49. Đinh Thị Phương Lan, interview, July 2015.

50. Ibid.

246 Notes to Chapters 5 and 6

51. Phòng lao động thương binh và xã hội, huyện Ba Tơ [DoLISA, Ba Tơ district], *Báo cáo tình hình thực hiện công tác xuất khẩu lao động 3 năm* [Report on the implementation of the first three years of the labor export program], 1.

52. Ibid., 2, 4–5.

53. Ibid., 5.

54. GMS TRIANGLE Project Quarterly Briefing Note, Thailand, January–March 2017. Maryann Bylander's work on Cambodian migrant workers in Thailand likewise shows that they rely on temporary, quasi-legal tourist visas to work in Thailand and need to return to Cambodia to get their passports and to make the jobs they already have in Thailand legal. All these activities are very costly to the migrants. Bylander, "Absurd Journeys."

55. At the time of the interview in June 2014, there were protests and unrest in Thailand.

56. These Muslim Chăm's networks in Cambodia are based on the Chăm's historical migrations to Cambodia in the seventeenth century, with some evidence of a Chăm colony in Cambodia back in the fifteenth century. Sources are cited in Chapter 1.

57. This transnational migration is beyond the extra-local movements described in Taylor, *Chăm Muslims of the Mekong Delta*.

58. I also document this escape story in "Weaving Life across Borders." Here, I present new material: her account of the risks she faced as an undocumented working for a Malay Muslim shop.

59. Weber, "The Cham Diaspora in Southeast Asia," 176–77.

60. Ford, Michele, and Lorene Lyons. "Travelling the Aspal Route: Grey Labour Migration through an Indonesian Border Town." In *The State and Illegality in Indonesia*, edited by Edward Aspinall and Gerry van Klinken, 107–22.

Chapter 6. Metaphorical Third Space Empowerment

1. Bhabha, *The Location of Culture*; Frenkel, "The Multinational Corporation as a Third Space"; Gutiérrez, "Migration, Emergent Ethnicity, and the 'Third Space.'"

2. Mrs. Giầy, conversation. Mrs. Giầy also mentioned that she was very appreciative of the services of the Polish government and the free public education for her daughter. However, according to Boski, only primary schools are free for non-Polish citizens; for secondary and beyond, non-Polish citizens have to pay tuition. Unlike in the United States, children who are born in Poland of immigrant parents are not automatically Polish citizens. Pathways to citizenship in Poland are complicated. Undocumented parents can apply for temporary and permanent residencies. (Conversation, June 2, 2017.)

3. Frenkel, "The Multinational Corporation as a Third Space."

4. Rutherford, "The Third Space."

5. These facts are consistent with Boski's argument (conversation, June 2017).

6. Non-Vietnamese tourists came in and tried to order food, but the female owner did not speak English, so they left without ordering anything.

Notes to Chapter 6   247

7. Bhabha, *The Location of Culture.*

8. Fahlander, "Third Space Encounters"; Scott, *Domination and the Arts of Resistance.*

9. Viện khoa học lao động và xã hội [Institute of Social and Labor Science], "Báo cáo tóm tắt" [Summary report], 17.

10. Hoang and Yeoh, "Transnational Labour Migration, Debts and Family Economics in Vietnam."

11. Chin, *In Service and Servitude.*

12. They were Mr. Thức, Ms. Cúc, Mr. Ngãi, Ms. Trúc, Ms. Kim-Ly, Mr. Việt, Ms. Loan, Ms. Hà.

13. Table 2 in the Report of Early returnees in Ba Tơ district: 2011 to July 2015.

14. According to Đinh Thị Phương Lan (interview, 2015), these loan statistics are estimates, since her office had not been able to obtain all the data from the Social Policy Bank branch at the Ba Tơ district level. Before 2015, the loan amount was only đ25 million. UBND huyện Ba Tơ [Ba Tơ District People's Committee], "Báo cáo về việc thực hiện một số quy định của pháp luật về lao động" [Report on the implementation of the legal provisions on labor at the departmental level], 8.

15. Bộ lao động thương binh và xã hội, huyện Ba Tơ [Ministry of Labor, Invalids, and Social Affairs, Ba Tơ district]. *Báo cáo tình hình thực hiện công tác xuất khẩu lao động 3 năm* [Report on the implementation of the first three years of the labor export program], 4.

16. In this case, Mr. Tuấn's experience abroad was a good one, and he was to come home at the end of his three-year contract. Apparently, the interest was not automatically deducted from his monthly paychecks while he was working in Malaysia.

17. This is a "gendered" dream: I did not see any photos of women standing next to a motorbike during my field trips!

18. Tử Trực and Phạm Anh, interview.

19. Võ Duy Yên, interview, July 2015.

20. Bhabha, "Of Mimicry and Man."

21. Father of Châu Hùng, interview, 2014.

22. Father of Châu Tiro, interview, 2014.

23. Neng Suvanna, interviews, 2012 and 2014.

24. Ms. Alvi, interview, 2014.

25. Ibid., 2016.

26. I assume that Malaysian Muslims working in the plants would also have been getting time to pray well before the arrival of these Chăm migrants. I thank Joe Lubow for this insight.

27. Abraham and van Schendel, "Introduction."

28. Since the loan was taken out under the name of his mother, Ms. Baqri, Mr. Sadat moved on with his life and delegated the loan repayment to his mother. As of 2014, Ms. Baqri still owed đ26 million, or đ20 million in principal and đ6–7 million in interest.

Chapter 7. Aspirations after Malaysia

1. Oishi, *Women in Motion*.

2. Ibid.

3. Yosso, "Whose Culture Has Capital?"

4. Strong ties and weak ties are social networks that often help migrants improve their economic outcomes. Strong ties include close contacts of families, friends, or neighbors, whereas weak ties are outside of those circles and include support from nonfamily ties and friendships, even from other ethnic and religious networks. Sources are cited in the Introduction.

5. Châu Anurak did not mention whether those companies are owned by Chinese Malaysians or Chinese from the mainland proper.

6. "Đề Án Hỗ Trợ Các Huyện Nghèo Đẩy Mạnh Xuất Khẩu Lao Động: Chưa đạt mục tiêu," *Nguoi Lao Dong* [Laborer], Blog Post (February 18, 2011), http://nld.com.vn/nhip-song-cong-nghiep/chua-dat-muc-tieu-2011021810120386.htm.

7. Interview with Ms. Đinh Thị Phương Lan, 2012.

8. Ba Tơ District DoLISA Office, "Báo cáo tình hình."

9. Geographical agency is a concept coined by Taylor, who argued that in response to Vietnam's move to a market-based economy, the Chăm have reinvented economic space through local and extra-local (still within Vietnam) trading practices that draw on their cultural competencies and institutions (Taylor, "Economy in Motion," 248). I argue that the Chăm's geographical agency goes beyond economic purposes and includes religious purposes.

10. These two centers are 153 kilometers apart, or several hours' drive.

11. Interviews with Mr. Phan Văn Dốp and Ms. Nguyễn Thị Nhung, who shared a lot of good insights on the Chăm's way of life based on their fieldwork, 2015.

12. Taylor, *Chăm Muslims of the Mekong Delta*, 78.

13. Phan Văn Dốp and Nguyễn Thị Nhung, "Quan Hệ Đồng Tộc và Văn Hóa – Tôn Giáo," 57.

14. This language is part of the Austroasiatic family, discussed in chapter 1.

15. Taylor, *The Khmer Lands of Vietnam*, 188–89.

16. I use his real name because he is a public clergyman at a recognizable public mosque.

17. Nakamura, "Chăm in Vietnam," 65.

18. This is in comparison to smaller temples. Taylor, "Economy in Motion" ; Yoshimoto, "A Study of the *Hồi giáo* Religion in Vietnam."

19. This salary was 50 percent higher than the 2015 regional minimum average of đ2.4 million per month. Prime Minister Decree 103/2014/NĐ-CP, November 11, 2014.

20. At that point, Mr. Lê (the jobber) interjected and hinted that Mr. Bình may have violated some contract terms and that his lifestyle may not have been suitable for a Muslim country.

21. Pamela McElwee argues that the sedentarization policy, "fixed cultivation, fixed residence" (định canh định cư), began in 1968 in the former Democratic Republic of Vietnam (before Vietnam's reunification in 1975 as the Socialist Republic of Viet-

Notes to Chapter 7 249

nam), affecting 3.1 million ethnic minority people. McElwee, "Becoming Socialist or Becoming Kinh?," 198–99.

22. Trần Hoài, email correspondence, May 2015.

23. This is consistent with McElwee's argument that this policy has not been very successful because there are no reliable statistics on the percentage of the minority people who continue to engage in swidden cultivation, or who have fixed residence (*định cư*) yet do rotational agriculture (*luân canh*). It is beyond the scope of this study to explore this topic further, but I hypothesize that the scope of the Hrê's swiddening activities became much more limited because of the privatization of mountainous/communal land by fewer owners (the Kinh and the rich Hrê) to cultivate cash crops.

24. These simple brick houses are called "*nhà gạch cấp 4*." Email correspondence with Trần Hoài, May 2015.

25. Kontum is less than 200 kilometers southwest of Quảng Ngãi. The Hrê migrants also pick coffee in the other two major central highland coffee bean provinces: Gia Lai and Đắk Lắk. Buôn Ma Thuột coffee town is located in Đắk Lắk province. While both provinces have similar rainy patterns, Kontum province receives half as much precipitation as Quảng Ngãi.

26. Trần Hoài confirmed that cassava can be both a food crop and a cash crop (such as for animal feed). Skype communication, May 2015.

27. Prime Minister Decision 167 and Decision 67, Mỹ Ái – Mai Hương.

28. Taylor, *The Khmer Lands of Vietnam*, 188, made a similar argument and pointed to the cycle of debt burden and land ceding as the reason.

29. Interview with Trần Duy Hiếu, Labor Department in Tri Tôn District, January 2014; interview with Ms. Thái Thị Bạch Lan and Mr. Nguyễn Văn Lâm, January 2014.

30. Interview with Phan Văn Dốp, April 2015.

31. Ibid.

32. Interview with Mr. Tôn Long Quốc Vinh, the human resource director at Samho, July 2014. At the end of 2014, Samho had opened another factory in An Giang. Vietnam Samho Company, Ltd., "About Us," http://vnsamho.com/company-introduction-35A51B56/en.

33. The 2012 Labor Code reasserted gender-related accommodations that had been introduced in the 1994 Code but were never widely implemented. These provisions give women a paid thirty-minute break daily during menstruation and give working mothers a sixty-minute break while nursing infants under the age of twelve months. While these long-overdue reforms were to take effect in 2013, they were not implemented until late 2015 due to employer delays and resistance. The 2019 Labor Code, ratified in November 2019 by the Vietnamese National Assembly, took effect on January 1, 2021. Responding to strong campaigns by the VGCL, the Women's Union, and other women's organizations, the code maintains all of these workplace accommodations, despite management's rigorous efforts to eliminate them. Moreover, Article 139 provides maternity leave for not only the female employee but also the male employee whose wife gives birth, an employee who adopts a child under six months of age, and a female employee who becomes a surrogate mother. Article

250 *Notes to Chapter 7 and Conclusion*

140 ensures employment security after maternity. Trần, Bair, and Werner, "Forcing Change from the Outside?," 410; The Labor Code 2019 (No. 45/2019/QH14), the Vietnamese National Assembly, Hanoi, November 20, 2019, http://nhankiet.vn/vi /r2579/The-Labor-Code-2019--Effective-Jan-01-2021.html.

34. She mentioned that her sister has to work all three shifts with this cycle: shift 1 in week 1, shift 2 in week 2, and shift 3 in week 3. She herself was very fatigued with work.

35. Taylor, *The Khmer Lands of Vietnam*, 2, 143.

36. She had worked at Samho five months at this point, too early for a home visit.

37. A "công" equals 1,000 square meters, or one-tenth of a hectare.

38. I pointed out to her that Samho had a decent childcare facility for workers, free of charge; she could send her infant and the three-year-old there so that the older ones could go to school. Unfortunately, I had no chance to follow up with her to see how she was doing.

39. Taylor, "Economy in Motion." It was unclear whether the local government had recruited and sent these Chăm workers to work in those factories, as in the Khmer's case.

40. This case has been cited in Trần, "Weaving Life across Borders."

Conclusion

1. World Bank, "COVID-19 Crisis Through a Migration Lens," https://documents .worldbank.org/en/publication/documents-reports/documentdetail/9897215875 12418006/covid-19-crisis-through-a-migration-lens, 16.

2. World Bank, "COVID-19 Crisis Through a Migration Lens," 7.

3. Xiang and Lindquist, "Migration Infrastructure"; Rodriguez, *Migrants for Export*; Guevarra, *Marketing Dreams, Manufacturing Heroes*.

4. The Labor Code, No. 45/2019/QH14, November 20, 2019, Articles 150 (p. 28), 179 (p. 33), and 188 (p. 35) and Amendment to Article 32 on the prerogative of the court to adjudicate labor disputes (p. 43).

5. The Law on Contract-Based Vietnamese Overseas Workers, 69/2020/QH14, Articles 6 (p. 3), 7 (p. 4), 17 (p. 8), 23 (pp. 11–12), 42 (p. 21), and 46 (p. 23).

6. I reached out to the VGCL for further information about the implementation of this plan of action but received no response.

7. GEFONT is an acronym for General Federation of Nepalese Trade Unions.

8. Crinis and Tran, "Migrant Workers in the Clothing Industry," 92–93.

9. http://www.poea.gov.ph/programs/programs&services.html.

10. Crinis and Tran, "Migrant Workers in the Clothing Industry," 89.

11. Long Nguyen, "Stranded Vietnamese face the brunt of resurgent Covid in Malaysia," *VnExpress*, June 11, 2021, https://e.vnexpress.net/news/life/trend/stranded -vietnamese-face-the-brunt-of-resurgent-covid-in-malaysia-4292350.html.

12. Giang Nam, "Tạm dừng đưa lao động sang Malaysia," *Người Lao Động*, September 30, 2020, https://nld.com.vn/cong-doan/tam-dung-dua-lao-dong-sang -malaysia-2020093020331948.htm.

13. The Law on Contract-Based Vietnamese Overseas Workers, 69/2020/QH14, Articles 19 (p. 10) and 72 (p. 31).

Notes to Conclusion and Appendices 1–2   251

14. Lam Le, "Migrant workers need better protection at home and abroad," December 29, 2020, https://e.vnexpress.net/news/news/migrant-workers-need-better-protection-at-home-and-abroad-4211496.html.

15. Moving testimonies from women who escaped demonstrate powerlessness and abuses hidden behind closed doors, as do some private recordings. Mahdavi, "Gender, Labour, and the Law; BBC News, "I wanted to die."

16. In one tragic case, a thirty-three-year-old female domestic worker died in Saudi Arabia in November 2020 due to Covid-19, leaving behind an elderly father and two young children in Cà Mau province in the deep south of Vietnam. The Vietnamese recruitment leaflet, which specifically looks for female workers, states, "The head of household directly pays the migrant domestic workers." This stipulation gives the Saudi Arabian sponsor-cum-employer tremendous power to treat the workers as he sees fit. It is difficult to verify whether the head of household in this particular case had, prior to the young woman's death, actually paid her the approximately US$14,000 her work would have been worth (based on an average $390 per month for three years). In communications with the journalist, I learned that the woman's father only received from the recruitment company about US$5,200 as part of her earnings (correspondence with Duy Nhân, April 2021). See Duy Nhân, "Xót xa gia cảnh nữ lao động tử vong nơi xứ người vì Covid-19," and Nam Việt Joint Stock Company, "Notice of Hiring Domestic Workers in Saudi Arabia."

17. Lâm Lê, "Migrant Workers Need Better Protection."

Appendix 1. Descriptions of the Samples

1. Suleco was still a state-owned overseas employment service company under the management of the Hồ Chí Minh City Labor Federation. Lịch Sử Hình Thành [History of Suleco Begins], suleco.vn, http://suleco.vn/lichsu-hinh-thanh/ (accessed January 10, 2016).

2. Many Hrê were still working in Malaysia or migrating to do short-term manual work (such as picking coffee beans in neighboring Kontum) in nearby provinces during the off-seasons in their own villages.

3. Rahman and Fee, "Towards a Sociology of Migrant Remittances in Asia," 693–95, 700, 702.

4. Mỹ Ái and Mai Hương, "Giảm nghèo vùng đồng bào Khmer" [Poverty reduction in the Khmer region].

5. The remaining two communes are Nhơn Hội and Khánh Bình, where I did not conduct any interviews.

Appendix 2. Land Issues Faced by the Five Ethnic Groups in This Study

1. Lưu Hùng argues that the Hrê have been practicing wet rice planting since the sixteenth century ("Góp phần nghiên cứu tỉnh song hệ ở dân tộc Hrê" [A contribution to the study of the double filiation of the Hrê people]).

2. McElwee, "Becoming Socialist or Becoming Kinh?," 198–99.

3. Nguyễn, "From Swidden Cultivation to Fixed Farming and Settlement."

252   *Notes to Appendices 3–4*

Appendix 3. Chronology of the Transnational Labor Brokerage State System, 1950S–2020

1. Bộ lao động thương binh và xã hội [Ministry of Labor, Invalids, Social Affairs], "Quy định chức năng, nhiệm vụ, quyền hạn và cơ cấu tổ chức của Cục quản lý lao động ngoài nước" [Defining functions, tasks, and organizational structure of the Department of Overseas Labor].

2. Achariam, "SUARAM."

3. Phan Anh, "75,000 Vietnamese repatriated amid coronavirus pandemic," *VnExpress*, December 28, 2020, https://e.vnexpress.net/news/news/75-000-vietnamese -repatriated-amid-coronavirus-pandemic-4213029.html.

Appendix 4. Legal Documentation of Labor Export Policies

1. Prime Minister Decree 50/2010/QD-TTg, Decision 15/QD-HDQT (2011) and an attachment, and Decision 7/QD-HDQT (2013).

2. In August 2012, the state added three more poor districts in the South (Trà Vinh, Bạc Liêu, Cà Mau), bringing the total to sixty-four districts (interview with Mr. Văn Thạnh, August 15, 2012).

3. International Organization for Migration, *Viet Nam Migration Profile 2016*, 71–72. "Those who sacrificed for the country" refer to people who fought in the (anti-French and anti-American) wars of liberation; they receive special status, recognition, and a small monthly financial compensation.

4. International Organization for Migration, *Viet Nam Migration Profile 2016*, 72.

5. See https://thuvienphapluat.vn/van-ban/Tien-te-Ngan-hang/Thong-tu-31-2013 -TT-NHNN-Bao-cao-thong-ke-don-vi-Ngan-hang-Nha-nuoc-to-chuc-tin-dung -216422.aspx#.

Bibliography

Abraham, Itty, and Willem van Schendel. Introduction to *Illicit Flows and Criminal Things: States, Borders, and the Other Side of Globalization*, edited by Willem van Schendel and Itty Abraham, 1–37. Bloomington: University of Indiana Press, 2005.

Achariam, Noel. "SUARAM: Bosses Must Stop Holding Foreign Workers' Passports." *Free Malaysia Today*, January 30, 2017. https://www.freemalaysiatoday.com /category/nation/2017/01/30/suaram-bosses-must-stop-holding-foreign-workers-passports.

Aguilera, Michael B., and Douglas S. Massey. "Social Capital and the Wages of Mexican Migrants: New Hypotheses and Tests." *Social Forces* 82, no. 2 (2003): 671–701.

Amarthalingam, Sangeetha. "Malaysia Defers Foreign Workers' Levy Payment to 2018: Malaysian Employers Express Relief, Call for Holistic Management of Issue." *South China Morning Post,* March 14, 2017. http://www.scmp.com/news/asia/southeast -asia/article/2061521/malaysia-deferrs-foreign-workers-levy-payment-2018.

Amly, Wan Syamsul. "RM1,000 Minimum Wage Beginning July." Translated by Najiah Najib. *Astro Awani,* April 5, 2016. http://english.astroawani.com/malaysia-news /rm1-000-minimum-wage-beginning-july-101208.

Anh Phương. "Đơn hàng tốt từ những đối tác tốt" [Good orders from good partners]. Hà Nội: Bộ lao động thương binh và xã hội [Ministry of Labor, Invalids, and Social Affairs], 2009. http://www.dolab.gov.vn/index.aspx?mid=1156&sid=11&nid=1437, accessed December 31, 2009.

Anh Thư, "Tạm dừng đưa lao động Việt Nam sang làm việc tại Malaysia," *Lao Động,* January 10, 2020. https://laodong.vn/cong-doan/tam-dung-dua-lao-dong-viet -nam-sang-lam-viec-tai-malaysia-840772.ldo.

Ba Tơ District, Department of Labor, Invalids, and Social Affairs. *Báo cáo tình hình thực hiện công tác xuất khẩu lao động 3 năm* [Report on the implementation of the first three years of the labor export program]. Ba Tơ District, Quảng Ngãi: Department of Labor, Invalids, and Social Affairs, August 2012.

254 Bibliography

Ba Tơ District People's Committee. *Báo cáo về việc thực hiện một số quy định của pháp luật về lao động việc làm trên địa bàn huyện giai đoạn 2011–2014* [Report on the implementation of the legal provisions on labor and jobs at the district level during the 2011–2014 period]. Ba Tơ district, Quảng Ngãi, 2015.

———. *Báo cáo về công tác xuất khẩu lao động năm 2012* [2012 report on the task of exporting labor]. Ba Tơ District, Quảng Ngãi: 2013.

Baláž, Vladimir, and Allan M. Williams. "Path-Dependency and Path-Creation Perspectives on Migration Trajectories: The Economic Experiences of Vietnamese Migrants in Slovakia." *International Migration* 45, no. 2 (2007): 37–67.

Ban chỉ đạo tổng điều tra dân số và nhà ở trung ương/Central Population and Housing Census Steering Committee. *Tổng điều tra dân số và nhà ở việt nam năm 2009: Kết quả toàn bộ/The 2009 Vietnam population and Housing Census: Completed Results*. Hanoi: Tổng cục thống kê /General Statistics Office, 2010. https://www .gso.gov.vn/default_en.aspx?tabid=515&idmid=5&ItemID=10799.

Baulch, Bob, Truong Thi Kim Chuyen, Dominique Haughton, and Jonathan Haughton. "Ethnic Minority Development in Vietnam." *Journal of Development Studies* 43, no. 7 (2007): 1151–76. https://doi.org/10.1080/02673030701526278.

BBC News. "'I wanted to die': The 'Hell' of Kafala Jobs in the Middle East." *BBC Africa Eye*, October 24, 2018.

Bélanger, Danièle. "Labor Migration and Human Trafficking among Vietnamese Migrants in Asia." *American Annals of Political and Social Science* 653, no. 1 (2013): 87–106. https://doi.org/10.1177/0002716213517066.

Bélanger, Danièle, Dương Lê Bạach, Trần Linh Giang, Khuất Thu Hồng, Nguyễn Thi Vân Anh, and Belinda Hammoud. "International Labor Migration from Vietnam to Asian Countries: Process, Experiences and Impact." Report presented at the "Labour Migration from Vietnam to Asian Countries: Sharing Research Findings and NGOs Experiences" workshop. Hanoi, Vietnam, March 15, 2010.

Bélanger, Danièle, Kayoko Ueno, Khuat Thu Hong, and Emiko Ochiai. "From Foreign Trainees to Unauthorized Workers: Vietnamese Migrant Workers in Japan." *Asian and Pacific Migration Journal* 20, no.1 (2011): 31–53. https://doi .org/10.1177/011719681102000102.

Bentham, Jeremy. *Selected Writings*. Edited by Stephen G. Engelmann. New Haven, CT: Yale University Press, 2011. http://public.eblib.com/choice/publicfullrecord .aspx?p=3420818.

Beresford, Melanie, and Đặng Phong. *Economic Transition in Vietnam: Trade and Aid in the Demise of a Centrally Planned Economy*. Cheltenham, UK: Edward Elgar, 2000.

Berger, Alan. "Vietnamese Workers in USSR." *Boston Globe*, May 23, 1982.

Bernama. "Employers to Bear Full Levy Payment for Foreign Workers." Bernama .com, September 25, 2018. http://www.bernama.com/en/news.php?id=1646221.

———. "Higher Levy Will Deter Foreign Workers to Malaysia." *Malaysiakini*, February 3, 2016. https://www.malaysiakini.com/news/329268.

Bhabha, Homi. *The Location of Culture*. London: Routledge, 1994.

Bibliography 255

———. "Of Mimicry and Man: The Ambivalence of Colonial Discourse." *Discipleship: A Special Issue on Psychoanalysis* 28 (Spring 1984): 125–33. https://www.jstor.org/stable/778467.

Biao Xiang and Johan Lindquist. "Migration Infrastructure." *International Migration Review* 48, no. S1 (2014): S124, S136.

Bloch, Alice, and Sonia McKay. "Employment, Social Networks and Undocumented Migrants: The Employer Perspective." *Sociology* 49, no. 1 (2015): 38–55. https://doi.org/10.1177/0038038514532039.

Bộ lao động thương binh và xã hội [Ministry of Labor, Invalids, and Social Affairs], Department of Overseas Labor (DOLAB). *Thị trường Malaysia 6 tháng đầu năm 2009* [The Malaysian market in the first six months of 2009]. Hà Nội: MoLISA, 2009. http://www.dolab.gov.vn/index.aspx?mid=1156&sid=11&nid=1369.

———. "Quy định chức năng, nhiệm vụ, quyền hạn và cơ cấu tổ chức của Cục Quản lý lao động ngoài nước" [Defining functions, responsibilities, mandates/charges, and organizational structure of the Department of Overseas Labor]. http://www.molisa.gov.vn/Pages/gioithieu/cocautochucchitiet.aspx?ToChucID=1476.

Boski, Pawel. "A Psychology of Economic Migration." *Journal of Cross-Cultural Psychology* 44, no. 7 (2013): 1067–93. https://doi.org/10.1177/0022022112471895.

Boyd, Monica. "Family and Personal Networks in International Migration: Recent Developments and New Agendas." *International Migration Review* 23, no. 3 (1989): 638–70.

Bruckmayr, Phillipp. "Between Institutionalized Syncretism and Official Particularism: Religion among the Chams of Vietnam and Cambodia." In *Rituale als Ausdruck von Kulturkontakt: "Synkretismus" zwischen Negation und Neudefinition*, edited by Andreas H. Pries, Laetitia Martzolff, Robert Langer, and Claus Ambos, 11–41. Wiesbaden: Harrassowitz, 2013.

Bylander, Maryann. "Absurd Journeys: The Costs of Becoming Legal." Paper presented at the UC Berkeley–UCLA Conference on Global Migration in Southeast Asia, Berkeley, CA, April 2018.

Carvalho, Martin, and Rahimy Rahim. "Reduced Extension Levy Fees for Foreign Workers Finally Enforced." *Star Online*, May 2, 2019. https://www.thestar.com.my/news/nation/2019/05/02/reduced-extension-levy-fees-for-foreign-workers-finally-enforced#lxt1IR336zDKOk3C.99.

Central Population and Housing Census Steering Committee. *The 2009 Vietnam Population and Housing Census: Completed Results.* Hanoi: General Statistics Office of Vietnam, June 2010.

Chandler, David P. *A History of Cambodia.* Boulder, CO: Westview Press, 2008.

Chin, Christine B. N. "Diversification and Privatisation: Securing Insecurities in the Receiving Country of Malaysia." *Asia Pacific Journal of Anthropology* 9, no. 4 (2008): 285–303. https://doi.org/10.1080/14442210802485070.

———. *In Service and Servitude: Foreign Domestic Workers in the Malaysia "Modernity" Project.* New York: Columbia University Press, 1998.

256   Bibliography

Coe, Neil, Philip Kelly, and Kris Olds. "Globalization, Transnationalism, and the Asia-Pacific." In *Remaking the Global Economy: Economic-Geographical Perspectives*, edited by Jamie Peck and Henry Wai-chung Yeung, 45–60. London: Sage, 2003.

Collins, Patricia Hill. "Intersectionality's Definitional Dilemmas." *Annual Review of Sociology* 41 (2015): 1–20. https://doi.org/10.1146/annurev-soc-073014-112142.

Collyer, Michael. "When Do Social Networks Fail to Explain Migration? Accounting for the Movement of Algerian Asylum-Seekers to the UK." *Journal of Ethnic and Migration Studies* 31, no. 4 (2005): 699–718. https://doi.org/10.1080/13691830500109852.

Constable, Nicole. *Maid to Order in Hong Kong: Stories of Filipina Workers*. Ithaca, NY: Cornell University Press, 1997.

Consular Department, Vietnam Ministry of Foreign Affairs. Viet Nam Profile 2016. Hanoi: International Organization for Migration, August 2017. https://publications .iom.int/system/files/pdf/mp_vietnam.pdf.

Cox, Judy. "An Introduction to Marx's Theory of Alienation." *International Socialism* ser. 2, no. 79 (1998). http://pubs.socialistreviewindex.org.uk/isj79/cox.htm.

Crinis, Vicki. "Continuities and Discontinuities: Malay Workers and Migrant Workers in the Manufacturing Industries." *Intersections: Gender and Sexuality in Asia and the Pacific* 36 (2014). http://intersections.anu.edu.au/issue36/crinis.htm.

———. "The Devil You Know: Malaysian Perceptions of Foreign Workers." *RIMA* 39, no. 2 (2005). https://www.researchgate.net/publication/30386686_The_Devil_You_Know_Malaysian_Perceptions_of_Foreign_Workers.

———. "Global Commodity Chains in Crisis: the Garment Industry in Malaysia." *International Journal of Institutions and Economies* 4, no. 3 (2012): 61–82.

———. "Malaysia: Women, Labour Activism and Unions." In *Women and Labour Organising in Asia: Diversity, Autonomy and Activism*, edited by Kaye Broadbent and Michele Ford, 68–83. London: Routledge, 2008.

———. "Sweat or No Sweat: Foreign Workers in the Garment Industry in Malaysia." *Journal of Contemporary Asia* 40, no. 4 (2010): 589–611.

———. "Vietnamese Migrant Clothing Workers in Malaysia: Global Production, Transnational Labour Migration, and Social Reproduction." In *The Global Political Economy of the Household in Asia*, edited by Juanita Elias and Samanthi J. Gunawardana, 162–77. Basingstoke, UK: Palgrave Macmillan, 2013.

Crinis, Vicki, and Angie Tran. "Migrant Workers in the Clothing Industry: Networking in Christian Spaces." In *Labour in the Clothing Industry in the Asia Pacific*. Edited by Vicki Crinis and Adrian Vickers, 80–96. London: Routledge, 2017.

Đặng Nghiêm Vạn, Chu Thái Sơn, and Lưu Hùng. *Ethnic Minorities in Vietnam*. Hà Nội: Thế Giới, 2014.

Davis, Benjamin, Guy Stecklov, and Paul Winters. "Domestic and International Migration from Rural Mexico: Disaggregating the Effects of Network Structure and Composition." *Population Studies* 56, no. 3 (2002): 291–309.

Department of Education and Training of An Giang Province. *Global Initiative on Out-of-School Children: Report on Out-of-School Children in An Giang Province*. Hanoi: UNICEF, 2013. https://www.unicef.org/vietnam/media/851/file/Out-of school%20children%20in%20An%20Giang%202014.pdf.

Dezan Shira and Associates. "Remittances to Vietnam on the Rise." *Vietnam Briefing*, May 4, 2018. https://www.vietnam-briefing.com/news/remittances-vietnam-rise.html.

Đổng Thành Danh. "Bàn thêm về sự du nhập của Hồi giáo ở Champa" [The introduction of Islam to Champa].Tạp chí nghiện cứu tôn giáo 3, no. 53 (2016): 80–93.

Dương Thị Bích Thủy. "Nâng cao chất lượng vận động trong đồng bào Khmer ở An Giang" [Improving the quality of mobilization among the Khmer people in An Giang]. Tạp chí *Xây dựng đảng* [Party building magazine], May 17, 2014. http://www.xaydungdang.org.vn/Home/Dan-voi-dang/2014/7391/Nang-cao-chat-luong-van-dong-trong-dong-bao-Khmer-o-An.aspx.

Duy Nhân. "Xót xa gia cảnh nữ lao động tử vong nơi xứ người vì Covid-19" [Grieving for the family situation of a female domestic worker who passed away due to Covid-19 while working abroad]. *Người lao động* [Laborer], December 27, 2020, https://nld.com.vn/ban-doc/xot-xa-gia-canh-nu-lao-dong-tu-vong-noi-xu-nguoi-vi-covid-19-20201227111344391.htm.

Duy Quốc. "Giao lưu trực tuyến: Những thông tin cần thiết cho người lao động đi làm việc ở nước ngoài" [Online exchange: Essential information for workers going abroad]. *Người lao động* [Laborer], May 30, 2007. http://nld.com.vn/viec-lam/giao-luu-truc-tuyen-nhung-thong-tin-can-thiet-cho-nguoi-lao-dong-di-lam-viec-o-nuoc-ngoai-190885.htm.

———. "Hết đường trốn ở Malaysia" [End of the road in Malaysia]. *Người lao động* [Laborer], October 1, 2013. http://nld.com.vn/cong-doan/het-duong-tron-o-malaysia-20131001084149371.htm.

———. "Rắc rối thẩm định hợp đồng" [Trouble appraising labor contracts]. *Người lao động* [Laborer], August 18, 2009. https://nld.com.vn/viec-lam/rac-roi-tham-dinh-hop-dong-20090817114317980.htm.

———. "Xuất khẩu lao động sang Malaysia: Lại thêm một vụ . . . đem con bỏ chợ" [Export labor to Malaysia: Another case of . . . leaving a baby stranded in the marketplace]. *Người lao động* [Laborer], June 9, 2004. http://nld.com.vn/46856P1017C1051/lai-them-mot-vu-dem-con-bo-cho.htm.

Elias, Juanita. "Gendered Political Economy and the Politics of Migrant Worker Rights: The View from South-East Asia." *Australian Journal of International Affairs* 64, no. 1 (2010): 203–22. https://doi.org/10.1080/13563460500144751.

Engelbert, Thomas. "The Khmer in Southern Vietnam: Cambodians or Vietnamese?" In *Nationalism and Ethnicity in Southeast Asia*, edited by Ingrid Wessel, volume 1, 176–85. Proceedings of the Nationalism and Ethnicity in Southeast Asia conference at Humboldt University, Berlin. Boulder, CO: Westview Press, 1995.

Fahlander, Fredrik. "Third Space Encounters: Hybridity, Mimicry and Interstitial Practice." In *Encounters, Materialities, Confrontations: Archaeologies of Social Space and Interaction*, edited by Per Cornell and Frederik Fahlander, 15–41. Newcastle upon Tyne, UK: Cambridge Scholars Publishing, 2007.

Felluga, Dino. "Modules on Foucault: On Panoptic and Carceral Society." *Introductory Guide to Critical Theory* website, January 31, 2011. https://www.cla.purdue.edu/english/theory/newhistoricism/modules/foucaultcarceral.html.

258 Bibliography

Ford, Michele, and Lorene Lyons. "Travelling the Aspal Route: Grey Labour Migration through an Indonesian Border Town." In *The State and Illegality in Indonesia*, edited by Edward Aspinall and Gerry van Klinken, 107–22. Leiden: KITLV Press, 2011. https://doi.org/10.1163/9789004253681_007.

Foucault, Michel. *Discipline and Punish: The Birth of the Prison*. New York: Pantheon, 1977.

Frenkel, Michal. "The Multinational Corporation as a Third Space: Rethinking International Management Discourse on Knowledge Transfer through Homi Bhabha." *Academy of Management Review* 33, no. 4 (2008): 924–42. https://doi.org/10.5465/amr .2008.34422002.

Giang Nam. "Đài Loan mở thêm 7 nghề cho lao động nước ngoài" [Taiwan opens 7 more job categories for foreign workers]. *Người lao động* [Laborer], December 2, 2020. https://nld.com.vn/cong-doan/dai-loan-mo-them-7-nghe-cho-lao-dong -nuoc-ngoai-20201202210905644.htm.

———. "Lao động ra nước ngoài làm việc được hưởng nhiều quyền lợi" [Laborers working abroad enjoy many benefits]. *Người lao động* [Laborer], December 16, 2020. https://nld.com.vn/cong-doan/lao-dong-ra-nuoc-ngoai-lam-viec-duoc -huong-nhieu-quyen-loi-20201215222814323.htm.

———. "Sang Nhật làm kaigo: Hấp dẫn!" [Going to Japan to work in home-care for the elderly: Interesting!]. *Người lao động* [Laborer], March 15, 2021. https:// nld.com.vn/cong-doan/sang-nhat-lam-kaigo-hap-dan-20210314210604513.htm.

Ginsburgs, George. "Imported Asian Labor in the USSR." *Asian Perspective* 14, no. 2 (1990): 5–45. https://www.jstor.org/stable/42703942.

Giulietti, Corrado, Jackline Wahba, and Yves Zenou. "Strong Versus Weak Ties in Migration." *European Economic Review* 104 (March 2018): 111–37. https://www .sciencedirect.com/journal/european-economic-review/vol/104/suppl/C.

Global Services Manpower Services Joint Stock Company. "Work in Malaysia." http:// www.gmas.com.vn/viec-lam/viec-lam-tai-malaysia.

GMS TRIANGLE Project Quarterly Briefing Notes, Vietnam. Various dates. Hanoi: International Labour Organization.

GMS TRIANGLE Project Quarterly Briefing Note, Thailand. January–March 2017. Bangkok: International Labour Organization.

Goscha, Christopher. *Vietnam: A New History*. New York: Basic Books, 2016.

Gramsci, Antonio. *Selections from the Prison Notebooks*. New York: International Publishers, 1971.

Guevarra, Anna Romina. *Marketing Dreams, Manufacturing Heroes: The Transnational Labor Brokering of Filipino Workers*. New Brunswick, NJ: Rutgers University Press, 2009.

Gutiérrez, David G. "Migration, Emergent Ethnicity, and the 'Third Space': The Shifting Politics of Nationalism in Greater Mexico." *Journal of American History* 86, no. 2 (1999): 481–517. https://doi.org/10.2307/2567042.

"Hà Tĩnh: Xót xa cảnh mẹ chờ 3 tháng nhận xác con lao động tử vong ở nước ngoài" [Ha Tinh: Mourning mother waits three months for confirmation of the death of her child who went to work abroad]. *Tin tức* [Vietnam news], November 17, 2014.

Bibliography 259

https://tintuc.vn/ha-tinh-xot-xa-canh-me-cho-3-thang-nhan-xac-con-lao-dong-tu-vong-o-nuoc-ngoai-9398/.

Hagan, Jacqueline Maria. "Social Networks, Gender, and Immigrant Incorporation: Resources and Constraints." *American Sociological Review* 63, no. 1 (1998): 55–67. https://doi.org/10.2307/2657477.

Hahamovitch, Cindy. "Creating Perfect Immigrants: Guestworkers of the World in Historical Perspective." *Labor History* 44, no. 1 (2003): 69–94. https://doi.org/10.1080/0023656032000057010.

Hammarström, Harald, Robert Forkel, and Martin Haspelmath, eds. "Sabine." In *Glottolog 3.0*. Jena, Germany: Max Planck Institute for the Science of Human History, 2017. https://glottolog.org/resource/languoid/id/sabi1245.

Hardy, Andrew. "From a Floating World: Emigration to Europe from Post-War Vietnam." *Asian and Pacific Migration Journal* 11, no. 4 (2002): 463–84. https://doi.org/10.1177/011719680201100406.

Harianto, Farid. "Business Linkages and Chinese Entrepreneurs in Southeast Asia." In *Culture and Economy: The Shaping of Capitalism in Eastern Asia*, edited by Timothy Brook and Luong Van Hy, 137–54. Ann Arbor: University of Michigan Press, 1997.

Hector, Charles, Mohd Roszeli Majid, and Pranom Somwong. "Employers Should Pay the Levy, Not Migrant Workers." Letter to the editor, *Malaysiakini*, February 11, 2016. https://www.malaysiakini.com/letters/330115.

Heywood, Andrew. *Political Ideas and Concepts: An Introduction*. London: Macmillan, 1994.

Hiệp hội xuất khẩu lao động Việt Nam [Vietnam Association of Manpower Supply]. "Giới thiệu về hiệp hội xuất khẩu lao động Việt Nam" [About the Vietnam Association of Manpower Supply], May 4, 2017. http://www.vamas.com.vn/gioi-thieu-ve-hiep-hoi-xuat-khau-lao-dong-viet-nam_t221c666n44438.

Hoàng, Lan Anh, and Brenda S. A. Yeoh. "Transnational Labour Migration, Debts, and Family Economics in Vietnam." In *Transnational Labour Migration, Remittances and the Changing Family in Asia*, edited by Lan Anh Hoàng and Brenda S. A. Yeoh, 283–310. London: Palgrave Macmillan UK, 2015.

Hodges, Laura. "Reincarnating Knowledge: Training the Lay Buddhist Priesthood of Khmer Achars in Cambodia." Georgetown University, *World Faiths Development Dialogue*, October 9, 2012. https://berkleycenter.georgetown.edu/posts/reincarnating-knowledge-training-the-lay-buddhist-priesthood-of-khmer-achars-in-cambodia.

Holmes, Seth M. "'Oaxacans Like to Work Bent Over': The Naturalization of Social Suffering among Berry Farm Workers." *International Migration* 45, no. 3 (2007): 39–68. https://doi.org/10.1111/j.1468-2435.2007.00410.

Hồng Vân, and Hà Nam. "Labor Export: Opportunities in 2015." *Voice of Vietnam World Service Online*, February 27, 2015. http://vovworld.vn/en-US/Current-Affairs/Labor-export-opportunities-in-2015/314083.vov.

Hüwelmeier, Gertrud. "Bazaar Pagodas: Transnational Religion, Postsocialist Marketplaces and Vietnamese Migrant Women in Berlin." *Religion and Gender* 3, no. 1 (2013): 76–89. https://doi.org/10.1163/18785417-00301006.

Iglicka, Krystyna. "Migration Movements from and into Poland in the Light of East–West European Migration." *International Migration* 39, no. 2 (2008): 3–32. https://doi.org/10.1111/1468-2435.00133.

Institute of Social and Labor Science, Ministry of Labor, Invalids, and Social Affairs. "A Brief Report: Assessment of the Realities of the Overseas Labor Returnees in Vietnam." Hanoi: MoLISA, June 2012.

International Labour Organization. "Malaysian and Vietnamese Trade Unions to Collaborate on Protecting Migrant Workers' Rights." *ILO in Asia and the Pacific*, February 20, 2018. https://www.ilo.org/asia/media-centre/news/WCMS_618220/lang--en/index.htm.

———. "Tripartite Action to Protect Migrant Workers within and from the Greater Mekong Subregion from Labour Exploitation (GMS TRIANGLE Project)." *ILO in Asia and the Pacific*, May 2015. http://www.ilo.org/asia/projects/WCMS_304802.

———. "Vietnam, Malaysia's Trade Unions Ink Agreement to Strengthen Protection of Migrant Workers." *ILO News*, March 16, 2015. http://www.ilo.org/hanoi/Informationresources/Publicinformation/newsitems/WCMS_353252/lang--en/index.htm.

Kaur, Minderjeet. "Home Ministry: 1.78 Million Foreign Workers in Malaysia." *Free Malaysia Today*, July 27, 2017. https://www.freemalaysiatoday.com/category/nation/2017/07/27/home-ministry-1-78-million-foreign-workers-in-malaysia/.

Kerkvliet, Benedict J. Tria. "Agricultural Land in Vietnam: Markets Tempered by Family, Community and Socialist Practices." *Journal of Agrarian Change* 6, no. 3 (2006): 285–305.

Kiến Quốc. "Xuất khẩu lao động 2021: Đâu là điểm đến chất lượng, an toàn?" [Labor export 2021: Where is a safe, quality destination?]. *Người lao động* [Laborer], February 18, 2021. https://nld.com.vn/cong-doan/xuat-khau-lao-dong-2021-dau-la-diem-den-chat-luong-an-toan-20210218105944858.htm.

Kiernan, Ben. *Việt Nam: A History from the Earliest Times to the Present*. New York: Oxford University Press, 2017.

Lã, Hải Anh, and Suiwah Leung. "Remittances from Migrants: Experience of Vietnamese Households." *Journal of Vietnamese Studies* 7, no. 4 (2013): 10–31. https://doi.org/10.1525/vs.2012.7.4.10.

Lâm Lê. "Migrant Workers Need Better Protection at Home and Abroad." *VN Express*, December 29, 2020. https://e.vnexpress.net/news/news/migrant-workers-need-better-protection-at-home-and-abroad-4211496.html.

Lan, Pei Chia. "Among Women Migrant Domestic Workers and Their Taiwanese Employers Across Generations." In *Global Women: Nannies, Maids, and Sex Workers in the New Economy*, edited by Barbara Ehrenreich and Arlie Russell Hochschild, 169–89. London: Granta, 2002.

Lê Thị Liên. "Sự Khác Biệt Về Tên Gọi Của Người HRê Trong Những Khu Vực Cư Trú Khác Nhau ở Miền Núi phía Tây tỉnh Quảng Ngãi." Bảo tàng lịch sử Việt Nam, unpublished manuscript as of July 2016.

Lê Thu Huong. "A New Portrait of Indentured Labor: Vietnamese Labor Migration to Malaysia." *Asian Journal of Social Science* 38 (2010). https://doi.org/10.1163/156853110X530787.

Lee, Charles T. "Bare Life, Interstices, and the Third Space of Citizenship." *Women's Studies Quarterly* 38, nos. 1/2 (2010): 57–81. http://www.jstor.org/stable/25679826.

Letts, Kristin. *Complaint Mechanisms for Migrant Workers: An Overview of Law and Practice*. Hanoi: ILO Regional Office for Asia and the Pacific, 2015. https://www.ilo.org/wcmsp5/groups/public/---asia/---ro-bangkok/---ilo-hanoi/documents/publication/wcms_482928.pdf.

Lian, Kwen Fee, Rahman, Md Mizanur, and Yabit bin Alas, eds. *International Migration in Southeast Asia: Continuities and Discontinuities*. Singapore: Springer, 2016.

Lim, Li Lin, and Nana Oishi. "International Labor Migration of Asian Women: Distinctive Characteristics and Policy Concerns." *Asian and Pacific Migration Journal* 5, no. 1 (1996): 85–116. https://doi.org/10.1177/011719689600500105.

Lindquist, Johan. "Labor Recruitment, Circuits of Capital and Gendered Mobility: Reconceptualizing the Indonesian Migration Industry." *Pacific Affairs* 83, no. 1 (2010): 115–32. https://www.jstor.org/stable/25698399.

Liu, Mao-Mei. "Migrant Networks and International Migration: Testing Weak Ties." *Demography* 50, no. 4 (2013): 1243–77. https://www.jstor.org/stable/42920553.

Lohman, Larry. "Who Defends Biological Diversity? Conservation Strategies and the Case of Thailand." In *Biodiversity: Social and Ecological Perspectives*, edited by Vandana Shiva, Patrick Anderson, Heffa Schücking, Andrew Gray, Larry Lohman, and David Cooper, 77–104. Penang: World Rainforest Movement, 1991.

Lưu Hùng. "Góp phần nghiên cứu tính song hệ ở dân tộc Hrê" [A contribution to the study of the double filiation of the Hrê people]. *Dân tộc học* [Journal of Ethnography] 3 (1983): 38–42.

———. "Mấy ghi nhận qua tìm hiểu làng của dân tộc Hrê" [Some records from researching on the village of the Hrê ethnic group]. *Sưu tập dân tộc học* [Ethnographic Collection] (VNU University of Social Sciences and Humanity, Museum of Anthropology), unnumbered volume (1979): 164–66.

———. "Sự du nhập hình thái canh tác ruộng nước vào vùng dân tộc Hrê" [The introduction of wet rice cultivation into the Hrê ethnic area]. *Sưu tập dân tộc học* [Ethnographic Collection] (VNU University of Social Sciences and Humanity, Museum of Anthropology), unnumbered volume (1981): 33–35.

———. "Tìm hiểu quan hệ xã hội ở dân tộc Hrê" [Research on the social relations among the Hrê ethnic people]. *Dân tộc học* [Journal of Ethnography] no. 3 (1980): 32–40.

Mae Chee Huynh Kim Lan. "A Study of Theravada Buddhism in Vietnam." Master's thesis, University, Bangkok, Thailand, 2010. https://www.academia.edu/8383837/a_study_of_therav%c4%80da_buddhism_in_vietnam.

Mahdavi, Pardis. "Gender, Labour and the Law: The Nexus of Domestic Work, Human Trafficking and the Informal Economy in the United Arab Emirates." *Global Networks* 13, no. 4 (2013).

"Malaysian Trades Union Congress Ticks Off Employers, Saying Probation Period Would Shortchange Foreign Workers." *Malaysian Insider*, July 30, 2013. http://www.mtuc.org.my/mtuc-ticks-off-employers-saying-probation-period-would-shortchange-foreign-workers.

Manguin, Pierre-Yves. "The Introduction of Islam into Champa." In *The Propagation of Islam in the Indonesian-Malay Archipelago*, edited by Alijah Gordon, 287–328. Singapore: Malaysian Sociological Research Institute, 2001.

Massey, Doreen. "Politics and Space/Time." *New Left Review*, November 1, 1992, 65–84. https://newleftreview.org/I/196/doreen-massey-politics-and-space-time.

Massey, Douglas, and Felipe García España. "The Social Process of International Migration." *Science*, August 14, 1987, 733–38. https://doi.org/10.1126/science.237.4816.733.

McElwee, Pamela. "Becoming Socialist or Becoming Kinh? Government Policies for Ethnic Minorities in the Socialist Republic of Viet Nam." In *Civilizing the Margins: Southeast Asian Government Policies for the Development of Minorities*, edited by Christopher Duncan, 182–214. Ithaca, NY: Cornell University Press, 2004.

"Migrant Workers Issue: Samsung Terminates Contract with Labour Supply Company in Malaysia." *New Straits Times* (Kuala Lumpur, Malaysia), December 13, 2016. https://www.nst.com.my/news/2016/12/196510/migrant-workers-issue-samsung-terminates-contract-labour-supply-company-malaysia.

Mills, Mary Beth. "Gender and Inequality in the Global Labor Force." *Annual Review of Anthropology* 32 (2003): 41–62. https://doi.org/10.1146/annurev.anthro.32.061002.093107.

Mỹ Ái and Mai Hương. "Giảm nghèo vùng đồng bào Khmer" [Poverty reduction in the Khmer]. *Báo An Giang* [An Giang newspaper], January 12, 2016. http://www.baoangiang.com.vn/An-Giang-24-Gio/Thoi-su/Giam-ngheo-vung-ong-bao-Khmer-1.html.

Nakamura, Rie. "Cham in Vietnam: Dynamics of Ethnicity." PhD diss., University of Washington, 1999.

Nam Dương and Duy Long. "Bốn ngày tìm Thằng Malai" [Four days in search of Thằng Ma Lai]. *Người lao động* [Laborer], March 8, 2010. http://nld.com.vn/xuat-khau-lao-dong/bon-ngay-tim-thang-malai-2010030812035562.htm.

Nam Viet Joint Stock Company. "Notice of hiring domestic workers in Saudi Arabia." July 26, 2017. https://www.xuatkhaulaodongnamviet.com/thong-bao-tuyen-lao-dong-giup-viec-gia-dinh-tai-a-rap-xe-ut.

National Institute of Statistics. *General Population Census of Cambodia 2008*. Phnom Penh, Cambodia: Ministry of Planning, 2008. http://www.stat.go.jp/english/info/meetings/cambodia/pdf/pre_rep1.pdf.

Người Lao Động [Laborer, pseud.]. "Đâu Là Sự Thật" [Where is the truth?]. *Tạp chí Xuân 2008: Tiếng nói lao động Việt Nam tại Malaysia* [Spring magazine 2008: Voice of Vietnamese workers in Malaysia] 4.

Nguyễn Duy. "Bức tranh màu xám của XKLĐ" [The grey picture of export labor]. *Người lao động* [Laborer], September 3, 2009. https://nld.com.vn/viec-lam/buc-tranh-mau-xam-cua-xkld-20090902100847294.htm.

Bibliography 263

———. "Chưa đạt mục tiêu" [Goal not yet reached]. *Người lao động* [Laborer], blog post, February 18, 2011. http://nld.com.vn/nhip-song-cong-nghiep/chua-dat-muc -tieu-2011021810120386.htm.

———. "Đi XKLĐ đong được vay đến 75 triệu đồng" [Export labor can obtain up to a 75VND million loan]. *Người lao động* [Laborer], September 12, 2009. http://nld .com.vn/viec-lam/di-xkld-duoc-vay-den-75-trieu-dong-2009091201025386.htm.

———. "Tạo mọi thuận lợi cho người lao động" [Creating favorable conditions for the workers]. *Người lao động* [Laborer], February 9, 2010. http://nld.com.vn/xuat -khau-lao-dong/tao-moi-thuan-loi-cho-nld-20100208110745319.htm.

———. "Thất bại với đề án ngàn tỉ" [Failure of project worth thousands of billions of Vietnamese đồng]. *Người lao động* [Laborer], September 2, 2014. http://nld.com .vn/cong-doan/that-bai-voi-de-an-ngan-ti-20140902213721036.htm.

———. "Xuất khẩu lao động: Vi phạm tràn lan" [Export labor: Widespread violations]. *Người lao động* [Laborer], September 15, 2009. http://www.nld.com .vn/20090915124728831P0C1051/xuat-khau-lao-dong-vi-pham-tran-lan.htm.

———. "Yêu cầu ngưng hợp tác với 3 công ty môi giới Đài loan" [Stop working with three Taiwanese companies]. *Người lao động* [Laborer], March 1, 2004. http://nld .com.vn/46683P0C1051/yeu-cau-ngung-hop-tac-voi-3-cong-ty-moi-gioi-dai-loan .htm.

Nguyễn Lương Trào, and Nguyễn Thanh Hoa. *Code of Conduct Applied to Vietnamese Enterprises Sending Workers for Overseas Employment.* Hanoi: Vietnam Association of Manpower Supply, 2015. http://www.ilo.org/dyn/migpractice/docs/188/Text%20 of%20the%20code.pdf.

Nguyễn Quyết. "Đi XKLĐ rồi . . . biến mất!" [Joined the labor export program, then disappeared!]. *Người lao động* [Laborer], March 1, 2010. http://nld.com.vn/xuat -khau-lao-dong/di-xkld-roi-bien-mat--20100301121738642.htm.

Nguyễn Thái Sơn. "Đột tử: Nỗi kinh hoàng của NLĐ" [Sudden death: The horror of workers]. *Người lao động* [Laborer], February 25, 2008. http://nld.com.vn /viec-lam/dot-tu-noi-kinh-hoang-cua-nld-216132.htm.

Nguyễn Thi Minh Hoa, Tom Kompas, Trevor Breusch, and Michael B. Ward. "Language, Mixed Communes, and Infrastructure: Sources of Inequality and Ethnic Minorities in Vietnam." *World Development* 96, no. 2 (2017): 145–62. https://doi .org/10.1016/j.worlddev.2017.03.004.

Nguyễn, Văn Chính. "From Swidden Cultivation to Fixed Farming and Settlement: Effects of Sedentarization Policies among the Kmhmu in Vietnam." *Journal of Vietnamese Studies* 3, no. 3 (2008): 44–80. https://doi.org/10.1525/vs.2008.3.3.44.

Nguyễn, Việt, Tim McGrath, and Pamela White. "Agricultural Land Distribution in Vietnam: Emerging Issues and Policy Implications." *Munich Personal RePEc Archive* Paper No. 25587 (October 2010): 1–26. https://mpra.ub.uni-muenchen .de/25587.

Nguyễn-võ, Thu-Huong. *Khmer-Viet Relations and the Third Indochina Conflict.* Jefferson, NC: McFarland, 1992.

Nhã Trân. "Vì sao nhiều công nhân Việt Nam ở Malaysia bị tử vong?" [Why did so many Vietnamese workers die in Malaysia?]. *Radio Free Asia*, May 3, 2008. http://

www.rfa.org/vietnamese/in_depth/Vietnamese_Workers_in_Malaysia_and_the_
High-Rate_Deaths_NTran-20080305.html.

Noseworthy, William B. "Articulations of Southeast Asian Religious Modernisms: Islam in Early 20th Century Cambodia and Cochinchina." *Suvannabhumi* 9, no. 1 (2017): 109–32. http://suvannabhumi.iseas.kr/index.php?mid=svn04&ck attempt=1.

Oishi, Nana. *Women in Motion.* Stanford, CA: Stanford University Press, 2005.

Ong, Aihwa. *Spirits of Resistance and Capitalist Discipline: Factory Women in Malaysia.* Albany: State University of New York Press, 1987.

Parrenas, Rhacel Salazar. *Servants of Globalization: Women Migration and Domestic Work.* Stanford, CA: Stanford University Press, 2001.

Paul, Anju Mary. "Stepwise International Migration: A Multistage Migration Pattern for the Aspiring Migrant." *American Journal of Sociology* 116, no. 6 (2011): 1842–86. https://doi.org/10.1086/659641.

Pfeffer, Max J., and Pilar A. Parra. "Strong Ties, Weak Ties, and Human Capital: Latino Immigrant Employment Outside the Enclave." *Rural Sociology* 74, no. 2 (2009): 241–69. https://doi.org/10.1111/j.1549-0831.2009.tb00391.x.

Phạm Quỳnh Phương and Chris Eipper. "Mothering and Fathering the Vietnamese: Religion, Gender, and National Identity." *Journal of Vietnamese Studies* 4, no. 1 (2009): 49–83. https://doi.org/10.1525/vs.2009.4.1.49.

Phan Hữu Đạt. "Lại bàn về chế độ song hệ ở các dân tộc nước ta" [The division in our nation]. Blog, March 6, 2013. http://phanhuudat.blogspot.com/2013/03/lai -ban-ve-che-o-song-he-o-cac-dan-toc.html.

Phan Văn Dốp and Nguyễn Thị Nhung. "Quan hệ đồng tộc và văn hóa—tôn giáo: Mạng lưới cho hoạt động mưu sinh xuyên quốc gia của người Chăm ở Tỉnh An Giang" [Ethnic and cultural-religious relations: A network for Cham transnational livelihood activities in An Giang province]. *Tạp chí dân tộc học* [Journal of ethnology], February 1, 2018, 50–59.

Piper, Nicola. "Rights of Foreign Workers and the Politics of Migration in South-East and East Asia." *International Migration* 42, no. 5 (2004): 71–97.

Pohjola, Anneli. "Social Networks—Help or Hindrance to the Migrant?" *International Migration* 29, no. 3 (1991): 435–44.

Portes, Alejandro. "Migration and Development: Reconciling Opposite Views." *Ethnic and Racial Studies* 32, no. 1 (2009): 5–22.

———. "Social Capital: Its Origins and Applications in Modern Sociology." *Annual Review of Sociology* 24 (1998): 1–24.

Quesada, James, Laurie K. Hart, and Philippe Bourgois. "Structural Vulnerability: Latino Migrant Laborers in the United States." *Medical Anthropology* 30, no. 4 (2011): 339–62. https://doi.org/10.1080/01459740.2011.576725.

Rahman, Md Mizanur, and Lian Kwen Fee. "Towards a Sociology of Migrant Remittances in Asia: Conceptual and Methodological Challenges." *Journal of Ethnic and Migration Studies* 38, no. 4 (2012): 689–706. https://doi.org/10.1080/1369183X .2012.659129.

Bibliography 265

Ramayah, Jeffrey. "PM: Strive to Strengthen Ties." *New Straits Times* (Kuala Lumpur, Malaysia), March 26, 1994. https://news.google.com/newspapers?id=bNNQAA AAIBAJ&sjid=mxMEAAAAIBAJ&pg=1042,2262444&dq=malaysia+vietnam +relations&hl=en.

Ratha, Dilip, Supriyo De, Sonia Plaza, Kirsten Schuettler, William Shaw, Hanspeter Wyss, and Soonhwa Yi. "Migration and Remittances: Recent Developments and Outlook: Migration and Development." *Brief* 26 (2016). https://openknowledge .worldbank.org/handle/10986/24012.

Ratha, Dilip, Christian Eigen-Zucchi, Sonia Plaza, Hanspeter Wyss, and Soonhwa Yi. "Migration and Remittances: Recent Developments and Outlook: Migration and Development." *Migration and Development Brief* 21 (2013). https://www.knomad .org/publication/migration-and-development-brief-21.

Reid, Anthony, *Charting the Shape of Early Modern Southeast Asia*. Chiang Mai, Thailand: Silkworm Books, 1999.

"Robber Kills Guard, Sets Building on Fire." *New Straits Times* (Kuala Lumpur, Malaysia), February 4, 2008.

Rodriguez, Robyn Magalit. *Migrants for Export: How the Philippine State Brokers Labor to the World*. Minneapolis: University of Minnesota Press, 2010.

Rutherford, Jonathan. "The Third Space: Interview with Homi Bhabha." In *Identity: Community, Culture, Difference*, edited by J. Rutherford, 207–21. London: Lawrence and Wishart, 1990.

Schwenkel, Christina. "Rethinking Asian Mobilities. Socialist Migration and Post-Socialist Repatriation of Vietnamese Contract Workers in East Germany." *Critical Asian Studies* 46, no. 2 (2014): 235–58. https://escholarship.org/uc/item /7mjo33q8.

———. "Socialist Mobilities: Crossing New Terrains in Vietnamese Migration Histories." *Central and Eastern European Migration Review* 4 (2015): 13–25. http://www .ceemr.uw.edu.pl/vol-4-no-1-june-2015/articles/socialist-mobilities-crossing-new -terrains-vietnamese-migration.

Scott, James C. *Domination and the Arts of Resistance: Hidden Transcripts*. New Haven, CT: Yale University Press, 1990.

———. *Weapons of the Weak*. New Haven, CT: Yale University Press, 1985.

Sittamparam, R. "Ministry to Probe Nike Claims of Worker Abuse." *New Straits Times* (Kuala Lumpur, Malaysia), August 5, 2008.

Soja, Edward. *Thirdspace: Journeys to Los Angeles and other Real-and-Imagined Places*. Cambridge, Mass.: Blackwell, 1996.

"Southeast Asia: ASEAN 2015." *Migration News*, 20, no. 4 (2013). http://migration .ucdavis.edu/mn/more.php?id=3868_0_3_0.

Southern Poverty Law Center. "Close to Slavery: Guestworker Programs in the United States." 2013. https://www.splcenter.org/20130218/close-slavery-guestworker -programs-united-states.

Storm, Anna. "Sapa, Prague's 'Little Vietnam.'" PragueTV, April 17, 2015. https:// prague.tv/en/s72/Directory/c209-Shopping/n2584-Sapa-Prague-s-Little-Vietnam.

Tan, Marsha. "Robbery, Rape Gang Busted." *Star* (Petaling Jaya, Malaysia), November 15, 2005. https://www.thestar.com.my/news/nation/2005/11/15/robbery-rape-gang -busted.

Taylor, Keith. *History of the Vietnamese.* Cambridge, UK: Cambridge University Press, 2013.

Taylor, Philip. *Cham Muslims of the Mekong Delta: Place and Mobility in the Cosmopolitan Periphery.* Singapore: NUS Press, 2007.

———. "Economy in Motion: Cham Muslim Traders in the Mekong Delta." *Asia Pacific Journal of Anthropology* 7, no. 3 (2006): 237–50.

———. Introduction to *Minorities at Large: New Approaches to Minority Ethnicity in Vietnam,* edited by Philip Taylor, 3–43. Singapore: ISEAS, 2006.

———. *The Khmer Lands of Vietnam: Environment, Cosmology and Sovereignty.* Singapore: Singapore University Press, 2014.

———. "Redressing Disadvantage or Re-arranging Inequality? Development Interventions and Local Responses in the Mekong Delta." In *Social Inequality in Vietnam and the Challenges to Reform,* edited by Philip Taylor, 236–69. Singapore: ISEAS, 2004.

———. *Social Inequality in Vietnam and the Challenges to Reform.* Singapore: Institute of Southeast Asian Studies, 2004.

Temko, Ned. "Soviets Defend 'New Form of Cooperation': Vietnamese Workers in USSR." *Christian Science Monitor,* May 4, 1982. https://www.csmonitor.com /1982/0504/050430.html.

Thelen, David. "Rethinking History and the Nation-State: Mexico and the United States as a Case Study: A Special Issue." *Journal of American History* 86, no. 2 (1999): 439–52. https://doi.org/10.2307/2567038.

Thông Tấn Xã Việt Nam [Vietnam News Agency]. "Ra mắt ban thường vụ lâm thời hội đồng hương Nghệ Tỉnh tại Séc" [The launching of the provisional standing committee of the Nghe Tinh Association of Councils in the Czech Republic]. *Que Viet Europe,* November 18, 2014. http://queviet.eu/cong-dong/sec/114701-ra-mat-ban -thuong-vu-lam-thoi-hoi-dong-huong-nghe-tinh-tai-sec.

Thông báo tuyển lao động giúp việc gia đình tại A rập Xê-út. [Notice of hiring domestic workers in Saudi Arabia]. https://www.xuatkhaulaodongnamviet.com /thong-bao-tuyen-lao-dong-giup-viec-gia-dinh-tai-a-rap-xe-ut.

"Three Rape Vietnamese Worker after Robberies." *New Straits Times* (Kuala Lumpur, Malaysia), August 18, 2013. https://www.asiaone.com/singapore/three-rape -vietnamese-worker-after-robberies.

Thu Hằng. "'Chợ' Sapa, hương Việt giữa lòng Praha, CH Séc" ["Sapa" market: The Vietnamese essence in the heart of Prague]. *Radio France Internationale,* September 23, 2016. http://vi.rfi.fr/viet-nam/20160909-%E2%80%9Ccho%E2%80%9D-sapa -huong-viet-giua-long-praha-czech.

Thulstrup, Andreas Waaben. "Livelihood Resilience and Adaptive Capacity: Tracing Changes in Household Access to Capital in Central Vietnam." *World Development* 74, (2015): 352–62.

Tintucdulich.vn. "Văn hóa truyền thống của dân tộc H'rê (Quảng Ngãi)" [Traditional culture of the Hrê people (Quảng Ngãi)]. *Quê hương* [Hometown magazine], July 7, 2014. http://quehuongonline.vn/tu-dien-van-hoa/van-hoa-truyen-thong-cua-dan-toc-hre-quang-ngai-40699.htm.

Tống Thanh Tùng. "Đi để sắm trâu, xây nhà." [Working overseas to buy buffaloes and build houses]. *Người lao động* [Laborer], August 13, 2009. http://nld.com.vn/viec-lam/di-de-sam-trau--xay-nha-2009081209439949.htm.

Trần, Angie Ngọc. "Contradictions of Multi-Stakeholder Labor Relations in Vietnam." In *Routledge Handbook of Contemporary Vietnam*, edited by Jonathan London. Oxford, UK: Routledge, 2021.

——. *Ties That Bind: Cultural Identity, Class, and Law in Flexible Labor Resistance in Vietnam*. Ithaca, NY: Southeast Asia Program and Cornell University Press, 2013.

——. "The Third Sleeve: Emerging Labor Newspapers and the Response of Labor Unions and the State to Workers' Resistance in Vietnam." *Labor Studies Journal* 32, no. 3 (2007): 257–79. https://doi.org/10.1177/0160449X07300716.

——. "Weaving Life across Borders: The Cham Muslim Migrants Traversing Vietnam and Malaysia." In *International Migration in Southeast Asia: Continuities and Discontinuities*, edited by Lian Kwen Fee, Md Mizanur Rahman, and Yabit bin Alas, 13–37. Singapore: Springer, 2015.

Trần, Angie Ngọc, Jennifer Bair, and Marion Werner. "Forcing Change from the Outside? The Role of Trade-Labour Linkages in Transforming Vietnam's Labor Regime." *Competition and Change* 21, no. 5 (2017): 397–416. https://doi.org/10.1177/1024529417729326.

Trần, Angie Ngọc, and Vicki Crinis. "Migrant Labor and State Power: Vietnamese Workers in Malaysia and Vietnam." *Journal of Vietnamese Studies* 13, no.2 (2018): 27–73. https://doi.org/10.1525/vs.2018.13.2.27.

Trân Nhã. "Vì sao nhiều công nhân Việt Nam ở Malaysia bị tử vong?" Radio Free Asia (May 2008). http://www.rfa.org/vietnamese/in_depth/Vietnamese_Workers_in_Malaysia_and_the_High-Rate_Deaths_NTran-20080305.html.

Trần Quang Vinh, "Cuộc sàng lọc nghiệt ngã," Tuổi Trẻ Online, May 12, 2007, https://tuoitre.vn/cuoc-sang-loc-nghiet-nga-200712.htm

Tran Thi Thanh Tu, Nguyen Phu Ha, and Tran Thi Hoang Yen. "Socio-Economic Impact of Rural Credit in Northern Vietnam: Does It Differ between Clients Belonging to the Ethnic Majority and the Minorities?" *Asian Social Science* 11, no. 10 (2015): 159–67. http://www.ccsenet.org/journal/index.php/ass/article/view/47764.

Trần Tuấn. "Vừa đi xuất khẩu lao động Malaysia 1 tháng, lao động Việt Nam đột tử" [Only working in Malaysia for one month, Vietnamese workers suddenly died]. *Lao động* [Labor], June 26, 2014. http://tamlongvang.laodong.com.vn/xa-hoi/vua-di-xuat-khau-lao-dong-malaysia-1-thang-lao-dong-viet-nam-dot-tu-219519.bld.

Trankell, Ing-Britt. "Songs of Our Spirits: Possession and Historical Imagination among the Cham in Cambodia." *Asian Ethnicity* 4, no. 1 (February 2003): 31–46. https://doi.org/10.1080/14631360301645.

268　　　　　Bibliography

Trúc Quỳnh. "Vài nét về dân tộc chăm ở An Giang" [Some characteristics of the Chăm people in An Giang]. *Tin An Giang* [An Giang news], n.d. http://www .angiang.gov.vn/wps/wcm/connect/web+content/agportal/sa-tin-tuc/a9f022804 d63df71b9eeffca90694990?presentationtemplate=PT-Print.

Trường Thọ. "Phương Thành: Traconsin 10 năm một chặng đường" [Phuong Thanh: The long, ten-year journey of Traconsin]. *Tạp chí giao thông vận tải* [Transportation magazine], June 28, 2014. http://www.tapchigiaothong.vn/phuong-thanh--traconsin-10-nam-mot-chang-duong-d3518.html.

Ueno, Kayoko. "Strategies of Resistance among Filipina and Indonesian Domestic Workers in Singapore." *Asian and Pacific Migration Journal* 18, no. 4, (2009): 497–515. https://doi.org/10.1177/011719680901800403.

Unrepresented Nations and Peoples Organization (UNPO). *Member Profile: Khmer-Krom; Khmers-Krom Federation (KKF)*. Report. Brussels, Belgium: UNPO Advocacy Office, 2018. http://unpo.org/downloads/2372.pdf.

U.S. State Department, Bureau of Democracy, Human Rights, and Labor. "Vietnam 2013 International Religious Freedom Report." Washington, DC: U.S. State Department. https://2009-2017.state.gov/documents/organization/222393.pdf.

Vietnamese General Confederation of Labor. "Report on the Protection of Labor Migration." No date.

Viện dân tộc học [Institute of Ethnology]. "Lễ Tàreo Bìnme Của Người Hrê" [The rain-praying ritual of the Hrê]." *Tạp Chí Cẩm Thành* [Cẩm Thành magazine], no. 46 (January 2006): 1–5.

Viện khoa học lao động và xã hội [Institute of Social and Labor Science]. "Báo cáo tóm tắt: Đánh giá thực trạng lao động đi làm việc ở nước ngoài đã trở về Việt Nam" [Summary report: Assessment of the working status of laborers in Vietnam who have worked abroad]. Hà Nội: Viện khoa học lao động và xã hội, 2012.

"Viet Nam, Malaysia's Trade Unions Ink Agreement to Strengthen Protection of Migrant Workers." *ILO News*, March 16, 2015. http://www.ilo.org/hanoi /Informationresources/Publicinformation/newsitems/WCMS_353252/lang--en /index.htm.

Vietnam News Agency. "Czech Republic Considers Vietnamese Integral Part in the Society." *The Voice of Vietnam: VOV World*, June 13, 2016. https://vovworld.vn /en-US/news/czech-republic-considers-vietnamese-integral-part-in-the-society -444807.vov.

———. "Malaysia Issues New Rules for Vietnamese Workers." *VietnamPlus*, November 2, 2015. http://en.vietnamplus.vn/malaysia-issues-new-rules-for-vietnamese -workers/84073.vnp.

Vietnam News Service. "Khmer Monks Open Summer Class." *Việt Nam News*, June 29, 2019. https://vietnamnews.vn/life-style/521962/khmer-monks-open-summer -class.html.

———. "Labour Export Companies Have Licences Revoked." *Việt Nam News*, November 7, 2017. https://vietnamnews.vn/society/416994/labour-export-companies -have-licences-revoked.html.

Bibliography

———. "Promising Year for Labour Export." *Việt Nam News*, January 3, 2019. https://vietnamnews.vn/society/483074/promising-year-for-labour-export.html.

Vu The Lan. "Ma-lai-xi-a, thị trường lao động nhiều tiềm năng." VINAEXIMCO website, http://xkld-hanoi.com/malaixia-thi-truong-lao-dong-nhieu-tiem-nang -n1070.html.

Wang, Hong-zen, and Danièle Bélanger. "Exploitative Recruitment Processes and Working Conditions of Vietnamese Migrant Workers in Taiwan." In *Labour in Vietnam*, edited by Anita Chan, 309–34. Singapore: Institute of Southeast Asian Studies, 2011.

Weber, Nicolas. "The Cham Diaspora in Southeast Asia: Patterns of Historical, Political, Social and Economic Development." In *Vietnam's Ethnic and Religious Minorities: A Historical Perspective*, edited by Thomas Engelbert, 157–201. Frankfurt am Main: Peter Lang, 2016.

———. "Exploring Cam Narrative Sources for History of the Cam Diaspora of Cambodia." Nalanda-Sriwijaya Centre Working Paper, no. 17, February 2015. https://sealinguist.files.wordpress.com/2015/02/cam017.pdf.

Williams, Allan M., and Vladimir Baláž. "Winning, Then Losing, the Battle with Globalization: Vietnamese Petty Traders in Slovakia." *International Journal of Urban and Regional Research* 29, no. 3 (2005): 533–49. https://doi.org/10.1111/j.1468 -2427.2005.00604.x.

Wilson, Tamar Diana. "Weak Ties, Strong Ties: Network Principles in Mexican Migration." *Human Organization* 57, no. 4 (1998): 394–403.

World Bank Group. "COVID-19 Crisis Through a Migration Lens." Migration and Development Brief 32, April 2020. https://documents1.worldbank.org/curated /en/989721587512418006/pdf/COVID-19-Crisis-Through-a-Migration-Lens.pdf.

Xiang, Biao, and Johan Lindquist. "Migration Infrastructure." *International Migration Review* 48, no. S1 (2014): S122–S148. https://doi.org/10.1111/imre.12141.

"Xuất khẩu lao động ở Malaysia: Bị đột tử có được bồi thường?" [Labor export in Malaysia: Sudden death compensation?]. *Tin mới chủ nhật* [New Sunday news], May 17, 2009. http://www.tinmoi.vn/Xuat-khau-lao-dong-o-Malaysia-Bi-dot-tu -co-duoc-boi-thuong-0123080.html.

Yen Duong, "Overworked, abused, hungry: Vietnamese domestic workers in Saudi." https://www.aljazeera.com/features/2018/9/19/overworked-abused-hungry -vietnamese-domestic-workers-in-saudi, 19 Sep 2018

Yeoh, Brenda S. A., Heng Leng Chee, Thi Kieu Dung Vu, and Yi'en Cheng. "Between Two Families: The Social Meaning of Remittances for Vietnamese Marriage Migrants in Singapore." *Global Networks* 13, no. 4 (2013): 441–58. https://doi .org/10.1111/glob.12032.

Yeung, Henry Wai-chung. "The Dynamics of the Globalization of Chinese Business Firms." In *Globalization of Chinese Business Firms*, edited by Henry Wai-chung Yeung and Kris Olds, 75–104. New York: St. Martin's Press, 2000.

Yeung, Henry Wai-chung, and Kris Olds, eds. *Globalization of Chinese Business Firms*. New York: St. Martin's Press, 2000.

Yi, Beh Lih. "World's Top Glovemaker Vows Clean-up as Migrant Workers Toil in Malaysia Factories." *Reuters*, December 6, 2018. https://in.reuters.com/article/malaysia-migrants-rights-glove/worlds-top-glovemaker-vows-clean-up-as-migrant-workers-toil-in-malaysia-factories-idINL8N1YA27Y.

Yoshimoto, Yasuko. "A Study of the *Hồi giáo* Religion in Vietnam: With a Reference to Islamic Religious Practices of Cham Bani." *Southeast Asian Studies* (Center for Southeast Asian Studies, Kyoto University) 1, no. 3 (2012): 487–505. https://www.jstage.jst.go.jp/article/seas/1/3/1_KJ00008190239/_pdf.

Yosso, Tara J. "Whose Culture Has Capital?" *Race, Ethnicity and Education* 8, no. 1 (2005): 69–91. https://doi.org/10.1080/1361332052000341006.

Index

actions, collective: class moments, 10, 110, 113, 117, 122

Agreement on Border Regulations, 216

alleviate poverty, 15, 205

aspirations, worker: "buying buffaloes and building homes," 83–84, 153, 158; cultural and religious resources, 9, 173, 200; education for themselves, 51, 197; entrepreneurship, 49, 194; fear of indebtedness, 177; help relatives, 108, 128, 179, 181–83; higher education 179, 182–83; language competency, 174; own motorbike, 36, 48, 83–84, 153, 160, 175; to serve their communities, 122, 182; "Traveling one day, learning tons of wisdom," 173

authorities, competing: local religious leaders, 170–71, 199; village leaders, 6, 95, 166–67, 169, 171

bankruptcy, 104, 155; early return home (2008–9), 96, 120; global financial crisis, 84, 100, 104, 171; Malaysian economy, 62, 96; workers stranded, 135, 204

banks, 6, 87, 96–97, 109; Agriculture and Rural Development, 66; "bank for the poor," 155; cosigners, 154–56; debt write-offs, 161–63; loan forgiveness, 162, 167, 170; loan process, 75–77; paying principal, 158; private, 66; recouping interest, 94; recruitment companies, 67, 87–88, 91; Social Policy Bank, 66–67, 216, 218–19, 247n14. See also recruitment and outsourcing companies; specific ethnic group

Buddhism, 27, 40, 230, 261; Mahayana, 27; Theravada, 40, 230n68

buffaloes, 32, 34, 158–59, 172; "buying buffaloes and building homes," 83–84, 153; Hrê consumption pattern, 167; "iron," 110; owning motorbikes, 36, 153; significance of, 36–37. See also Hrê

Cambodia: Agreement on Border Regulations, 216; Chăm in 43–48, 147–48, 176, 178, 229n52, 231n90, 246n56; crossing borders, 15, 37, 47, 200, 230n62, 246n54; history of, 37–40, 44–46, 229n52, 229n93, 231n90; kinship ties, 121, 232n108, 242n46; population, 37, 229n104, 229n105, 231n101, 232n102; tensions with Vietnam, 91–92; wars, border, 92

capital, cultural, 51, 225

Chăm, the: circular migration patterns, 10, 144–46, 194–95, 246n57; đi đường dưới, đi chui, 145; education, access to, 28–29, 40–42, 50–51, 227n16, 227n17, 230n70; education, alternatives to, 147, 178–79; education, becoming teachers, 122, 185, 197; education, gendered differences in, 122, 185, 197; education, higher, 179; education of relative, remittances for, 108, 122; entrepreneur, 61, 127–28, 195–97; fasting during Ramadan, 166; gendered division of labor, 140, 143–44, 149; history, 44–46; Islam, 43–46, 106, 120, 165, 179, 201; mimicries, 163–66; mosques, 51, 53–54, 185, 201, 230; praying, 48, 164–66;

Chăm, the (continued): Ramadan, 48, 120, 165–66, 211, 242n40; religious leader, 170–71; religious studies, 51, 122, 178–79, 183–84, 201, 230n70; Sunni Muslims, 43–46, 164
circular migration, 9, 10–11, 144–45; Chăm, 15, 144–45, 194–95, 196; Hrê, 210, 251n2 (appendix 1); Khmer, 15, 139–41, 176
circulars, Vietnamese government; Circular 31/2013/TT-NHNN, 217, 220; Circular No. 21/2013/TT-BLDTBXH, 217, 219; Circular No. 22/2013/TT-BLDTBXH, 217, 219; Joint Circular No. 32/2013/TTLT-BLDTBXH-BNG, 219 No. 1034/NHCS-TD, 216, 218
classes, cultural orientation, 65, 78–80
class moments, 10, 110, 113, 117, 122
collective actions, 110–14, 117–21
complaints, worker, 58, 63, 68–69; contract system, 115; denial of basic benefits, 58; gender responses, 98; hostel conditions, 103, 111–13; indigenous leaders, 21–22, 25, 31, 170–71; media coverage, 22, 72; "No one came to help," 114, 118, 120; overtime, 58, 76, 79, 83, 99, 104, 113, 136; pain of separation, 102, 116, 120, 134–35; robbery, 103–4, 106, 111, 114, 120, 241–42, 266; shift rotation, 112; speedup, 103, 130–32; termination, 11; working conditions, 62, 84, 96, 100, 102, 105, 118, 181, 193–94, 218, 221, 233, 269
conditions, global, 98, 100
công, 92–93, 193, 240n36, 250n37
consent, manufacture or (manipulation) of, 5, 7, 55, 74, 199; employment centers, role of, 75; false consciousness, 132, 244n28; gender differences, 18–19; Gramsci, 5, 222n18; LBS, 5–8, 13–15, 50, 52, 55; recruitment and marketing, 7, 36, 63, 65–67, 80–86; ruling through consent (civil), 5; ruling through force (political), 5; subordination, 244
contracts, 3, 7, 10, 86–88, 134; "carte-blanche," 65, 77; one-employer, 98–99, 110, 115
coping mechanisms, 98–99, 101, 105, 107, 109, 115, 117, 119, 121–22, 240; becoming undocumented, 132–33; collective actions, 110–14; cultural resources, 5–6, 10, 14, 27, 37; cultural wealth, 14–15, 51, 129, 199, 225n65; false consciousness, 132, 244n28; feigning ignorance, 11; foot dragging, 11; garlic peeler, 132–34; Ghostman, 135–37; hiding products, 123, 132; mimicry, 12–13, 152–53; mimicry, ironic, 156–58, 161–62, 164, 167–68, 170–72; mimicry,

"performance," 159; mimicry, subversive, 153–56, 167–72; naps in restroom, 130–31; personal empowerment, 107–10; public protests, 15; religious and cultural networks, 50, 100, 105–7; sending remittances home, 100, 137; strikes, 111, 113, 117–19, 121, 141, 234n35, 242n33. See also metaphorical third space; physical third space; specific ethnic groups
Council for Mutual Economic Assistance, 26, 61, 226n4
COVID-19, 204, 206–7, 217, 251n16
Czech Republic/Czechoslovakia: "Little Hanoi," 125–26; mediating dependency, 129–30; Prague, 13–14, 123–24, 126, 129, 151–53, 243n10; Sapa Center, 124, 126, 130, 152

debts and remittances, 87, 90, 94; Agriculture and Rural Development Bank, 66; debt collection, 67, 154, 163, 169; debt forgiveness, 155, 162, 167, 171–72, 200; gambling, 96, 104, 137, 239n27, 243n9; interest paycheck deduction, 94, 158; land as collateral, 66, 91, 93, 154, 170, 240n35; loan application, 77; money, pooling, 78, 109, 164; robberies, 98, 103–4, 116, 121–22; Social Policy Bank, 66–67, 87–88, 155–56, 161–63, 218–19, 247n14. See also loans and collateral; specific ethnic group
decisions: Decision 15/QD-HDQT (2011), 219, 252; Decision No. 630/QD-LĐTBXH, 219; Prime Minister Decision 71/2009/QĐTT, 3–4, 62–63, 187, 219, 222n11, 234n37, 235n54, 237n79
decrees: MoLISA Decree 1083/QLLDNN-KHTC, 219; Prime Minister Decree 50/2010/QD-TTg, 219, 252; Prime Minister Decree 103/2014/NĐ-CP, 220, 248

education: access to, 28–29, 33, 54, 199; achievement, low educational, 29, 41, 51, 147; aspirations, 17, 108, 177, 179–83; children's, 147, 194; costs, 65; escape poverty, 51, 122, gender differences, 42–43, 56, 185; helping relatives, 108, 183; hierarchy, 17, 50–51; higher 179, 182; rates, dropout, 50, 147, 227n16, 227n17, 232n115; religious studies, 51–52, 122, 178–79, 183–84; to teach, 30, 40, 51, 121, 180, 181; at temples and mosques, 40–42. See also language issues; vocational training; specific ethnic groups

Index

employers, Malaysian, 233n12, 235n52, 242 n37, 249n33, 251n16; conditions, unsafe working, 118–19; contracts, 58, 98, 142, 218, 233n12, 242n37; housing, 100; language of, 52, 121, 157; levy, foreign worker, 60, 77; one-employer, 58, 98–99, 110, 115, 117, 118; passport, 57–58, 65, 98–99, 110, 142, 244n32; quotas, production, 114; recruitment companies as employer of record, 57–58, 133, 233n12; responsibilities, 32, 77, 79, 160, 163, 168, 202, 255; rotations, shift, 114

empowerment, 6, 15, 51; accommodations, gender-specific, 249n33; barriers, women's education, 42, 122, 179, 182; early return, 139, 186; equity, 149, 196; escape from Malaysia, 143; family ties, 8, 16; financial independence, 107, 122; gender, 18–20, 23, 32, 42–43, 101; groups, religious, 106–7, 164–65; internal, 6, 15, 98, 112; labor, gendered division of, 86, 140, 141, 143–45, 148; languages, 18, 39, 52, 182, 200, 206; metaphorical third space, 12–13, 150–72, 203; migrants, socialist, 124–30; multilingual, 84, 90, 130, 140–41; napping, on-the-job, 131; new skills, 15, 107, 173–74, 179, 200; orders, gender-specific, 237n2; personal, 107, 141, 145; physical third space, 11, 13–14, 123–49; products, hiding, 132; remittances, 108, 241n22; responses by gender, 98, 100; roles, gender, 148, 173, 200; sensitivity, gender, 207; stepwise international migration, 16–17, 175–76, 206; strikes and protests, 98, 111; structural, 6, 15, 113, 117; subjective, 134; underground, 104, 135–37, 141, 147; undocumented, 133–34; visas, tourist, 139–43, 145. See also *specific ethnic groups*; *specific languages*

ethnicities: circular migration and entrepreneurship, (Chăm), 194–96; cultural factors, 18, 110, 124; differences, crossethnic (group), 18, 23, 25, 124; differences, cultural, 3, 98; differences, gender, 15, 18, 25, 28, 101, 228n31; economic constraints, 173; economic factors, 9, 18, 50; hierarchies, aspirations for stepwise mobility, 16; hierarchies, cultural rankings 51; hierarchies, educational, 33; hierarchies, ethnic, 17–18, 26, 50, 199; hierarchies, ethnic, and gender differences, 15; mimicries of competing ethnic authorities (Hrê), 166–68; mimicries of

competing ethnic authorities (Khmer), 169–70; mimicries of a religious leader (Chăm), 170–71; minorities, 4, 14–15, 18, 82, 152, 173, 228n36; minorities, access to education, 50–52, 182; minorities, cultural resources, 171; minorities, domestic migration patterns, 185–96; minorities, Kinh/Hoa and, 27–29, 177; networks, social (Kinh/Hoa), 129–30; risks, third space, 145–47; third space, 6, 9–10, 66; third space, metaphorical, 10–13; third space, physical, 13–15; third spaces in Malaysia (Hrê), 137–39, 158–60; third spaces in Malaysia (Kinh/Hoa), 130–37, 153–58; third spaces in Thailand and Malaysia (Khmer), 139–41, 160–63; traveling the Chăm Way, 141–45, 163–66; uneven power relations, 18, 207. *See also* aspirations; empowerment; *specific ethnic groups*

Europe, Eastern: Council for Mutual Economic Assistance, 26, 61, 226n4; Czechoslovakia, 26, 61, 127–28, 226n4; Czech Republic, 25, 124, 126–30, 221n4, 243n25; export labor, 26, 124; Kinh Migrants, 150–52; Marywilska shopping center, 124–26; Poland, 26, 61, 124–26, 150–51, 226n4; Sapa Center, 124, 126, 130, 152, 243; Soviet Union, 26, 61, 216, 218, 221n4, 226n4

gender and inequality issues: abortion, 101; family separation, 57, 116, 134, 240n6; health, 18, 29, 32–33, 64–65, 131, 156; health care (services), 18, 28, 58, 90, health checks (exams), 4, 64–65, 77, 84, 96, 168, 219; health clinics, 82, 113; health expenses 90, 93, 134, 158; health, mental, 206; laws, 192; tests, mandatory periodic pregnancy, 65; workers, domestic: resistance, 11, 13, 157, 206; workers, domestic: 2019 Labor Code, 201–2, 206, 220, 222n17, 223n22, 224n47–48, 244n29, 251n15–16

geographical agency, 14–15, 225n65, 248n9; Chăm, 46–49, 145, 147, 178, 194, 195, 225n65, 242n41, 246n57; circular migration patterns, 9, 11, 144–45, 194–96; Khmer, 139, 229n62, 230nn70–71, 249n28, 250n39; local and extralocal trading practices, 225n65; rural-urban, 147; Taylor, Philip, 15, 147; Vietnam, 51, 226n10, 248n9, 249n18

274   Index

GMS TRIANGLE Project, 236n61; Thailand, 234n37, 246n54; Vietnam, 7, 69, 221n7 222n11, 222nn15–17, 244n32
guest workers, 1–6, 9–11, 221n3; actions, collective, 117; alleviation, poverty, 162, 219; costs, 50; costs, international migration; crisis, global, 133, 171, 239n23; death, sudden, 104; debt collection, 67; defined, 1; direct dialogue on risks and benefits, 83; era, socialist, 26–27, 61, 67, 124; internal empowerment, 200; labor brokerage state, 67; language, 157; in Malaysia, 60, 67; passports, 244n32; precarity, 98; pre-departure, 56, 65, 79, 219, 222n10; and private recruitment companies, 84; remittances, 88–89; third space, 135; violations, contract, 99

Hanic Company, 85–86
history: Berlin Wall, fall of, 27, 128, 221n42; Bracero Program (1942–1964), 1; Chinese colonization (Hoa), 27–28; Cochinchina, 45, 264; Democratic Republic of Vietnam, 1; French colony, 26; guest worker programs, 1–2; Hrê, 34; Kampong Chăm, 45, 184, 229, 232; Khmer, 37–39, 92–93; kingdom of Champa, 44; migrants, Kinh and Hoa (socialist era), 26–27; Nguyễn dynasty, 45; Socialist Republic of Vietnam, 1; Udong, 45; U.S. War, 26, 40; Vietnam and Cambodia, Chăm in, 44–46, 229n52. See also Philippines; specific ethnic groups
Hoa, the, 28, 30, 52, 171; Chinese colonization, 26–27; Chinese Malaysians, 20, 28, 84–85, 118, 120; coping mechanisms, 105–14; cultural resources, 27–28; debts and remittances, 87–89; precarity, 101–5; Trường Giang Company, 84–85. See also Kinh; specific subject listings
Ho Chí Minh City Muslim Representative Committee, 184
hostel living conditions: gambling, 96, 104, 137, 239n27; robberies, 98, 103–4, 116, 121–22; sexual violence, 98, 103, 122; water, lack of, 112–13
Hrê, the, 21, 210; acacia trees, 34–35, 82, 158–59, 214; access to credit, 29, 90; access to education, 33, 50–51, 227n17; animism, 32; aspirations, 122, 158–59, 178, 179–82; beef and Heineken beer, 160; "brothers of Ba Tơ district," 148; buffalo ceremony,

227–28; buffaloes, 34, 36–37, 83, 153, 158, 167; cash crops, 31, 34–35, 84, 187, 189, 249n23; coping mechanisms, 115; created an economic space, 187; default, loan, 172; double filiation, 32, 228n31; elders, village, 31, 166–70; food crops, 30–31, 34, 187, 189–90; gendered division of labor, 32, 140, 143–44, 149; giảm nghèo và quản lý dân cư, thôn bản, 186–87; lack of water irrigation, 189; land, 33–34; mimicry, 158–59, 162; Nghĩa Hành district, 31, 187; population, 30, 221n8, 227n20; precarity, 115–16; returnees, 168 185–90; rituals, spiritual, 31; Sơn Hà District, 78, 187; third space, 137; U.S. war, 166; Vùng Tái Định Cư, 187; water, 32; wet rice cultivation, 30–32, 187–88, 214. See also specific subject listings
hybrid cultural space and practices, 123–24, 150–51; food culture, 151; next generation, 151

Indonesian Riau Islands, 146
intercultural hybridity, 130
International Labour Organisation, 235. See also GMS TRIANGLE Project
International Organization for Migration, 252n3
intersectionality, 18, 23; cultural differences, 3; ethnic differences, 3, 18; gender relations, 3, 18–19, 32
Islam: Bani, Cham, 43, 45
Islam, Sunni: Chăm, adopted by, 43–46, 165, 179, 201, 231n90, 242nn40–41; Imam, 184–85, 211–12, 242; Malay influence, 45–46, 52, 120, 165, 178–79, 183–84; mosque, 46, 48–49, 51, 120, 170–71, 183–85, 211, 248; Sunni, 43–46, 164, 185

Japan, 4–5, 81, 87, 180, 222n11; fear of indebtedness, 177; loan origination, 87; media coverage, 70; pay, higher, 56, 67; preferred destination (stepwise international migration), 16–17, 56, 175, 176, 178, 235n55; production of paper from acacia trees, 34; unauthorized workers, 222n10

Khmer, the, 91, 164, 177, 200; access to education, 29, 40–41, 50–51, 54, 147, 227nn16–17; adopting "the master's tools," 161; agencies, local employment, 76, 88; An Giang province, 21, 41, 43–44, 46, 92–93; aspirations, 177–79, 182–83,

190–94; Bình Dương province, 195; border crossings, 39; Buddhism, Theravadist, 40; conditions, restrictive working, 131; coping mechanisms, 15, 101, 116–19; crisis, global economic, 93; debts, 91, 161; hierarchies, 50–52; history, 37–40, 91–92; issues, gender, 42–43, 200; Khmer Krom, 37–39, 92; Khmer Rouge, 92–93; land, agricultural, 92; land as collateral, 91, 93, 154, 170; land ceding, 91–93, 169, 249; landlessness, 25, 29, 91–93, 169, 232; languages, 39–42, 52; leaders, hamlet, 25, 39–40, 169–70; leaders, village, 169–70; Mekong River, 39; mimicry, 161–63; monks, Theravadist Buddhist, 25, 40; population, 29, 37; poverty, abject, 115, 171; precarity, 116–19; relocation, 31, 93, 210; resources, linguistic, 40; resources, religious, 40, 42, 51; rights, land-use, 92; roots, Cambodian, 54, 176; temples (wats) and monks, 25, 40, 230n71; third space, hamlets as, 40; third space, languages, 54; tourist visa usage, 139–41, 176; Tri Tôn and Tịnh Biên districts, 41, 92, 190–91, 211; work in Thailand, 141. See also *specific subject headings*
Kinh, the, 18, 29, 85–86, 117, 147; access to credit, 29; access to economic resources, 18, 28; access to education, 28, 29, 128, 176, 179, 227nn16–17, 246n2; access to health care, 28; access to social capital, 28; aspirations, 176; conditions, working, 102; coping mechanisms, 103, 105–14; debts, 156; dependency, path, 129; empowerment, 107–10; gender, 5, 65; hierarchies, 18, 50–52; issues, language, 28; migrants, socialist, 176; migration, stepwise international, 16, 176, 199; networks, religious, 105–7; population, 226n5; precarity, 101–5; resources, cultural, 29; resources, economic, 28, 29, 176; third space, 135; working conditions, 102, 105, 133, 218. See also *specific subject headings*

Labor Brokerage State, Malaysia, 57–60; Contracts, "carte blanche," 77; outsourcing, 7, 55–59, 62–63, 65, 71, 239n25; recruitment systems, 57, 216; 2015 memorandum of understanding, 202
Labor Brokerage State system, Vietnam, 6–8; agencies, employment, 80–81; banks, 66, 75–76, 87, 96, 109, 201; banks, local branch, 87, 155, 163; benefits to the LBS,

64–65, 201–3; capitalist labor export system, development of, 61–64, 216–17; Châu Hưng Recruitment Company, case of, 82–84; classes, orientation, 78–80; committees, people's, 71, 75, 80, 139, 219; companies, private recruitment, 84–86, 238n12; companies, state-owned recruitment, 80–81; complaint mechanism, 68, 235n53, 236nn61–62; complaints, DOLAB's role, 63; contracts, 76–78; costs to work overseas, 65–66; COVID-19, 204; debt collection, 67, 94–96; DOLAB, 71, 83, 99, 117, 204, 222n11; gender, 98, 100, 122; indebtedness, 29, 86, 87, 91, 93, 94; infrastructure, financial, 67–68; infrastructure, LBS, 55; infrastructure, migration, 6–7, 19, 79, 190; Law 72/2006/QH11, 62; LBS, internal contradictions, 70–72; loans, 76–78; marketing, 63, 158–59, 168–69; markets, labor, 55–56; media, 70–73, 136; MoLISA, 63, 66, 68–69, 74–76, 219, 238n17; networks, social, 8–9; organizations, quasi-state, 81–82; recruitment, 7, 55, 74–76, 80–86, 201–4, 218–20, 233n12, 236n62, 251n16; risk management, 67; socialist labor export system, 60–61; stakeholders, 19, 21–22, 55, 70, 202; Trường Giang case, 84–85; VAMAS, 75, 218, 237n1; VGCL, 68–72, 81, 203–5, 218, 220, 236n65; wage differential, 62; waiver, fees for classes, 238n6; women's union, 82, 91, 189, 249. See also *specific ethnic groups*
labor export policies, 7, 12, 201, 207, 218–19; after reunification, 1; challenges to, 12; dissent from, 6; Employment Service Center, 67, 190; "eradicate hunger and reduce poverty," 171; internal contradictions, 70–72; Labor Brokerage State system, 61–65; low-interest loans, 219; mass organizations, 81–82; response to workers' complaints, 97; socialist period, 26–27; training, history, 26, 128; training, language, 4, 74, 85, 157, 206; training, predeparture, 56, 236n64, 238n15; training, skills, 4, 219; training, vocational, 26, 61, 128, 175, 206, 219
land issues, 29, 33–34, 214–15, 251; deforestation, 214; fixed settlements, 214; Kmhmu people, 214; landlessness, sedentarization policy, 214, 248n21; swidden cultivation, 30–31, 36, 187–88, 214, 249n23; wet rice cultivation, 30–32, 187–88, 214

Index

language issues: Arabic, 44, 51–52, 144, 147, 183–85; barriers, language, 28, 51, 83; gendered division of labor, 140, 143–44, 149; language, Chinese, 30, 52, 157, 174; language, Japanese, 16; language, Khmer 40–42, 52, 182–83; language, Korean, 177, 178; language, Malay, 52, 79–80, 111, 118, 136, 141; Pattani Malay, 179; training, language, 157, 206, 219; verbal abuse, 131, 157

laws, 13–14, 201–3, 220; gender, 192, 202; Labor Code, No. 45/2019/QH14, 250; Law 021/2011/QH13, 68–69; Law 72/2006/QH11, 62, 216, 218; Law on Contract-Based Vietnamese Overseas Workers, 69/2020/QH14, 250; laws, implementation of, 99, 133

leaders, local: competing authorities, 39; hamlet, 7, 20, 25, 42, 47, 74–75, 91; hamlet chief, 39; hamlet deputy chief, 25, 40, 169, 211; Imam, 184–85, 211–12, 242; local mosque keeper, 170; medicine man, 31–32; Quảng Ngãi People's Committee, 160; village chief, 31; village elder, 31–32, 37

legal-illegal activities, 122–23; dissent, third space of, 6, 9–14; empowerment and protest, 15–16; strategies for survival, 14, 26, 54, 123, 150; third space, metaphorical, 12–13; third space, physical, 13–15, 123–24; working for other employers, 123. *See also under* Hoa; Kinh; Marywilska Commercial Center in Warsaw; Sapa Center in Prague; Third Space

liminal third space, 9, 13–14

loans and collateral: accountability, 58, 78, 97, 172, 202; application, 77–78; default, 67, 153, 160, 189; land as collateral, 91, 93, 154, 170; payment postponement, 155. *See also* banks; debts and remittances; *specific ethnic groups*

Malaysia, 3–6, 19–20, 57–60, 217, 235n44; alienation, 57, 105–6, 120, 256; Batu Pahat, 89, 106, 111, 133, 173; dislocation, 57; employment centers, 75, 81–82, 91, 139; family separation, 57, 116, 134, 240; Johor Bahru, 19, 103, 106, 164, 235n44; Kuala Lumpur, 63, 73, 99, 105–6, 117–18, 136, 241n31; Ministry of Home Affairs, 60; MTUC, 69–70, 203–4, 220; outsourcing companies, 7, 55, 57–59, 62, 65, 71, 239n25; Printing Presses and Publications Act of

1984, 60; Tenaganita, 7, 56, 58, 60, 72, 223; 2015 passport law, 99; undocumented workers, 10, 132–33, 142, 221; vulnerabilities, 7, 122, 168, 186, 241n31

Marywilska Commercial Center, 124–25, 130, 150

mass organizations, Vietnam, 6–7, 63, 66, 67, 81; peasant employment centers, 82; women's union, 21, 51, 189

media participation: internal contradictions, 5, 7, 55, 70, 199; in recruitment, 158

migration patterns, 8, 10–11, 144–46, 175–76, 178; gender differences, 18–19, 100; migration, domestic, 11, 13, 185–89, 193–94, 194–97; to work in Malaysia, 9–10, 11, 14–17, 19, 25; to work in Thailand, 118, 139, 246. *See also specific ethnic groups*

networks, migrant: family, 8–9, 25–26, 28, 66, 128; religious, 8–9, 46, 52, 54; social capital, 8–9, 28, 145; strong ties, 8, 39, 176, 195–96, 248n4; weak ties, 8, 176, 223, 248n4

non-governmental organizations: Catholic Migrant Ministry, 106, 204; Committee to Protect Vietnamese Workers, 59, 204; Suara Rakyat Malaysia, 99; Tenaganita, 7, 58, 60, 72; Vietnamese Family in Malaysia, 106

passports, 57–58, 98–99, 134, 220, 244n32, 246n54

path dependency, 10, 61, 85; defined, 12, 14, 110, 227, 244; locked into, 243; mediating, 129

Philippines, 3, 17, 45, 205, 221n7; infrastructure, 6–7, 19, 79, 190, 223n22; overseas Filipino workers, 63, 203; Philippine Overseas Employment Administration, 63, 203; Philippine Overseas Labor Office, 63, 204

Poland, 26, 61, 124–25, 150–51, 246n2; "Little Hanoi," 125; Marywilska Commercial Center, 124–25, 150–51; Vietnamese Bazaar, 125; Warsaw, 10, 13–14, 200

police, Malaysia: arrests, 95, 136, 244n31; and the Chăm, 141–46; extortion and theft by, 99, 115, 142–43; fear of, 8, 103, 111, 113, 177; harassment, 96, 98, 99, 142, 240n4; undocumented migrants, 6, 8–9, 135, 148–49, 224, 244n31

Index

practices of the five ethnic groups, 25–54. See also *specific ethnic group listings; subject categories*
precarity, 4, 98–101, 103–5, 119–22, 239n27; abuse, 157, 202, 206, 233, 265; contract violations, 68, 76, 113, 117–19, 121, 134; death, 104, 105, 115, 241n13, 251n16; fear, 103, 119, 142, 177, 241n18; fear of robbery, 103–4, 111, 114; health, 33, 58, 64–65, 90, 131, 168; isolation, 17, 19, 98; Kafala, 205, 254; police, 8, 103, 111, 113, 177; shift rotations, 101–2, 114
productivity, 96, 100, 102–3, 110, 132; quotas, 114, 130, 244n26; resistance, 6, 11–12, 57, 83, 96, 114, 224n45, 224n47, 224n51, 244n28; third space, metaphorical, 150, 171; third space, physical, 123, 171, 214

recruitment and outsourcing companies, 7, 55; and banks, 87, 109; "carte blanche," 58, 71, 77, 84; employment centers, 75, 81–82, 91, 139, 190; fees, 65, 77; media investigation, 71; orientation classes, 65, 78–79, 96, 157, 174; outsourcing defined, 239n25; peer pressure, 159, 169, 177, 181; preference for female workers, 63; private, 22, 84–86, 238n12; quasi-state, 80–81, 216, 218; state-owned, 80, 238, 245, 251; training, 157, 190, 219, 222n10, 229n60, 238n15. See also *specific ethnic groups*
religion, 19, 26, 50, 185, 248n18; animism, 32; Buddhism, Mahayana, 27; Chăm, 44; and education, 41, 42; gender, 32, 51, 122, 140, 197; Hinduism, 45; Hoa, 27, 30, 50–53, 105–7; Hrê, 210, 227, 267; Islam, religious studies in, 51; Khmer, 25, 40–42, 54, 86, 93; Kinh, 27, 30, 78, 105–6, 150; language and culture, preservation of, 42, Malay-Chăm, connections between, 147; Mexican communities in California, 14, 126; networks, 8–9, 46, 52, 54; organizations, Christian, 106, 204; praying at work, Muslim workers, 164–66; resources, cultural, 50; rituals, 31, 32, 36, 40; Theravada, Buddhism, 40, 230, 261
remittances, 3, 6, 8, 15–16, 21; "buffalo, house, and motorbike," 64, 158, 180; debts, repaying previous, 86, 90; empowerment, 108, 241n22; for education, 180, 201; for their families' needs, 100, 158; as investment, 109–10; LBS, benefits to, 36; loans, percentage of GDP, Vietnam, 201, 221n7,

225n67, 235n47; loans distributed, predeparture, 65, 87–88; to pay for childcare, 132; pooling money, 109, 164; repayment of loans, 94, 163
resistance of the weak, everyday forms of, 96
resources, cultural, 5–6, 10, 14, 27–28, 30, 37. See also third space of dissent, metaphorical; third space of dissent, physical; *specific ethnic groups*
retail trade competency, 47
returnees, 12, 160–64, 174–77, 182, 185–87; apply relevant new skills, 200; debt, forgiveness of, 155, 156, 160; early, 104, 116–18, 141–42, 149, 154–58; experienced new cultures, 200; interest, cancellation of, 155; learned new languages, 200; leverage, negotiating, 137–39; policies, contradictions in, 155–56; psychological difficulties, 169; as recruiting assistants, 85; repayment of loans, 94, 154, 156, 163; responsibility for debt, transference of, 160–61; threatening for payment, 67; worldviews, broader, 200
rights, worker: passports, 57–58, 98–99, 134, 146, 202; visa, tourist, 9, 85, 140–45, 195
robberies, 98, 103–4, 116, 121–22; dormitories, 72; police, 111, 203; on the street, 99, 145

Sapa Center, 124, 126, 129–30, 152, 243; family networks, 8–9, 25–26, 28, 66, 87, 128, 196; intercultural hybridity, 130; "Little Hanoi," 125–26; native place bonding, 152, 197; Prague, 10, 13–14, 123–24, 126, 129, 150–53, 200, 210, 243; 265–66; smuggling apparel, 127
Social Policy Bank, 66–67, 77, 87, 91, 94, 155–56; "bank for the poor," 155; loan forgiveness, 67, 162, 168, 170, 200
society, global civil, 7, 55, 72, 204
standards, global labor, 55, 72, 85
stepwise international migration, 16–17, 175–76, 206, 225, 264; costs, 16, 175–78, 181, 207; upward mobility, 124, 151, 177–78, 183
support for workers overseas: General Federation of Nepalese Trade Unions (GEFONT), 203–5, 250; Malaysian Trades Union Congress (MTUC), 59–60, 69–70, 72, 203–4; migrant resource centers, 70, 203; religious ties, 43, 54, 145;

support for workers overseas (*continued*): social networks, 8–9, 61, 129, 224n31, 248n4; targeted support services, 70, 203; Textile, Clothing, and Footwear Workers Union of Australia, 59; union, 7, 68–69, 75, 81, 202, 204–5; VGCL, 21–22, 68–72, 81, 203–5, 220

Thailand, 174, 178–79, 222n11, 222n17, 246n54; crossing borders, 45–47, 52, 54; third space, diverse forms, 147–48; tourist visas, Chăm, 141–43; tourist visas, Khmer, 123, 139–41, 176
third space of dissent, 12, 122, 152, 166; authorities, competing, 9, 14, 154, 166, 172; Bhabha, Homi, 6, 12, 14, 130, 152; causes, 57, 105, 110; Chăm, 141–43; cultural, 124, 126, 129, 150; defined, 12, 14, 110, 227, 244; discourses of dissent, 12, 150, 152; in the factory, 132, 134; gender, Chăm's division of labor, 143–45; Ghostman, the story of, 135–37; in Greater Mexico, 14; hiding products, 123, 132; Hrê, outside LBS, 137–39; hybrid cultural, 124, 150–51; irony, 156, 171; Khmer, using tourist visas, 139–41; Kinh and Hoa, 130–37; in Malaysia, 123, 130–36, 141–45, 147–49, 156–59; metaphorical, 150–53, 155, 157, 159, 161, 163–65; mimicries, 154, 163, 166–67, 199; networks, social, 6, 8–17, 49, 61; networks, social-mediating dependency, 129–30; physical, 1, 13–15, 23–25, 40, 127, 129–31, 133, 135; in Prague, 14, 124, 126, 151, 153; religious, 8–9, 12, 126, 138–39, 144–45, 147–48; resistance, everyday forms of, 83, 96, 123, 171, 214; risks of, 67, 145–47; rituals, 14, 31–33, 36–37, 40, 90; social, 19, 21, 27–28, 30, 32, 40; taking naps in restrooms, 130–31; undocumented, becoming, 132–35; in Warsaw, 13–14, 123, 150, 200
transnational migration, 3, 7, 17–18, 187, 246n57
transnational oversight, 76

undocumented migrants, 6, 8–9, 135, 149, 203, 224
unions, 7, 68–69, 75, 81, 202, 204–5; General Federation of Nepalese Trade Unions (GEFONT), 203–5, 250; Malaysian Trades Union Congress (MTUC), 59–60,

69–70, 72, 203–4; Textile, Clothing, and Footwear Workers Union of Australia (TCFUA), 59; VGCL, 21–22, 68–72, 81, 203–5, 220; women's union, 21, 51, 82, 189, 249n33

Vietnam: An Giang province, 37–39, 41–42, 76, 88, 177; An Phú district, 48, 120, 194, 211; Ba Tơ district, 33–34, 36, 137–38, 148, 158, 167–68; Chăm Bani, 43, 46, 231; Chăm Sunni Muslims, 43, 45, 119–21; Cochinchina, 45, 264; Dak Lak, 185–86; Department of Overseas Labor (DOLAB), 62–63, 83, 99, 117, 204–5, 222n11; Đồng Nai province, 163; Gia Lai, 185–86, 249; history, 25–30, 37–43, 43–46, 60–62; Khmer, 37–43, 116–19; Labor Brokerage State (LBS) system, 55–56, 64–65, 70–72; Mekong Delta, 20, 29, 37–40, 43, 45–46; Ministry of Foreign Affairs (MoFA), 63, 71, 217, 219; Ministry of Labor, Invalids, and Social Affairs (MoLISA), 63, 74–76, 82, 167, 219; MoFA, 63–64, 68; Phú Nhuận district, 48; Quảng Ngãi city, 33; Quốc Thái commune, 120, 170, 194, 211; Red River Delta, 29; resettlement policy, 186–87, 189; sedentarization policy, 214, 248; Sơn Hà district, 78, 82, 138, 159, 210; Tịnh Biên, 41, 92, 141, 169, 190–91, 211; Tri Tôn district, 39, 92, 183, 211–12
Vietnam Association of Manpower Supply (VAMAS), 21, 75, 85, 218, 237
Vietnam General Confederation of Labor, (VGCL), 21, 68–72, 135, 203–5, 249n33
visas, 123–24, 139–40, 143–44, 176, 179
vocational training, 26, 69, 128, 175, 206; acquisition, language, 85, 182, 183, 206, 222; classes, 41–42, 78–79, 106, 176, 238n6; cultural orientation, 65, 96, 157, 174, 222; legal instructions, 222

wealth, cultural, 14–15, 116, 129, 199–200, 225n65
weapons of the weak, 11–12, 123, 224, 265
working conditions, exploitative: glass windows, 102; low wages, 54, 118–19, 142, 177, 194; management surveillance, 102; panopticon, 102; shift rotations, 101–2, 114; speedup, 103, 130–32; verbal abuse, 157

Angie Ngọc Trần is a professor of political economy at California State University, Monterey Bay. She is the author of *Ties That Bind: Cultural Identity, Class, and Law in Vietnam's Labor Resistance.*

Studies of World Migrations

The Immigrant Threat: The Integration of Old and New Migrants
in Western Europe Since 1850   *Leo Lucassen*
Citizenship and Those Who Leave: The Politics of Emigration and Expatriation
Edited by Nancy L. Green and François Weil
Migration, Class, and Transnational Identities: Croatians in Australia
and America   *Val Colic-Peisker*
The Yankee Yorkshireman: Migration Lived and Imagined   *Mary H. Blewett*
Africans in Europe: The Culture of Exile and Emigration
from Equatorial Guinea to Spain   *Michael Ugarte*
Hong Kong Movers and Stayers: Narratives of Family Migration
Janet W. Salaff, Siulun Wong, and Arent Greve
Russia in Motion: Cultures of Human Mobility since 1850
Edited by John Randolph and Eugene M. Avrutin
A Century of Transnationalism: Immigrants and Their Homeland Connections
Edited by Nancy L. Green and Roger Waldinger
Syrian and Lebanese Patrícios in São Paulo: From the Levant to Brazil
Oswaldo Truzzi, translated by Ramon J. Stern
A Nation of Immigrants Reconsidered: US Society in an Age of Restriction,
1924–1965   *Edited by Maddalena Marinari, Madeline Y. Hsu, and
Maria Cristina Garcia*
Ethnic Dissent and Empowerment: Economic Migration
between Vietnam and Malaysia   *Angie Ngọc Trần*

The University of Illinois Press
is a founding member of the
Association of University Presses.

University of Illinois Press
1325 South Oak Street
Champaign, IL 61820-6903
www.press.uillinois.edu

Printed by Printforce, United Kingdom